PEGGY SEEGER

MUSIC IN AMERICAN LIFE

*A list of books in the series appears
at the end of this book.*

# PEGGY
# SEEGER

## A LIFE OF MUSIC, LOVE, AND POLITICS

JEAN R. FREEDMAN

**UNIVERSITY OF
ILLINOIS PRESS**
Urbana, Chicago, and Springfield

Publication of this book was supported by grants
from the Manfred Bukofzer Endowment of the
American Musicological Society, funded in part by
the National Endowment for the Humanities and
the Andrew W. Mellon Foundation, and from the
L. J. and Mary C. Skaggs Folklore Fund.

Library of Congress Control Number: 2016961776
ISBN 978-0-252-04075-7 (hardcover)
ISBN 978-0-252-09921-2 (e-book)

Permissions to reproduce copyrighted materials
appear on pages xv–xvi.

*To Jonathan and Rachel, with love*
*and*
*to the memory of Leon David Freedman (1921–2013),*
*Myrle Neistadt Freedman (1921–2015),*
*and Peter Seeger (1919–2014)*

# Contents

Preface . . . . . . . . . . . . . . . . . . . . . . . . . . . . . . . . . . . . . . . . ix

Acknowledgments . . . . . . . . . . . . . . . . . . . . . . . . . . . . . . xiii

Permissions . . . . . . . . . . . . . . . . . . . . . . . . . . . . . . . . . . xv

Introduction . . . . . . . . . . . . . . . . . . . . . . . . . . . . . . . . . . . . 1

1. Very Good Stock . . . . . . . . . . . . . . . . . . . . . . . . . . . . . . 5

2. The Early Years . . . . . . . . . . . . . . . . . . . . . . . . . . . . . . 23

3. Coming of Age in Chevy Chase . . . . . . . . . . . . . . . . . . . . 39

4. A Rendezvous with Death . . . . . . . . . . . . . . . . . . . . . . . 54

5. The Rover, Part One . . . . . . . . . . . . . . . . . . . . . . . . . . . 72

6. The First Time Ever . . . . . . . . . . . . . . . . . . . . . . . . . . . 82

7. The Rover, Part Two . . . . . . . . . . . . . . . . . . . . . . . . . . . 93

8. New Day Dawning . . . . . . . . . . . . . . . . . . . . . . . . . . . . 107

9. At Home Abroad . . . . . . . . . . . . . . . . . . . . . . . . . . . . . 118

10. What Is a Folk Song? . . . . . . . . . . . . . . . . . . . . . . . . . . 133

11. High Noon . . . . . . . . . . . . . . . . . . . . . . . . . . . . . . . . . 144

12. Beginnings and Endings . . . . . . . . . . . . . . . . . . . . . . . 160

13. Different Stages . . . . . . . . . . . . . . . . . . . . . . . . . . . . . 173

14. Things Fall Apart . . . . . . . . . . . . . . . . . . . . . . . . . . . . 187

15. Late in the Day . . . . . . . . . . . . . . . . . . . . . . . . . . . . . . . 199
16. The Day Is Ending . . . . . . . . . . . . . . . . . . . . . . . . . . . . 216
17. The Long Road Home . . . . . . . . . . . . . . . . . . . . . . . . . 239
18. Heading for Home . . . . . . . . . . . . . . . . . . . . . . . . . . . . 248
19. Old New England . . . . . . . . . . . . . . . . . . . . . . . . . . . . 268
20. Everything Changes . . . . . . . . . . . . . . . . . . . . . . . . . . . 278
21. What Is a Folk Revival? . . . . . . . . . . . . . . . . . . . . . . . . 294

    Notes . . . . . . . . . . . . . . . . . . . . . . . . . . . . . . . . . . . . . . 305
    References Cited . . . . . . . . . . . . . . . . . . . . . . . . . . . . . 339
    General Index . . . . . . . . . . . . . . . . . . . . . . . . . . . . . . . 353
    Index of Selected Recordings and
    Publications by Peggy Seger . . . . . . . . . . . . . . . . . . . . 365

*Illustrations follow page 186*

# Preface

I first met Peggy Seeger on an autumn evening in London in 1979. The setting was the Singers Club, a folk club that Peggy and her husband, Ewan MacColl, had begun in the early 1960s. I was in London studying theater through that most American of adventures: the junior year abroad. Having grown up in a much smaller city, I was entranced by the cultural offerings that only a major metropolis can afford. But on that October evening, I was still a newcomer and a stranger, a long way from home and bemused by cultural differences I had never anticipated: I didn't know my shoe size or the proper way to buy vegetables; the cars were unfamiliar and drove on the wrong side of the street; and I needed a new vocabulary for ordinary things—*lift*, *aubergine*, *petrol*, *chemist's shop*, *surgical spirit*. I had never seen Peggy before, but her accent was familiar, and she sang the songs I knew: "The Single Girl" and "Jenny Jenkins." After the performance, I introduced myself and said, "Thank you for taking me home."

Throughout that long and extraordinary year, the Singers Club became an essential part of my routine. In a small room above a Bloomsbury pub, I could hear some of Britain's finest folk musicians for a price of £.50, and in the middle of the evening, anyone who wanted could sing a song "from the floor." I particularly looked forward to the nights when Ewan and Peggy sang. I loved their unique combination of old and new music: eighteenth-century ballads and nineteenth-century sea shanties mixed with musical polemics about apartheid or Margaret Thatcher. I loved their combination of intellectual rigor, political clarity, and musical skill. I joined the committee that ran the Singers Club, and at my first committee meeting, Ewan began telling me of his days in the theater. When I indicated my interest in hearing more, Ewan and Peggy invited me to dinner at their home, where we ate, talked, and sang long into the night. They encouraged me to sing from the floor at the Singers Club and gave me useful suggestions and warm praise when I did so.

After I returned home, we exchanged letters and postcards and saw each other occasionally, when I visited England or when they were on tour in the United States. But as time passed, our connection grew more tenuous. After Ewan died in 1989, Peggy and I maintained only occasional and sporadic contact. For several years, we lost touch entirely. But I never forgot her music or the keen intelligence behind it.

Ewan and Peggy's influence on my life was perhaps greater than they knew. After my year in London, I returned to the United States and completed my degree in theater. Then I moved to New York, where I found myself spending more and more time with folk music: singing, writing songs, helping to run a small folk club in Greenwich Village. In 1988, I began graduate school in folklore and ethnomusicology at Indiana University. I wrote my MA thesis on Scottish ballads and dedicated it to Ewan's memory. My PhD dissertation was a study of London during World War II; in particular, it examined the interplay between culture and politics. Once again, I spent a year in London, but the Singers Club no longer existed, and the folk music community—still creative and vibrant—was very different from the one I had known.

Time passes. In the 1990s, a friend from the New York City folk revival put Peggy and me in contact via email. A friend from graduate school asked me to review a book about Peggy's mother, Ruth Crawford Seeger, for the *Journal of American Folklore*. I had questions about the book and emailed them to Peggy; she preferred to discuss the matter by telephone. I spoke to her on a cold Sunday afternoon in winter; half a world away in New Zealand, Peggy replied from a warm Monday morning in summer. In the course of our conversation, she asked if I knew anyone who was interested in writing her biography. I suggested myself. Six months later, we saw each other for the first time in years when she visited my home in Montgomery County, Maryland, only a few miles from where she grew up. Our work as biographer and subject had begun.

For the next eight years, I interviewed her, pored through her papers, visited archives, and spoke to her family, friends, and acquaintances. Telling the life story of another is a fearsome responsibility, and this book would not have been possible without Peggy's unstinting help and generosity. She answered all my questions completely and with candor, allowed me access to her private papers, and provided contact information for important people in her life.

She read every word I wrote, made comments, and corrected errors of fact, but she never told me what to write or tried to control my telling of her story. When we disagreed, she would graciously say, "This is your book." To supply a subjective telling of her life, she began to write a memoir, which will serve as a complement to this book.

For the past eight years, it has been my honor and my pleasure to immerse myself in the music of a gifted, creative, and innovative artist. Peggy Seeger has been a major figure in the Anglo-American folk music revival for more than sixty years, but she is less well known than some members of her extraordinary family. I hope that, through this biography, readers will come to know a remarkable artist and to appreciate the music that she has created.

# Acknowledgments

My first thanks go to Peggy Seeger herself. No biographer could have had a more cooperative, generous, and honest subject. She gave me access to a myriad of private papers, allowed me to tape-record her memories, fed and housed me during research trips, and entrusted me with the great responsibility of telling her life story. Her warmth, intelligence, and sincerity made her a pleasure to work with, and I am proud to call her my friend.

Peggy's family, friends, and acquaintances have likewise been generous with their time. I would like to thank Frankie Armstrong, Jay Ball, Bob Blair, Elias Bouquillon, Guy and Candie Carawan, Jim Carroll, Shirley Collins, Peter Cox, Sonya Cramer, Lin Frothingham Folsom, Kerry Harvey-Piper, Joe Hickerson, Stan Kelly-Bootle, Sandra Kerr, Calum MacColl, Kitty MacColl, Neill MacColl, Jean Newlove (MacColl), Pat Mackenzie, Jim McKiernan, Barbara Seeger Miserantino, Lorraine Murphy, Sheelagh Neuling, Barry Olivier, Noel Osheroff, Brian Pearson, Ruth Perry, Annette Dapp Poston, Nina Powell Scheider, Irene Pyper-Scott, Tony Saletan, Chris Arley Seeger, Jeremy Seeger, John Seeger, Kate Seeger, Naomi S. Seeger, Pete Seeger, Tinya Seeger, Alexia Smith, Judith Tick, Maurice Van de Putte, and Clark Weissman. Sadly, Mike Seeger died before I had the opportunity to interview him, but I will always be grateful for his warm interest in this project.

Copyright holders have also been generous. I am grateful to James Robinson for permission to quote from a letter from the late Earl Robinson. For permission to quote from a letter from the late Manny Greenhill, my thanks go to Mitch Greenhill, courtesy Folklore Inc./Estate of Manny Greenhill. Thanks to folklorist Millie Rahn for permission to quote from a presentation she gave at the Seeger family tribute held at the Library of Congress in 2007. I am grateful to Ewan MacColl Ltd., The Bicycle Music Company, and Harmony and Bucks Music for permission to quote from a multitude of songs (listed separately in the "Permissions" section).

A good archivist is a biographer's best friend. At the Library of Congress, I worked with many fine archivists at the Music Division and the American Folklife Center. In particular, I would like to acknowledge Kate Rivers of the Music Division and Catherine Hiebert Kerst of the American Folklife Center for archival assistance beyond the call of duty. At the Ewan Mac-Coll/Peggy Seeger Archive at Ruskin College, I would like to thank Valerie Moyses, Raymond King, and the rest of their fine team. I am also grateful to Stephanie Brown and Gail Sansbury of the Chevy Chase Historical Society in Montgomery County, Maryland.

At the University of Illinois Press, I have been privileged to work with editors whose dedication, knowledge, and insight are second to none. Special thanks to Laurie Matheson for guiding this project from beginning to end.

My friends provided help, encouragement, and much-needed distraction. Jill Terry Rudy initially got the ball rolling when, as book review editor of the *Journal of American Folklore*, she asked me to write a review of a book about Peggy's mother, Ruth Crawford Seeger. Terri Farrow Winkler gave me the benefit of her sterling music-theory skills. Joan Bolker, through our weekly emails, gave me advice, encouragement, and the occasional nudge. Jessica Bolker read my work and cheered me on. My friends from the New York City folk revival showed me that folk music continues to be a living, breathing art. My friends from the world of academic folklore provided another and equally important point of view: folk music is a fascinating object of study and analysis.

To my family I owe my greatest debt. My mother, Myrle Freedman, a conservatory-trained singer and pianist, bequeathed to me a love of music and an unshakable belief in its importance. My father, Leon Freedman, a university professor, taught me the joy of intellectual inquiry and the importance of social justice. My husband, Jonathan D. Pollock, read and commented on my work, kept the home fires burning while I was away on research trips, and provided unstinting encouragement and love. My daughter, Rachel Pollock, remained infinitely patient as this project consumed my time, starting with my initial meeting with Peggy back in 2008, which required me to miss Rachel's dance concert.

Three important nonagenarians died during the course of writing this book. My father died in April 2013 at the age of ninety-one, and my mother died in December 2015 at the age of ninety-four. Peggy's brother Pete died in January 2014 at the age of ninety-four. To their example of intelligence, joie de vivre, and insistence on fighting the good fight, this book is partially dedicated.

# Permissions

Thank you to Ewan MacColl Ltd. for kind permission to reproduce lyrics taken from the following songs: "Bring the Summer Home," "Daddy, What Did You Do in the Strike?," "The Day of the Fight," "John Axon Was a Railwayman," John Axon's final song, "The Joy of Living," "Only Doing Their Job," "Parent and Child," "Seven Days of the Week," "Shellback Song," "There's No Place for Me," "We Are the Engineers," and "We're Young but We're a-Growing."

Thank you to Bicycle Music for permission to quote from the following songs: "The Ballad of Springhill," "I'm Gonna Be an Engineer," "It's All Happening Now," "Love for Love," "The War Game," and "When I Was Young," © Stormking Music, Inc. (BMI) administered by Figs. D Music c/o The Bicycle Music Company. All rights reserved. Used by permission.

Thank you to Simon Platz, managing director of Bucks Music Group, for permission to quote from the following songs: "Ballad of Jimmy Massey," "Billy and George," "Birds of a Feather," "Bring Me Home," "Carry Greenham Home," "Dick and the Devil," "Doggone, Occupation Is On," "Enough Is Enough," "Everything Changes," "45, 85," "Four-Minute Warning," "Go to Sleep," "Heading for Home," "Hello Friend," "Home Sweet Home," "The Invader," "I Remember," "The Judge's Chair," "Love Call Me Home," "Love Unbidden," "Love Will Linger On," "Lullabye for a Very New Baby," "My Friend Pat," "My Son," "Nero's Children," "New Spring Morning," "North Carolina Home," "Obama Is the One for Me," "Old Friend," "One plus One," "Plutonium Factor," "Primrose Hill," "Reclaim the Night," "Sing about These Hard Times," "Sit Down Occupation," "Song for Calum," "Song for Charles Parker," "Song of Myself," "Talking Matrimony Blues," "That's How the World Goes On," "Thoughts of Time," "Tomorrow," "Tree of Love," "Vil-

PEGGY SEEGER

# Introduction

There are moments in one's life that, when viewed in retrospect, take on such a transformative importance that the slightest deviation from what actually happened would have altered the course of one's entire existence. When viewing these moments through the glass of memory, one plays the childish game of "what if?": "What if I had not answered the phone?" "What if I had turned left instead of right?" Such a moment occurred in Peggy Seeger's life in March 1956.

It had been a hard winter, though an interesting one. Peggy had arrived in the Netherlands the preceding autumn, just a few months after her twentieth birthday, in order to stay with her brother Charles and study at the University of Leiden. During the summer, she had studied the language with a Dutch immigrant in California, near where her father lived with his new wife, Mar, whom he had married two years after the death of Peggy's mother. It was understood that Peggy would spend a year in Leiden and then return to the United States to finish her college education. For a while, all had gone well; Peggy enjoyed the lovely old city and made an agreeable circle of friends. But tensions within her brother's family ultimately convinced her that it was time to go. Always an adventurer, she did not pack her bags and return home, perhaps because she had no home to return to. The big house in Chevy Chase, where she had spent most of her youth, had been sold after her mother died, and she never felt comfortable in her father's new home, for it was really Mar's house. In fact, during the summer in California, she and her sister Barbara had lived in the servants' quarters while five large bedrooms stood empty in case any of Mar's children chose to visit.

Peggy was a long way from the comfortable suburbs of Washington, D.C., where she had grown up, and the ivy-covered halls of Radcliffe College, where she had spent two years. But she was in no hurry to return to America. Europe fascinated her, though it was cold and dark and without central heating, and still recovering from the Second World War. When friends invited her to join them on a trip to Scandinavia, she accepted, eager to see new countries before returning to her own. Shortly before her departure, she received a telephone call from an old family friend, Alan Lomax, who offered her a job singing and playing the banjo if she could come to London. Initially, she turned him down; she was committed to the trip to Scandinavia and had no money to travel to England. But when he said that she could delay her arrival for several weeks and offered to pay her travel fare, she accepted. So she arrived in London, disheveled and travel-weary, on the morning of March 27, 1956.

Peggy had been on the train from Copenhagen all night. Her clothes were dirty and unfashionable, her long hair tangled and in desperate need of a comb. Alan's girlfriend, Susan Mills, was a fashion model, and she accepted the challenge before her with the enthusiasm of a Picasso attacking an empty canvas. Within a few hours, Peggy emerged clean and glamorous, sporting a beehive hairdo, layers of makeup, high-heeled shoes, and Susan Mills's clothes. Clutching her long-neck banjo, she went to meet the musicians with whom she would work if they liked the way she sang. She made an incongruous figure in her fashionable getup, perched on a stool so high that her feet tapped the air, playing an American instrument that few of these British musicians had ever seen, singing "The House Carpenter," an American variant of a European ballad—a tale of love and betrayal and magical revenge that was totally beyond her personal experience yet entirely within her musical skill. She had never met Hobart Smith (whose banjo playing she aspired to) or Texas Gladden (whose singing she emulated), but she played with the innate musicality of someone to whom music is as natural as seeing and with a sureness and intensity of someone twice her age. Smith and Gladden would no doubt have approved.

Peggy was twenty years old, and in a sense everything in her life had prepared her for this moment. American folk music had been as much a part of her upbringing as the air she breathed. When she was two years old, confined to a hospital bed because of a burned foot, her parents found her room by following the sound of her singing "Barbara Allen." This was the music that her classically trained parents believed was on a par with that of the European masters. This was the music that her musicologist father had collected in large cities and isolated hamlets, that her composer mother had adapted and arranged and played over and over again from Alan Lomax's field recordings, so that the music was as constant a feature of the house as food or clothing or love, and every bit as important. This was the music that had accompanied all of Peggy's childhood activities, from getting dressed in the morning to coming home from school; this was the music that had sent her to sleep at night, that had permeated her very dreams. This was the music that her brother Mike sought in the hills of Virginia, that her brother Pete had made famous. Peggy may have been very far from her own country and dressed in a fashion completely alien to her taste, but she carried her home in her hands and her voice and her banjo case.

The other musicians, a fledgling folk group called the Ramblers, were impressed. One, a singer and playwright named Ewan MacColl, was captivated. In a moment, his life changed forever, and though Peggy did not yet realize it, so did hers. This was the moment that Ewan would later immortalize in his most famous song, "The First Time Ever I Saw Your Face." If one wished to view life teleologically, this was the moment that Peggy had prepared for since the day she was born.

# CHAPTER 1

# Very Good Stock

I heard my mother's birthing cry
The day that I was born.
I saw the light in my father's eye
And knew that I was home.

—Peggy Seeger, "Bring Me Home"


The year 1935, the midpoint of what W. H. Auden called a "low, dishonest decade," was a good year for Charles Seeger. After years of financial insecurity and pieced-together part-time work, Seeger had landed a steady job with the Special Skills Division of the Resettlement Administration (RA), a New Deal organization charged with creating new communities for unemployed workers and impoverished farmers. The Special Skills Division incorporated the arts into this project by teaching practical skills such as weaving and woodworking and by using the arts to build community and foster a spirit of togetherness. Seeger's initial assignment as director of the music program was to place three hundred musicians in three hundred new communities within six months, a task that seemed impossible and would turn out to be. But the steady salary meant security for his family, and financial stability was rare during the Depression. The job also allowed him to integrate the two passions to which he was devoted but had never, to his satisfaction, combined: music and politics. So Charles accepted the position, and in November 1935 he and his wife, Ruth Crawford Seeger, took their household goods and their two small children to Washington, D.C.

Charles was nearly fifty years of age when this happy confluence of events brought him and his family to Washington. His life had been a combination of brilliant successes and disappointing failures. He had known both luxury and poverty; he had been praised for his idealism, and he had been fired for sticking to his ideals. He was born in 1886 in Mexico City to a genteel businessman of New England extraction. Charles Seeger Sr. had built a successful import-export business that required frequently moving his family between Mexico and the northeastern United States. Home base was a lavish house on Staten Island, with a large barn and an extensive yard filled with fruit trees. Charles called it "an idyllic spot for childhood."[1] Charles and his younger siblings, Alan and Elizabeth, were free to roam the neighborhood with their friends, playing hide-and-seek, organizing secret societies (complete with brutal initiation rituals), and fostering fledgling romances.

The large house required a retinue of servants; cook, nurse, gardener, and waitress lived in, while a woman came daily to do the sewing. Children were forbidden to visit the servants, but this prohibition was often winked at, especially when the scent of freshly baked bread beckoned from the kitchen. Dennis, the gardener and coachman, was a beloved figure who told wonderful stories, yet the only time Charles entered Dennis's house, he was appalled at the squalor in which Dennis's family lived—at wages paid by the Seegers. Charles's mother, Elsie Adams Seeger, "ruled the establishment like a queen," though like many women of her age and class, she had relatively little to do.[2] She had been raised for no occupation other than marriage, yet servants relieved her of the burdens of housework and child care. Charles described his mother as "extraordinarily intelligent" but also "incredibly uneducated."[3] She had gone to good schools but had shown little interest in studying, preferring instead to read Victorian novels. She remained tenaciously proud of her heritage, having come from pure British stock (unlike the Seegers, who also had German blood) and claimed several ancestors who came over on the Mayflower. "You come from very good stock," she would inform her grandson Pete, who, to her disappointment, could not have cared less.[4] Charles loved her, in the dutiful way that Victorian children did, but one wonders if he respected her.

He did, in any case, respect his father, who exhibited the unwavering integrity that is a hallmark of Seeger character. In 1900, Charles Sr.'s business failed, and he was required to appear in bankruptcy court in New York. Bankruptcy law would have allowed him to renege on his debts, but he refused to do so. He had given his word to repay his creditors, and his word was his bond: he eventually repaid every cent, with interest. But Charles Sr. was, in his son's words, "more of a Hamiltonian than a Jeffersonian"; he did not think highly of the common man.[5] He believed that only 10 percent of humanity comprised the world's natural leaders, and he did not doubt that the Seegers belonged in the talented tenth. Women were to be respected and protected but kept firmly in their place. Boys went off to college and then to their rightful duty of governing the world with a firm but virtuous hand, while girls were kept within the family circle until they married, when their care and guidance could be passed on to their husbands.

Charles Jr. enjoyed his peripatetic childhood, retaining throughout his life a deep appreciation for Latin American culture, particularly its music. From 1902 to 1908, he spent the academic year in the United States, initially at boarding school and then at college, and returned to Mexico for summers with the family. His 1908 graduation photograph from Harvard shows a well-dressed, somewhat arrogant young man peering at the world from behind rimless glasses. It was customary for Harvard graduates to spend time abroad before settling down, but Charles Sr. felt that his son should work for a living rather than continue to live on family wealth. This vision of middle-class thrift so horrified Charles's Harvard classmates that eventually the elder Seeger relented, and Charles spent two and a half years in Europe. His desire to be a musician (either a composer or a conductor) appalled his businessman father, who advised him to go into business for ten years, make enough money to retire, and then spend his life as a musician if he wished. This plan had no appeal for young Charles. Late in 1908, with a magna cum laude degree in music composition, Charles sailed for Europe, where he wrote music in Berlin, made love in Paris, and served as an apprentice conductor at the Cologne Opera. Beginning to suffer from hearing loss, which would plague him throughout his life, he realized that conducting as a profession would not be possible. But his original compositions were beginning to garner critical acclaim, and he returned to the United States in 1911, sure of his future as a composer.

That year brought great change to the Seeger family. The Mexican Revolution ended a quarter-century sojourn in Mexico. The ship that left Mexico with many of the Seeger possessions sank, leaving a somewhat impoverished family to start over again in the United States. But within a relatively short time, Charles Sr. was sent to Europe as a corporate executive for the United States Rubber Company. As he had advised his son to do, the elder Seeger made enough money to live for the rest of his life, and the family retired to a large house called "Fairlea" in Patterson, New York.

Charles Jr. lived nearby, in a small apartment in New York City, and composed music that was both published and praised, a rare accomplishment for a twenty-four-year-old composer. Shortly after his arrival in New York, he met a talented young violinist named Constance Edson. Constance came from a patrician but highly unstable family, and she planned to use her musical gifts to support herself. She had had excellent training; she had studied at the

Paris Conservatory of Music while her mother was the mistress of a French aristocrat. Back in New York with her mother, the affair with the aristocrat having ended, Constance was looking for an accompanist with whom she could give concerts and recitals. Charles fit the bill. Mrs. Edson's connections with New York's upper crust meant a ready-made audience, and the musical duo was a modest success. By the end of the year, they were married.

Marriage required more than a hand-to-mouth existence with some composing on the side. Constance was soon pregnant, and Charles, true to his upbringing, sought ways to support his bride in comfort. The solution came in May 1912, when he was offered a job as a full professor of music at the University of California at Berkeley with an annual salary of three thousand dollars. The couple moved to a pleasant home in Berkeley, where, in September, they welcomed their first child, Charles Seeger III.

Berkeley was then a semirural community in the shadow of San Francisco, long the largest city on the West Coast (a designation it was to lose by 1920). The university's music department was virtually nonexistent when the Seegers arrived, and Charles threw himself into the job of building the department from the ground up. He introduced radical changes into the History of Music course by including modern music and, even more unusually, folk music. He implemented a four-year curriculum in music and taught a complete course in musicology, the first in the United States. He gave a concert of folk songs in seventeen different languages, conducted a large chorus, and gave occasional chamber music recitals with Constance. He began to develop his theory of dissonant counterpoint, which would later impress composers such as Paul Hindemith and Arnold Schoenberg; in 1914 he shared his theory with his best student, a very young Henry Cowell. Financially, the Seegers were doing well enough to buy an attractive home with a separate studio for Charles's work. His second son, John, was born in February of 1914.

Charles's years at Berkeley marked the awakening of his social conscience. Horrified by the conditions of migrant laborers in California, he sought ways to ameliorate the suffering caused by poverty. He befriended members of the Industrial Workers of the World (IWW or "Wobblies"), read radical thought, and—influenced by Bertrand Russell—became an avowed pacifist. He frequently associated with and gave talks to radical organizations in the area, actions that were starting to get him into trouble on campus. But they might have been overlooked had it not been for a conflict that occurred seven thousand miles away.

The First World War laid a heavy hand on the Seeger family. The Great War that produced great carnage and great literature took Charles's younger brother Alan, author of one of the classics of World War I poetry, the eerily prescient "I Have a Rendezvous with Death." Alan had joined the French Foreign Legion in 1914, and he died on July 4, 1916, in the French town of Belloy-en-Santerre. His poems were published the following year and received a glowing review from his Harvard classmate and fellow poet T. S. Eliot.

Charles Seeger opposed the war that had taken his brother's life, and he paid for this opposition with his livelihood. His stance had been in tune with most Californians until the United States joined the Allies in 1917. After that, his opinions were seen as cowardice, possibly even treason. Colleagues derided him; friends snubbed him. He was worn out from teaching a full schedule, building a music department, developing his own theories of music, composing, and, in his spare time, delving into radical politics. He gladly took a sabbatical for the academic year of 1918–19, and he and Constance returned east, where they lived with Seeger's parents.

Charles was emotionally exhausted, and his health was suffering. Hard work was the least of it. He was grievously disappointed in the unthinking jingoism that drove the United States into World War I. His opinions had earned him the enmity of many in Berkeley, and it soon became clear that he would not be welcomed back at the university. But he was disappointed in himself as well. The music that he composed seemed increasingly esoteric and removed from real life. He later remarked, "In the late teens and early twenties, I [gave] up composition because I couldn't approve of the music I liked and I couldn't like a music that I approved, and I couldn't make either one of them connect in any way with the social situation I found."[6]

The brightest spot of 1919 was the birth of his third son, Peter, in May. But with three children to support, he needed a way to earn a living. Deeply interested in combining music with political and social activism, he developed a plan to bring good music to the impoverished. "Good music" in those days meant Western art music; Seeger derided popular music, was horrified by jazz, and believed that folk music was nearly dead. He planned to travel the country giving free concerts in churches, schools, and other public places, financing the venture by giving paid concerts in homes of the well-to-do. He and Constance built a trailer where they could live and keep their equipment. In November 1920, in a caravan laden with instruments, a cast-iron pot for doing laundry, and three young boys, they set off for the rural South.

Their initial goal was to reach California, but bad roads and bad weather ended their journey in North Carolina. Living in a trailer—and for several months, a log cabin—and traveling from town to town might have been a glorious adventure for the children, but it was an impractical way to raise a family. Financially, the scheme failed; they could never make enough money to support themselves. Moreover, it turned out that impoverished rural folk weren't so music hungry, after all. They were polite at the free concerts but not much interested, for they had music of their own. After Charles and Constance played Mozart and Beethoven, the local people brought out their banjos and fiddles. Charles was fascinated; the music he had thought on its deathbed was alive and kicking, with a sophistication and subtlety he could barely have imagined. His son Peter was too small to have any memories of these impromptu concerts, but perhaps seeds were planted that would later bear fruit. As a teenager, Pete Seeger returned to North Carolina with his father and heard some of the virtuosos of traditional southern folk music. Thus began Pete's love affair with folk music, a love that burned brightly for more than seven decades.

The summer of 1921 found the Seeger family back in New York, looking for more substantial ways to earn a living. The solution came in August, when Frank Damrosch, a close family friend of Constance, offered them jobs teaching at the Institute of Musical Art, which would later become the Juilliard School. Constance taught violin, and Charles developed an innovative music program that included musicology, general musicianship, and the study of myth and epic. Their colleagues were among the leaders in their fields—the concertmaster of the New York Philharmonic was one of them—and Charles was swept up in the intellectual excitement of devising a new curriculum and sharing ideas with his colleagues. It seemed that, at the age of thirty-five, Charles had finally found his niche.

The idyll did not last long. The Seegers' marriage had begun to fray. Charles's work increasingly took him away from home, and his time at home was marred by quarrels and misunderstandings. In 1927, Constance put her money into a separate bank account, an action that infuriated Charles and caused a separation. The couple made a few more attempts at reconciliation, and they remained married for five more years, but for all intents and purposes, the marriage was over.

Once again, Charles felt himself a failure. His family's tradition of high ideals had led him to expect great happiness from marriage, but such happiness had proved elusive. However, he was determined to succeed at fatherhood. His children attended good boarding schools and spent happy summers at the Seeger estate in Patterson. During those summers, Charles Sr. and his wife lived in their large, well-appointed house, while Charles Jr. and the boys occupied the barn, where they wore old clothes, played raucous games, and sang at the top of their lungs. Once a week, they changed their clothes and dined at the house, where the boys learned the manners and mores appropriate to their class, including the proper way to behave with servants. When dinner was over, they returned to the barn, where life consisted of preparing their own meals, sleeping in the hayloft, and using an outhouse. For the rest of his life, Charles was to maintain this balance between his patrician upbringing and more democratic inclinations of his own.

Earning a living remained a problem, particularly as the Depression deepened. Frank Damrosch, annoyed at Charles's separation from Constance, reduced his teaching load. Charles began to teach part-time at the New School for Social Research, an institution dedicated to progressive education and a haven for scholars whose politics placed them to the left of the American mainstream. He also began accepting private composition students. In 1929, Henry Cowell suggested that he teach a remarkable young composer named Ruth Crawford, who was then studying in Chicago. Charles was reluctant, for he did not think highly of women composers and said so in a rather tactless letter to Crawford. But he needed the money and he prized Cowell's judgment, so he agreed to an initial six weeks of lessons. After the trial period, they would continue the lessons if both wished to do so; if not, they would part without further responsibility to each other. As it turned out, they did not part for twenty-four years.

Ruth's background was in some ways similar to Charles's: both were of northern European, Protestant stock; both were raised in a tradition of uncompromising moral integrity; and both had had a peripatetic childhood. There the similarities ended. The Seeger tradition of morality was based on class elitism; only a virtuous ruling class could produce a virtuous society. The Crawford tradition was based on Christian universalism; a Christian behaved well because God had his eye on the small as well as the great. Ruth's father, Clark Crawford, was a Methodist minister whose calling took him from Ohio (where Ruth was born in 1901) to Missouri to Indiana and finally to Jacksonville, Florida. The Seeger notion of virtue did not preclude worldly pleasures, but Ruth lived within a tighter sphere; dancing and circuses were forbidden the preacher's daughter. Yet her childhood was primarily a happy one; Ruth was a devout and serious child, eager to please and readily accepting her position as an exemplar for her father's congregation. These happy days ended when Clark Crawford died of tuberculosis at the age of fifty-nine. Ruth was twelve years old at the time, her brother Carl a few years older.

With Clark's death, the family had to vacate the parsonage where they had lived. The small pension provided by the Methodist Conference was insufficient to their needs, so Ruth's mother, Clara Crawford, opened a boarding-house near the church and tried to keep up the accoutrements of middle-class life. Ruth had attractive clothes for school and continued the piano lessons she had begun at the age of six. Like many serious and introspective teenagers, she kept a diary. Her diary entry for Christmas of 1917 describes a dreary holiday due to the lack of money. Her description recalls the opening pages of *Little Women* (which Ruth would surely have read), in which another set of impoverished preacher's children struggle and ultimately triumph over hardship and austerity. Like Jo March, the unconventional heroine of *Little Women*, Ruth turned to writing to express and analyze her adolescent point of view. Like Jo, Ruth wanted to be a writer; she published her poems in magazines and produced a literary journal with her friends. Her writing is rather conventional and often highly romantic; she was seeking a way to reconcile the spiritual world in which she had been raised with the more earthly love of beauty that she was discovering on her own. Had the money been available, she might have continued her quest in college. But after Ruth Crawford finished high school, she had to earn a living, and she did so by turning to the art that most perfectly combines the spiritual and the sensual: music.

Music is the art form that is the least material and simultaneously the most completely embodied. Music has no outward physical products: no painting, no photograph, no essential spectacle. Music can be written down, but transcriptions are no more "music" than a recipe is food. Yet music's lack of an external project means that it exists entirely within the human body: in the human ear and the human brain. Its sensuality comes not from our connection with the physical world but from our production of sound from within.

Then as now, music had a practical side. America in 1918 had a growing market demand for music teachers. Teaching had become a woman's profession by the turn of the twentieth century, when the image of the educated, self-supporting "new woman" supplanted the older notion of the passive, sexless Victorian lady. Bertha Foster, owner of Jacksonville's School of Musical Art, was a perfect example of the new woman, a career woman who never married but retained the feminine virtues of beauty, warmth, and charm. Foster hired Ruth as a junior music teacher, and the salary enabled the Crawfords to sell the boardinghouse and buy a single-family home. Recognizing Ruth's talents, Foster had her continue her piano lessons with the school's best teacher, Valborg Collett. For three years, Ruth was a popular teacher at the School of Musical Art and a respected pianist in the Jacksonville community. She even began composing a few small works of her own.

By 1921, the school had grown so much that Bertha Foster decided to relocate to the larger city of Miami. This change allowed Ruth to follow her own ambition; it was clear she would not spend her life as a junior teacher in someone else's school. Her talent was such that it needed the guidance of a world-class mentor, and she chose to study with Heniot Levy, head of the piano department at the American Conservatory of Music in Chicago. Ruth's plan was to spend one year in Chicago, earn a teaching certificate, and return to Jacksonville with the qualifications and expertise to open a studio of her own. The plan was expensive and Mrs. Crawford would be left on her own, but a cousin offered to finance the year, and Clara Crawford encouraged her daughter to obtain the training that would make her financially independent. In September 1921, Ruth Crawford moved to Chicago.

For the sheltered preacher's daughter, living alone in Chicago was a new world. Chicago boasted a world-class symphony orchestra and a world-class opera and was a popular destination for touring European and American musicians. Levy recognized her talent and insisted that she switch to a more advanced program than she had originally considered, a course of study that included harmony and composition as well as piano pedagogy. This program also required long hours of practice, which resulted in Ruth developing severe neuritis in her left arm. Following doctor's orders, she cut back on her time at the piano, a serious matter in a field that requires extensive practice to achieve technical virtuosity. Yet she ended the year as fourth in her class and was the only one of Levy's students who received a gold medal and was invited to compete for end-of-the-year student prizes. These accomplishments gave her the confidence she needed to return for a second year and follow her growing interest in harmony and composition.

Ruth recognized that, given her physical limitations, a concert career was probably not within her grasp, and she concentrated instead on her composition lessons with the renowned Adolf Weidig. In June 1924, she received her bachelor's degree, and her work was showcased in Weidig's annual concert of student composers. In the fall, she entered the master's program at the American Conservatory and simultaneously was hired as a member of the conservatory's piano teaching staff. Her new piano teacher, Djane Lavoie Herz, arranged for Ruth's compositions to be professionally performed in Chicago and New York, and she introduced Ruth to composers such as the French émigré Dane Rudhyar and the up-and-coming American Henry Cowell. Cowell was particularly taken with Ruth's work, as was Alfred Frankenstein, a writer and musician who introduced her to Chicago's poet laureate, Carl Sandburg. Sandburg was looking for a piano teacher for his daughters, and the fatherless Ruth got on so well with the family that she was accepted as an "informal adopted daughter."[7] Moreover, he hired Ruth to arrange some of the songs for his *American Songbag*, a collection of American folk songs. Songbooks with piano accompaniment were popular at the time; they were intended to facilitate family singing around the piano, an extension of the Victorian "cult of domesticity." What made the *American Songbag* different was its use of folk songs, not Tin Pan Alley ditties or watered-down classical music, and it was one of the first introductions of American folk song into popular culture. Ruth's experience with Sandberg's project was one that she would build on decades later.

The 1920s were a fruitful period for Ruth. Her teaching schedule was full, but she found plenty of time to compose. She set several of Sandburg's poems to music and composed for piano, violin, and orchestra. Success followed success: in 1926 she won a scholarship in composition from the Institute of Musical Art; in 1927 she received her master's degree summa cum laude; and in 1928 she was awarded the conservatory's Weidig gold medal, its highest honor in composition. Ruth's compositional style is generally known as "ultramodernism." Ultramodernists rejected Romantic harmony and tonality; they attempted to produce new musical techniques while simultaneously reinterpreting and reinventing older ones. Ruth was attracted to dissonant counterpoint, a compositional strategy that violates Romantic aesthetics with its deliberate use of dissonance and infuses the old technique of counterpoint with modernist sensibilities. Her mastery of form showed both discipline and playfulness, an ability to follow any formal structure while varying it and making it her own.

Ruth had become known as one of Chicago's premier composers, and paradoxically this prominence led to her decision to leave the city. Henry Cowell suggested that her radical style would find wider acceptance in New York and encouraged her to study with his former teacher, Charles Seeger. In 1929, two opportunities to further her musical career presented themselves, but both required Ruth to leave Chicago. The first was a chance to spend the summer in New Hampshire at the MacDowell Colony, where she would be free to do nothing but compose. The second was an opportunity to spend a year in New York at the home of Blanche Walton, a well-to-do music patron, and to study privately with Charles Seeger. Ruth accepted both challenges.

Marian MacDowell had designed the MacDowell Colony to free artists from any other work, either remunerative or household. Residents lived alone in small cabins, where lunch magically appeared on their doorsteps at 1:00 p.m. They ate breakfast and dinner together in the dining hall and could enjoy discussions with one another in the evening. Ruth's summer at the MacDowell Colony was a highly successful one. She composed music that pleased her and made friends who shared her interests. In the autumn of 1929, she moved to New York, where Blanche Walton's apartment provided the setting for informal meetings with well-known musicians, and where concerts of Ruth's music were performed to critical acclaim. But the most important event of that year was meeting her new teacher, Charles Seeger.

Charles's low opinion of women composers had hurt and angered Ruth, and she was determined to prove him wrong. It is unlikely that she did so from any self-consciously feminist position. The U.S. feminist movement had collapsed in exhaustion after its most hard-won victory—the vote—and it remained in this semi-quiescent state for the rest of Ruth's life. Though individuals such as Alice Paul continued to fight for women's rights, most feminist leaders believed that their work was largely done and women should channel their energies into the good of society as a whole. It was common for remarkable women in the 1920s and 1930s to avoid women's organizations and rebel against being classed with women as a group; to do otherwise, many believed, was to accept living in the ghetto. Ruth had avoided women's musical groups in Chicago, seeing them as essentially second-rate. Considered from this viewpoint, Charles's real mistake was not his unreflective dismissal of women composers but his inability to see that Ruth was an exception to the rule.

Charles's skepticism about Ruth's talent and Ruth's anger at his insensitivity disappeared at their first meeting in the autumn of 1929. Each found in the other an exciting intellectual and musical partner. Their lessons were highly successful, with Charles providing expert guidance and Ruth always moving beyond it. Charles was pleased by the improvement in her work, and she was eternally grateful to her teacher. But he was no Pygmalion molding a passive Galatea, nor did he want to be. Lyn Ellen Burkett suggests that the two ultimately worked symbiotically: "If Seeger's ideas on dissonant counterpoint provided a young Crawford with the mechanisms to wind together the still raveled fibers of her own compositional aesthetic, then certainly it must be said that Crawford's mature compositions weave Seeger's ideas into tapestries more spectacular than anything he could have envisioned emerging from his nascent theories."[8]

Despite the passion and intensity of their work together, the relationship between Crawford and Seeger was initially platonic. Seeger was fourteen years older than Crawford and still married, though separated from his wife. In the winter of 1930, he began an affair with Mona Dunlop—a woman even younger than Ruth—and asked Constance for a divorce. Constance refused, and the affair ended soon afterward. Ruth did not dissipate her energies on romance, and her hard work paid off in the spring. Several of her new pieces were performed in New York, in the company of composers such as Charles Ives, Henry Cowell, and Marc Blitzstein. Marian MacDowell invited her to spend another summer at the MacDowell Colony. Even more impressive was her receipt of a Guggenheim Fellowship in composition, making her the first woman to win that honor.

The Guggenheim's only requirement was residence in Europe, a sign of the artistic inferiority complex that Americans still suffered. Ruth's initial plan was to spend the summer at the MacDowell Colony and leave for Europe in the fall. She was reluctant to end her lessons with Charles, and he, equally reluctant, suggested that she spend June with him in Patterson, helping him write a manual on composition and dissonant counterpoint. Ruth agreed. She stayed on a farm nearby and spent her days in the Seeger barn, working with Charles and taking her meals with him and the boys, who were home from boarding school. This was Ruth's first opportunity to see Charles in his role as a family man, and she liked what she saw. As might be expected, the Seeger household was musical: the boys held elaborate singing contests, and singing together after dinner was a regular part of the day. Four Seegers were occasionally overwhelming for the shy midwesterner; John recalls, "We boys acted like three boys—we never stopped talking."[9] But she was genuinely fond of the boys and they of her. Friendly, cheerful, and unaffected, Ruth became an accepted part of the Seeger ménage.

The book could not be finished in one month, so Ruth abandoned her plan to go to the MacDowell Colony. The book was still unfinished in mid-August, when Charles drove Ruth to Quebec, her departure point for Europe. A four-day sojourn in Vermont ended the platonic phase of their relationship. Their friendship had turned into a love affair in which music was a central component.

Ruth composed steadily and well during her Guggenheim year. During this time, she wrote her most celebrated work, the String Quartet 1931. She applied to stay for a second year and was devastated when the Guggenheim Foundation turned her down. Charles visited her in the summer and suggested that they "were going to get married and [they] would have some lovely children."[10] Ruth assented, but there was one problem: Charles was married to someone else. He was still married when Ruth moved into his Greenwich Village apartment in the autumn of 1931. Constance eventually granted him a divorce, and in the autumn of 1932, Charles and Ruth were married. By December, she was pregnant. Charles's mother was furious at the scandal and refused to see her new daughter-in-law.

Charles was still teaching part-time at the Institute for Musical Art and the New School for Social Research. In keeping with the ethos of the day, he insisted that he should be the breadwinner, and Ruth should stay home and concentrate on her composing. Artistically, this worked well—Ruth's work was performed, published, and recorded—but financially, they were barely making ends meet. To save money, they gave up the apartment and stayed with friends. On August 15, 1933, Ruth gave birth to their first child, Michael. After she and the baby left the hospital, the family stayed with friends before moving to a cheerless railroad apartment on the Upper East Side. Home on vacation from boarding school, the teenaged Pete Seeger loaned his father money to buy milk for the baby.

Poverty may have been new to Charles Seeger, but it was no rarity during the Depression. The 1930s rekindled Charles's interest in using music to improve the world, and he enlisted Ruth as a comrade-in-arms. Ruth was a relative latecomer to politics. She had spent most of her Guggenheim year in Berlin without ever mentioning the Nazis in her many copious letters to Charles. But she was eager to join in Charles's new enthusiasm. With Henry Cowell, they helped create the Composers' Collective, an organization of radical musicians who wanted to use music to further left-wing political causes. Originally part of the Pierre Degeyter Club, one of the cultural arms of the American Communist Party, the Composers' Collective began in 1931 and included musicians such as Elie Siegmeister, Earl Robinson, Marc Blitzstein, and Aaron Copland.[11] They were primarily conservatory-trained composers, and their aim was to produce music that could be used as a "weapon in the class struggle."[12] They focused on art music and had little use for folk or popular music. In his 1934 article "On Proletarian Music," Seeger went so far as to say, "First, there is the question of music *for* the proletariat. Needless to say, the proletariat has not produced any music of its own *as such*."[13] But the lush harmonies of the past seemed intimately connected with the upper class, too enmeshed in the status quo to further a message of radical social change. For this task, members of the Composers' Collective sought to create a revolutionary form consistent with the revolutionary content that the music would convey. In the same article, Seeger elegantly debunks the notion that art can exist apart from the society in which it is created: "Art, then, is always and inevitably a social function. It has social significance. It is a social force. It is propaganda: explicit, positive; implied, negative. The better the art, the better propaganda it makes; the better the propaganda, the better art it is. . . . The liberal composer who has sat in his ivory tower and said, 'whether or not there is a class struggle, music has nothing to do with it,' is broadcasting negative propaganda (tacit approval) for the social system that gives him a tower and allows him to sit in it."[14]

Some members of the Composers' Collective were members of the Communist Party, while others were not, and party membership was never required. It is unclear exactly when Charles Seeger joined the Communist Party. By 1934, he was the music critic for the Communist *Daily Worker*, under the pseudonym "Carl Sands." In his FBI file, however, he stated that he joined the Communist Party only after leaving New York, from 1936 to 1939 and briefly again in the early 1940s. Charles was to become disillusioned with the Communist Party after the Moscow purge trials and would formally leave in 1943. But in the 1930s, he and many others saw Communism as a beacon of hope in a world dominated by failed capitalism and growing fascism. As a teenager, Pete once asked him, "If there is good and bad in everything, what is bad in communism?" Charles replied optimistically, "It's all good."[15]

The hero of the Composers' Collective was German composer Hanns Eisler. A student of Schoenberg who rejected his teacher's technique (though he remained an admirer of Schoenberg's music), Eisler had done precisely what the Composers' Collective wanted to do: he had turned his back on the bourgeois tonalities of the past and created music that was fresh, exciting, and filled with revolutionary content. His songs (many of which had words by Bertolt Brecht) were sung as far away as China, and his music filled the cabarets and films of the Weimar Republic. A Jew and a Marxist, Eisler left Germany in 1933, and Charles Seeger was instrumental in bringing him to the United States.

Eisler shared Seeger's low opinion of folk music—at least in theory. Seeger had enjoyed fiddle and banjo playing in North Carolina, but he did not think that these vestiges of a dying culture could contribute to the political task at hand: "Many folksongs are complacent, melancholy, defeatist . . . intended to make slaves endure their lot—pretty but not the stuff for a militant proletariat to feed upon."[16] Eisler believed that true folk music had been killed by the Industrial Revolution and that attempts to revive it were, at best, reactionary and sentimental yearnings for a precapitalist era. His distrust was well founded, for he had witnessed the most vicious folk revival in history: the Nazis' use of German folk culture to support their racist ideology and murderous regime. But in practice, Eisler could not slough off folk culture quite so easily. His "Capriccio on Jewish Folk Songs," written for an independent German film in 1931, is an ingenious combination of traditional Jewish melodies with the unconventional rhythms and jazz-inspired instrumentation of German and French cabaret music. In 1932, he wrote an adaptation of Brecht's "O Fallada, There You Are Hanging," a text inspired by "The Goose Girl," a tale from Germany's ur-folklorists, the Brothers Grimm. And in 1935, he praised "The Peatbog Soldiers," a song created in the Börgermoor concentration camp, as "one of the most beautiful revolutionary songs of the international working-class movement."[17] Börgermoor was a camp designed primarily for political prisoners, and the song quickly became an antifascist rallying cry. It was sung in many concentration camps, among the soldiers of the International Brigades during the Spanish Civil War, and in concerts. "The Peat-Bog Soldiers" remains the most famous concentration camp song, and Eisler wrote the tune by which it is best known. That Eisler recognized it as a folk song is apparent in his remark, "This song did not arise spontaneously, as bourgeois folk song experts have assumed."[18] His knowledge of the genre is manifest as he details the song's attributes, which are the hallmarks of a folk song: it was composed to express the ideas and to fulfill the needs of a group; it was composed by amateur musicians; and the melody was based on the traditional music of an earlier age.

The Composers' Collective never achieved what Eisler did. They had no Brecht to write texts, and their music was frequently too complicated to be understood by anyone outside their own circle. Ultimately, many members of the Composers' Collective turned to folk music as a more effective way to reach the working classes. Even those who remained firmly committed to art music began to see folk music as a foundation on which the composer could build.[19] Aaron Copland would become the most distinguished American composer of his generation, and some of his best-loved compositions involve the creative use of American folk melodies. Earl Robinson's song "Joe Hill," written in 1936 about the slain labor leader, takes the form of a traditional Anglo-American ballad and has become a folk revival standard. Elie Siegmeister used American folk songs in his own compositions and created the American Ballad Singers, a group of classically trained musicians who sang his arrangements of traditional American songs. Hanns Eisler sought to rehabilitate German folk music in 1950, when he and Johannes R. Becher published *New German Folk Songs*, an attempt to wrest German folk culture from the poisonous embrace of Nazi propaganda. Joy H. Calico describes the songs as blending the best of prewar German folklore with modern antifascist ideology: "Original songs designed for the new generation of German citizens and yet self-consciously referential to the storied German folk song tradition, they are uniquely positioned to create an appropriate past and link the antifascist socialist present to it."[20] But no one embraced folk music more completely or more thoroughly than Charles and Ruth Seeger.

Despite his somewhat doctrinaire remarks in the early 1930s, Charles had never considered "music" to be synonymous with Western art music. His appreciation of music had always been relatively broad, going back to the Mexican songs he had learned as a child and the folk songs he had performed as a professor at Berkeley. He insisted that musicologists should study all the world's music, not just the concert hall music of the West. Guido Adler, one of the founders of musicology and its first major theorist, had divided the field into two parts: historical musicology, which focused on the history of Western art music; and systematic musicology, which comprised music theory and "comparative musicology," the study of all other kinds of music. Adler's schema asserted that musicology should include all forms of world music, yet by the designation "comparative," it set up Western art music as the gold standard by which other kinds of music would be judged. Charles Seeger was one of the few scholars to bridge the divide.[21]

During the 1930s, Charles began to think that composers, instead of creating music for the proletariat, might do well to look at the music that the working classes had already made: folk music. Several factors contributed to his changing point of view. One was the experience of playing the guitar in Thomas Hart Benton's string band. Charles found that audiences responded to the traditional music of Benton's Ozark background far more readily than to the abstruse work of the Composers' Collective. John and Alan Lomax's *American Ballads and Folk Songs*, published in 1934, was further evidence that folk music was alive and well if one took the trouble to look for it. John Lomax was a Texas folklorist who, like Charles, had been a student of the great ballad scholar George Lyman Kittredge at Harvard. Lomax was also an indefatigable folk song collector; his *Cowboy Songs*, published in 1910, was one of the first published collections of American folk songs. That folk songs could be used for progressive political causes was made manifest by the labor songs of Aunt Molly Jackson, who came to New York from the coalfields of Kentucky in 1931. An appearance at the Composers' Collective left her and the composers mutually mystified; her harsh Kentucky twang was as unintelligible to them as their ultramodernist creations were to her. But Charles Seeger soon understood the value of her music. He later reflected, "I learned her songs and discovered that they were folk songs simply dolled up, with new words and perhaps a few touches of her own, and that the people could sing their songs and they couldn't sing our songs. So I went up to her and I said, Mollie [*sic*], you're on the right track and we're on the wrong track and I gave up the Collective. We were all on the wrong track—it was professionals trying to write music for the people and not in the people's idiom."[22]

Though Charles and Ruth Seeger were enjoying a rich intellectual and musical life, they were still having trouble making a living. Charles had been fired by the Institute of Musical Art, in part because of his association with radical politics, in part because Frank Damrosch was annoyed by the divorce from Constance. Charles was teaching part-time at the New School for Social Research, and Ruth had a few private pupils, but money was a constant worry. The year 1935, which would end so well, began with grave uncertainty: Ruth was pregnant with their second child, and Charles was eager to find a permanent home for his growing brood. In the summer, he planned to earn money picking blueberries at a farm near his parents' home in Patterson. He delayed his departure until after his child was born. After four boys, Charles hoped for a girl. His wish was granted on June 17, 1935, when his daughter Margaret was born.

Charles named his first daughter after Margaret Taylor, a rich and beautiful woman he had loved in his youth. Ruth, showing either saintly forbearance or serene confidence that no woman could replace her in her husband's affections, acquiesced. "As far as I know, my mother thought it was a hoot," Peggy Seeger recalls. "She liked the name Margaret, but I was immediately Peggy."[23] Satisfied that Ruth was recovering well and Peggy was healthy, Charles took Mike and decamped for Patterson. A rapprochement had been reached with Elsie Adams Seeger, who welcomed her small grandson and was eager to see her first granddaughter. But Ruth was in no hurry; she was enjoying the time alone with her baby daughter. The housing that awaited her—a trailer with no running water or other amenities—was hardly inviting for a mother with a newborn and a toddler. In July, Mike became ill, and Elsie wrote her daughter-in-law a worried letter: Charles was exhausted from working on the farm and taking care of Mike. The letter urged Ruth to hurry and take up her familial duties; it also contained a rather belated welcome: Elsie thanked Ruth for making Charles happy and for giving him two children. Shortly thereafter, Ruth and Peggy joined the family in Patterson.

Back in New York City for the autumn, the Seeger family continued the struggle to make ends meet. Charles recalled having money for "the rent of the apartment and . . . suppers but not much else."[24] The call to join the Resettlement Administration could not have come at a better time. Not only would it provide his family with a steady income; it would allow him to do what he most wanted: use music to improve the world. He and Constance may have failed to interest rural North Carolinians in the music of Bach and Beethoven; he may have been unable to write music that could be used as a weapon in the class struggle; but this time he had the New Deal as a comrade-in-arms. Adrian J. Dornbush, director of the Special Skills Division, saw the arts as a way to implement progressive social policy: "The music and dramatic activities of the Division are not engaged in as ends in themselves, but rather as means by which larger social aims may more readily be achieved."[25] Charles was still ambivalent about folk music; despite his experiences with Benton, the Lomaxes, and Aunt Molly Jackson, he could write in January 1935, "Until recently the American was the most music-less worker in the world. . . . The traditional country (folk) music practically died out by 1900."[26] But he and many other progressives were starting to see folk music as the authentic creation of the common people. The philosophy of the Popular Front, which urged Communists, socialists, liberals, and other reformers to cooperate in the fight against fascism, also encouraged respect for the culture of "the common man," as the idiom of the day would have it. So while Spanish Republican forces attempted to repel the armies of Francisco Franco and while Nazis forged the iron bars that would turn Germany—and much of Europe—into a prison, Charles Seeger went to Washington to fight the good fight with music as his weapon. It was more than a job. It was a blow for democracy.

# CHAPTER 2

# The Early Years

The house I lived in, when I was a child,
Had woods, we all ran wild,
You could hide, then come home after a while.
The town I lived in when I was young,
Everybody knew my name,
The world was my own,
Safe in the dark, playing games,
Till Mama called me home.

—Peggy Seeger, "Everything Changes"

The Seegers' first home was in Clarendon, Virginia, in a rented house so close to the District of Columbia line that letters mailed to "Washington, D.C." got there. Ruth rejoiced in the space after years of cramped New York City apartments. In early 1936, Ruth wrote, "The baby? She still has curly hair and dimples, is healthy and fat . . . and likes the new job because it means a sunny porch and the whole day spent on it. Michael loves and fondly torments and pummels the butter ball whenever he gets the chance."[1] Charles's income was sufficient for their daily needs and even allowed the Seegers to pay off debts and hire a woman to help Ruth with household chores.

But financial security came at a price: Charles's job required frequent absences from home. During the next few years, he would travel hundreds of miles by car and train, from Tennessee to Alabama, from Florida to Texas. As head of the RA's music program, Charles was responsible for musical activities in newly created communities, or "homesteads," composed of people whose livelihoods had been shattered by the Depression. The homesteads had a somewhat ersatz quality: residents included unemployed miners and urban factory workers as well as farmers and sharecroppers whose land no longer afforded a living. Religious differences were a frequent source of strife. The raison d'être of the Special Skills Division was the belief that "participation in organized, leisure-time activities such as dances, community sings, pageants, and performing groups, would help ameliorate the discord rife among the newly resettled populations."[2]

The philosophy behind the Special Skills Division partook of that heady blend of idealism and activism that characterized many New Deal projects. Yet the process by which these ideals could become reality was not clearly developed, and much of the work of the Special Skills Division proceeded by trial and error. Fieldworkers specializing in music, drama, painting, and other arts went to live in the homesteads for periods of time ranging from a few weeks to six months. There they attempted to use the arts to alleviate tensions that emerged among a diverse group of people thrown together by chance and disaster. Charles believed that the participation of the homestead residents themselves was the key to the program's success; moreover, he believed that RA programs should build on the music that the residents already knew and enjoyed.

Within a few months of starting his new job, the man who had viewed folk music as moribund or reactionary had a fundamental switch in perception, and he embraced folk music with the fervor of a religious convert. Folk music was plentiful in the communities that Charles visited, and the ease with which new words could be written to old tunes made them ideal vehicles for progressive messages, a technique that Aunt Molly Jackson had shown him years earlier. Not all his fieldworkers followed this path; some scorned the local music and refused to use it in their work. Nor was admiration for folk music universal among the homestead residents; some preferred classical music or jazz or hit songs from the radio. But folk music was simple enough and familiar enough to be used for the primary purpose of the RA: fostering cooperation among the homestead residents in a common pursuit. Many residents had come from rural areas where folk music was still the common musical coin. In a 1937 report prepared with Margaret Valiant, the music division's best fieldworker, Charles argued for the centrality of folk music not only in RA homesteads but in the "musical culture of the nation": "The basis for musical culture is the musical vernacular of the broad mass of the people—its traditional (often called 'folk') idiom; popular music (jazz) and professional (high art) music are elaborate superstructures built upon the common base. . . . There is no ground for the quarrel between the various idioms or styles, provided proper relationship between them is maintained—jazz need not be scorned, nor professional music artificially stimulated, nor folk music stamped out or sentimentalized."[3]

The abundance of folk music in the homestead communities led Charles to an important innovation in the music program's agenda: the preservation and collection of traditional music. His initial request for a recording machine was met with skepticism by bureaucrats who did not see its relevance; the intervention of President Roosevelt was necessary before the request was honored. Despite Charles's dictum that other kinds of music should not be scorned or neglected, the collection project focused specifically on folk music. In this project, Charles was assisted by two of the music division's best workers: Sidney Robertson (who later married Henry Cowell) and Herbert Haufrecht, a composer and friend from the Composers' Collective.

Charles's excitement about discovering folk music in its native—or at least recently transplanted—habitat was tempered by loneliness for his family and the strangeness of life in the rural South, a part of the country unknown to the sheltered northeasterner. During his many absences, Charles and Ruth wrote each other nearly every day, and their letters reveal an extremely affectionate family life. Ruth detailed the minutiae of daily life and the children's accomplishments. When the children were old enough, they sent their own messages and dictated letters that Ruth dutifully typed.

While Charles was traveling, Ruth was left alone with two small children in a city where she initially had few friends and no professional outlets. The burdens of the household rested heavily on her shoulders. She received help from a series of housekeepers, but for the first few years at least, she did the bulk of the housework and child care. In a letter dated January 2, 1936, she wrote to Charles, "It is 10:07 and time to go to bed, and the day is just begun."[4] She had just finished dealing with a flooded basement and garage on an evening of heavy snow, though she insisted she felt "fine fresh and fit" after a supper of café au lait. The cheerful complaints turned serious toward the end of the letter when she wrote, "How terrible it would be if you traveled like this steadily and we were always living in the future or the past, with only a scattered day here and there in the actual present."[5]

Occasionally, she was able to join him in his travels. In the summer of 1936, Ruth and Pete traveled with Charles to some of the best-known folk festivals in the South, including the White Top Folk Festival in southwestern Virginia and Bascom Lunsford's Mountain Dance and Folk Festival in Asheville, North Carolina. Ruth's interest in American folk music, first kindled when she worked with Carl Sandburg on *The American Songbag*, was reignited by Charles's ventures into folk music's home territory. It was in Asheville that seventeen-year-old Pete became acquainted with the five-string banjo, the instrument that later became his trademark.

In 1937, the Seegers left Virginia for a rented property on P Street in Washington, DC. In May, Ruth gave birth to their third child, a daughter named Barbara Mona ("Mona" was an homage to Charles's fling in the winter of 1930). In the summer, John Lomax asked Ruth to transcribe songs for an upcoming book based on his recent fieldwork. *American Ballads and Folk Songs* had been a commercial success but had been sharply criticized for the poor quality of its transcriptions. A subsequent book, on the Louisiana-born African American musician Huddie Ledbetter (better known as Leadbelly), had been transcribed by the eminent ethnomusicologist George Herzog, but the transcriptions were so precise and minute that they were virtually useless to musicians who wanted to learn the songs. Lomax was searching for a transcriber who could combine technical accuracy with practicality. Ruth accepted the offer. Unlike composing, transcribing was a paid position and would provide the family with much-needed funds. It was also work that Ruth could do at home, no minor consideration for a mother with three small children and a frequently absent husband. For the next four years, this work would absorb her, and the sounds of American folk song, played over and over again by the meticulous transcriber, would fill the Seeger home.

In the autumn of 1937, Ruth returned to composing. This time, she turned away from the abstruse tonalities of ultramodernism and toward American folk music. She arranged twenty-two American folk songs with piano accompaniment, intended for beginning piano students. All these songs came from published collections: Carl Sandburg's *The American Songbag*, John and Alan Lomax's *American Ballads and Folk Songs*, Cecil Sharp's *English Folk Songs from the Southern Appalachians*, and Bascom Lamar Lunsford and Lamar Stringfield's *30 and 1 Folksongs from the Southern Mountains*. The use of American folk songs was an exciting departure for Ruth as a composer, but she had little time to develop it. Professionally, her transcription work for the Lomaxes came first. The money that she earned was important, for Charles's job at the Special Skills Division would last only a few years. The RA's idealistic director, Rexford Tugwell, came under attack for his left-wing sympathies; Tugwell eventually resigned at the end of 1936. The Special Skills Division was incorporated into the Department of Agriculture in 1937, but funding was reduced, and Charles's job ended by the beginning of 1938. For six months he was out of work. Ruth was not particularly well paid for her transcribing work, but the fact that she was paid at all may have kept the family from poverty.

During this time of financial uncertainty, Charles III became engaged to a young woman named Inez Wolf. This happy event was marred by Elsie Adams Seeger's reaction: Inez was Jewish, and Grandmother Seeger declared that young Charles's bride would never be welcome in her home. Charles Jr.'s immediate support for his son and future daughter-in-law showed the same unblinking integrity that he had shown in his opposition to World War I. In the winter of 1938, he wrote to Charles III and Inez and embraced the young couple as fellow victims of Grandmother Seeger's intolerance: "Welcome to the Happy Brotherhood of GM Seeger's disapproval! . . . It is not so very hard for Charles and me to grind our teeth and laugh at the same time but it is hard for Ruth and Inez to put up with such gutter-behaviour on the part of a member of the family they marry into. The only thing I can think of that might help mitigate their righteous wrath and real deep hurt . . . is to analyse the motives back of the writers innate vulgarity and discourtesy."[6] These lines encapsulate the many aspects of Charles Seeger's personality: the man of principle fights prejudice wherever it occurs; the patrician New Englander adopts a stiff upper lip while simultaneously defending his womenfolk; the scholar approaches all problems with analysis (and prefers British spelling); while the human being is so upset he makes minor grammatical errors. In time, Elsie Adams Seeger did accept her daughter-in-law, in part because of Inez's kind and courteous behavior to Charles Sr. when he was in the hospital. And when Pete became engaged to Toshi Ohta, who was half-Japanese, during World War II, Elsie Adams Seeger gave up trying to understand her descendants' marriage patterns. Bowing to the inevitable, she put on her hat and went down to the Ohtas' Greenwich Village home to introduce herself.[7]

In June 1938, Charles was hired to oversee programs of traditional music for the Federal Music Project, a division of the Works Progress Administration (WPA). Once again, he was frequently away from home, traveling to Tennessee and Oklahoma, Mississippi and Arkansas. His job included the creation of recreational programs that featured folk music, the collection and documentation of traditional music, and the promotion of American folk music in the schools. He and Ruth were adamant that American composers and music teachers should base their work on American folk music and not try to imitate Europeans. The Seegers found a close personal and professional ally in Benjamin Botkin, a poet and folklorist from the Federal Writers' Project. The city-bred son of Jewish immigrants, Botkin argued that the city was a place where folklore was continually being created anew, and he stressed the importance of immigrants' contributions to American culture.

Charles's WPA salary allowed the Seegers to leave their rented accommodations and buy a home of their own in September 1938. Peggy has a few memories of the apartment on P Street—memories still as snapshots and vague as dreams—but her clearly remembered childhood began when the family bought a house on Fairway Avenue (renamed Dallas Avenue in 1940) in Silver Spring, Maryland. Ruth described her new home as a "charming peculiar house" with a large fireplace and no closets.[8] Finances were still tight, so the Seegers initially shared the house with Adelaide and Alfred Truesdale, a single mother and her son. By October, Ruth had found a housekeeper named Bertha, whom she considered "very good with the children—firm but patiently firm."[9] With Bertha at the helm, Ruth was able to leave the children at home and go into Washington, where she could work undisturbed at Margaret Valiant's apartment.

Like many working mothers, Ruth often felt torn between her desire to work and her desire to be with her children. In August 1938, she wrote, "The work goes slowly, with many interruptions. When I am working, I feel restless about the children and heartless because I am so little with them; then when I go out to see how they are getting on, am not content till I get back to work."[10] Ruth's attempts to balance work and family—a topic of frequent discussion and analysis for second- and third-wave feminists—had no context in the 1930s. She treated the difficulties purely as personal problems, as most women did in those days. Unable to neglect her family and unwilling to neglect her work, Ruth drank innumerable cups of coffee and carved out time for herself while the rest of the world was sleeping, a pattern that would continue much of her life. By the time she was three years old, Peggy saw her mother running a household and pursuing her own career, without rest or complaint or acceptance of second-rate work. Ruth was relentless in her self-criticism. Years before, during her Guggenheim year, she had lamented her "weakness of will in making [herself] do anything regularly. Eve's great sin in the garden, which according to Charles Louis Seeger Jr. was laziness, was in other words selfishness."[11] The preacher's daughter did not allow selfishness; the award-winning musician could not afford laziness. The woman laid these sins at the door of the mythic first woman and, following Charles's advice, preferred the company of men. But she could not avoid the woman's dilemma that pitted work against family.

As a small child, Peggy was close to her sister Barbara, playing happily with her while Mike and Alfred were in school.[12] Yet Mike was always the sibling to whom she was closest; as small children, they occasionally slept in the same bed. In the summer of 1938, Mike visited the Seeger grandparents by himself, spending his birthday at Fairlea. When his birthday cake arrived, he asked if he could save it to take home to his sister. His grandmother explained that birthday cakes do not keep but promised that another cake would be provided for Peggy. Elsie Adams Seeger praised Mike's unselfishness (and his table manners) and remarked on his strong attachment to Peggy: "I said at table 'Grandmother will write Mother and Father and tell them what a nice time we are having'—and he said, 'I write to Peggy.' 'Michael loves you.'"[13]

Peggy remembers Silver Spring as "a great place to bring up children."[14] Despite its proximity to the nation's capital, it still had a country feel that she appreciated. The Seegers' next-door neighbor was a chicken farmer, and the children could hunt for four-leaf clovers in nearby fields. Children walked to school and played games outdoors: jump rope, hopscotch, London Bridge is falling down. Charles built a wooden merry-go-round and erected a badminton set in the backyard. In one corner of the large central living room, Ruth set up a treadle sewing machine, a desk for transcription, and eventually a piano. There was no radio or television, but music filled the house: Charles played the guitar and sang the Spanish songs of his Mexican childhood; Ruth played the piano like the conservatory-trained musician that she was; and the Lomax field recordings were constantly being played. In February 1939, Ruth heard Peggy singing in the bathroom, "Oh, pretty my condition, just as you would your own / Lolly tru dum tru dum tru dum lolly day."[15] At the age of three, Peggy hadn't quite gotten the words right (it should be "*pity* my condition"), but she had already absorbed the structure and could reproduce the vocables of the Anglo-American ballad.

The amenities of life were largely homemade. Money was still in short supply, and the family could not afford store-bought presents when the children were invited to birthday parties. Instead, Ruth baked cookies with iced letters that spelled out "happy birthday" and the name of the child. Handmade paper chains adorned the Christmas trees. Peggy and Barbara's dolls wore dresses that Ruth and Peggy had crocheted. Charles taught Mike woodworking and carpentry, and Mike supplied furniture for his sisters' dolls. Despite Charles and Ruth's political progressivism, the sexual division of labor was upheld and passed on to the children with gender-appropriate toys. However, Ruth was never content with the traditional woman's role and refused to allow her daughters to accept it. In February 1939, she wrote to Charles: "Peggy is getting the idea that some of the things she can't do, like going to school and concerts, are due to the sad state of being a girl. I . . . must disabuse her of it, poor young one."[16]

The arrangement with the Truesdales eventually proved untenable; the house was small, and Ruth worried about Alfred's frequent illnesses, which were usually passed on to the Seeger children. But supporting a family of five on a WPA salary was a challenge. In addition to her transcription work for the Lomaxes, Ruth decided to go back to piano teaching. Before the family could afford a piano, Ruth went to other people's homes to give lessons. Housekeepers came and went, some staying for months, others for only a day. Peggy remembers women knocking on the door in the morning, asking if "Mrs." needed help that day. Many of these women were African American migrants from the South; some were experienced housekeepers, while others were simply trying to make a living in one of the few professions open to black women at the time.

The Seeger household was a mixture of New England decorum and bohemian nonconformity. Constance's boys addressed their parents as "Father" and "Mother" (though Pete would sometimes write letters to "Pop" or "Pa"), but Ruth's children called their parents "Charlie" and "Dio." ("Dio" came from Mike's childish attempt to imitate Charles's New England pronunciation of "dear," and the nickname stuck.) Ruth and Charles frequently went without clothes in the house, and the children bathed together when they were small. When Pete became engaged to Toshi Ohta, the young couple had little privacy: Pete was in the Army and lived in a group house in New York City when on furlough; Toshi lived with her parents. When Charles discovered that the engaged couple had never slept together, he offered his bed for their use. Pete and Toshi gratefully accepted.

Yet informality coexisted with propriety. At the age of three, Peggy was sent to her room for whining and stamping her foot, "it being explained that she must play alone if she could not be agreeable."[17] Peggy recalls, "You weren't allowed to lose your temper in our house. You were not allowed to scream and shout and have tantrums, and if you started doing that, you had to go to your room."[18] This tranquil temperament was natural to Charles, less so to Ruth. Their differences are apparent in a note that Ruth wrote to Charles when Michael was small: "Please forgive me for losing temper with Michael this morning—and love me even more if possible."[19] Peggy remembers few occasions when her father got truly angry. Mike concurred; at the age of eight, he wrote: "My father never gets angry—except that time he came home at night and we were taking a bath by ourselves, Peggy and me, . . . and we got the bath mat soaking wet. But that only happened once."[20] When Ruth's temper showed signs of erupting, Charles would put his hand on her shoulder and say, "Now, Dio, don't get peppy."[21] "Peppy" was Charles's word for Ruth's occasional lapses of self-control; anger was so foreign to his nature that he didn't even call it by name.

Charles's equanimity was natural to him, but it was probably helped by the fact that he was not the children's primary caretaker. Even when he was no longer traveling for work, Ruth organized the household, kept track of the children's schedules, and acted as disciplinarian. Charles preferred to ignore signs of discord; if the children became too noisy at the dinner table, he simply turned off his hearing aid. Ruth was not so easy-going. When Peggy was six, the Seeger family bought a piano after many years of saving. Peggy, who had recently learned to write, was delighted: "They saved up so long for this piano, and it arrived and it was so shiny—the perfect thing to write on. . . . I took a stylus and carved my brother's name right along the keyboard cover. . . . My mother went nuts. She spanked me in every room in the house."[22]

This was the harshest punishment that Peggy ever received. Ruth's spankings were usually minor affairs, and Peggy was normally a well-behaved child, the apple of her father's eye and a great favorite among family friends. In August 1938, Ruth wrote to Charles: "Everybody thinks she is very beautiful as well as very superior in intelligence."[23] At the age of three, she was able to have conversations with adults, and even when Ruth found Peggy's behavior frustrating, the frustration was mingled with maternal pride. In January 1939, Ruth wrote to Charles: "Her whining and impatience hit me I can't tell you how! Yet how beautiful she is! And when her eyes twinkle and she is gay, or dream and she is soulful, one should be able to say, 'Now next time she whines I won't mind.'"[24]

With both parents professionally involved with music, it is no surprise that the Seeger children considered music a normal part of everyday life. Peggy remembers: "Music was part of life very, very early on. My mother accompanied what we did with music. . . . If galoshes had to be put on, there was a song for it. If you had a pretty dress, there was a song for it."[25] In the years when B. F. Skinner was applying his benign behaviorism to the tasks of child-rearing, Ruth used music to effortlessly mold her children's behavior: "Barbara didn't want to put her galoshes on? Remake 'Mary Wore Her Red Dress' and—hey, presto!—Barbara's galoshes were on before the verse was ended. . . . We'd start dancing up to bed the minute 'Cindy,' our goodnight song, was broached on the piano. In the end, Dio only had to play the *chord sequence* and up we'd go."[26]

Peggy was the most musically precocious of Ruth's children and began piano lessons at the age of six. Ruth was an unusually creative teacher, turning the whole experience into an interesting game. Peggy recalls: "My 'lessons' began before I even knew they were lessons—and they were very unorthodox. We sang songs and played the chords on the piano; we made up stories and poems in which the words began with the letter of whatever note she was playing; she would set the theme of the 'Moonlight Sonata' to a sequence of folksong chords with a thumping bass, or play 'Barbara Allen' in the style of a Bach Invention."[27] Mike never learned to read music, but he had an excellent ear, which eventually allowed him to master a variety of musical instruments. Barbara, on the other hand, was less musically inclined. Ruth attempted to teach her to play the piano, but Barbara recalls, "She said my fingers were too short, and I just didn't catch on."[28] Like Michael, Barbara never learned to read music. But all the Seegers loved to sing.

Visits from their banjo-playing big brother, Pete, were eagerly awaited. Mike and Peggy would cry, "He's here!" and Ruth would allow them to stay home from school, figuring they could learn more from Pete than from attending school that day. Pete would sit by the fire in the Dallas Avenue living room, playing the banjo while the Seeger children sang along, his large feet beating in robust time to the music. Peggy recalls her mother's warm relationship with Pete: "My mother . . . loved him. . . . I don't think she ever looked on herself as his 'stepmother.' . . . Pete was always our brother. . . . Other people correct me: 'Oh, your half-brother' . . . yeah, but he's my brother."[29] Mike agreed. In 1941, eight-year-old Mike described his "big brothers" as "very old" (twenty-two, twenty-seven, and twenty-nine years of age) and added, "I am very proud of them. I like them. They come to see us every Christmas and they sing and we sing."[30]

Pete had dropped out of Harvard in 1938, hoping to become a journalist, though the field was flooded at the time. He also had an interest in painting, and John wrote to Charles, asking if any money was available to further Pete's art education. But Charles was financially strapped, and there would be no art school in Pete's future. Instead, he spent his time practicing the banjo and touring the country—with companions such as Woody Guthrie—in search of songs. He became as sturdy a champion of American music as his father and stepmother and was soon getting jobs singing for unions and left-wing organizations.

By the close of the 1930s, the U.S. economy was starting to recover after years of financial insecurity. But Europe, which had suffered just as grievously from the worldwide depression, was plagued by fascism, which grew till it covered much of the continent like an evil black cloud. In September 1939, Europe plunged once again into war. The United States stayed out of the war for more than two years. Opposition to intervention came from both the right and the left. On the right were isolationists who felt that the United States should stay out of European problems; there was also a small group of genuine fascist sympathizers. Opposition from the left was harder to understand. Throughout most of the 1930s, the Communist Party had been a staunch opponent of Nazism and fascism, whether in Germany, Italy, or Spain. Yet when the Soviet Union signed a nonaggression pact with Nazi Germany in August 1939, Communist Parties throughout the world followed suit, declaring the war an imperialist project that should be opposed. In the United States, the Communist Party never had the influence or the numbers that it enjoyed in Europe, but it had a few well-known members, including the young Pete Seeger, who had joined the Young Communist League while still at Harvard. With the Almanac Singers, a group he helped create in 1941, he gained a certain notoriety singing antiwar songs in the early months of that momentous year. When Germany attacked the Soviet Union in June, the Communist Party reversed its position and supported the war as a heroic antifascist cause.[31] The Almanac Singers stopped singing antiwar songs. Pete's hatred of war and violence was genuine, though his equal hatred of fascism must have made the decision to countenance appeasement uneasy. His biographer David Dunaway explains: "Underlying his political back-and-forthing was the basic truth of the Almanacs' antiwar songs: A good cause didn't make war any less horrible. Many would later criticize these flip-flops as coldhearted, which overlooks the deep roots of both anti-Nazi and antiwar instincts in the thirties. Then, radical youth seesawed between pacifism and antifascism, first taking the antiwar Oxford Oath, then pledging to fight for Collective Security in Spain. In these contradictions Seeger was by no means alone."[32]

Pete was getting involved with the Communist Party at the same time that Charles was severing his ties with it. In public at least, Charles and Ruth's left-wing convictions had softened into New Deal reformism. Charles held a government job that he did not want to lose; Pete occasionally changed his name when singing for controversial causes, to avoid embarrassing his father. Charles and Ruth's politics had lost its intensity; Peggy remembers no political discussions at the dinner table. While Charles crisscrossed the country in search of American folk songs, he focused on domestic matters, not international ones. If Ruth was horrified that the country where she had composed so happily had turned into a colony run by murderers, if Charles grieved to see his beloved Paris trampled by Nazi boots, their letters did not show it. The cozy homestead on Dallas Avenue did not shut out the world, but it did make family the first priority.

In February 1939, Ruth remarked wistfully that, for the first time, she had a twenty-two-month-old child but no baby inside. Having a fourth child was impossible at the time, not only for financial reasons but also for "the pull of the work."[33] Her piano teaching was a financial necessity, and her work on the Lomax book took far more time than she or the Lomaxes had envisioned. Alan and she chose the songs from field recordings, and she agonized over making the transcriptions precisely mirror the recordings. Bess Lomax Hawes, Alan's younger sister, recalls frequent arguments about what the field recordings actually said:

> A mammoth battle over the blues song "Go Down, You Little Red Rising Sun" went on for weeks, the point at issue being whether in the second line the singer had sung "you redder than rouge rising sun" with a voice break or "redder than ruby rising sun."
>
> Alan's position was that no blues singer he had ever recorded would consider singing such an awkward and unpoetic line as "redder than rouge" while Ruth maintained that the only problem with that was that it was just what had indeed happened. And she had listened a sufficient number of times to prove it—eighty-five, perhaps, or eighty-six?[34]

Despite their disagreements, Alan had great respect for Ruth. In 1939, he arranged for her and Charles to be awarded commissions to compose new works based on American folk melodies. Charles's composition, an adaptation of the Anglo-American ballad "John Hardy," is tuneful and pleasant, if rather conventional. Ruth was more daring: instead of adapting one song, she wove together two songs and one fiddle tune, all of which she had recently transcribed for the Lomax book. The result, "Rissolty, Rossolty," is an attempt to stretch the boundaries of classical music by infusing it with the genius of folk music—melodically, rhythmically, and even in terms of performance practice. Judith Tick writes, "By using more than one version of the title tune, which she transcribed from different field recordings, she honored the dynamic nature of oral tradition. . . . 'Rissolty, Rossolty' does not really 'end'—it shuts down abruptly as the three tunes mix it up. . . . The composer pays homage to the way traditional singers and players did not really come to an applause-seeking cadence . . . but stopped in readiness to start again."[35] With "John Hardy" and "Rissolty, Rossolty," Charles and Ruth bequeathed to their children concrete examples of their musical credo: folk music and art music are both valuable and on a par with each other; moreover, these two musical traditions can be creatively combined.

Even as Alan celebrated Ruth the composer, he was becoming impatient with Ruth the transcriber. He was not alone. Editors at the Macmillan publishing company wrote threatening letters and eventually reduced her long, scholarly introduction to an eighth of its size. And the children missed her; in 1939, Mike declared, "I wish the world didn't have so much work to do."[36] In September 1940, stuck in a doctor's waiting room, Ruth wrote a seven-page letter to her Macmillan editor, Miss Prink, in which she detailed the difficulty of attending to her work because of the many demands on her time: housework (except Sundays when Mamie, the maid, came), cooking (including baking her own whole-wheat bread because Charles preferred it to anything she could buy), and taking care of three small children. Ruth invited Miss Prink to imagine taking charge of the Seeger household during the previous week, when Ruth and all three children had colds:

> I must remind you always to remain cheerful. . . . and when Peggy's fire-siren rises, . . . calling you up from the basement (where you are washing the children's weekly 42 socks and 21 shorts and other delicacies not trustable to the laundry)—and when you discover the cause of her excitement to be the momentous ascent from the jar-bottom to jar-top of her corn "wormie" (salvaged from the last batch of corn-husks and lovingly housed in a mayonnaise jar with corn to munch and a hole for air)—at this point do not fail to express to Peggy your delight that the worm showed such enterprise, at the same time taking advantage of occasion to note . . . whether Peggy's legs are covered, her forehead hot, her neck moist, her water-cup empty. Also it might be wise to be sure that the top of the worm-jar is secure, unless you want to go chasing the worm under the furniture.[37]

In 1941, *Our Singing Country* went to press, and the Seeger family breathed a collective sigh of relief. At the same time, Charles's work with the federal government had come to an end. A conservative Congress had made major cuts in New Deal arts agencies, and Nikolai Sokoloff, director of the Federal Music Project, had never been very interested in folk music to begin with. In February 1941, Charles became director of the Pan American Union's Inter-American

Music Center and chief of the Musical and Visual Arts Division. With Europe at war, collaboration among the American states took on greater urgency. "It is my firm belief, and that of many of my distinguished colleagues," Charles wrote, "that we can have peace in this hemisphere, that peace is dependent to a large extent upon cultural coöperation in place of cultural competition, and that music is a very important factor in cultural coöperation."[38] By the time he retired from the Pan American Union in 1953, Charles had an impressive list of accomplishments: he had published the work of Latin American composers; sponsored Latin American tours for North American musicians; created brochures, bibliographies, periodicals, and libraries dedicated to Latin American music; and ended the practice, then common in the North American music industry, of paying Latin American composers less than their North American counterparts.

As Charles began his work for the Pan American Union, Ruth was eager to begin new projects as well. She recognized the toll that *Our Singing Country* had taken on her and her family, but the children were older now. Mike and Peggy were in school, and four-year-old Barbara was eager to join them. When Ruth received a letter inviting her to join the Silver Spring Cooperative Nursery School, she debated long and hard. Barbara's eagerness to attend school was a factor in its favor, as was the prospect of mornings free to compose. Ruth worried about the cooperative nature of the venture: she would be required to attend meetings with other mothers and to participate at the school one day a week. Her thoughts show the wholesale dismissal of women's work common in the 1940s, even from a woman who baked her own bread:

> I can't quite see myself . . . cooperating with a lot of women. I've always avoided women like the plague. . . . When I have found myself in a roomful of charming voices, with smiles Polyannaing briskly about and the sisterhood of man being spread on as thick as Charlie spreads our granulated honey on my home-made whole-wheat bread—well, I have frowned at myself for every sweet smile I gave in return. . . . Maybe I feel so vinegary, on such occasions, because I myself am criticizing myself for the same sugar-coated characteristics. Probably I'm too durn sweet myself down underneath and see myself in the mirror.[39]

Ruth was pleasantly surprised when the meetings turned out to be interesting and the other women intelligent, politically astute, and well informed about pedagogical practice. Ruth was assigned to do "something musical" with the children, but her first morning on the job, Charles found her "in a panic. . . . [He] couldn't help laughing at her and . . . said, 'Why, just walk in, smile at the children not too broadly, sit down on the floor and do just what you do with our children."[40] And Ruth did. With the songs from *Our Singing Country* burned into her brain, the improvisational nature of folk music fresh in her mind, Ruth adapted the song "Mary Wore Her Red Dress" and sang about the clothes that each child had worn that day.[41] The children were eager to join in the singing, especially since the songs were all about them.

Ruth's success in using folk songs in the nursery-school setting led her to create a book, "American Songs for American Children," which supplied appropriate songs (most of which were taken from field recordings) with her own piano accompaniment. Eventually the book grew into Ruth's most successful publication, *American Folk Songs for Children*, published in 1948. Ruth was adamant that American songs were the appropriate vehicles for teaching American children, a significant departure from the praxis of most music educators of the time, who favored European folk and art songs. The composer in her appreciated the dynamism and fluidity of the folk process: "What we are doing, then, teacher and children, is making something together, fresh each day—a sort of composition."[42] She was soon in demand as a music teacher at nursery and elementary schools in the Washington area, work that she continued for many years. With her teaching and her song books, Ruth bequeathed to generations of American children the gifts she had already given her own: the insistence that American music was as valuable as its European counterparts, an appreciation of folk music as a precious component of national heritage, and the tools for making music an integral part of everyday life.

In December 1941, life changed abruptly when the United States entered World War II. Isolationism was quickly replaced by interventionism for most Americans. Pete and the Almanac Singers adapted the fiddle tune "Old Joe Clark" and sang, "Round and round Hitler's grave / Round and round we go." Woody Guthrie took the melody of the Carter Family song "Wildwood Flower" and wrote "The Sinking of the Reuben James" about the first American ship torpedoed in the war. The Almanacs, finally swimming in the political mainstream, enjoyed a brief success. Yet by 1942, investigators at the FBI discovered the group's Communist ties and its previous antiwar stance. When this information was made public, bookings became scarce. But the war would have interrupted their plans anyway. Several members of the Almanac Singers went to work in war factories; Woody Guthrie joined the merchant marine. Pete was drafted in the summer of 1942 and became a private in the U.S. Army. His initial posting was in Alabama, where he won an amateur contest by singing "Round and Round Hitler's Grave" on his first day in the service.

Like most American children, Peggy's life was brushed by the war but not saturated with it. The war was filtered through newspaper headlines and *Life* magazine photographs; pictures of starving children made an especially strong impression. Blackout curtains were issued, and practice air raids were held; butter disappeared and was replaced by margarine that had to be dyed yellow by the customer. There were occasional visits to Pete when he was transferred to Fort Meade, Maryland, in 1943, shortly after he and Toshi were married.

By 1943, the Seegers' life was more stable and prosperous than it had ever been. Charles traveled occasionally for the Pan American Union, but not as often as when he had worked for the federal government. Ruth continued to teach and took an occasional transcription job. It was finally possible to have what she longed for: another baby. On Christmas Eve 1943, a child was born whom Ruth named Penelope. Peggy suggests that the name was in remembrance of the long-suffering but highly resourceful wife of Odysseus, a woman who had much in common with Ruth.

With four children, the Dallas Avenue house was becoming too small. A larger house would also be helpful for Charles and Ruth's careers: Ruth would be able to expand her piano studio, and Charles would be able to entertain dignitaries in an appropriately magisterial style. In the summer of 1944, the Seegers bought a large white clapboard house on West Kirke Street in Chevy Chase, Maryland, an exclusive suburb of imposing homes and mature trees. Much closer to the District of Columbia than Dallas Avenue and filled with well-to-do families for whom piano lessons would provide a veneer of culture, West Kirke Street was a convenient and prestigious address. It was also expensive and plunged the Seegers into debt. The property cost $15,000 and required more than $1,000 worth of repairs before it was livable. Both Ruth and Charles would have to work long hours to pay for their new home. In retrospect, Mike described the process as, "Buy the big house—to get the piano to teach—to buy the big house."[43] But Peggy remembers the years in Chevy Chase as the golden ones of her childhood.[44]

# CHAPTER 3

# Coming of Age in Chevy Chase

I was brought up in plenty until I was twenty,
A joy to myself as but children can be;
A joy to my father, a joy to my mother,
The pain of my country was nothing to me.

—Peggy Seeger, "Song of Myself"

"We moved when the lilies of the valley were out and the lilac was in bloom," Peggy remembers.[1] The Seegers' new home was a large three-story house with an extensive basement and a wide, tree-filled corner lot. Chevy Chase was (and is) Montgomery County's most prestigious neighborhood, a planned community begun in 1890. Chevy Chase's founders provided the churches, schools, and clubs that would attract the desired clientele, and even in its earliest days, the "village" (as many residents referred to it) boasted luxuries such as electricity, telephones, piped-in water, and streetcars that provided easy access to Washington, D.C. In the oldest section of Chevy Chase, restrictive covenants ensured that the enclave would remain exclusive: no house could cost less than $3,000, and houses on Connecticut Avenue had to cost at least $5,000. In some sections, though not the one where the Seegers lived, restrictive covenants also forbade houses to be sold, rented, or "otherwise place[d] in the possession of any one of the African race."[2]

Chevy Chase's tangle of elegant streets and patches of tidy green lawn provided an endless playground for the neighborhood children. Outdoor play was the norm: in winter, the Seeger children dressed in snowsuits and galoshes and went sledding in the golf course; in fairer weather, they rode bicycles and roller-skated on the bumpy brick sidewalks. Free of the fears of violence that plague suburban neighborhoods today, children roamed the streets with impunity, playing hide-and-seek after dark and catching fireflies on long summer nights. Mike, Peggy, and Barbara were so close in age that they frequently played together, though Mike and Peggy's closeness occasionally made Barbara the odd one out. Penny was the much-loved baby of the family, and Peggy in particular enjoyed taking care of her, but she was too young to join in their games. Peggy had playmates in the neighborhood and at school, but her closest friends were her family.

Mike missed his friends back in Silver Spring, but Peggy adored the new neighborhood. West Kirke Street was only a few blocks from the bustle and convenience of Washington, yet it afforded a semblance of country life. Peggy picked wildflowers in the yard, planted a garden, and played with lizards and turtles in a nearby stream. A fence enclosed the backyard, providing a safe place for Penny to learn to walk and then to play unattended. Near the post office on Connecticut Avenue was a forsythia bush large enough for a child to hide beneath it and watch, undetected, the dramas of the neighborhood.

Peggy remembers the house on West Kirke Street as "a patrician house, the house [her] father always thought he deserved."[3] Charles may have championed the common man, but he had no real desire to live like one. The house came equipped with two staircases, a remembrance of the days when family and friends walked through the front door and servants slipped unseen in the back. A bell under the dining-room table summoned the help when anything was wanted at meals. Having household servants may have been an echo of Charles's childhood, but it was also a shrewd financial decision: Ruth's earnings as a piano teacher were necessary to pay for the house, and housekeepers' salaries were small. It was an irony that reflected the complex intertwining of gender, race, and class in the 1940s: economic necessity required the cash-poor, debt-ridden Seegers to hire three housekeepers on a regular basis.

All the housekeepers were African American women from the South, but they were very different in temperament and background. Mamie Harrison had worked for the Seegers in Silver Spring, and she continued to come on Sundays in Chevy Chase. A deeply religious woman (Charles called her a "first-century Christian"), the intensity of her spiritual life seemed to negate her physical needs: she never married and lived on bread, onions, and sassafras tea. "She was like a walking skeleton," Peggy recalls.[4] She had had little education and asked the Seeger children to correct her grammar, even paying them a penny when she made a mistake.

By contrast, Mary Ann James was a college graduate who corrected *their* grammar. Mamie was thin from eating too little, but Mary Ann was plump from eating too much of her own good cooking. A qualified teacher, she either could not find a teaching job or discovered that housekeeping paid more than teaching in the underfunded, segregated school system of the Washington area. She helped the Seeger children with their homework and cooked wonderful meals, which she served to the family in the dining room and ate by herself in the kitchen. Ruth formed a bond with Mary Ann; having grown up in a boardinghouse, Ruth knew what it was like to do someone else's housework. The two women drank coffee together at the kitchen table, but Ruth could never convince Mary Ann to call her anything other than "Mrs. Seeger."

In 1948, another housekeeper joined the ménage after rescuing a lost Seeger child in a downtown department store. (The details of this story are not entirely clear: Pete thought that the lost child was Peggy; Mike and Peggy thought it was Penny; while Barbara simply remembers a chance meeting.) Elizabeth (Libba) Cotten took the lost child to the store's office, where a relieved Ruth arrived a few minutes later. Ruth struck up a conversation with the gentle lady who had rescued her daughter and, needing additional coverage for the days when neither Mamie nor Mary Ann could come, offered her a job. Did she know that Libba was a talented musician? Libba had played the guitar as a young girl but had stopped when she married while still in her teens. Now a grandmother, she took up her guitar again, playing in her own special fashion—turning the guitar around without restringing it, fretting with her right hand, and picking with her left. (In the 1950s and 1960s, when Libba gained some fame as a folk musician, this style of playing became known as "Cotten picking.") As a teenager, Mike walked into the kitchen and found her singing a song that she had written as a girl in North Carolina, listening to the lonely sounds of the freight trains that passed her house. Mike and Peggy copied her style of playing—Peggy also played the song in conventional guitar fashion—and soon the Seeger household rang with the refrain, "Freight train, freight train, going so fast . . ." Libba was also a fine cook and a reliable, affectionate presence for the Seeger children; Barbara called her "our surrogate mother."[5]

Having three housekeepers did not free the Seeger children from household chores. Peggy and Barbara cleaned the bathrooms and sometimes made the job more interesting by pulling down the shades and cleaning by candlelight. Mike was free of this "feminine" task; he cut the grass. As the children grew older and Ruth's piano lessons became more extensive, the children were frequently responsible for shopping and cooking dinner. Charles was not expected to help around the house on a daily basis, but he did wash dishes: this was a family activity in which all participated, with one person supplying the music that made the work go more smoothly, like a shantyman on a nineteenth-century sailing vessel. When the dishes were finished, the music making moved to the living room, with its straight-backed chairs and its two pianos, and the sounds of "Barbara Allen" and "Lolly Tudum" would fill the air.

World War II ended when the Seegers had been in their house for a year. The war's end brought ticker-tape parades and joyful homecomings, but also the photographs of Buchenwald and the newsreels of Dachau, and the eerie, science-fiction-like destruction of the atom bomb. Having experienced no fighting on its own soil, the United States emerged as the most powerful country in the world. After four hundred years of hegemony, Europe had lost its place as the center of power. But with Europe's decline went also the certainties of the past, the belief that education and science lead to progress and enlightenment; the entirety of Western civilization was on trial. This realization was perhaps best expressed by Holocaust survivors such as Bruno Bettelheim, whose ultimate madness did not preclude moments of terrifying clarity: "In World War II Auschwitz and Hiroshima showed that progress through technology has escalated man's destructive impulses into more precise and incredibly more devastating form. . . . Progress not only failed to preserve life, but it deprived millions of their lives more effectively than had been possible ever before."[6]

In the United States, institutionalized racism became harder to defend after four years of fighting fascism abroad. In 1946, President Truman appointed a committee on civil rights, and in 1948 he banned racial discrimination in the armed forces and in hiring for the federal government. Restrictive covenants based on race or religion, which had been relatively common in the early decades of the twentieth century, were challenged in the courts. The civil rights movement would not make extensive strides for more than a decade, but the seeds had been sown.

Yet the horrors of the war also brought about a yearning for a "return to normalcy," (to use Warren G. Harding's phrase after the First World War), an embracing of the comforts of an imagined past. Though American women had contributed to the war effort in factories, hospitals, and the armed services, their involvement was deemed appropriate "for the duration only." Rosie the Riveter was no longer a beloved role model; a proper woman quit her factory job before she was fired, gussied up her appearance, and had babies. Fear of the Soviet Union and belief in a worldwide Communist conspiracy led to redbaiting so severe that thousands of suspected Communists and leftists lost their jobs. Charles's old friend, Hanns Eisler, was deported in 1948. The experimentation of the war years was over, and the dominant ethos valorized tidy apolitical suburbs, replete with schools and churches, peopled by nuclear families with a working father, a homemaking mother, and a wide range of electrical appliances.

In the immediate postwar years, the Seegers shared in their nation's prosperity, even taking an occasional family vacation together. The postwar baby boom kept Ruth in constant demand as a music teacher, with mornings typically spent at schools and afternoons and Saturdays with private pupils. Mary Ann greeted the children when they arrived home from school. Annette Dapp Poston remembers walking home with Peggy from Rosemary Elementary School; the girls frequently stopped at the Seeger house for a snack and a chat with Mary Ann before going off on their own. It was, Annette recalls, a friendship characterized by relatively serious conversation; the Seeger home was filled with music but not with raucous laughter.[7]

The Seegers continued their musical collaborations with the Lomaxes. In 1947, the songbook *Folk Song U.S.A.* was published. Charles and Ruth had served as joint music editors; Ruth had provided transcriptions and piano accompaniment for most of the songs, while Charles undertook the rest. The book was a critical and commercial success. In its wake, Charles and Ruth began collaboration with Duncan Emrich, then director of the Archive of American Folk Song, on the production of a mammoth collection of American ballads and folk songs. Charles was to serve as music editor, and Ruth's job was to produce transcriptions of a thousand songs. For this task, Ruth pressed her two oldest children into service. Mike could not read music, but he could copy transcriptions and type lyrics. Peggy also served as a copyist, but since she could read music, she learned to transcribe as well. After months of intensive work on the project, the book deal fell through, but Peggy had gained a skill she would use the rest of her life: "When I hear a tune or get an idea and am nowhere near a tape recorder I can just write it down."[8]

The failure of the collaboration with Emrich only inspired Ruth to work harder on other projects. In the autumn of 1948, *American Folk Songs for Children* was published to universal critical acclaim. Praised by academics, educators, and composers, the book received glowing reviews in periodicals as different as the *Journal of American Folklore*, the *New Yorker*, *Parents' Magazine*, and the *Daily Worker*. Peggy first sang folk songs in public with her mother, to promote and publicize Ruth's most celebrated book.

The Seegers were fast becoming known as the first family of American folk music. On Saturday evenings, the house on West Kirke Street was a gathering place for square dances and informal jam sessions. Alan Lomax and Ben Botkin were family friends who might stop by; Alan or Pete might bring Woody Guthrie or Leadbelly as well. Ruth followed up the success of *American Folk Songs for Children* with two additional folk song collections: *Animal Folk Songs for Children* in 1950 and *American Folk Songs for Christmas* in 1953. Charles promoted folk music as part of his job at the Pan American Union and published scholarly articles on American folk songs, one of the few ethnomusicologists to do so. Peggy continued piano lessons with her mother, learning folk music as part of a rigorous study of classical music. She recalls, "I remember spending several challenging weeks learning to play one tune right through the circle of fifths. Then I would take the tune through every mode in every key—and unless you've played 'The Irish Washerwoman' in C# in the Lydian mode at the age of ten, you haven't lived."[9] She also began to play the guitar, learning the music of her father's Mexican childhood, and helped her mother transcribe songs for Ben Botkin's *Treasury of Western Folklore*, published in 1951. But the Seeger whose fame would eclipse them all was Pete.

Pete had begun making records of folk music while still in the army. After the war, he threw himself into being a folk musician with a social conscience. With several like-minded friends, he founded People's Songs, an organization that promoted folk music in tandem with progressive political causes. When People's Songs went bankrupt in 1949, Pete formed a folk quartet called the Weavers with Lee Hays (a former member of the Almanac Singers), Fred Hellerman, and Ronnie Gilbert. Initially, the Weavers' venues were similar to that of the Almanac Singers: political rallies, unions, and hootenannies. By the end of 1949, they had recorded Pete and Lee's new song "If I Had a Hammer," but their paying gigs were few. They considered their options: breaking up or turning to more commercial venues instead.

Pete's first love was political music—and would remain so. But America in the postwar years was growing increasingly conservative. Pete had encountered violence when singing for the Progressive Party candidate Henry Wallace in 1948 and with the great African American bass-baritone Paul Robeson at Peekskill in 1949. The Weavers chose to continue their poorly paid (or unpaid) work for political causes while also performing in nightclubs, where they sang more neutral fare, such as Christmas carols and the South African chant "Wimoweh." Audiences loved their close harmony, lively presentation, and exciting banjo music. Ruth's old friend Carl Sandburg praised them while quoting the nineteenth-century radical poet Walt Whitman: "When I hear America singing, the Weavers are there."[10] In 1950, their recording of the

Leadbelly song "Goodnight Irene" and "Tzena Tzena" (a Hebrew song from the infant nation Israel) sold more than a million copies.

By this time, Charles Seeger was the paterfamilias of a very diverse brood, which included a brilliant academic astronomer who had trouble finding a job (Charles III), an apolitical educator (John), three folksingers (Pete, Mike, and Peggy), and two young schoolgirls (Barbara and Penny). His eldest child was thirty years older than his youngest. Among his children by Constance (what Barbara calls "batch number one"), Pete was the one to whom Charles was closest; they shared musical, political, and intellectual passions. Among Ruth's children ("batch number two"), Charles's attitude made it implicitly clear that Peggy was his favorite. Bookish, musical, and gentle, Peggy shared her father's interests and his temperament; she was all that he wanted a daughter to be. After four sons, Charles was delighted with his baby girl and felt his family was complete. As Peggy grew older, Charles confided in her, telling her things he did not tell the others. He acceded to his wife's desire for more children, but it was Ruth who wanted them. Barbara felt hurt by his lack of interest, and Ruth attempted to make up for it by giving her special attention. More interested in socializing than schoolwork, Barbara did not get the high grades that Peggy did, much to Charles's disapproval. Later calling herself the "white sheep" of the family, Barbara loved the things that the other Seegers disdained: high heels, makeup, television, ballroom dancing, popular music. In a family of gifted, left-leaning intellectuals who learned music from field recordings, folk festivals, European émigrés, and American vagabonds, Barbara wanted only to be a normal American teenager.

"I was encouraged to do whatever I wanted," Peggy remembers, perhaps because what she wanted melded so easily with the family ethos.[11] Schoolwork was easy for her, and after school she read or practiced, pursuits her parents approved of and shared. Unlike Barbara, Peggy had little interest in the fashionable or the conventional, though she was sometimes embarrassed because Ruth was so different from the elegantly dressed and coiffed matrons of Chevy Chase. "She just wasn't like anybody else's mother," Peggy remembers. "The strange thing is—I didn't want her to be like other people's mothers, but part of me didn't want her to stand out so much."[12] Other mothers did not write books and compose music and wear men's shoes to school functions. Conventional standards of femininity meant little to Charles and even less to Ruth, who wore the same style of dress every day (in different colors), braided her hair like a nineteenth-century peasant, eschewed jewelry and makeup, and wore men's shoes because they were more comfortable.

Who could be surprised that her eldest daughter was a tomboy who climbed trees, wore blue jeans, and rode a bicycle to school? Neither Ruth nor Peggy could decode the useless talents that thrived during the years of the feminine mystique: the cultivation of popularity, the ability to mask one's intelligence, the intense focus on personal appearance. Ruth had rebelled against the frills and the limited sex roles of her childhood, but Peggy walked through such gendered expectations as though they were not there.

Perhaps it was her complete absorption in the Seeger mentality that made Peggy feel that she "never belonged" at school.[13] The Seegers had been in tune with the artistic ferment of the 1920s, the radical politics of the 1930s, the self-sacrifice and antifascism of the war years. But in the postwar world of conformism and Cold War hysteria, they were marching to a markedly different drummer. Peggy felt that she had little in common with the other girls in her class: she wore glasses, dressed unfashionably, read constantly, and got excellent grades; she had little interest in boys and no talent for small talk. "I loved my home," she says. "I loved the musical instruments, the music going on in it. I loved getting home from school and sitting in the kitchen with a hot chocolate while Mary Ann ironed and talked. . . . Perhaps I was isolated because I did get good grades. . . . I didn't feel I had anything to offer [other girls], and I wasn't interested in what they had to offer."[14]

"She was quiet," Annette recalled. "At times, she could kind of meld into the background, and you weren't aware that she was there. . . . I don't think she very often raised her hand to answer a question, but she knew it. . . . If she was called on, she could always answer. . . . She was smart, and she knew what was going on."[15] The yearbook of Leland Junior High confirms this opinion: in 1950, at the close of ninth grade, the following couplet accompanied Peggy's school picture: "Peggy Seeger has a mind / That is Leland's treasure find." Peggy remembers being somewhat of a loner and a misfit in school, but the yearbook lists an impressive number of activities: she was class president in the seventh grade and class publicity representative in the ninth grade. She also sang with the chorus, was a member of the yearbook staff, and played intramural sports. Though Peggy loved sports, she disliked the competition associated with organized athletics. She explains, "No matter how good you are, there's always someone better than you are, and you feel bad about it. Or if you're better than somebody else, you feel bad about that too. It's like the game of Monopoly: I can't bear to win it; I can't bear to lose it. I hate it. Because it makes someone else below you, and you feel you're not as good as somebody."[16]

Competitive sports and games have long been linked to capitalism; Monopoly makes this connection explicitly clear. Peggy remembers few political discussions in her growing-up years, but perhaps she absorbed Charles's philosophy of "cooperation rather than competition" without realizing it. As a musician, Peggy aspires to a personal ideal that does not depend on the judgment of others: "I enjoy doing my best. Whether people know I'm doing my best or not, that doesn't matter; I know when I'm doing my best. And that's what I owe to the people who have taught me and to the tradition."[17]

Despite her love of home, Peggy spent the academic year 1950–51 at boarding school. Mike was attending Woodstock Country School in Vermont, and Peggy spent her sophomore year at the nearby Putney School. On vacations, she and Mike took the train home together, meeting in Brattleboro Station in the cold predawn and enjoying the time spent free of adult supervision. Putney boasted a working farm where all the students worked, and it was Peggy's ambition at the time to become a farmer's wife. After a year of rising at 4:00 a.m. to milk the cows, traversing deep snow in winter, Peggy changed her mind about living the farming life, but the year at Putney was a very happy one. Lin Frothingham Folsom, one of Peggy's Putney roommates, remembers the school as a "wonderful escape from reality."[18] Located on a Vermont hilltop, the school combined beautiful natural surroundings with first-class teachers and high expectations for students. A progressive school founded in 1935, Putney stressed scholarship, the arts, community service, and the dignity of labor. From its inception, it strove to be economically and ethnically diverse. Its celebrated music program focused on classical music; popular music was frowned upon, and radios were forbidden. Its values were utterly in line with the Seeger mentality.

Putney's founder, Carmelita Hinton, was an educator whose husband had made a fortune by inventing the jungle gym. She was still head of the school when Peggy was a student there. "Carmelita Hinton had arrived at the hilltop with two goats and a lot of ideals," said Peggy. "She believed in toughening us up."[19] Students did much of the work on the farm and in the school and lived in Spartan quarters with little privacy or heat. The toughening-up process included spending the night outdoors in the Vermont hills in December, in tribute to two former Putney students who had died while camping on the West Coast. Peggy had only a sleeping bag shell to shield her from the New England cold; she spent the night "walking the mountain and crying."[20] The temperature inside Kelly House, where Peggy shared one room with four other girls, was only slightly better. Peggy and her roommates kept warm by piling their beds together, putting on layers of clothing, and sleeping in a heap like puppies. Peggy's guitar accompanied her to Putney, and Lin recalls her sitting cross-legged on her bed, playing the guitar, and singing "All the Pretty Little Horses": "Her voice was just beautiful, but so quiet and so delicate—she didn't want to impose on anybody."[21]

For all her good-girlism, Peggy had a streak of rebellion. From an early age, she was fearless. When Peggy was three years old, Ruth wrote Charles that, for the second time, she had to send Peggy to her room for playing on the street. (Ruth prefaced her remark with a commonplace of Anglo-American folk music: "Peggy weeps and Peggy mourns.") At the age of four, Peggy wandered out of parental sight at a swimming pool and ended up making her way around the deep end by holding onto the side. Eight-year-old Mike remarked that Peggy could do many things better than he, although she was two years younger: "She gives the numbers to the telephone operator, and she is not afraid of doing it wrong. I guess that's it. She's not afraid of things."[22] At Putney, away from the father who adored her and the mother who depended on her, Peggy's rebellious streak had freer rein.

The housemistress at Kelly House was Peggy Miller, a shy young woman whose primary interest was the chemistry teacher she was dating. At five feet zero, she commanded little authority and received little obedience. At night, when the girls were supposed to be indoors and in bed, they easily escaped Peggy Miller's gaze (focused on the chemistry teacher) and wandered the campus, down the lanes and across the fields, beneath the country-dark sky blanketed with stars. For a girl from the suburbs of Washington, it was a magic place. Boyfriends were de rigueur, and a few girls managed to slip through the lax discipline at Kelly House long enough to "do it." Peggy was not among them—her "womanly manifestations" (as Ruth termed the menses) began at Putney, but her boyfriends were more sources of confusion than passion. What she did find at Putney was a circle of friends who were like her.

At Putney, the misfit of the Montgomery County public schools found other misfits, other children of left-wingers, other people who didn't quite fit in. Some were from well-known families: there were children of the Hollywood 10, and Peggy found a friend in Mike Vidor, son of film director King Vidor. Lin recalls the children of Norman Rockwell, Rudolf Serkin, Alexander Calder, and Alger Hiss among her classmates.[23] There were people who listened to folk music, who recognized the Seeger name, who were impressed that Peggy was "Pete Seeger's sister." They sang along as she played folk songs on the piano or guitar; they applauded when she and Mike Vidor (a talented guitar and banjo player) performed at school assemblies. When Pete came to give concerts, Peggy Miller cooked a special breakfast, and everyone wanted an invitation to attend. "As long as we kept feeding him pancakes, he'd play," Lin remembers.[24]

Why did Peggy stay for only one year? Finances may have had something to do with it. Mike graduated Woodstock Country School at the close of Peggy's year at Putney, and perhaps the Seeger purse had been stretched too far. Perhaps it was felt that boarding school was more important for Mike than Peggy: he had been an indifferent student in public school but had done much better at Woodstock. Peggy, on the other hand, had excelled at public school and had done less well at Putney, with its many attractive distractions. Perhaps her failure to return resulted from her placing a snowball in Carmelita Hinton's bed—and then owning up to it, as honor demanded. Or perhaps Ruth wanted all her chicks in the nest with the specter of the Korean War on the horizon and Mike's draft status in doubt. Whatever the reason, Peggy returned home and began her junior year at Bethesda–Chevy Chase High School in the autumn of 1951.

It was hard enough to be a suburban misfit; it was harder to be a misfit who had been away for a year. But at least all the family was together. Mike was in a kind of leisured limbo. When he graduated Woodstock in 1951, he did not follow the Seeger tradition of college at an Ivy League school. He was about to enter the University of Maryland when he discovered that it required male students to participate in the Reserve Officers' Training Corps (ROTC), a program designed to train officers for the U.S. military. Instead, he attended George Washington University (which had no military requirement) for one semester before dropping out. An opponent of the Korean War, Mike applied for (and eventually received) conscientious-objector status, following in his father's antiwar footsteps if not in his academic ones. Charles saw in his son's refusal to fight a continuation of the Seeger tradition of independent thinking and principled action. In November 1952, Charles wrote the Selective Service Board to support Mike's request for conscientious-objector status. Charles detailed the family history, which included warriors and conscientious objectors in the same generation: Charles had been a conscientious objector in World War I, while his brother Alan had died fighting; Charles III had been a Navy researcher during World War II, while Pete was in the army, and John was a Quaker and conscientious objector who spent the war years working in hospitals and schools. One wonders how the bureaucrats of the Selective Service Board responded to Charles's intellectual (and patriotic) defense of the conscientious objector:

There is a great multitude of men ready and anxious to take up arms. And an even greater one can be persuaded. In our time, the Government of the United States will never lack soldiers. But there are very few who have the nature to say this "No" and the courage to back it up. And far from being a danger to the freedom we have enjoyed, these few are the very sign and symbol of it. To the extent these few are respected, that freedom may last. To the extent they are persecuted, that freedom may be lost.[25]

While Mike waited for the decision of the Selective Service Board, he dedicated his time to learning traditional southern music. He recalled, "My mother was very upset that I didn't go to college, but what I was doing in a way was going to my own version of college. I was going around to square dances, hanging out with these musicians, trying to learn the banjo, and listening to these old-time music tapes, just educating myself about traditional music. . . . I began meeting traditional musicians and recorded a few of them with the family tape recorder."[26] Mike had fallen in love with southern mountain music after years of listening to field recordings and commercial records. He also realized that he lived near the area where the music existed in rich abundance. "Mike was always adventurous in going out from where we were," said Peggy, "while I was content to just sit at home and play."[27] Not satisfied with books and recordings, Mike traveled to the countryside and sought out traditional musicians, learning the "subtle nuances of vocal inflections, melodic variations, and rhythmic irregularities that characterized much southern mountain folk music."[28]

Always her closest friend, Mike became Peggy's musical partner. Both learned to play the banjo by following the instructions in Pete's book, *How to Play the 5-String Banjo*, and practicing on the one banjo that the family owned. In September 1952, nineteen-year-old Mike and seventeen-year-old Peggy traveled to the National Championship Country Music Contest in Warrenton, Virginia, where an Arlington disc jockey heard them playing an impromptu session and pronounced them "hotter than a 'tater.'"[29] Mike auditioned and participated in the contest, while Peggy, suffering from an attack of nerves, did not. Interestingly, even by 1952, the contest was primarily a product of the folk revival. A reporter from the *Washington Post* noted, "On Saturday, not one genuine old-time fiddler or banjo-picker showed up for the program. The old-timers stayed in the hills while the youngsters had their day."[30] It took a determined youngster like Mike Seeger to go into the hills and learn the music as played by its traditional masters, not the sweetened and prettified offerings of hillbilly radio.

Mike was temporarily a man of leisure, but Peggy was still a high school student. She continued to get excellent grades and sat alone at lunchtime with her chicken leg and her honey sandwich and her book. "I wasn't a total misfit at school because I never really deep down wanted to fit in," remembers Peggy. "I had what I needed at home so I tolerated school."[31] She participated in fewer activities in high school than in junior high, though she did sing with the Madrigal singers and the junior choir and was a member of the National Honor Society. After school, Ruth was frequently busy with her piano students, so Peggy often shopped for and cooked dinner, in addition to playing with Penny, practicing, doing homework, and keeping a 10:00 p.m. bedtime. In the early mornings, she had a paper route, in the days when few girls rose in the dark to deliver newspapers by bicycle.

Academically, she was a leader; sexually she was several paces behind her classmates. Charles had told her the facts of life after a party that featured kissing games, but she had little interest in the subject. She disliked dirty jokes and competing for boys' attention. "I was probably very puritanical," she remembers.[32] "She was gorgeous," Annette recalls, and high school photographs of Peggy bear out this assessment, but she had little sense of her own attractiveness.[33] Despite her beauty, she was not a magnet for high school boys: she had inherited Ruth's lack of interest in clothes and personal adornment; she got intimidatingly high grades and made no apology for them; she was a quiet person when she was not singing and sometimes even then.

Eventually, Mike's friends noticed Peggy. Jeremy Foster, a friend of Mike's from Woodstock, was handsome, romantic, and a lover of folk music. Peggy was astonished when he returned her affection. In her senior year of high school, Jeremy became her boyfriend and her first lover. Her virginity ended beneath the forsythia bush on Connecticut Avenue, hidden from passersby by a narrow curtain of leaves and flowers. It was an awkward beginning to an affair in which intimacy took place in cars, in Jeremy's bedroom, in any place that offered a modicum of privacy. Like Peggy, Jeremy sang folk songs, went square dancing, and played the guitar and the banjo. It was a problem that she was a much better musician than he.

The year 1953 began pleasantly enough. Peggy was in her last semester of high school, and Mike and Jeremy were on hand for social and musical companionship. In January, Ruth's piece "Rissolty, Rossolty" was performed by the National Symphony Orchestra at Constitution Hall, and she was hard at work on her book of Christmas songs. Yet by February, problems appeared that would change the Seeger family forever. FBI investigation of the Seegers' left-wing associations intensified. The Weavers, early victims of the blacklist, found it virtually impossible to get gigs and officially disbanded. Charles, a scholar who frequently represented his country at international meetings, had enjoyed a diplomatic passport until 1951, when, without explanation, his diplomatic privileges were revoked. In 1952, his passport limited him to official travel, and in 1953, it was taken away entirely. To avoid further harassment, Charles retired from the Pan American Union on February 28, 1953. But a more bitter blow had come two weeks earlier, when Ruth was diagnosed with intestinal cancer.

Ever one to ignore personal discomfort, Ruth continued teaching, composing, and working on her folk-song books. Charles and she maintained a facade of normality and for months did not inform their children of Ruth's illness. In June 1953, two days after her eighteenth birthday, Peggy graduated from Bethesda–Chevy Chase High School and was awarded the Washington Radcliffe Club Scholarship to attend Radcliffe College in the fall. It was her last summer to sleep late, work a part-time job, and lounge around the house, reading and sewing and listening to music. With Mike and Jeremy, she frequented square dances and informal singing sessions. In August, Ruth entered the hospital for an operation, and Peggy realized, for the first time, that her mother had cancer. But Charles and Ruth retained hope for a full recovery and did not discuss the seriousness of the disease with their children. After returning home from the hospital, Ruth plunged back into her work, composing and planning books and even sketching out ideas for a children's record. No one made the slightest suggestion that Ruth's illness might interrupt Peggy's plans for college.

Peggy spent the last few weeks of the summer shopping for college, playing music with Mike and friends, and sorting out her feelings for Jeremy. On September 16, her shopping and sewing finished and her bags almost completely packed, the reality of her departure hit her: "My reluctance to leave increases. I really DON'T WANT TO GO. I can't fathom the change for I was quite eager a few days ago. I really feel unable especially to face the receptions, teas and arrangements of orientation week."[34] Leaving the snug Seeger cocoon also meant leaving Jeremy, who was headed for Antioch College in Ohio. Jeremy recognized the dichotomy in Peggy's personality, the good girl and the rebel, and worried about it; on September 17, she wrote, "He is under the impression that I shall change radically at Radcliffe, shall break loose from parental concern and go wild. I agree with him; I probably shall. For a while. But, as at Putney, it is probable that I shall return to the straight and narrow after my fling is over."[35] Though not yet able to integrate the two sides of her personality, she had no worries that such integration would eventually occur. A family history of Puritan radicalism had shown her the way it might be done.

The following day, she and Charles left Chevy Chase to spend a few days in New York, visiting Aunt Elsie and doing some final shopping before heading to Cambridge. Peggy was aware that momentous changes were in store. But she could not know—nor could anyone else—how completely her childhood had ended.

# CHAPTER 4

# A Rendezvous
# with Death

The cradle and grave, the fruit and the seed,
The seasons mirror my own.
The geese flying south are calling to me,
And I'm thinking of heading for home,
And I'm thinking of heading for home.
—Peggy Seeger, "Heading for Home"

The population density increased and the signs of autumn grew more pronounced as Charles and Peggy drove north from Chevy Chase. In the industrial towns that hugged the New Jersey Turnpike, Peggy was horrified by the man-made destruction she witnessed: the oil refineries that spewed smoke into the air and trash into the marshes. She wrote in her diary, "It was beyond conception the horror it filled me with—this society so intent on bettering its status that it degrades itself in the process of amelioration. The idea of employing living beings in those man-made hells of furnaces and mazes of smog, odor and dirt is overwhelming. But then I am on the outside looking in. Thank God."[1] For perhaps the first time, Peggy felt the benefits and the burdens of her privileged background, just as Charles had so many years earlier in California.

In New York, they stayed in an apartment near where Charles's sister lived with her companion, Downie. Peggy was very fond of her aunt Elsie, whom she resembled physically and intellectually. On her first full day in town, Peggy noticed how well dressed New Yorkers seemed, and Aunt Elsie was no exception. Peggy had thought herself well prepared for college: she had good luggage, a typewriter, and engraved calling cards that read, "Miss Margaret Seeger," but her clothes were the dirndl skirts and bobby socks she had worn in high school. Aunt Elsie made sure that she had a smart gray flannel suit to take with her to Radcliffe. The following day, Charles and Peggy arrived in Cambridge, and Peggy was installed in Peach House, a small student dwelling on the outskirts of the campus. Peggy liked its homey feel and was pleased that she could keep her pet parakeet, Marcus Aurelius, in her room. But she was lonely at first, particularly after Charles left: "The college populace seems very distant and nothing at all like me."[2]

The loneliness did not last long. She quickly found old friends (such as Mike Vidor) and made new ones. The folk revival was starting to take off, and singing sessions (also called "hootenannies") became a regular part of her schedule. She became a song leader at the weekly hootenanny at Harvard's International House, and at a session at MIT, she taught an African song so well that she "felt, with no self-deception, like Pete for a moment when he teaches."[3] When classes began, she threw herself into her studies with a seriousness she had not previously shown. Her diary entry of September 30, 1953, written in response to her natural science class, shows the wonder and excitement of a young mind grappling with new ideas:

I was walking home . . . and looked at the clouds which obscured the star, very bright, directly overhead. The clouds were moving quite fast and disintegrat-ing into the horizon in this movement and the constant disappearance of the star quite bewildered me. . . . I became unable to comprehend the largeness and fruitlessness of all animate and inanimate existence. Life did seem but a grain of dust which any puff of wind or even a breeze could toss about and confuse with no system or motive. . . . I believe that I almost perceived my proper position in the view of the universe—that of a microscopic entity on a microscopic shoal of time, doing microscopic acts which seem frightfully necessary but which really are not necessary or permanent at all.[4]

Peggy was enjoying her independence; at the same time, she missed Jeremy and she missed home, "home in which there are people [she] love[d] rather than just like[d] and respect[d]."[5] Occasionally, she saw Pete when he came to the Boston area to give concerts. After a concert in which Pete and Peggy sang together, she wrote to the family at Kirke Street, "It is wonderful: people know Pete and are his friends, everywhere in this country. Even if people have never met him before except through hearsay, they will walk up to him 'hi Pete' and get a friendly reception from him. Music."[6] Peggy was meeting people from broken homes, people who did not get along with their parents, and these new acquaintances prompted in her an intense appreciation of her own family. A more touching tribute to Charles and Ruth's parenting can hardly be found than Peggy's letter of that autumn:

The real reason . . . for my being here at all, is not to gain a smattering of words or an artificial coating of book-learning. It is to find for myself a place in the order on earth, a harmony with myself. So I thought again that I could hardly be anything else, for I sprang from harmony and lived in it all my life. Is there any way to tell you both, you the harmony that produced me, how much I treasure the unity of my life, or the richness of being in a family? . . . I can hardly say: "I am *lucky* to have such a life" for it was skill and action with intention and work behind it that created such an atmosphere to live in. By beginning with yourselves then adding annexes you have done what a million in a million wish to do, what two in a million are capable of doing.[7]

What parent would not be overjoyed to receive such a letter? Yet Charles and Ruth's joy at receiving Peggy's letter was tempered by the heartbreaking knowledge that their harmonious family life would soon end. Perhaps Peggy's letter was prompted by a letter that Charles had written, without Ruth's knowledge, on October 31. Ruth was much worse: she was confined to her room except for daily radiation treatments. Ruth had not wanted to worry Peggy with the bad news, but Charles felt that it was time she knew the truth. He counseled her, however, not to let Ruth know that he had written and to write letters "as if everything were going on as usual. It is best not to remind her, but rather to take her mind off into the affairs of others. . . . We are living, for the moment, in the present and not contemplating eventualities."[8] They had told few people of the change in Ruth's health, though some had guessed, and Charles had taken over Ruth's piano teaching. As much as possible, they were trying to hold death at bay by never mentioning its name.

Initially, Peggy was worried but hopeful, even commenting that though Ruth was confined to bed, she would still be able to write books. But such optimism was short-lived. On November 14, Charles telephoned Peggy to tell her that Ruth was dying. Peggy was home the following day, and she was shocked by the change in her mother. Ruth had been a lively, plump, rosy-cheeked woman in September, but now she was thin and weak and pale, with barely enough strength to hug Peggy in greeting. For three days, Ruth drifted in a drug-laced delirium, while Peggy and Charles tended her, trying to appear normal for the sake of Barbara and Penny, never crying unless alone. Mike could not bear sitting with his mother; the pain was too great.

Ruth's book of Christmas songs was published her final autumn, and Peggy had enjoyed playing the songs at Radcliffe. Yet Ruth did not live to see the Christmas that followed its publication. At 9:30 a.m. on November 18, Mike and Peggy sang songs from their mother's new book to "an uninhibited audience" of young listeners at the *Washington Post*'s Children's Book Fair.[9] A few hours later, they were home. At noon, Charles and Peggy were by Ruth's side, and Peggy held her mother as she drew her last breath.

"It is hard to avoid resenting the injustice of the situation," Peggy wrote the following day. "Dio just beginning to become known internationally in music circles, then she dies."[10] Ruth had recently returned to composing after a hiatus of many years, and her work had been well received: in 1952 she won a prize sponsored by the Washington chapter of the National Association for American Composers and Conductors. Excited by the success, she had attacked composing with renewed vigor and declared, "If I live to be 99 as my grandfather did, that gives me 48 more years."[11] Yet only one of those 48 years had been left to her. Undaunted and unresigned, she continued working on a new folk-song book until a few days before her death.

If Peggy resented the loss of Ruth the composer, it was the loss of Dio the mother that grieved her most deeply. "When the mother dies, the whole hub of the house is gone," recalled Peggy.[12] It was Ruth who had held the household together, who had made sure that the meals were cooked and the laundry done, and who had, for years, earned the majority of the Seeger income. Charles was stunned by Ruth's death and almost immobile with grief. He spoke frankly to Peggy of his life with Ruth, of their "23 years of heaven," but his younger daughters were shut out of these confidences and were confused and bewildered.[13] Penny did not even know that her mother had died until several days after it happened.

As the eldest Seeger female, Peggy began to organize the household. She wrote the obituary that appeared in the *Washington Post* on November 20. She listened to her father's confidences and tried to comfort him. She went with Charles and Mike to take Ruth's body to the crematorium. She sorted through Ruth's clothes and with Barbara wrote polite responses to letters of condolence. Gradually, the sober reality of the situation began to sink in. "Never is a long time," wrote Peggy.[14]

Charles insisted that Peggy return to Radcliffe. The pleasure that she had initially found in college was gone, however; she found it hard to concentrate on her studies and was desperately lonely and homesick. She realized that her longing for home was in large part a longing for her mother, a desire to return to a time rather than a place. "My fear of death has vanished completely," she wrote to Charles, "which is a great comfort, for I do not like fearing anything. I only fear the effect of my death on others, so refrain from throwing myself around recklessly."[15] For the rest of the semester, she wrote to Charles every day, sang songs from her mother's books to honor her memory, attained a 3.0 average (with an A in music), played a concert at MIT so well she credited "divine inspiration," and started planning Christmas, particularly for the sake of Penny.[16] She wrote a fugue that astonished her music professor, a real tribute to Ruth's training: "I guess he isn't used to his pupils trotting around writing contrapuntal imitative compositions!" she observed.[17] The fugue was so difficult that Peggy could not play it herself, and she wrote to Charles, "I see now the pleasure Dio got out of composing and remember with somewhat of a pang all the composing she was going to do when we went away and she didn't have to teach so much."[18]

The Christmas vacation that Peggy had anticipated so eagerly at the beginning of the semester was a bitter mockery of the holiday her mother had loved. Though Ruth had completely rejected her religious upbringing, she took great pleasure in the Christmas rituals of decorating the tree and choosing presents and preparing a festive meal. The holiday had become a celebration of that which was most holy to her: her family. It was hard to celebrate in the wake of her death. Peggy had looked forward to seeing Jeremy all semester, but when she actually saw him during Christmas vacation, she was indifferent and eager for him to leave. It was her father whose company she sought. Charles and Peggy spent hours together, taking long walks and talking about their feelings of loss. On December 19, after preparing a birthday dinner for Penny (whose tenth birthday was on Christmas Eve), Peggy noted in her diary the different phases her grief had taken: "It is as if someone's right hand had been viciously chopped off: first the blinding hurt; then the surface healing of the wound; then the realization that there is no use fooling oneself, for the hand is gone; then the re-learning."[19]

Peggy also confided in Mike but found it difficult to communicate with her younger sisters. On Christmas Day, she was astonished when Barbara said that Christmas didn't seem like Christmas "because there is no snow." "Does she feel it so deeply that she doesn't realize it?" Peggy wondered.[20] When Charles left on December 26 for a five-day trip to Chapel Hill, Peggy took over running the house, doing most of the housework and listening sympathetically when Barbara described how she felt different from the rest of her energetic, driven family. Aunt Elsie came for a visit, which helped immensely, but when she left, Peggy slipped back into the maternal role. This pattern continued when Charles came home on New Year's Eve. In her diary Peggy wrote, "It's wonderful how Charlie tells me the things he used to come home and tell Dio: things people said, sometimes how he outfoxed a particularly disliked or biased person and he even said, when speaking of some things, that he 'wouldn't tell these things to anyone but me.' I feel as if I'm being of some use when I am brought into confidences like that and I can take mine to him as I was always hesitant to do with Dio."[21] Once, Peggy noticed, her father called her "Dio."

Peggy returned to Cambridge shortly after New Year's Day. "Nice a vacation as possible but both Charlie and I realize the vacancy of it," she wrote in her diary, showing the characteristic Seeger love of wordplay.[22] She continued to mourn Ruth and to analyze her own grief: "I do miss so much all the closeness we had, the further closeness we were to have . . . The books yet left for us to do together, the talks about college and friends."[23] But music, studies, and friends began to distract her. In the spring, she decided to major in music. Surprisingly, she noted, "It used to be willy-nilly the LAST thing I wanted to major in. I wish I could have told Dio, too: she always hoped I would change my mind."[24] She began to get regular paying gigs in Cambridge and had an active social life. Mike Vidor remained a friend and singing companion. Jay Ball and Clark Weissman, MIT undergraduates who had learned folk songs in summer camp and in the burgeoning New York City folk revival, were Peggy's constant companions. (Jay figured that folk song gatherings were a good place to meet girls, and indeed, he met his future wife at one.) Jean-Pierre Radley was slightly older, an MIT student who played the guitar with Peggy; he also took her to movies and the symphony and parties where people spoke French. Tony Saletan was also slightly older, a Harvard student who first learned music from his father, a Russian immigrant who played the balalaika (when he was not practicing dentistry). Tony had learned folk music in summer camp and at the Walden School in New York City; he rounded out his music education with piano lessons from Leonard Bernstein. Benji Hayeem was an Israeli who sang in Hebrew, cursed in Arabic, and spoke Yiddish with his landlady; he had big eyes and short stature and was in love with Peggy. She talked to him easily and made love with him sporadically and wondered if she could truly love him back—"I love him in spasms," she wrote in March.[25]

Most of her friends were men, and sex was frequently a complication. Peggy enjoyed sexual experimentation with some, while others became cross when she turned them down. "I want to fall in love," she declared but worried that she could not.[26] She had few women friends; the giggling and gossiping of the women in her house annoyed her: "These girls are perfectly intelligent but it seems as if they do their best to hide it."[27] Peggy noted in her diary the revelation of a rare woman friend: "MIT people are rather in awe of me and although this is flattering to me it doesn't bring friends."[28] She was growing weary of being admired as "Pete Seeger's sister."

Peggy's closest confidants remained her family—particularly Charles and Mike. Yet the household in Chevy Chase was unraveling. The big house on West Kirke Street was becoming a financial burden, and the Seegers were living beyond their means. When Charles had retired in February 1953, he had had to apply for financial aid to cover Peggy's Radcliffe tuition. At the age of sixty-seven, Charles had no wish to return to full-time employment. His unconventional musicological ideas and his refusal to sign a loyalty oath would have made him difficult to employ in any event. Though he took over many of his wife's piano students, he lacked her skill and pleasure in teaching children with "macaroni-like fingers."[29] His great desire was to devote himself to full-time scholarship, to become the kind of gentleman scholar his father had envisioned so many years earlier. But he could not do so and remain in the gentleman's house that his family had come to love.

He discussed the situation with Peggy when she was home for Easter vacation. They considered selling the house in Chevy Chase and building another near Pete's home in Beacon, New York. But Pete was mired in controversy at the time and was under investigation because of his left-wing ties. He was also frequently away from home, performing at colleges, schools, and summer camps—the only places that would employ him because of the blacklist. (At this point, Peggy did not know that Pete had actually been a member of the Communist Party, an ignorance that may have been designed to protect her and Pete. Her father had deliberately not told his children of his own previous membership in the Communist Party, and it would be years before Peggy discovered this fact.) Charles was no longer the omniscient paterfamilias who could do anything; he was coming to rely on Peggy's judgment as she had always relied on his. On April 13, 1954, she wrote with some alarm: "Once when we were talking in Charlie's room and he turned to me, saying in a most hopeless, almost helpless voice, '*what* shall I do, Peggy?' It stunned me, the combination of words and tone of voice, neither of which I had never [*sic*] heard from Charlie. I do not know whether he is weakening mentally or not, but he is listless and sad almost all the time, except when we play two piano or have some excited discussion on religion or something intellectual."[30] Accepting the fact that her father was growing old may have been almost as hard as accepting the fact that her mother never would.

Back at Cambridge, Peggy confided in Jay and Clark. She feared she might not have enough money to return to Radcliffe for her sophomore year. Jay recalls, "Clark and I looked at each other—here's this wonderful musician from a famous folk music family—and we said, 'Why don't you make a record?'"[31] Without wasting a moment, Jay and Jean-Pierre formed a record company, which they called Signet Records. "I've always had the attitude," says Jay, "that if I haven't tried and failed, then I don't know that I can't do it, so I'm going to assume that I can."[32] They arranged to use the acoustic lab studio at MIT to do the recording and made arrangements with a division of RCA to turn their tape into a record. Jean-Pierre would serve as sound engineer, and Clark would accompany Peggy on the guitar.

Peggy was on her way to becoming a professional musician. A visit to the Swarthmore Folk Festival in late April—where she, Mike, and Pete performed—further increased her reputation. While standing in line for an event at Swarthmore, Peggy shivered in the cold air, and the friendly young man in front of her offered her his sweatshirt. It was Ralph Rinzler, then a Swarthmore student, a folk musician who would make a name for himself with the Greenbriar Boys and would later found the Smithsonian Folklife Festival and become one of the nation's most respected folklorists. Shortly after the festival, Ralph wrote Peggy a letter that cheered her immensely:

I really think you ought to know how much you and Mike did down here. I know that I am speaking for a great many of us when I say that you both "made" this festival for us. . . . by just playing and singing with us in a way which only Pete Seeger himself could have done. . . . We were all sitting around on Sunday evening after everything had ended . . . and musing on the fact that the spirit didn't appear until after (and during) the Seeger concert and jam session last year. This year we were luckier in that we didn't have to wait until the last event. It seems to be an undeniable fact that if it's not one Seeger it's two others that save the Folk Festival for so many of us. . . . Everyone has just been in a state of bewilderment over the effect you two had on the whole weekend. I don't want this to sound like a fan letter, but we all certainly admired your spirit as well as your phenomenal way with a banjo.[33]

Peggy and Ralph became lifelong friends. Peggy cherished Ralph's honesty, musicianship, and good humor—and the fact that, unlike many of her male friends, he never tried to seduce her.[34]

By the end of the semester, buoyed by her music and her friends, Peggy wrote, "I am finding my peace, I think. Or making it."[35] She made the Dean's list "by the skin of my teeth," with one A-, one B, and two B-'s.[36] "Considering the painfully little studying that I did for those exams, I came off remarkably well," wrote Peggy, "but Charlie was horrified at the B-'s. He tells me to take it easy and sacrifice marks to a certain degree, but he still hopes secretly that I'll get all A's."[37] She recorded her album shortly before leaving Cambridge for the summer. It was a warm day, and the humidity wreaked havoc with the high-fidelity condenser microphones, causing them to pop and hiss in ways that threatened to ruin the recording. The ever-resourceful MIT students used silica gel as a desiccant, packed it in a condom, and hung it on the end of the microphone. (It worked.) According to Jay, a condom was chosen "because we needed some way of surrounding the microphone with this stuff and yet something that wasn't going to ruin the high-frequency response of the microphones."[38] The bawdy prop was highly appropriate for the subject matter of the album, entitled *Folk Songs of Courting and Complaint*.[39]

By summer, it was clear that the Chevy Chase house would have to be sold, though it was unclear where the Seeger family would live. Barbara went to visit her uncle Carl in California and was considering his invitation to stay. In June, Charles, Peggy, and Penny visited Pete and Toshi in Beacon, then drove to Vermont so that Penny could attend Camp Killooleet, a summer camp run by John Seeger and his wife, Ellie. Afterward, Peggy and Charles vacationed in Vermont, Connecticut, and Quebec before returning to Beacon, where Peggy faced down a copperhead with characteristic sangfroid:

> Event of the day: a copperhead snake that crept up behind Peggy in the raspberry patch. I looked at him: he looked at me. Each figured the other was bad business. Both edged away cautiously. I ran up to Pete (still in bed, Toshi asleep) with a breathless, "there's a copperhead . . ." Toshi thought I meant it was in the house and leapt up with phenomenal alacrity. We killed the poor creature who was only doing his natural business. I felt so badly at killing it that I silently apologized to it beforehand, my apologies mingling with "it's either him or us."[40]

Peggy was happy to return to Chevy Chase in July, but it was a bittersweet homecoming: she had to prepare the house for sale. On July 18, the house was sold to Bernard and Joan Hollander for $32,500, though the Seeger family could continue living there for the rest of the summer. Peggy chose the Hollander family because they, like the Seegers, had four children and two pianos.

Being back in Chevy Chase threw Peggy once again into the company—and the arms—of Jeremy Foster. The reconciliation was brief but intense; they even considered marriage. By the end of the month, however, Peggy was back in Cambridge working on her record with Jay and Jean-Pierre. Afterward, she took them to visit Pete and Toshi's home in Beacon. Charles joined them, and he and Peggy continued to discuss the possibility of building a home nearby. But there were practical difficulties: hiring people to clear the land and build the house was an expensive proposition, and they did not have sufficient time or ability to do the work themselves. It had taken Pete and Toshi, when they were young and strong and without children, a year to build a house sufficiently large for two people.

After the visit to Beacon, Peggy and Charles returned to Chevy Chase. Peggy became worried by Charles's fits of depression, during which he would say, "It would have been so much simpler if I had died instead of Dio" and "There is no goal in life for me anymore. . . . If you have no goal then you die."[41] But shortly after their arrival home, he was greatly cheered by a visit from his childhood sweetheart, Margaret Taylor (whom he called Mar), and her son Rufus. By the end of the summer, unbeknownst to Peggy, Charles and Mar were considering marriage. For the immediate future, however, Charles had decided that the Seeger family should move to Cambridge so that Peggy could continue to attend Radcliffe. There was no money to support a separate household for Charles and the other children. On September 21, Peggy found a two-bedroom apartment at 1039 Massachusetts Avenue in Cambridge. Charles had one bedroom, while Peggy and Penny shared the other; Barbara remained behind in Washington, babysitting for a family.

It was difficult for Charles, with his patrician background, to move from a stately three-story house to a small two-bedroom apartment, with no yard and only one bathroom, often crowded with hand laundry. Much of the family furniture was stored in Pete's barn, but a grand piano followed the Seegers to Cambridge. "It was a great year," Peggy remembers. "We took care of each other."[42] The pain of Ruth's death was beginning to lessen, and Peggy relished living with her family once again. There was no money for housekeepers and, in tune with the ethos of the 1950s, Charles was exempt from housework, so Peggy organized the household. "I was little mother," she recalled.[43] After singing Penny to sleep at night, Peggy would retire to the linen closet to study, the only place she had a modicum of privacy and quiet.

In addition to keeping house for herself, her father, and her sister, Peggy was taking a full load at Radcliffe (including intensive Russian, which required three to six hours per day of studying), organizing hootenannies at International House, teaching guitar at a community center, and leading an active social life. She drank too many cups of coffee (as Ruth had done) and got only five hours of sleep at night; her grades suffered, and her nerves were frayed. She missed Jeremy, but in his absence took up with Gilles, a French aristocrat and devout Catholic who was fifteen years older than she. Gilles, an MIT student, was different from her other friends: he was not a folk musician; his old-world manners guided his treatment of her; and his faith limited their sexual activity.

Peggy's first album, *Folk Songs of Courting and Complaint*, came out in the autumn of 1954. Jay peddled the records to the shops of Cambridge, and after they had paid back expenses, the profits were enough to help finance Peggy's sophomore year.[44] *Folk Songs of Courting and Complaint* was a project filled with Peggy's family and friends: Jay produced it, Clark played guitar, Jean-Pierre was the recording engineer, and Charles wrote most of the liner notes. The songs were primarily childhood favorites; a few had been gleaned from books in the Harvard library. Peggy was pleased with the result, and indeed, it is a record that any nineteen-year-old would be proud of. There are no false notes, no embarrassing lapses of taste that so often bedevil the recordings of neophyte musicians. The introductory notes describe her style well, calling it "midway between the 'raw' material of rural folk song and the 'consciously polished' material of its urban adoption. . . . It reduces to a minimum the usual excesses of urban rendition of rural music—uncalled-for dramatization of words or phrases, over-precise articulation of degrees of the scale, exaggerated contrasts of loud and soft, fast and slow, etc.—at the same time avoiding affectation of the nasal or whining voice found in some—but by no means all—good rural singers."[45]

The light, delicate voice that had so enchanted Lin at Putney is the voice that one hears in *Folk Songs of Courting and Complaint.* Peggy's voice lacks the rich vocal timbre that it would develop a few years later, but it has a naive sweetness that emphasizes her youth and lends poignancy to the songs of love and sorrow. (Years later, her son Neill would express appreciation for the light, delicate voice of his mother's early recordings.) Her diction is perfect: she takes care that the words be understood but does not overemphasize them to an unnatural degree. Occasionally, she produces microtones and vocal decorations, but she uses these techniques sparingly and with a subtlety that heightens their effectiveness. Those who are familiar with the singing of the mature Peggy may not recognize her in this album, for she had not yet developed the distinctive style that she would use for most of her career. Her voice here lacks a personal stamp; it could belong to any talented newcomer. The accompaniment is simple—just Clark on guitar and Peggy on banjo and guitar—and contrives to make singing the focal point of the album.

In this album, one can hear both the strengths that Peggy would build on and the weaknesses that she would later overcome. A case in point is the traditional Anglo-American song "When First unto This Country a Stranger I Came." Vocally, it is her best song: the register is just right for her; her voice is sweet and controlled and exceptionally pretty; the flowing guitar accompaniment adds to the overall musical effect. But she doesn't seem to be paying much attention to the lyrics. Occasionally, she sings too fast for the words to be understood, and the complaints of the luckless, lovesick immigrant are sung with little emotion. Essentially, she uses the words as fodder for her musicianship, as many art singers do. This is the voice of a young, inexperienced singer who knows a lot about music but little about the troubles she is singing of.

The song that follows, "All of Her Answers to Me Were No," is completely different—a two-part song in which she sings both parts and shows a good sense of the song's dramatic potential. She sings more slowly here and concentrates more on the words. Her vocal timbre is richer and fuller, though it lacks the pristine vocal beauty of "When First unto This Country a Stranger I Came." The song is pitched a bit too low (the chorus is at the very bottom of her register), but the song is the focus here, not the skill of the singer.

In many ways, the song that best points to Peggy's future is the third song of the album, "The House Carpenter." An American variant of the Child ballad "The Demon Lover" (Child 243), "The House Carpenter" was one of Peggy's favorites; she later referred to it as her "comfort song."[46] The banjo accompaniment is exceptionally skillful, but it does not detract from the singing. Unlike some songs on this album, in which the words are essentially pegs on which to hang the music, the narrative structure of the ballad forces her to pay close attention to the lyrics, causing the listener to become intensely interested in the story. The singing is especially good, with a lovely clear tone and occasional microtones and vocal decorations, simply and effectively done. The pace is a bit rushed—a common failing of this album—and occasionally leaves her breathless, but the words are never sacrificed.

Probably the weakest part of the album is the penultimate song, "Katy Cruel." It is a fragmentary song with undistinguished lyrics, and she sings it much too fast; the sense of the words—such as they are—occasionally gets lost. Yet even in "Katy Cruel," Peggy's musicianship is sure, her diction is precise, and her voice is pleasant and always on key. If this is the weakest link in the chain, then it is a chain with enormous promise. Peggy's self-awareness and self-criticism helped her to steer clear of the faults she disliked in other musicians: "I am becoming so cynical about performers of folk music who use it merely as a medium for personal elevation/fame and not at all socially or even in good musical taste; so many who employ almost grotesque instrumental technique purely for their own amazement at their ability."[47]

Christmas of 1954 may have lacked the magic that Christmases had when Ruth was in charge, but neither did it have the bleak desolation of the previous year. On December 21, Charles wrote a long letter to Mar, a letter ripe with possibilities: he promised to finish the song he had begun for her in 1907 and confessed that he had wanted to marry her when he was a young man. Barbara came to Cambridge for Christmas and returned to Washington shortly thereafter. Ralph Rinzler came for Christmas dinner, and his gentle presence (and "magnificent" banjo frailing) added to the festivities.[48] Gilles left when Christmas vacation began, and Jeremy came to visit, leaving Peggy's feelings to vacillate wildly between the two.

Jeremy left early in the new year, after quarrels that left Peggy drained and hurt. She found Gilles more cheerful than the moody Jeremy but admitted that the latter "will accept anything I do, even if it's sending him away."[49] Gilles, on the other hand, was concerned with propriety and sometimes frowned at Peggy's slapdash behavior; as she remarked in her diary, "I am too unrespectable. I enjoy throwing myself around in slacks all the time, sitting on the floor, swearing when necessary, listening to smutty stories."[50] He was not the only one of her Cambridge acquaintances who occasionally found her unladylike. When others criticized her, she was charitable enough to consider if their criticisms were just, and if so, she strove to improve herself. But in external matters, such as conventional behavior or fashionable dress, she had little interest or patience and concluded, "I am what I am," a remark she attributed to Jonathan Swift.[51] Years later, her inability to "be a lady" would be an underlying theme of her most famous song.

In late January, Charles went to California to visit Mar and told Peggy frankly that he was considering marriage. Peggy was skeptical, but her faith in her father remained absolute: "I know he would not marry her for love, but for companionship—he has told me that. I cannot fathom, with knowledge of my needs and reasons in marriage, his sort of need at all, but grant him guideship in his own life. Whatever he does I approve of it."[52] When he returned several weeks later, he announced his engagement to Mar. Peggy sorted out her feelings about it in her diary: "Charlie has changed by much persuasion my viewpoint on the marriage—mostly by pointing out the different kinds and degrees of love and how they correspond to the ages of their participants.

. . . He is quite changed with the prospect of a summer in California and this new outlook on his old age. Even though he never talked a great deal of it, being alone in old age has been a terrible thing since Dio died."[53] The marriage simplified certain practical matters: Mar was wealthy and owned a large house, and Charles would no longer have to worry about making ends meet. Barbara had left Washington—the chore of babysitting six children had proved too much for a sixteen-year-old—and had moved into Peggy and Penny's room in Cambridge; the small apartment was bursting at its seams. Charles planned to marry and move to California in the spring and have Penny and Barbara join him in the summer. Peggy did not want to remain behind in Cambridge, miles away from her family; it felt "almost like being deserted."[54] But she had no desire to go to college in California. Instead, she decided to go to the Netherlands and stay with her elder brother Charles, who had an academic position at the University of Leiden. "I have always wanted to go," wrote Peggy, "and I'm sure I would be welcome and find a rewarding family-ness that I feel so lost without."[55] Her father approved of the plan, at least for a year, after which time it was assumed that Peggy would return to the United States and complete her college education. She was looking forward to the challenge of being in a place where neither her musical ability nor the Seeger name would guarantee immediate entrée.

On March 28, Peggy noted in her diary, "Have forgotten to record Charlie's marriage to Mar, several weeks ago. I have become so used to the idea and the actuality that I have not mentioned it or written it."[56] Peggy, Barbara, and Penny were all in school and did not attend their father's wedding. In the summer, Charles and Mar planned to return to Cambridge, pack up the Seegers' belongings, and drive to Mar's home near Santa Barbara. In the meantime, Peggy's life continued at its usual fever pitch. A weekend in the country with Gilles deepened their relationship but also pointed to an irreconcilable difference—religion. Gilles's Catholicism was an essential part of his being. Peggy's religious education had been limited to Sunday morning Bible readings interspersed with readings from the *Decameron*. Charles and Ruth had combined a few trappings of American Protestantism (such as Christmas trees) with a strong moral sense that did not depend upon belief in a deity. Realizing that marriage with Gilles would be impossible without an agreement on religion, she accompanied him to mass on Easter Sunday. But she found the experience empty, particularly after a solitary two-hour walk she had taken the previous evening. Alone with nature, she celebrated a personal and rather Spinozan conception of religion:

It was shortly after sundown and I was fascinated by the presence of the stars. I worshiped without a church. . . . God was those stars, the earth, life and lights. . . . It was me, as part of the creation, as a work of art so beyond my comprehension. I found this thing in myself to worship—just the principle of life, the manifestations of it. Why try to place a cause behind it? What can be more glorious and worthy of worship than a creation that can create itself? A flower that, let alone, can produce eternally likenesses or mutations of itself?[57]

Peggy was willing to adapt herself to Gilles in mundane matters, but in matters of principle, she—like other Seegers—would not budge. "I may not earn salvation in heaven," she wrote, "but I must have it on earth."[58]

Peggy's lack of sympathy with mainstream religion did not limit her affection for Christmas. With Penny, Barbara, and a group of children from the South Boston Music School, she began recording songs from her mother's final book, *American Folk Songs for Christmas.* In this book, Ruth presented Christmas as a celebration of homegrown American traditions, rejecting both the commercialism and the European borrowings that had in large measure replaced them. Ruth chose the songs from books and field recordings; all the songs were of American origin, but they were not the songs that most Americans knew. Many of them came from isolated areas and were little known outside their home communities. Ruth's concern was to introduce mainstream America to the forgotten gems created on its own soil. *American Folk Songs for Christmas* presents a Christmas of a different time and place, a predominantly rural America of small hamlets and villages, far from department-store windows filled with tinsel and candy canes. In championing homegrown material, she also celebrated the artistry of those with little power or prominence. Ruth approached this book as a folklore scholar as well as a composer, and the result reflects a common folkloristic conundrum: progressive politics mixed with cultural nostalgia.

Folkways Records produced the album *American Folk Songs for Christmas* in 1957. Most of the songs on the record are from the South; many are of African American origin, though white shape-note hymns are presented as well. All the songs are religious, though not all of them specifically mention Christmas. The three sisters receive equal billing, but it is Peggy's voice that predominates. Children from the South Boston Music School provide an enthusiastic, if occasionally off-key, backup. Particularly well done are the shape-note songs, such as "Bright Morning Stars Are Rising," which later became popular among folk revival singers, and "Babe of Bethlehem," a folk rendering of the gospel. The songs are presented simply and with dignity, but without the exuberance that one might expect of a holiday album. The record, like the book on which it is based, reflects more a scholarly interest in the history and folklore of Christmas songs than an attempt to record what Americans actually sang in the 1950s. The secular, cosmopolitan Seegers presented a vision of Christmas that was remote, old-fashioned, and intensely religious.

This antiquarian, noncontroversial rendering of folk song dominated much of the 1950s folk revival. Jay and Clark recalled that most folksingers of their acquaintance concentrated on old, traditional songs, not on new, topical songs written in the folk idiom. Tony, who had been a member of People's Songs while a high school student in New York, also recalled political music as part of the folk scene but agreed that an interest in traditional music was paramount.[59] The 1950s folk revival was predominantly one of old-fashioned lyrics and beautiful melodies; it celebrated a kind of homemade simplicity that was cherished in the age of television and record players, of slickness and specialization. If there was any political subtext, it was that of democratic populism: the songs had been created by ordinary people in the course of their daily lives, not by professionals with specialized training or by entrepreneurs who wished to make money. It was the artistry of those who did not consider themselves artists.

The great exception to this grand generalization was, of course, Peggy's brother Pete, the unassailable leader of the folk revival from the 1940s until his death in 2014. But in the 1950s, few followed him down the path of political singing and songwriting. In the McCarthy years, controversial words could have frightening consequences. While Peggy was preparing Christmas songs, Pete was preparing to appear before the House Un-American Activities Committee (HUAC). Anti-Communist fervor was at its height, with government prosecutions based on a broad interpretation of the Alien Registration Act of 1940 (the Smith Act), which forbade advocating forcible overthrow of the government or even belonging to an organization that did so. According to this interpretation—later deemed unconstitutional by the Supreme Court—membership in the Communist Party could be grounds for criminal prosecution. Peggy knew that Pete was in difficulty and was staunchly supportive of her big brother, but political ideas and activism did not, as yet, loom very large in her life.

Eventually, Peggy's overextended schedule caught up with her. Returning from the Swarthmore Folk Festival in April, she described the trip in wry and humorous detail—a twenty-four-hour ordeal involving exploding tires, stripped brakes, and melted bearings. The last paragraph is strikingly reminiscent of Ruth's "Letter to Miss Prink":

> When you haul into Cambridge 24 hours after departure from Swarthmore only to remember that (1) Penny must be taken to the dentist (2) none of the weekend duties of defrosting and cleaning up were done . . . and consequently must be done during the week (3) you must bus it all the way over to the South End to work with some children who are preparing for the Christmas record with you. Above all, you must be prepared for the next day's Russian class and stay up until 2:00 AM to do it . . . then sleep through the class on Tuesday.[60]

By May, Peggy was in the hospital with mononucleosis. For more than a week, Barbara and Penny were on their own, while Peggy lay in her hospital bed, occasionally delirious, physically so weak that she slept most of the day. She had so many visitors that they sometimes taxed her limited strength, but it was Gilles who visited her most faithfully, and it was he whom she depended on to relax and cheer her.

By late May, she was well enough to recuperate at home. Mar and Charles arrived to pack up the apartment and move the family to California. On May 27, Peggy described, with some unease, the changes in the household:

> Mar is here now and I am having more difficulty adjusting than I reckoned I would have. . . . Somehow I feel out of this household, do not feel so close to Charlie now that his need of me as a companion has diminished. Mar keeps him happy, is cheerful and good to us. But I do not feel at home with her yet. . . . I guess when I come right down to it, my uneasiness is just because of the state of flux this household has been in for the past two months—without Charlie and yet a home. I long to find, as Charlie has, some permanence emotionally as well as geographically.[61]

The longing continued, though the semester ended well. On June 7, her friends gave her a surprise going-away party, which touched and pleased her. Her grades were good, especially considering the weakened state she had been in while she studied for exams: she received an A– in ballads, a B in music, and two B+'s in Russian. In mid-June, she visited Beacon with her family and Gilles. She rejoiced in Pete and Toshi's new baby, but their happiness only intensified the aching within her: "I felt so envious of Toshi and Peter and all people with husbands and babies. . . . I felt like some unnatural limb without a tree."[62] She and Gilles discussed marriage, but she doubted that it would ever happen because of their many differences.

Briefly, the Seegers returned to Cambridge in order to finish packing and prepare for the journey. Gilles would be driving cross-country as well, and she looked forward to seeing him in California over the summer. The future seemed wide open, with all the possibilities and all the uncertainty that such freedom entails. The day before Peggy's twentieth birthday, the Seegers packed their car and, as so many of their compatriots had done, headed west.

# CHAPTER 5

# The Rover, Part One

Always on the move, with banner unfurled,
Yet gathering moss on the stone,
I sing for the children and cry for the world,
And I'm thinking of heading for home,
And I'm thinking of heading for home.

—Peggy Seeger, "Heading for Home"

Penny stayed east to attend Camp Killooleet for the summer, while Charles, Mar, Peggy, and Barbara set off for California. The cross-country drive was a time of unaccustomed leisure, and Peggy used it for intense self-examination. It was not always a pleasant process; she was relentlessly self-critical, and her usual sources of stability—home and family—were in a state of flux. On her twentieth birthday, near Niagara Falls, she wrote, "I have always shied away from being like other people. I want to be common without looking it, dress nicely without dressing like other people. . . . I spend more time living differently than actually living happily, for I would no doubt be less of a misfit in many groups if I would accustom myself to being and thinking like them."[1] In Cleveland, the Seegers stayed with Mar's daughter Edith and her husband, Joel, and Peggy's sense of differentness became a source of discomfort. Mar's family was chic and wealthy and conventional—the polar opposite of the nonconformist and increasingly cash-strapped Seegers. A musical evening in Cleveland consisted of Edith and Joel playing classical music, while Charles and Peggy played folk music. "I was the quaint touch," said Peggy and felt she had played badly before their uncomprehending and possibly condescending eyes.[2] Her disappointment was not due to any personal ego; if she had done poorly that night, she knew she could do better. What distressed her was the thought that she had represented the tradition badly and had done a poor job of presenting music that Mar did not understand and might look down on. In addition, she was being thrust into the midst of a tight family unit while her own family ties seemed to be loosening. Mar and Edith's closeness only emphasized Peggy's own loss: "When we arrived, and Edith rushed into Mar's arms, my heart almost hurt with the need to do that myself, to have Dio alive and near again."[3] Her father was a close intellectual companion but not someone who easily showed physical affection. Perhaps even more unnerving was the fact that Charles seemed quite at home with his new family, leaving Peggy—the darling of his old family—somewhat bereft.

Peggy hoped that these feelings of insecurity would disappear when they reached California and established a new home base. In the meantime, she proved to be a canny observer of an America she had never seen before. In the Midwest, she wrote, "Everything looks like silence, a visual translation of an aural sensation. . . . Nature is in her own here, but the life of man seems terribly slowed down."[4] In Oklahoma, along the fabled Route 66, she wrote, "We stay in one of the facets of a string of neon jewelry along the usual motel main street. I like these places inside, but their external setting is usually somewhat grim. Truckers, diners, snappy come-ons and advertisements, sunglasses and foot-long hot dogs. The more I look at travel scenery the more I am convinced that here is universal characterization of America, different as her regions may be. I'm glad Gilles is taking a better route than 66, for he must go back with a decent impression of the USA."[5]

The vast inhuman beauty of the West moved her deeply. But she was troubled by a growing distance between her and her father. Charles and Mar were so attentive to each other that they frequently left Peggy and Barbara out of their plans. Peggy noted that such things had never happened with Charles and Ruth: the family had functioned as a unit, and the children were automatically included in everything. On June 23, the day before they arrived in California, she wrote, "It isn't that I wouldn't give in to Charlie's desires first—I always have. But we [Peggy and Barbara] would both like to be consulted, even if we give in afterwards. . . . I am, on one hand, grateful to her [Mar] for her relation and companionship to Charlie and, on the other hand, quite jealous. Actually jealous—for I hardly ever see him by himself anymore. . . . And I feel worse because Mar is such a nice person."[6]

Mar may have been nice, but she was not Ruth. "You couldn't have had anyone more different from my mother than Mar," Peggy remembers.[7] Mar was an upper-class lady, a giver of cocktail parties, a churchgoing Episcopalian unaccustomed to scandalous behavior or passionate politics. Always elegantly coiffed and perfumed and bejeweled, she was a lady of leisure who could support Charles's preference for the finer things in life. In no way did she resemble the plainly attired, hard-working intellectual that Ruth had been, a woman who had never cared much for things—fine or otherwise.

Peggy struggled to get to know her new stepmother, but she never felt at home in California. "Of course she didn't get along with Mar," Barbara remembers. "She was used to having Charlie to herself. . . . I think she didn't get along with Mar partly because she was named after her and partly because it was somebody who took Charlie's affections." [8] Barbara, who had always felt different from the other Seegers, took to Mar much more easily. "Peggy was the favorite," Barbara explains. "And I think it damaged her more than it damaged me. . . . It made me more of a fighter. . . . But Peggy had a harder time, I think, when she got out on her own . . . because she was just used to being . . . treated differently." [9] Peggy's position as adored first daughter made it difficult for her to accept a family structure where such was not the case.

As her relationship with Charles grew more emotionally distant, Peggy turned more and more to Gilles, eagerly anticipating his letters, even quoting poetry in her diary: "Oh that my love were in my arms, and I in my bed again." [10] Gilles visited Santa Barbara shortly after the Seegers' arrival, but the visit was brief, and the two had little privacy. Immediately thereafter, Peggy went to Pasadena to visit her Crawford relatives. Back in Santa Barbara, she became bored with her leisured schedule of tennis, swimming, and piano. It was a relief when she started learning Dutch from Mr. Pollman, a Dutch immigrant who spiked their language lessons with tales of the resistance during World War II. She began to enjoy the pleasant house and lovely surroundings, though she had her doubts about the marriage:

> There are many flaws in this merger of a household. To Mar, we are still "Charlie's children" and supported by him. When Barbara buys a dress, Charlie pays for it, even though Mar took her shopping. . . . It bothers me considerably, as I remember the give and take of Kirke Street. Joint accounts in money as well as love and children. I know Mar has a considerable income and Charlie is living off capital which will dwindle soon. Then what . . . ? I have a faint feeling that Charlie is like a prince consort, even though Mar doesn't intend it to be that way. [11]

Charlie's children did not even live in the main house with Mar and Charles; they stayed in the servants' quarters, though several large bedrooms stood empty.

By August 12, Peggy had had enough of California. She returned to Cambridge and rented a room on Myrtle Street, where the highlight of her day was cooking dinner for Gilles and spending the evening with him. Charles was not pleased with the living arrangements; though his objections were practical rather than moral, he knew the dangers of violating the dominant moral code: "It's all right with me if you live with Gilles, but if Radcliffe finds out they won't let you back there, or I'm much mistaken."[12] Ironically, Gilles's religion and iron self-discipline kept the relationship from getting past the point where Radcliffe might not approve.

If Peggy's personal affairs seemed scandalous, they were very small beer compared to Pete's political ones. Several days after Peggy arrived in Cambridge, HUAC arrived in Washington, D.C., and subpoenaed several well-known folksingers, including Lee Hays and Pete Seeger. Lee Hayes testified before the committee on August 16 and refused to answer any questions, invoking the Fifth Amendment, the constitutional protection against self-incrimination. He was excused in short order, but the experience caused deep emotional stress: "I don't think I have ever felt so damned alone as on that day. . . . When I got home my heart hurt and I place the beginnings of my heart trouble at that day."[13] Pete in no way denigrated those who chose the path of the Fifth Amendment, but he felt it was not for him. Invoking the Fifth did nothing to lift the blacklist; besides, doing so made it look as if the defendant had something to hide. Pete wanted to turn the tables on the committee: rather than defending himself, he indicted the entire line of questioning. Since the First Amendment guarantees the rights of free speech and political association, Pete questioned the entire legality of the proceedings: "I am not going to answer any questions as to my association, my philosophical or religious beliefs or my political beliefs, or how I voted in any election or any of these private affairs. I think these are very improper questions for any American to be asked, especially under such compulsion as this."[14] In essence, he was saying what Paul Robeson would say explicitly the following summer, during his own HUAC testimony: "You are the non-patriots, and you are the un-Americans."[15]

Charles had nothing but praise for his son's unflinching *J'accuse*: Pete was upholding the Seeger standard of ethics by refusing to betray others and demanding that his country not betray the principles on which it had been founded. In a letter dated August 30, 1955, Charles wrote to Peggy, "He has really done a beautiful job. If he does not go down in history for his singing he should for his stand. I cannot help wondering if there was not someone on the Committee who could see that Peter was standing up for the America of the Founding Fathers while the Committee was impugning it. If you have not already talked with him about this and read his prepared statement carefully, you must make a point of doing so."[16] Peggy did visit Pete before departing for Europe, but her letter from Beacon was filled with family news, not political controversy. Pete and Toshi's family was "in wonderful shape," and Penny, Mike, and John were visiting as well.[17] With Mike and Penny, she spent her last night in the States at the home of Ralph Rinzler's family in Passaic, New Jersey. On September 9, Mike, Penny, and Ralph saw her off to Europe on the SS *Maasdam*.

The transatlantic voyage was filled with singing and playing chess and staying up all night to watch the sun rise. Peggy's first impression of Holland was unfavorable: "tiny shacks on the seaside, flat for miles and freighters chugging up and down."[18] The ship continued past a town that looked "EXACTLY like Newark, New Jersey" before docking in Rotterdam.[19] Her brother Charles, his wife, Inez, and their three sons met Peggy at the ship and took her to Leiden. She wrote to her family:

> At last a place which came up to my romantic expectations. . . . Everything is small . . . that is, it is close together with narrow brick streets and canals all over. This particular house is quite large. . . . My own room, on the first floor and looking out on the canal, lawn and garden behind, with the gas lamps and reflections and everything one could want, is at least 15' high, twenty long and 12 wide. And the house is not cluttered or fussy, but made to live in—which I intend to do.[20]

Charles and Inez welcomed her and were delighted to hear the folk songs that they had known in the States—though they were somewhat shocked that these songs had succumbed to the folk process and were rather different from what they had remembered.

Leiden did not have the gritty, sensual glamour of Amsterdam, but it had its own charm. The University of Leiden was the oldest in the Netherlands, and it took its sixteenth-century motto, *Praesidium Libertatis* (Bastion of Liberty), seriously. Like René Descartes and John Locke before him, Charles Seeger III found in the Netherlands an intellectual freedom lacking in his own country. Though his work in radio astronomy was highly acclaimed, he had had difficulty finding an academic position in the United States. Internecine academic quarrels may have been part of the problem, but association with his radical brother Pete clinched the matter. Naomi S. Seeger, Charles's daughter by his second wife, explains:

I know for a fact that it was his family ties that prevented my father from getting a job in the U.S. He told me he was offered a plum job at MIT but couldn't take it—he would never be given security clearance to do the job because he was Pete's brother. . . . It wasn't until the 70s till he had a boss . . . that was willing to stand by him and fight to get him sufficient security clearance. Even then, during the interviews, he was asked more questions about Pete and Peggy, their actions, habits, and beliefs than about his own actions and views.[21]

Europe, which had lost so many scientists to exile and death, was happy to take advantage of the reverse brain drain. Charles and his family originally went to Gothenburg, Sweden, and a year later came to Leiden, where Charles worked at the university's world-class observatory. Initially, the arrangement seemed very satisfactory to Peggy: "The household seems very stable, is full to the brim of love and welcomes."[22] Jeremy Seeger, Charles's eldest son, remembers Peggy being like "an older sister" who sang to the boys at bedtime and was occasionally the target of harmless pranks.[23] Inez spent most of her time at home with the boys and took occasional work that could be fitted in around housework and child care, such as editing student theses.

Peggy enrolled at the University of Leiden to continue her Russian studies, but she attended few classes. The Netherlands was too full of interesting and distracting pastimes: skating on the canals, weekends in Amsterdam and the Hague, and spending time with her new friends. Her favorite part of university life was the tradition of organizing women students into groups called *vereenigingen*. Each *vereeniging* (literally "togetherness") functioned as a support group for new students, an instant family for those who had recently left home. Peggy's *vereeniging* was a group of thirteen young women who met frequently to sing and talk and drink "awful milky coffee."[24] The group was called the Woozle (*de Woezle* in Dutch) after a Winnie the Pooh character, and Peggy wrote the Woozle's official song: a musical setting, in the form of a round, of a Dutch translation of an A. A. Milne poem. The *vereeniging* sang the song during an evening when each *vereeniging* presented a skit for the others. After the skits was an initiation ceremony, with all the solemnity of a secret society, complete with candles, blindfolds, and pledges in a darkened room.

While things were going well at the university and with the *vereeniging*, life at Charles and Inez's home was not quite so happy. The pleasant facade that Peggy had witnessed initially was showing signs of marked strain. In a letter to her father, with the curious date of "Octobvember 11, 1955," Peggy wrote: "Scarcely a day passes without some angry outbreaks, and the boys reflect somehow the instability of their past four years. Perhaps it is idealizing on my part, perhaps slips of memory, but I remember no such atmosphere in our family. . . . I do not get actively embroiled in these things, but it disturbs me to be around them."[25] Though she tried not to take sides, her letters make clear that her sympathies lay with Charles. At this time, Inez had few activities outside the home and may have suffered from what Betty Friedan would later call "the problem that has no name"—Inez was a highly intelligent woman cloistered in the home, in charge of work that was not satisfying or respected or even recognized as real work.[26]

Peggy tried to help with the housework, but Inez's standards were strict, and Peggy's attempts came up short. "Inez and I were soon at loggerheads," Peggy remembers.[27] Peggy began to spend much of her time away from home—looking for a Russian family in Amsterdam with whom to practice the language, spending weekends in the Hague, celebrating St. Nicholas Day with her *vereeniging*, going with her friend Anneke Rueb to visit Anneke's family in Arnhelm. In December, a childhood friend, Nina Powell, who had been studying at the London School of Economics, appeared on Peggy's doorstep. Peggy decided it was time to quit Leiden and, with Nina, to hitch-hike around Europe. At about the same time that the Weavers reunited at a sold-out concert in Carnegie Hall, Peggy and Nina hit the road.

December was an awkward time to hitchhike in northern Europe, but Peggy and Nina had no trouble getting rides. Nina had many friends in Europe with whom they could stay; when no friends were available, they stayed in youth hostels. In Alkmaar, they attended a concert of organ music in the cathedral and discovered that the organist was one of Ruth's former piano students. On the road to Friesland, they were picked up by an avid Jehovah's Witness who, when he discovered that Peggy could speak Dutch, spent the trip trying to convert her. In Groningen, there was a power outage, and "everyone was wandering around with huge flares; it was like something out of Brueghel."[28] On a cold night near Christmas Eve, they arrived at a youth hostel to find it closed and locked for the winter. A neighbor woman supplied a key and blankets but no food; there was also no heat in the hostel. From there, they made their way into Luxembourg, where the northern European cold was seeping into the marrow of their American bones. They were hitchhiking in a blizzard, stranded at dusk on a country road, when Father Jos Vloeberghs gave them a ride.

Josef Ernst Vloeberghs was a Belgian Catholic priest with great energy and no compunction about picking up two bedraggled American hitchhikers.

He was involved in many projects, among them the oversight of a troupe of university students who performed the play *Das Spiel der heiligen drei Könige* (The Play of the Three Holy Kings) during Christmas vacation. Jos was intrigued by Peggy's banjo and guitar and invited her and Nina to join the troupe and accompany them on their tour of Germany. Most of the participants were Flemish-speaking students from the Catholic University of Leuven in Belgium. Maurice Van de Putte, one of the students, remembers Peggy as a "sweet, steady, wise, intelligent young lady" who got along very well with other members of the troupe.[29] Peggy quickly learned Belgian Christmas songs (and taught American folk songs in return) and provided musical accompaniment for the play. (Despite her knowledge of Dutch, she found Flemish incomprehensible.) Nina took the role of the Farmer's Wife. The last few days of 1955 and the first few days of 1956 found them in Berlin, performing in German and exploring the great, wounded city.

Peggy found Berlin somber, a place where people rarely smiled, a city of "ruined buildings and ruined people," still licking its wounds from the Second World War.[30] West Berlin impressed her as a "weird conglomeration of old and new architecture, punctuated by . . . ruins . . . skeletons of girders and brick walls and little mortar and shrapnel holes."[31] The Soviet sector was even worse: "It is everything that the west pictures it to be, yet worse. The ruins are appalling—not only from the war but from the several uprisings and revolutions held by the East Berliners themselves. There is no energy, will, no material, to build with."[32] The troupe held several performances at a refugee camp for people who had fled East Berlin for the West. Peggy was appalled by the conditions in the camps, even more so by the cramped and joyless appearance of the children. She wrote to Charlie, "I shall never forget some of those child faces that came into the theater hall, stern and rigid. It was like watching the accelerated growth of a flower that next 45 minutes. Their faces opened, they sang, clapped, and clamored as children ought. The more they wanted to laugh the more I wanted to cry at their helplessness to *live* as children ought. They are all locked into the camps, have no playthings, live in virtual dormitories."[33] Jos and the troupe took nineteen of the children back to Belgium for a holiday. Maurice and Peggy were designated "foster parents" to look after them on the journey. Finding places for thirty-five people to stay was frequently a challenge, as was the language barrier. "My speech is a potpourri of German, Dutch (which I venture only with caution, as the Flemish have a contempt for Dutch accent and general character,) English and Gesture," Peggy wrote to Charles.[34] She responded to the challenge as she always did—by singing.

Upon arriving in Belgium, Peggy and eleven of the children moved into Jos's house in the village of Montigny-le-Tilleul, near the town of Charleroi, in Walloon country. Peggy considered the house "barely large enough for Jos and the sister who live[d] here, much less for the 11 children . . . who [were] to remain here for six months."[35] For two weeks, Peggy cared for the children and did general housework, aspiring to the strict standards of the nun who lived there: "The nun there had a complex about dirt . . . and cleaned up the dirt before it arrived. The natural accessories for the day were a dust-rag, broom and patience."[36] Peggy sang to the children after dinner, "as if singing were the dessert for each meal," and at bedtime.[37] Jos approved of her willingness to help and was happy to have her stay for as long as she liked.

Jos Vloeberghs at the age of thirty-two was like no one whom Peggy had ever met. A deeply, even severely, religious man, he was also a cheerful and occasionally playful one—referring to his clerical uniform as his "clown suit," dancing in the streets of Berlin, reciting Shakespeare in the lobby of Berlin's Free University, rolling up his trousers and dancing a hornpipe in the kitchen at one o'clock in the morning. At the same time, he had contempt for anything nonreligious and was strict in enforcing religious orthodoxy among the children. Peggy wrote Charles, "It doesn't seem to bother him if I'm not Catholic, so long as I'm a good girl and do useful things and love people."[38] Nonetheless, he spent a good deal of time trying to convert her, even suggesting that she settle down in the local convent.

At this point, Peggy was a fish out of water, with little money and no immediate plans, somewhat estranged from her only near relatives, a well-fed American in a hungry part of Europe, a Protestant (though in name only) in the midst of a devoutly Catholic household. She wrote to Hugh and Sally Lindsay, American friends she had met on the *Maasdam*, who were spending the year in Amsterdam. The Lindsays decided that Peggy needed rescuing and arrived in Montigny near the end of January. They joined the household for a meal, then packed Peggy and her luggage and instruments into their tiny Fiat, and drove her back to Leiden.

Leiden was only a temporary solution. Relations between Peggy and Inez worsened. Peggy made plans to leave, but she did not want to return to the United States just yet. "I probably will not get over here again once I return to America or get married, so would really like to be here another year," she wrote to Charles.[39] She had made reasonably good money singing at an American air base and began to search for other gigs. She contacted Alan Lomax, the Seegers' old family friend, who was living in London and working on a myriad of folk music projects. Could he perhaps find her work? She was also eager to do more traveling, and when the Lindsays invited her to join them on a trip to Denmark in March, she accepted. Though she left some luggage in Leiden, it was clear she would not return.

The day before Peggy left Leiden, Alan Lomax telephoned and asked if she could come to London to play in the musical drama *Dark of the Moon*. She refused; after accepting the Lindsays' generous offer of a trip to Denmark, she did not feel she could suddenly back out. Besides, she did not have enough money to travel to London. But Alan was persistent. He called back a few hours later and offered to send the money for her travel fare. He also said that she could delay her arrival for several weeks, allowing her to keep her commitment to the Lindsays, and promised that there would be radio appearances and possibly other gigs in London. This time she accepted.

Peggy enjoyed Copenhagen, and the Lindsays were fine traveling companions. In the youth hostel where they stayed, Peggy became friendly with a young Israeli who told her that she had "eyes the color of time" and urged her to join him on a trip to Finland, where he heard that one could make good money in the logging camps. It was tempting, but she had already given her word to go to England. She assumed that the trip would be for just a few weeks and that she would then rejoin the Lindsays. She also assumed that she would return to the States in the fall and continue her college education. She had applied for financial aid at Radcliffe but was also considering the University of California at Berkeley, which would be less expensive and would allow her to be closer to her family. She hoped to do some traveling over the summer and was determined to see Paris before she left, but she assumed that, within a few months' time, her European adventure would draw to a close.

In all these things, her assumptions would prove to be quite wrong.

# CHAPTER 6

# The First Time Ever

The first time ever I saw your face
I thought the sun rose in your eyes—
And the moon and stars were the gifts you gave
To the dark and empty skies, my love,
To the dark and empty skies.
—Ewan MacColl, "The First Time Ever I Saw Your Face"


March 27, 1956, was a day that would be forever burned into Peggy's memory, but she had no such premonition when she arrived at London's Waterloo Station in the early hours of the morning, tired and unkempt, after a twenty-seven-hour journey from Copenhagen. Alan Lomax enfolded her in a bear hug and took her to the Chelsea flat that he shared with Susan Mills, a twenty-three-year-old model and artist. Alan had several plans for Peggy, and the production of *Dark of the Moon* was only one of them. He wanted to organize a folk group that Peggy characterized as an "English Weavers, junior style."[1] (The original Weavers were doing quite well after their reunion concert in December 1955.) Alan's partner in creating the folk group was a singer, playwright, and songwriter named Ewan MacColl. Alan named the group "the Ramblers" and envisioned a core of musicians supplemented by guest artists such as English folksinger A. L. (Bert) Lloyd, Irish uilleann pipe player Seamus Ennis, and West Indian calypso musician Fitzroy Coleman. The only thing missing was a banjo player, and Alan felt that Peggy would fit the bill perfectly. Without Peggy's knowledge, he had arranged an audition for her; it would occur that morning.

After a twenty-seven-hour journey, Peggy was in need of a bath, a change of clothes, and a night's sleep, but she would only be allowed the first two. She had inherited her mother's lack of interest in sartorial presentation, but Susan Mills understood the importance of first impressions. She ordered Peggy into the miniscule shower and then went through Peggy's clothes with increasing despair; Peggy's dirty jeans and cheap cotton dress would not do. Finally, Susan gave up and got her own clothes, jewelry, and makeup. Peggy recalls:

> She . . . gave me the first manicure of my life, and decorated me like a Christmas tree with earrings, bracelets, and necklace. She washed, untangled, trimmed, and back- combed my long, long hair, putting it up into one of those 1950s bouffant concoctions. At her dressing table she sat me down and expertly slapped on me one of those faces that cosmetic companies use to prove that all their products can be used at once. Saying, "Breathe in and hold your breath," she zipped me into a low-necked, wasp-wasted, 1956-feminine creation, then perched me on three-inch heels and nudged me compassionately into the little room where the audition committee was waiting.[2]

At the audition, Peggy sat on a stool in the middle of the room, somewhat disconcerted; the stool was so high that she could not tap her feet on the floor. But she had no fear of performing. She sang "The House Carpenter" and played her banjo as easily as if she were in her own living room. The banjo was not a common instrument in Britain in those days, though folk music aficionados had probably heard it on recordings and were familiar with its general sound. But this was something different. As Ewan MacColl later remarked, Peggy's banjo playing was "as far away from the metallic plinkety-plonk of the average tenor banjo as the cor anglais is from the kazoo."[3] The Ramblers happily accepted her into their company. The group might have been a mere interlude in her career as a folksinger had it not been for one thing: it was through the Ramblers that she met Ewan MacColl. She did not yet realize, on that morning in early spring, that she had met her second Waterloo of the day.

Ewan was a slight, intense forty-one-year-old writer and musician (though he originally told Peggy that he was thirty-eight) with thick black hair and a striking red beard. His "senses were utterly ravished" when he heard her play, and he was eager to know her better.[4] Peggy had met many extraordinary people, from Woody Guthrie to Hanns Eisler, but she would meet few people more remarkable than Ewan MacColl. He was equal parts poetry and politics, artistry and activism; he had a restless mind and a glorious baritone voice. Born James Henry Miller to a left-wing, working-class Scottish family in Salford, England, Ewan had left school at fourteen, the age at which British schooling ceased to be free of charge in those days. He had grown up in the same neighborhood that Friedrich Engels had described as "very unwholesome, dirty and ruinous" in *The Conditions of the Working Class in England*; according to Ewan's biographer, Ben Harker, it had changed little from Engels's day to

Ewan's childhood in the early decades of the twentieth century.[5] Ewan had worked in factories and offices, had been on the dole, and in 1929 had joined the Young Communist League. From an early age, he was exposed to folk music and radical politics—his parents and many of their friends were left-wing activists as well as devoted singers of traditional Scottish songs—and the two would remain intertwined in his work. His first songs, even those that were not about avowedly political subjects, such as "The Manchester Rambler," were shot through with political commentary. If Peggy was from folk revival aristocracy, Ewan was one of its intellectual shock troops.

By 1956, Ewan was an important member of the British folk revival, but his first love had been theater. He had been a writer, actor, and director of several agitprop theater troupes in the 1930s, and with his first wife, Joan Littlewood, had founded the highly successful Theatre Workshop shortly after World War II.[6] (This was also the time when he took the pseudonym "Ewan MacColl," the name of a nineteenth-century Gaelic poet.) Like much radical theater, MacColl's theater groups eschewed the fourth wall and other trappings of realism in favor of a more experimental style, which included street performance, political declamation, dance, and music. Theatre Workshop's unconventional and politically committed productions had garnered critical acclaim throughout Europe, and Ewan MacColl, as resident playwright, was often singled out for praise. In 1948, Hugh MacDiarmid called Ewan "the most important and promising young dramatist writing in English, or any dialect of English, at the present time"; Sean O'Casey prophesied that "Marlowe is in the wings"; and George Bernard Shaw called Ewan "the only genius working in the theatre of the day—apart from himself."[7]

MacColl and Littlewood divorced in 1948, but each remained an admirer of the other's work, and they continued to lead Theatre Workshop together for several years. Among Theatre Workshop's innovations was an emphasis on physical movement; Ewan recalled, "We talked longingly of a theatre where the actors could handle their bodies like trained dancers or athletes."[8] Their search for a movement teacher led them to the Hungarian émigré choreographer Rudolf Laban, who, with his assistant, Jean Newlove, trained the Theatre Workshop actors in dance and movement. The addition of Newlove to the company marked a major change for Theatre Workshop and for Ewan MacColl, who noted, "She [Newlove] turned out to be a magnificent teacher, serious but good-natured, full of ideas and quick to recognise the unique character of Theatre Workshop. Under her tutelage, the dormant capabilities of the actors in the group underwent a complete transformation and it wasn't long before our part-time tutor fell under the spell of the theatre and joined us. And it wasn't long before I fell under the spell of our dance teacher and married her."[9] The two married in April 1949.[10] In the summer of 1950, their son, Hamish, was born.[11]

Theatre Workshop's goal was to create a revolutionary theater that furthered the interests of workers and had workers as the primary audience. Though based in Manchester, the company spent much time touring. After years of hard work, Theatre Workshop had achieved a measure of success, but the effort had taken its toll: the actors had barely enough money to live on, and their health was suffering. Ewan suggested establishing a home base in Glasgow, a city with strong working-class traditions, and the company moved there briefly but could not find affordable permanent premises. When the Theatre Royal in London's East End became available at a price amenable to Theatre Workshop's shoestring budget, the company chose to settle there.

London had been the center of Britain's theatrical life for centuries, and Theatre Workshop would thrive there until the mid-1970s. Ewan and Jean moved to London in 1953, but his heart was not in it. Jean remained the company's movement coach and choreographer, but Ewan drifted away, only occasionally acting in and writing for Theatre Workshop productions. He had recently become involved with the Scottish Renaissance, and this involvement led him back to the Scottish songs of his childhood. At the Edinburgh Fringe Festival in 1951, while Theatre Workshop performed his play *Uranium 235*, Ewan sang in a concert of Scottish folk music organized by the Scottish poet and folklorist Hamish Henderson. In 1952, the English Folk Dance and Song Society subsidized his first two records, collections of traditional Scottish songs. But it was an American, Alan Lomax, who was the greatest catalyst of Ewan's nascent folk music career—and later of his personal life.

Ewan had been singing and writing songs—both for personal pleasure and for the theater—since the 1920s, but he had never considered himself a songwriter or musician. Music was simply something that he did, and like any folk poet, he based his compositions on the traditional songs he had learned from his family. Initially, he reworked older songs "the way a cobbler repairs shoes: cuts a bit of scuffed leather off here and adds a bit there, adds a rubber heel-tip to a run-down heel and cuts out a new sole for a bigger job." As he described it, "That's what I was doing—making cast-offs fit for use again."[12] Perhaps because they were based on time-tested, familiar models, his songs struck a chord. His first major song, "The Manchester Rambler," written in 1932, became an anthem for hikers throughout the country. But it was not until the 1950s that Ewan regarded songwriting as anything more than "a simple chore to be sandwiched between more important chores."[13] Some of his songs, such as "Dirty Old Town," "The Shoals of Herring," and "The First Time Ever I Saw Your Face," would travel far from their creator, metamorphosing in the hands of pop and rock and bel canto musicians, picking up new words and discarding old ones like a peddler with a trunk of ever-changing wares.

Ewan's growing disenchantment with Theatre Workshop coincided with Alan Lomax's arrival in England. Alan had begun collecting and recording folk music as an apprentice to his father, John Lomax, but by this time, Alan had far exceeded his father's collecting activities in both scope and breadth.[14] In 1950, he moved to Europe in order to record music for a multivolume series of world music sponsored by Columbia Records. (He also left the United States to escape the blacklist.) By early 1951, he was living in England, appearing on radio shows, collecting music for records, and developing his own folk music programs under the auspices of the BBC.

Folk music had enjoyed a following in the British Isles since the eighteenth century, but the focus had primarily been on the antiquarian type of music favored by Cecil Sharp and his brainchild, the English Folk Dance and Song Society (EFDSS).[15] In the 1950s, most people in Britain still considered folklore to be rural archaisms. When Alan began working with British folklorist Peter Kennedy on a recording of English folk music, they agreed that urban and industrial music should be included.[16] Peter suggested two folksingers for the project: A. L. Lloyd, who sang traditional English songs and working-class industrial songs, and Ewan MacColl.

Ewan had recorded for the EFDSS and on the tiny, left-wing Topic label, but not until he met Alan Lomax did he regard folk music as anything more than "a pleasant medium of relaxation."[17] "Alan had become deeply preoccupied with the idea of a British folk-song revival," wrote Ewan. "His enthusiasm was infectious and I began to see in my mind's eye an invading army of singers and fiddle players, of troupes of dancers, actors and storytellers."[18] On records, on the radio, and in concert, Ewan's rich expressive voice, dramatic presentation, intuitive musicality (he never learned to read music), and knowledge of songs soon garnered him an enthusiastic following. He began to see folk music as a treasure trove of working-class culture, an art form that gave voice to working-class ideas and experiences—in short, a tool that could be used to mold the future.

In 1953, Ewan and Alan collaborated on a series of radio programs entitled *Ballads and Blues*, designed to showcase the best in British, Irish, and American folk traditions. The series featured Ewan, Alan, A. L. Lloyd, Seamus Ennis, Scottish singer Isla Cameron, British jazz musician Humphrey Lyttelton, Appalachian singer and dulcimer player Jean Ritchie, and blues legend Big Bill Broonzy, among others.[19] The popularity of the series led to several concerts with similarly eclectic lineups; Scots ballads and English sea shanties shared the stage with jazz, calypso, and the latest national craze, skiffle music. Blues musicians in the United States had used the term *skiffle* in the early decades of the twentieth century, and in 1950s Britain, skiffle referred to music inspired by American blues, jazz, and folk song. Skiffle musicians revered the songs of Woody Guthrie and Leadbelly, and they accompanied these songs on guitar, washtub bass, kazoo, and other instruments. Skiffle clubs appeared throughout Britain in the 1950s, and skiffle musicians included Martin Carthy, Mick Jagger, Van Morrison, and a band called The Quarrymen, led by a young art student named John Lennon. In 1954, Alan and Ewan formed the Ballads and Blues Club at the Princess Louise pub in High Holborn—one of the first clubs to explicitly brand itself a "folk club" rather than a skiffle club. The British folk revival would spend much time and energy building an identity that was different from (and often in opposition to) the American folk revival; thus it is perhaps ironic that three of the engines that drove the British folk revival were American: Alan Lomax, the skiffle movement, and Peggy Seeger.

Peggy was initially unimpressed with the quality of the skiffle clubs; she described them as consisting of "four or five second or third-rate musicians who have learned their style of singing and playing from records of Leadbelly and Guthrie."[20] But she was an immediate hit there. A highly skilled musician, an American who had known Woody Guthrie and Leadbelly, she showed what a folk musician could be: someone who played the music of her own country with artistry and commitment. *Dark of the Moon* lasted for only a few days, but opportunities to play in clubs seemed endless. Alan's Chelsea flat was too small for her to stay for more than a few days, so he found her a furnished room in nearby Oakley Gardens. Peggy described the dwelling as "very bleak," but it made up in location what it lacked in charm.[21] She was excited by her independence and her ability to make a living as a musician, but work was only one reason she chose to stay in London. The other reason was Ewan MacColl.

At the time of Peggy and Ewan's first meeting, he was playing the Street Singer in Brecht and Weill's *Threepenny Opera* at London's Strand Theatre. "He was wonderful in the part," says Peggy, and she went backstage to congratulate him.[22] He invited her to come again. When she did so, he drove her home in his old blue Ford Vauxhall and told her that he loved her. "He said, 'I'm going to make love to you.' . . . Now this was not the college boy talk I was used to."[23] After this extraordinary declaration, Ewan gave her a kiss, and she exited the car, dazed and overwhelmed. It was only a matter of time before Ewan's prediction came true.

On April 11, less than three weeks after their first meeting, Peggy confided to her diary, "Ewan MacColl is in love with me. And I with him."[24] It was the start of an affair that was exhilarating and exhausting, passionate and all-encompassing yet filled with uncertainty, frustration, and secrecy. She was enthralled by Ewan's talent for words and music, his intellect, his passion for theater and politics and folk music—and her. "When Ewan talks I listen," she said. "My mind is at his command."[25] Yet she could think of no good or permanent outcome to their tortuous situation. Ewan adored his small son, Hamish, and though his marriage had its problems, he cared deeply for Jean and had no wish to hurt her. "I do think he loved Jean," says Peggy. "He just didn't love her as much."[26] Even if it were possible for Ewan to marry Peggy, she wondered if that would be the right course: "I would lose my personality were I to marry him—he is too pronounced a personality, too complete a person to really need me."[27]

A political neophyte, Peggy was now getting an accelerated education from Ewan, whose politics drew on Marxist theory, his visits to the "eastern democracies" (as some leftists referred to the Soviet bloc), and his own gut-level reaction to the poverty of his youth and the violence that had greeted his first forays into political activism. Though she would never be quite as political as he and would never join a political party other than, briefly, the British Labour Party and later the Green Party, she saw in Ewan's political analysis a way of understanding the world that made sense to her. "Ewan's sort of communism is very attractive," she confided to her father, who reacted with mild alarm.[28] He could not even bring himself to write the words "communism" or "left-wing"; instead, he counseled Peggy to stay clear of "all tendential organizations" and admitted that, in the past, both he and Pete had shown "definite attitudes."[29] Charles's caution was not misplaced. He knew from personal experience how membership in radical organizations could damage one. At that moment, Pete's livelihood was suffering because of the blacklist, and he expected to be cited for contempt of Congress for his "unfriendly" testimony before HUAC. (The citation came in July of that year, and Pete would spend years fighting it.) Though Charles understood the thrill of being part of a movement greater than oneself, he did not think that this particular battle was appropriate for Peggy: "For MacColl it's a different thing altogether. He comes from the working class. It is his fight. You and I come from the bourgeoisie. We can enter the fight. We can even become leaders. But it is never our fight, however hard we try to make it so."[30] Surprisingly, Charles had no worries about his daughter entering an apparently hopeless love affair with a married Communist twice her age. Indeed, he felt that a person who had not experienced an unsuccessful love affair was not truly adult.

The difficulty of pursuing a clandestine relationship was exacerbated because Ewan and Peggy were constantly in each other's company. Both were members of the Ramblers, which Peggy described as "a group consisting of a communist dramatist, a worker in an airplane factory, a classical guitarist, an African drummer, two jazz men for the bass and clarinet, Alan and myself, and a girl who works on the bus lines in London. The results are enough to chill the blood of a purist, but I think they will hit the right spot in British folksong movement."[31] By mid-April, they were rehearsing for a television series for Manchester's Granada television. In May, Peggy's work visa ran out, and Alan advised her to leave the country until Granada could issue her a new one. She left England for nearly a month, going to Belgium to visit Jos and the children and then to Leiden to stay with friends. During this time, Ewan and she wrote each other regularly. His last letter was a shock: he had told Jean about the affair (which Peggy had advised) and decided that it must end. They would remain friends and coworkers; after Peggy returned to England, they began to record an album together. Much of the recording was done at Ewan and Jean's house in Croydon, often with their son, Hamish, as recording engineer, a situation that was painful and awkward for all concerned. "I don't know how long I can take it," she wrote to Charles, "but somehow I feel that if he can, I can."[32]

Peggy was not the only one whose love life had undergone a transformation. Susan Mills had left Alan because he would not marry her. He had relocated to a larger house in North London, where there was room for Peggy—and Alan's ex-wife Elizabeth, their daughter Anna, Elizabeth's new lover, and Alan's new girlfriend, Shirley Collins, a singer from Sussex and member of the Ramblers. Though Peggy and Shirley were the same age, Peggy had a confidence and skill beyond her years, and Shirley found her somewhat intimidating. She recalls, "I was often a little nervous of Peggy, finding her cool and self-assured, and with a rather brisk manner, although she did have a very merry laugh. She certainly amazed and impressed all the fledgling folk singers and musicians with her guitar and banjo playing. It was far beyond anything we'd heard, and it inspired many young people to improve their skills."[33]

Peggy and Shirley would ultimately see the Ramblers as a failed experiment, but it began with high hopes. The television series with Granada was perhaps its greatest success. On Mondays, the cast traveled to Manchester, where they rehearsed and broadcasted, then returned to London the following day. Peggy had characterized Ewan as a "purist" who "sings only the most traditional and musically 'good' folk music," yet the television shows made little distinction between traditional music and modern songs composed in the folk idiom.[34] In fact, the term *folk music* was rarely used; Alan opened the June 18 broadcast by saying, "Now's the time for ballads, for skiffle music, with guitar and banjo."[35] Sometimes the similarities between old and new music were shown deliberately, as in the June 22 broadcast, when two labor songs were juxtaposed: Peggy's version of Woody Guthrie's "Union Maid" and Ewan's version of the traditional British song "Four Loom Weaver."

Several of Ewan's compositions were prominently featured in the programs. "The Manchester Rambler" was an obvious choice for the series theme song, but it was eventually eclipsed by "Dirty Old Town," which would prove to be one of Ewan's most enduring creations. Initially written for his play *Landscape with Chimneys*, "Dirty Old Town" drew on Ewan's memories of Salford and his love-hate relationship with the city of his birth. Without romanticizing poverty or minimizing the harshness of life in Salford's grim streets, he perfectly captures the beauty that can nonetheless exist therein, like a flower growing in a junkyard:

> I found my love by the gasworks croft,
> Dreamed a dream by the old canal;
> Kissed my girl by the factory wall.
> Dirty old town, dirty old town.[36]

With its spare, poetic lyrics and slightly bluesy melody, "Dirty Old Town" stands as an evocation of folk culture itself: a hopeful human reaction to adversity. Strangely enough, Ewan claimed minimal credit for his songs on the television series, presenting them instead as part of an unbroken line of folk poetry. He admitted to having written the ephemeral—and obviously modern—"Space Girl's Song" but not the artistically superior "Manchester Rambler" or "Dirty Old Town."

The intense, all-day work schedule of the Ramblers and the nights free of ordinary responsibility provided an atmosphere too powerful for Ewan and Peggy to resist. The affair began again with renewed urgency and continued after the Ramblers' television series ended in mid-July. Peggy's new work visa allowed her to do concerts and work for the BBC; she felt sure she could support herself. Nonetheless, she considered going home and finishing college. The affair with Ewan seemed hopeless, and it was becoming too painful to remain in his company with no hope of a joint future. She booked a flight that would leave London on August 18 and was making plans to study at the University of California at Berkeley. Strangely enough, Charles urged her not to "come running back to the U.S."[37] He assured her that he would support her no matter what and even registered her as a student at Berkeley, but it seemed a shame to him to abandon "such an eventful and profitable year, to come back and bury [her]self in books."[38] He did advise her to be careful, to take a deep breath and do things slowly, and to use birth control.

Much of the summer was depressing and lonely. The relationship between Ewan and Peggy seemed doomed, yet neither could bear to end it. On July 12, Peggy confided to her diary, "To think of doing anything that does not include him brings on me a despair and loneliness that is so tangible even in thought that my heart aches. . . . My heart has ached like that but once before, when Dio died. . . . The hurt of not being able to have him, of having to hide everything, is getting to be too much."[39] By late August, however, everything had changed. Peggy no longer thought about returning to the States; she was making records with Ewan and the Ramblers and was working on a book with Alan and Shirley.[40] She wanted to see more of Europe before coming home; most of all, she wanted to work things out with Ewan. She wrote to Charles lightheartedly, "Ewan is sure he wants at least 50 years of my life and I am agreeable. . . . I'm not coming home for quite a while because I have another sort of home here and am following a sort of Black Jack Davy."[41] Charles would surely have understood the reference to "Black Jack Davy," which Ruth had transcribed for *Our Singing Country*, an American variant of the British ballad "The Gypsy Laddie" (Child 200), the story of a well-born, married lady who leaves her comfortable home to follow a lover of a different culture and lower social class.

Charles never expected the affair to last, but he felt that Peggy would come away from it with the important knowledge that broken hearts can mend. He recognized certain similarities between Peggy and Ewan's situation and his own relationship with Ruth, but he pointed out that there were important differences as well. He and Constance were no longer living together when he first met Ruth, and Constance's reluctance to sever the marriage stemmed from the stigma that divorce still carried in the 1930s, not from any desire to repair her relationship with Charles. His two eldest children had been grown, and his youngest was thirteen years old and in boarding school; divorce did not change his relationship with his children, who were always welcome in Ruth's home. This situation was quite different from that of Ewan and Jean, who were living together with their young son, and Jean very much wanted to save her marriage.

Though Peggy did feel guilty about Jean and Hamish, she also felt that Ewan was happier with her than with his wife. Ewan's passion for her was overwhelming, even somewhat frightening, and she was utterly captivated. "Ewan was an entrancing man," she recalls. "He was fascinating. I was never bored by him."[42] She had no idea what the future would bring, but she was willing to risk it. She had thought herself in love before, but this was different. Her previous romances faded into insignificance; if she thought of them at all, it was with the amused and nostalgic tolerance with which an adult regards childish things. This was the love she had long imagined, and now it was here in reality—for the first time ever.

# CHAPTER 7

# The Rover, Part Two

I thought it no danger to follow a stranger,
But with time changing a friend he became.
—Peggy Seeger, "Song of Myself"

Peggy had purchased a Lambretta motor scooter, and Charles suggested that it could provide an inexpensive way to explore Europe. In August 1956, Peggy put this plan into action. First stop was Scotland, Ewan's historical—if not native—country. Ewan helped plan her itinerary and traveled with her as far as Lincoln; his many friends in Scotland provided her with places to stay. After traversing the north of England in the pouring rain, she arrived at the home of the poet Hugh MacDiarmid, whom Ewan and Peggy called by his given name, Christopher Grieve. She found the elderly Grieve "a beautiful person" despite his tendency to drink too much, and from his cottage she departed for Glasgow and Edinburgh.[1] In Fish Cross, a community of miners welcomed her warmly, gave her a tour of the mine, treated her to a ceilidh, and impressed her as "politically the most energetic and alive group of people [she had] met in [her] life."[2] Throughout Scotland, from Glasgow to Ullapool to Skye, she met people with whom she could sing and people who invited her to stay in their homes, sometimes complete strangers intrigued by her banjo and American songs. She met Jimmie MacGregor, Adam McNaughtan, and Norman and Janey Buchan, all of whom would become prominent in the Scottish folk revival. She spent several days in the Aberdeen home of Scots Traveller Jeannie Robertson, singing and talking because it was too wet to go out. At other times, she was alone with the breathtaking scenery of the Scottish Highlands.

Peggy returned to London in mid-September to discover that there was no longer room for her at Alan's home. She contacted Maud Karpeles, who had been Cecil Sharp's collecting partner in the Appalachians and was a longtime stalwart of the English Folk Dance and Song Society. Maud greeted Peggy warmly, invited her to stay in her flat, and departed for the Bartók Festival in Hungary. By the time she returned, Peggy had become a companion-cum-assistant to Diane Hamilton, founder of Tradition Records. (Diane used the pseudonym "Hamilton" to disguise her wealth and family connections; her real name was Guggenheim.) An avid collector of folk songs, Diane had recently introduced the Clancy Brothers to Tommy Makem and had recorded the first album-length record of Irish folksingers in Ireland. Peggy accompanied Diane to Italy and Ireland, where they continued Diane's collecting work. In mid-November, Peggy returned to London and tried to sort out her relationship with Ewan. Musically, they had begun to demonstrate the tight symbiosis that would last more than three decades. When Decca Records released a 1956 recording of the Ramblers, the album cover read "Alan Lomax and the Ramblers with Ewan MacColl and Peggy Seeger"—a sign that Ewan and Peggy were already considered a musical unit. They had also recorded an album, *Classic Scots Ballads*, for Tradition Records. Personal relations between Ewan and Peggy were still in a state of confusion and flux. As autumn progressed, Peggy became confused and depressed about the course her life had taken; she quarreled with Ewan for no apparent reason and thought him a saint for bearing her moods so patiently. Ewan was torn as well; whatever course he took, he felt he would deeply hurt someone he loved. Hamish was moody and bewildered, and Jean was still trying to keep her marriage intact. By December, Peggy decided that she needed a break and returned to the United States.

Peggy left England with a steamer trunk, a guitar, a banjo, and her Lambretta scooter. She crossed the ocean in a force 8 winter storm that made most of the passengers too ill to leave their cabins. She spent Christmas in Beacon, then flew to Santa Barbara for the winter. She had talked about going back to college when she returned to the United States, but when she actually arrived, she chose to pursue music rather than higher education. Ewan wrote to her frequently, but a resolution to their dilemma was no nearer than it had been during the summer. They rarely telephoned each other, for transatlantic phone calls were expensive at the time, but one telephone conversation proved memorable. Peggy mentioned that she needed a short, new love song for an upcoming gig. Did Ewan know of one? Deftly, her experienced songwriter-lover put one together on the spot and sang it for her. The song was a gift to her, and he called it "The First Time Ever I Saw Your Face."

Ewan never sang the song himself and said, "Only Peggy's singing matches the feelings that gave rise to it."[3] Yet dozens of musicians, from Elvis Presley to Johnny Cash to Celine Dion, have covered the song. Roberta Flack's version became a smash hit in 1972 and earned a Grammy for best song in 1973. It is unquestionably Ewan's best-known song, and current comments on the internet show that audiences still respond to these three simple stanzas:

> The first time ever I saw your face
> I thought the sun rose in your eyes—
> And the moon and stars were the gifts you gave
> To the dark and empty skies, my love,
> To the dark and empty skies.

> The first time ever I kissed your mouth,
> I felt the earth move in my hand—
> Like the trembling heart of a captive bird
> That was there at my command, my love,
> That was there at my command.

> The first time ever I lay with you
> And felt your heart beat next to mine—
> I thought our joy would fill the earth
> And last till the end of time, my love,
> And last till the end of time.[4]

Ewan would write many love songs during the course of his life with Peggy, from the politically and linguistically complex "Love for Love" to the lushly poetic "Sweet Thames, Flow Softly" to the achingly tender "Joy of Living." In many ways, those are more interesting and imaginative songs, yet none has come close to achieving the fame of "The First Time Ever I Saw Your Face." While many of Ewan's songs deal with specific political or personal situations, this one is universal, describing the joyous moment of first love—a factor that may explain its great popularity. Though it is shorter and simpler than many of his songs, it clearly shows his songwriting method: take the form of traditional Anglo-American folk song and vary it.

In common with many Anglo-American ballads, "The First Time Ever" is composed of five-line stanzas, each consisting of a quatrain and a repeated final line. Ewan also uses ballad "commonplaces"—catchphrases that appear in many different ballads.[5] "The first time I saw my love" is a well-known commonplace of Anglo-American balladry; Ewan's slight alteration to "the first time ever" gives it a more contemporary sound. Unlike traditional ballad makers, Ewan sometimes used catchphrases taken from ordinary speech (and, in other songs, from poetry). In the second stanza, he takes the modern cliché "I felt the earth move" and couples it to the strikingly original "like the trembling heart of a captive bird," a phrase that aptly describes the breathless intensity of early love. The first line of each stanza is the same except for slight variations, a technique known as "incremental repetition." In ballads, this technique is used to advance the course of the story; here, it is used to describe the course of the love affair. Perhaps the way in which "The First Time Ever" most violates the conventions of British folk song is in the direct address to the lover. British—and particularly Scottish—folk songs tend to be relatively objective; the singer may describe the emotions of others but rarely expresses his or her own. The direct address to the lover is, of course, the preferred style for pop music, and perhaps it was this subjectivity that made the song so appealing to the pop market. "The First Time Ever" was well received when Peggy sang it for the first time in California in 1957, and she has been singing it ever since.

In the spring of 1957, Albert Grossman offered Peggy a job singing at the Gate of Horn, a folk club he had recently opened in Chicago.[6] She flew to Philadelphia, where she had left her scooter with friends, then took off for Chicago, with her suitcase, guitar, and banjo strapped precariously to the passenger seat. Upon arrival, she moved into the housing provided for Gate of Horn performers: the fifth floor of an old warehouse. The Gate of Horn would launch the careers of many folksingers, including Odetta and Bob Dylan, and Albert Grossman would become the manager for an array of well-known musicians, including Joan Baez, Janis Joplin, and Peter, Paul, and Mary. This was Peggy's first regular gig as a solo artist; she shared the bill with blues legend Big Bill Broonzy. Her workday lasted from 9:00 p.m. to 3:00 a.m., and she arrived home in time to watch the sunrise. Each evening, she performed three thirty-minute sets of traditional American folk songs. A newspaper review praised Peggy's stage presence, musical skill, and rapport with the audience: "Talent broad enough to keep the rapt attention of the house for 30 minutes without pretentious stage tricks is scarce in the folk music field. Peggy Seeger reaches into a wide variety of folk idioms and offers them up with a sharpness of detail and a vibrant fresh-air voice that makes an intense and constantly varying imprint on the audience with each number." She also gave a children's concert at the University of Chicago, where Pete had sung a year earlier. Though Peggy was proud of her family connections, she disliked the "inevitable comparisons to Pete's performance": "People here remember Pete so well that it's very difficult to make one's own way—no matter how well you do, you can never come up to that infinitely high standard."[7] She had a brief romance with a Northwestern student named Peter Schlein, who (like Peggy) was the child of a critically acclaimed but not very well-known composer.[8] When Peggy's gig ended in the summer, she drove her scooter more than seven hundred miles to New York, with Peter as her passenger.

In New York, Peggy gave a concert at the Actors' Playhouse in Sheridan Square, the first concert produced by Izzy Young, who owned the Folklore Center on nearby MacDougal Street.[9] She visited Pete and Toshi in Beacon and was much impressed with the family's newest venture: making films of musicians. On June 18, Peggy traveled to Montreal, accompanied by Ralph Rinzler, and from there set sail for England. Her reunion with Ewan was less successful than she had hoped. After the freedom she had enjoyed in Chicago, she chafed under Ewan's demands to be always in his company—at least as far as was possible with a married man. When she told him about Peter Schlein, Ewan was so angry that he slapped her—and then collapsed in tears, horrified by his own behavior. "I've never hit a woman before," he said. "It won't happen again."[10] (It never did.) Peggy forgave the slap but was puzzled by her conflicting feelings—she could love him so deeply yet could quarrel with him over minutiae; she sometimes craved solitude and silence rather than the company of the intense, talkative Ewan. She did not know if she would stay with him or return to the United States and allow the memory of him to fade, as a fond youthful adventure. In the meantime, she chose to attend the World Youth Festival in Moscow.

The World Festival of Youth and Students was organized by the World Federation of Democratic Youth and the International Union of Students, left-wing organizations founded shortly after the end of World War II. The first World Youth Festival was held in 1947 in Prague, where seventeen thousand participants from 71 countries demonstrated the dance, music, and culture of their homelands. The festival has been held sporadically ever since, but the largest World Youth Festival was the one that Peggy attended in Moscow from July 28 to August 11, 1957. The event included thirty-four thousand participants from 131 countries, and its theme was "For Peace and Friendship." Peggy knew one of the American participants: a young Californian named Guy Carawan, who attended the festival with his wife, Noel.[11] Guy and Peggy had met at the Seeger home in 1953, where Guy had impressed Peggy by baking bread and doing his own laundry—things she had never seen a man do before.

The journey from London to Moscow took three days, "two of which were spent sleeping sitting up (in a baggage rack if you were lucky and short enough), and living on food handed out with welcomes at towns in Eastern Europe."[12] In Moscow, the Americans were taken to quarters that were clean and comfortable, if lacking in privacy. Participants slept five to a room but had access to hot water and laundry facilities, and their itinerary had been entirely arranged by their Soviet hosts. On the first day of the festival, trucks took the American delegation through the Moscow streets to the opening ceremony at Lenin Stadium. Crowds of people surrounded the trucks, waving, proffering gifts, shaking hands, and shouting "peace and friendship" in many languages. Peggy was deeply moved by the enthusiastic welcome that the Americans received: "My heart almost burst and our tears certainly did. I am hoarse from my own enthusiasm and shrieking."[13] In the stadium, delegations from Australia and Argentina, Israel and Egypt, France and Algeria, the United States and China (among others) marched in a huge parade. Hundreds of Russian dancers and athletes performed with clocklike precision, holding flags that spelled out "peace and friendship." The festival featured events both large and small: demonstrations of English folksinging and dancing, athletic competitions, ballet performances, an international song contest ("Moscow Nights" took first place), and a gymnastics demonstration by Soviet gymnast Alexander Sobolev while he was suspended from a helicopter.

The American delegation was small (approximately two hundred people) and disorganized. A *Life* magazine article describes them as "a mixed group, some bargain hunters, some curiosity-seekers, some fellow travelers."[14] They were not required to stay together, though frequently diplomats and members of the news media asked them to attend events as representatives of the United States. Looking back, Peggy recalls, "It was probably very bad diplomacy because most of us were completely ignorant, young, still wet behind the ears, green. In no way should we have been expected to represent our country."[15] They had planned no cultural demonstrations, certainly nothing to rival the extravagant displays provided by the Russians or the Chinese. But Peggy and Guy could play and sing American folk songs, which were warmly received by the Russian audiences, particularly since Peggy could introduce them in Russian. Back at the hotel, after an exhilarating and exhausting first day, a group of curious Russians sang along as Peggy played her banjo and sang "Michael, Row Your Boat Ashore." "I am tired and so happy I cannot sleep," she wrote.[16] Festival participants also appreciated "Down by the Riverside", with its chorus, "I ain't gonna study war no more," and its updated verse "I'm gonna lay down the atom bomb."

Many of Guy and Peggy's concerts were small, but there was also a performance at the Bolshoi Theater, where each delegation demonstrated the culture of its homeland. After a spectacular display of Chinese dragons, the American delegation trooped out—the men in blue jeans and the women in simple blouses, skirts, and saddle shoes—and sang along to Peggy and Guy's accompaniment. "The Russians loved the informality of the Americans," remembers Peggy. "It was fresh to them, the way children would be fresh."[17] Guy remembers singing Ed McCurdy's classic antiwar song "Last Night I Had the Strangest Dream" at the Bolshoi concert and remarks, "It seems like a dream to me now that we could have actually done that."[18] Indeed, the multinational audience singing about the decision to end war must have seemed the realization of McCurdy's strange dream.

Ewan and Jean attended the festival as part of the British delegation. Jean was busy with dance performances, and Ewan contrived to see Peggy as often as possible. The meetings were not always successful; both were tired and pulled in too many directions at once. One ill-fated day, Ewan arranged for Peggy and Guy to give a concert for a group of left-wing writers. It was not a success: Peggy and Guy delivered a program of gospel music in an officially atheist country, to a group of people who believed that religion is the opiate of the masses. Ewan was horrified, so angry that he told Peggy he was breaking off the relationship. (It was a resolution that he could not keep for long.) He and Jean returned to London.[19] Peggy and the other members of the American delegation had been invited to go to China.[20]

Traveling behind the Iron Curtain during the height of the Cold War was an unpopular choice for Americans; *Life* magazine reported that the festival participants "went despite State Department warning that the festival was a propaganda gimmick."[21] The State Department could not forbid them to go to the Soviet Union, but China was a different matter: the United States had no diplomatic relations with the People's Republic of China, and an American passport forbade travel there. According to *Time* magazine, a letter from Acting Secretary of State Christian Herter was delivered to the American delegates, advising them, "By traveling to Communist China at this time you will, in the considered view of your government, be acting as a willing tool of Communist propaganda intended, wherever possible, to subvert the foreign policy and the best interests of the U.S."[22] Frantic telephone calls ensued between the Americans and their families back home, and most chose to heed the State Department's warning. But forty members did not, among them Peggy Seeger, Guy and Noel Carawan, and the writer Sally Belfrage. (Sally Belfrage was the daughter of radical journalist Cedric Belfrage, who had been deported to his native England in 1955 for refusing to cooperate with HUAC.)

Charles was supportive of Peggy's decision to go to China, but he sent her a carefully crafted telegram, "Don't go China if contrary American law," to which she replied equally carefully, "Not contrary to law but to policy."[23] Charles felt these wires would give Peggy legal protection: they indicated that her family had told her to obey the law, and she had indicated her belief that she was doing so. The legal position of Americans traveling to China was hazy—they had been warned of the possibility of fines, prison sentences, and loss of passport—and Charles urged her not to return to the United States until the legal consequences were clear. He spent several days fielding calls from the news media and treated the whole affair with his usual equanimity. Mar did not. She was so horrified that she asked Peggy to stop saying she was from Santa Barbara.

Two years previously, Western Europe had seemed strange to Peggy. Now she was traveling to a vast, predominantly rural country where Westerners were rare, a country where she knew no one, spoke not a word of the language, and knew virtually nothing of its history and culture. The Trans-Siberian Railroad hosted a multinational crowd of World Youth Festival participants, who hopped from car to car, organizing parties, sharing ideas, and consuming a sugary soft drink called "people's pop." In China, the different delegations went their separate ways. The Americans stayed together; their Chinese hosts had arranged tours for them but also allowed free time to explore. "Some of the things you saw," says Peggy, "it was like going back in time. Not centuries—millennia."[24] Industrialization had started, and one of their first tours was to a truck factory in Changchun, but by and large, goods were still made by hand and transported by foot. To Peggy, China seemed a land of great optimism in the face of enormous change. Noel Osheroff (then Noel Carawan) described China in 1957 as "a country being born. The enthusiasm, the excitement, the hope—it was mind-blowing, like a release of energy."[25] After a meeting with the vice mayor of Changchun, Peggy wrote, "What beautiful, warm faces they have—they all ask 'please, if you have any suggestions, you must tell us, for we have so much to learn.' Americans, remember and learn this humility, for this is one of the aspects of this 'backward' country that is more forward than in our technically advanced land."[26] The Americans traveled vast distances and visited a multitude of sites, including a shipyard in Dairen, a meeting of trade union officials in Beijing, a Buddhist temple in Wuhan, a hospital in Nanjing (that combined Chinese and Western medicine), a jade factory in Shanghai, a community of expatriates in Canton, and music schools throughout the country. They saw slums in some cities and clean, inexpensive apartments for workers in others. They met with youth groups, representatives of the Chinese Christian community, and an official in Shanghai whose job was the reeducation of prostitutes. Through interpreters, they asked hard questions—about freedom of speech, the right to dissent, the right to a fair trial, and whether things had gotten better or worse since the Communist takeover—of journalists, ordinary people, and Chou En-Lai himself. They saw many examples of poverty and illness, yet also the will to overcome these evils. "Was there ever a land so full of extremes?" asked Peggy. "With so many mountains, rivers of natural beauties and human miseries?"[27]

Cultural misunderstandings and mistakes are inevitable in foreign travel, and the Americans knew little of Chinese mores. In Tientsin, they bought sugarcane—a Chinese treat—and proceeded to chew it while walking down the street. Children watching them could not control their laughter. "It turned out that not only is sugarcane a sweet only for children but you must remove the husk first. . . . Our action was equivalent to an adult in the U.S. buying a piece of bubble gum, putting it into his mouth without first removing the wrapping, then walking down a busy street blowing bubbles."[28] A more serious faux pas occurred when some of the Americans made bawdy jokes about a Chinese interpreter's upcoming wedding. The interpreter was deeply offended; such humor was not appropriate in China. Perhaps the greatest shock to the American mentality was the ancient patience that the Chinese people displayed. In cloth factories, some looms were mechanized, but much weaving was still done by hand, with artisans working slowly and carefully to create patterns learned by heart and handed down from generation to generation. At an ivory cooperative, they met an elderly ivory carver who had worked his entire life creating an intricate pattern in relief on an elephant tusk. At the Great Wall of China, Peggy was puzzled by the hordes of workers rebuilding that symbol of imperial power: "What pride is there in rebuilding a structure which took the lives of other thousands, in which, indeed, many workers are buried?"[29] It was backbreaking labor, slow, unhealthy work that left the workers exhausted and covered in lime dust. When Peggy inquired why the wall was being rebuilt, the interpreter grew "very indignant . . . and exclaim[ed] that the wall is one of China's oldest constructions and must be preserved, no matter whether men do inhuman toil to keep it in presentable shape."[30]

Peggy was impressed by what she saw in the Soviet Union and China. Though she did have her criticisms, she wanted to see more of the Communist world. "I am becoming a doubter of every conclusion that I do not arrive at by myself," she wrote to Charles, "and I cannot learn anything about other people's systems of living by listening to the conclusions of newspapermen, radio announcers or reading 'authoritative accounts' that may be just a pack of lies."[31] In early autumn, Peggy and the Carawans flew back to Russia, where Peggy and Guy performed in Moscow and Minsk. In November, Peggy and the Carawans traveled to Poland. This was the brief period of liberalization under the Gomulka regime, and she found Poland more open than Russia to Western ideas. The Soviets had seemed ignorant of the West and uninterested in learning more, but she noted, "The Poles *feel* themselves Western and have always had antagonisms to both their bordering countries, east and west. The Germans hauled them off to camps and razed their towns, but the Russians did them in ideologically."[32] Though Warsaw had been largely rebuilt, other towns still showed the gaping wounds of war. Peggy and Guy gave a concert in the old opera house in Łódź, only part of which was still standing. The theater was so cold that the audience sat wrapped in coats and blankets. Peggy recalls singing "Barbara Allen," her eyes closed as usual, and hearing the audience gasp. She opened her eyes and saw an enormous rat strolling across the stage.

Guy and Noel did not stay long in Poland, and Peggy was soon alone. She made friends in Warsaw with a group of Polish students who spoke English and helped her get cheap—though Spartan—accommodations in university housing. She joined a student cabaret and traveled with them to Wrocław, where the ravages of war were still apparent: "Children playing here are like flowers blowing through a graveyard," she wrote in her diary. "The children grow up in rubble, play with rubble—this morning on a walk, Janek saw some children trying to toss a rusty old bombshell, a foot long, over the wall of a former bunker."[33] By contrast, Kraków was relatively untouched, its medieval beauty still intact: "a place where the proverb 'time stands still' must have originated."[34] Students in Kraków asked for jazz and pop songs, but she pleaded ignorance and gave them "pseudo-jazz folksongs and . . . a fairly good cross-section of Americana."[35] Back in Warsaw in early December, she continued to perform until she became ill. She had no idea how to contact a doctor and lay shivering in her frigid room, too weak to leave her bed, for days until her fever broke. On December 9, she was well again and boarded a plane for Paris.

In Paris, she explored the city with Ralph Rinzler, who was studying French and living with a family in the Latin Quarter. The preceding six months had been a bit too breathless, and she needed a rest. Her hectic concert schedule in Russia and Poland had lessened the pleasure that music gave her, and she told Charles that she did not think she wanted to earn her living as a musician. But Paris, with its matchless beauty, quickly revived her. Diane Hamilton had asked Ralph to drive her Bentley from Paris to Florence; ever ready for adventure, Peggy joined him, and they took off for Italy in mid-December. They made a luxurious, ten-day journey of it, even stopping for a few days to earn money singing in the Italian Alps.

The year 1957 had been filled with extraordinary adventures and impressive musical achievement. Several of the recordings that Peggy had made in the United States were released that year. Peggy sang with Barbara and Penny on *The Three Sisters*; *Come Along, John*; *Shine like a Star*; and *American Folk Songs for Christmas*. Mike joined his sisters on *American Folk Songs Sung by the Seegers*. These recordings showcase traditional American folk music, and many of the songs were taken from Ruth's songbooks. Peggy's repertoire had remained relatively constant, but she had come a long way since *Songs of Courting and Complaint*. By this time, Mike and she were no longer talented amateurs but young professionals beginning to develop their own individual styles.

Mike had immersed himself in the old-time music of the southern Appalachians, music he had initially grown to love by listening to the field recordings that Ruth had played while she transcribed the songs. In 1954, he moved to Baltimore in order to work at the Mount Wilson Tuberculosis Hospital, his alternative to military service during the Korean War. In Baltimore, he met and played music with many talented musicians who had relocated from the Appalachians. Though he never learned to read music, he became a skilled performer on guitar, banjo, mandolin, autoharp, and fiddle. Mike was able to absorb the style and performance practice of old-time music while at the same time making it seem fresh and alive, not a sterile reproduction of a bygone era. He and Peggy were now putting into practice the lessons they had learned from their mother. In her introduction to *American Folk Songs for Children*, Ruth had stressed the importance of both tradition and innovation in folk music: "Strive to maintain a balance between two of the outstanding values which music like this possesses . . . the vigorous beauty of the traditional text, and an inherent fluidity and creative aliveness which invites improvisation as a natural development of the life of the song."[36] One can hear this synthesis of old and new in "Old Molly Hare," the first song on *American Folk Songs Sung by the Seegers*. According to the liner notes, which were written by Charles, "Old Molly Hare" is a "Scots-Irish fiddle tune, without words in the 'old countries,' but acquiring them in the new."[37] The first stanza is typical:

"Old Molly Hare,
What you doing there?"
"Sitting on the fireplace
A-smoking my cigar."

Mike sings these playful words with such tender joy, with such respect and love for the tradition that the listener envisions and delights in the absurdities described in the song. The timbre of Mike's voice is reminiscent of the Appalachian musicians who sang the song before him; his pronunciation is not what he had learned at school ("hare" and "there" rhyme with "cigar," for example). Yet he seems no more inauthentic than an American opera singer who attempts to perfect an Italian accent before singing the lead in *Madame Butterfly*. Peggy's banjo and Ralph's guitar provide a vigorous and subtly beautiful counterpoint to Mike's expert mandolin and fiddle playing.

Mike's musical style remains constant throughout the album—and throughout his career. He had already found his distinctive voice, while Peggy was still struggling to find hers. In some songs, such as "Dance to Your Daddy" (the only British song on the album), one can still hear the light, delicate voice, with its perfect diction, that she had demonstrated in *Songs of Courting and Complaint*. On others, such as "The Wedding Dress Song," she uses a rich, vibrato-less timbre with just a hint of nasality, similar to the traditional singing style of the Anglo-American South. Here, as elsewhere, Peggy excels at ballads: possibly her best song on this album is "The Rich Irish Lady," with its beautiful melody and poetic words. She sings the song simply and with restraint; her guitar provides a steady but nonintrusive backdrop. She is less successful with the African American song "Jane, Jane." Her attempts to add a few elements of African American singing style are dignified and respectful but not entirely convincing. Occasionally, the musicians' prowess is overwhelming, as in "Fair Ellender," an Anglo-American ballad with beautiful lyrics and a gruesome story. Here, Mike and Peggy sing in harmony and accompany themselves on mandolin and guitar, with Ralph Rinzler on autoharp. The musicianship is adequate, but there is too much going on, and it distracts from the story; the simple mountain ballad is dressed in clothes that are far too fine. This is a common failing of young musicians: the desire to showcase one's virtuosity at the expense of the dignity and restraint best suited to traditional music. But these are minor defects, and they detract little from the album as a whole.

Peggy also produced two solo albums in 1957: *Eleven American Ballads and Songs* and *Animal Folk Songs for Children*, both of which she recorded in England. American songs would remain the backbone of Peggy's repertoire, but in England she began to experiment with British music, initially as Ewan's accompanist. By 1957, her banjo and guitar could be heard on many of Ewan's albums, including *Scots Drinking Songs*, *Bad Lads and Hard Cases: British Ballads of Crime and Criminals*, *Bless 'Em All and Other British Army Songs*, *Thar She Blows* (whaling songs), and the most acclaimed, *Shuttle and Cage: Industrial Folk Ballads*. But the first album in which Ewan and Peggy are presented as equals is the 1957 *Matching Songs of Britain and America*. Here their real collaboration begins, with Ewan singing British versions and Peggy singing American versions of the same—or very similar—songs.

A brief look at some of the songs reveals the vibrancy of their musical partnership. The first matched pair are versions of "The Sweet Trinity" (Child 286). Ewan learned the Scottish version, "The Sweet Kumadee," from his mother, and here he is at the height of his vocal and dramatic power. His long experience in theater brings the song to life with all its dramatic potential; he knows just what to stress and just when to slow down, but nothing seems contrived or false. Peggy accompanies him on the banjo and joins in on the chorus, though her voice is a bit overpowered by his. The American variant, "The Golden Vanity," is a song that she learned from Pete. Her voice does not yet have the dramatic versatility of Ewan's, but it is strong and clear and confident and focused on the words, with the rich vocal timbre that she used on *American Folk Songs Sung by the Seegers*. The tentative quality that one hears in *Songs of Courting and Complaint* is gone. Ewan and Peggy's different musical traditions and individual musical strengths complement each other: Ewan's remarkable Scottish version of "The Gypsy Laddie" is well supported by Peggy's American banjo; when she joins in on the chorus of "There Was a Puggie in A Well," the two voices blend evenly, Peggy's bright soprano floating above Ewan's rich baritone.

Peggy and Alan Lomax also coauthored a book in 1957: *American Folk Guitar*, subtitled "A Book of Instruction including Chords and Lyrics of 15 Traditional American Folk Songs."[38] It had been a remarkable year, but 1958 would be even more so. In the winter, Peggy wrote to her father, "I seem to rotate around my center of gravity and always return to London."[39] She was staying at the home of Bert Lloyd and recording extensively. She recalled, "I don't remember ever being so busy in all my life, sitting before a microphone at least 8 hours a day recording for small and large companies."[40] She recorded two albums with Guy Carawan before he returned to the United States (and had his passport invalidated): *America at Play* (children's songs) and *We Sing America*. She joined other American folksingers on several albums, including *Our Singing Heritage*, and two Alan Lomax productions, *American Song Train* and *Folk-Song Saturday Night*.

She sang only two songs on *Our Singing Heritage*, which showcased many of the best American folksingers of the day, including Dave Van Ronk, Paul Clayton, and Ellen Stekert. These two songs clearly show her musical development. She sings the first song, "Rich Old Lady," in a style that is unusually dramatic for her, with vocal flourishes and ritards calculated for dramatic effect. She has overcorrected the mistakes of *Songs of Courting and Complaint*—the tentativeness, the lack of attention to the words—and the song seems histrionic and slightly false. In "Love Henry," by contrast, she reins in the dramatic excesses of "Rich Old Lady" and lets the drama of the story speak for itself. Her voice is stronger and more expressive than in her early recordings, though it has lost some of the pellucid sweetness of *Songs of Courting and Complaint*. While her first album might have been the work of any talented young musician, "Love Henry" is in the singular and unmistakable voice of Peggy Seeger: the voice of a grown woman, not a promising girl. If she has sacrificed some of the breathless youthful sweetness that she showed in *Songs of Courting and Complaint*, she has gained a voice that is uniquely her own.

Peggy continued her solo recordings in 1958, including a 78 rpm of *Freight Train* and an album of American songs entitled *Folksongs and Ballads*. She accompanied—and sometimes sang with—Ewan on several albums of British music, including *Second Shift*, *Still I Love Him* (with Scottish folksinger Isla Cameron), *Steam Whistle Ballads*, *Bold Sportsmen All* (with A. L. Lloyd), and *English and Scottish Love Songs* (with Isla Cameron and Ralph Rinzler). She was a resident singer at the Sunday night Ballads and Blues club, with Ewan, A. L. Lloyd, Seamus Ennis, Fitzroy Coleman, and others. But the most remarkable project that she would undertake in 1958 was the first of the Radio Ballads, *The Ballad of John Axon*.[41]

# CHAPTER 8

# New Day Dawning

We were a new spring morning,
You and me and the rising sun;
We were a new day dawning,
Our loving had only begun.

—Peggy Seeger, "New Spring Morning"

In the first half of the twentieth century, radio became the primary means of disseminating information and providing entertainment. It gave birth to new art forms, such as radio drama and radio documentary, devoted entirely to the sense of hearing. Just as film had evolved from a means of recording plays into an entirely new way of presenting drama, radio had evolved into a medium that exploited the creative possibilities of sound. Musicians, writers, and dramatists collaborated on productions that experimented with new techniques (such as sound effects) and revitalized older ones (such as incidental music). The tense immediacy of radio, the feeling that the action was happening just out of one's sight, made it ideal for productions about contemporary concerns. Radio also had the ability to bring historical events to life. In 1944, a folk cantata entitled *Lonesome Train*, which told the story of Abraham Lincoln's funeral cortège, was broadcast on CBS radio. *Lonesome Train* was produced by the progressive writer Norman Corwin and had been written by Earl Robinson (a former member of the Composers Collective) and Millard Lampell (a former member of the Almanac Singers). The popular folksinger Burl Ives provided a musical narration. *Lonesome Train* impressed a young BBC producer named Charles Parker, who found its combination of narrative and song extremely moving. In 1957, he decided to use the same format to tell the story of a different train, one driven by an Englishman named John Axon.

John Axon's story was simple, straightforward, and genuinely heroic. On the morning of February 9, 1957, he was driving a loaded freight train in north Derbyshire when its steam brake valve failed, filling the cab with steam and making it impossible to stop the train. Axon and Ron Scanlon, the fireman in the cab with him, were forced from the cab and onto a steel step outside it, where they clung precariously to the side of the train. As the train hurtled down a seven-mile drop, Axon advised Scanlon to jump to safety, and Scanlon did so. Axon chose to stay with the train, like a captain going down with his ship, in order to warn others on the route. He lost his life when his train crashed into another one at the bottom of the hill. In May of that year, he was posthumously awarded the George Cross, the highest civilian honor in the UK, for his selfless act of bravery.

Axon's story shares many attributes of the traditional British ballad: a heroic protagonist, a dramatic ending, an extraordinary act that transfigures an otherwise ordinary life. Parker's idea was to tell John Axon's story as a combination of radio drama, music, and interviews with Axon's friends and family (called "actuality" in radio parlance). Parker was an experienced radio producer, but he was out of his depth when it came to the music. He approached the person who seemed ideally suited to the project: Ewan MacColl. The two had met when Charles produced a BBC program in which Ewan had participated; they later worked together on a program written by Alan Lomax. Parker was familiar with Ewan's radio work and admired his creative mixing of folk song and drama. Ewan's songwriting skills and knowledge of folk music were essential to the project that Charles envisioned; his initial letter to Ewan, written on July 12, 1957, stated that the project "is going to hinge rather on whether or not you can participate."[1] Ewan, intrigued by the idea of combining music and drama in a tale of working-class heroism, accepted.

Initially, Parker and MacColl seemed an odd duo. Parker was no progressive intellectual like Norman Corwin or Alan Lomax, no working-class artist like A. L. Lloyd or Millard Lampell. Parker was conventional, religious, and conservative. He had a degree from Cambridge and had commanded a submarine during World War II, though his background was less privileged than it sounded: he was the descendent of railway workers (which may explain his enthusiasm for John Axon), and his mother (like Ruth Crawford's) had kept a boardinghouse. What Charles and Ewan shared was an enthusiasm for the artistic possibilities of radio.

In the autumn of 1957, Charles and Ewan traveled to Stockport with an EMI Midget recorder (the first portable tape recorder) to interview John Axon's coworkers and his widow, Gladys. Ewan intended to write a script in which actors would perform the dramatic action, but the high quality of the taped material caused him to change his mind: "As I listened it became obvious that on these tapes we had captured a remarkable picture of a way of life, a picture in words charged with the special kind of vitality and excitement which derives from involvement in a work-process. . . . It wasn't merely that the recorded speech had the true ring of spontaneity; there was something else—the excitement of an experience relived and communicated directly without dilution of additives, living speech unglossed by author's pen or actor's voice."[2] Ewan's script dispensed with actors entirely: Axon's coworkers and widow spoke for themselves, in their own words and their own voices. The script also contained songs, sound effects, and a small amount of narration.

Ewan had written two songs that could be easily incorporated into *John Axon*: "The Manchester Rambler" describes Gladys and John Axon's favorite pastime and was used virtually unchanged; "The Fireman's Not for Me," originally written for Ewan's play *You're Only Young Once*, was adapted and new words were added. Ewan wrote the other songs "in ten days, conceiving each song as an extension of a specific piece of actuality, as a comment on that actuality, or as a simple frame for a collection of actuality pieces."[3] In some cases, he used the tunes of traditional songs; in others, he took motifs from traditional music and used them as foundations for his own melodies. For the lyrics, he took pieces of actuality and the occasional phrase from traditional music, weaving them together into a pattern of his own. Here, he was on his home turf, acting like a traditional songwriter, borrowing bits of text and tune and grafting them onto his own creations. But he had no experience in arrangement or orchestration and, in fact, could not read music. Clearly, Peggy's skills were needed.

Within a few weeks of her arrival in London in January 1958, Peggy had arranged and orchestrated the songs, written incidental music to ease transitions between songs and actuality, and transcribed the music according to each musician's need. Peggy describes her arrangements as "very basic," but there was no time for anything more complex.[4] In the liner notes of *The Ballad of John Axon*, Laurence Aston wrote, "Seeger's arrangements were to transform the apparently disconnected sequences of recorded speech into a series of smoothly flowing episodes."[5] When the program was recorded on January 26 and 27, Peggy acted as musical director and played guitar, mandolin, and banjo. It would take months of Charles's careful editing and still more months of convincing the BBC that such an unorthodox piece should be aired before *The Ballad of John Axon* was finally broadcast on July 2, 1958.

The use of actuality rather than actors, which became one of the defining features of the Radio Ballads, was met with great skepticism at the BBC, and even Charles Parker initially had his doubts. But he set to work weaving together the various components—songs, sound effects, narration, and actuality—and became an enthusiastic proponent of the Radio Ballad form. Ewan and Charles's skills complemented each other: Charles's first-rate editing ability and Ewan's talent as a dramatist and songwriter brought Axon's story to life with sympathy, vigor, and clarity. It was a story of hardship and heartbreak, but also of loyalty to one's friends, pride in one's craft, and an inherent sense of dignity. The voices of the people who knew John Axon had an immediacy that could not have existed with the studied voices of professional actors. *The Ballad of John Axon* is like a finely wrought fabric with jagged edges, rough and imperfect in places, smooth and polished in others, with a raw honesty that embraces, rather than denies, this dissonance.

*John Axon* was unusual in several ways. Radio programs about working-class subjects were not unknown at the BBC; during World War II, praise of "the common man" was deemed essential to the war effort. Working-class accents had appeared on the radio, and working-class subjects were taken seriously. However, such fare was not typical of the BBC's output. In the wartime broadcasts, working-class voices were added to a tale created by their social and political higher-ups; by contrast, the trajectory of John Axon's story was set by the working-class subjects themselves. Axon's fellow railwaymen described their profession in thoughtful and sophisticated terms; they were proud of their work and the useful function they served. Axon's self-sacrifice was presented as the ultimate expression of a noble tradition.

Charles, Ewan, and Peggy noticed similarities between the recorded actuality and the language of traditional British folk song; both were composed of speech honed by oral tradition. In order to highlight and build on these similarities, the British traditional ballad became the framework within which the entire program took place. *John Axon* begins with Peggy's banjo, then with Ewan singing the following lines:

> John Axon was a railwayman, to steam trains born and bred,
> He was an engine driver at Edgeley loco shed,
> For forty years he followed and served the iron way,
> He lost his life upon the track one February day.[6]

With their spare, journalistic style, impersonal point of view, use of commonplaces ("born and bred"), and quatrain format, these lines sound like the beginning of a traditional Anglo-American ballad. Only the focus on trains betrays the modern origins. Throughout the broadcast, Ewan returned to this tune to tell John Axon's story, dropping stanzas throughout the program, creating a ballad that frequently broke off to allow actuality, incidental music, and other songs to be heard. This modern-day ballad ended only at the conclusion of the program.

The politics of *John Axon* is mixed. In some ways, the message of *John Axon* is a radical and progressive one: working-class men can act with judgment, discipline, and intelligence and can display as much honor as their social superiors. *John Axon* takes a subtle stand against racism in "Fireman's Calypso," performed by the Trinidadian singer and guitar player Fitzroy Coleman.[7] The song tells of the skill and devotion of a Jamaican fireman and was inspired by a comment from engine driver Jack Pickford: "It doesn't matter where you come from. What color you are, what religion, anything. It doesn't make any difference. If you got that feeling that you want to be a driver, if you've got it in your blood, you make a railwayman. . . . I had a West Indian fireman with me on long-distance trains, and he's been as good a fireman as I've ever had on the job. He definitely has it in his blood, and he comes from Jamaica."[8] In other ways, however, John Axon's world is a relatively conservative one. It is a primarily masculine world, in which women serve as helpmeets but rarely express desires of their own. "The Fireman's Not for Me," the one song sung by women, is a complaint that a railwayman's sweetheart will always come second to his demanding mistress, the locomotive:

> Come all you young maidens, take a warning from me:
> Shun all engine drivers and their company;
> They'll tell you they love you and all kinds of lies,
> But the one that he loves is the train that he drives.[9]

Indeed, the personification of the train as a difficult female who ultimately yields to masculine control is a thread that runs throughout the program. Engine drivers, like ships' captains, use the feminine pronoun to refer to their vessels and present themselves as men with the power to tame, lovingly but firmly, the machines that bear them. This masculinist control is never brutal, however; it has an old-fashioned, chivalric cast. In "Fireman's Calypso," which Peggy calls a "love song for a locomotive," the railway worker brags of his ability to keep his iron female in line.[10] At the same time, he ends each stanza with a statement of devotion: "Going to serve me steam locomotive."[11]

Service and devotion are constant themes in *The Ballad of John Axon*. John Axon's valedictory song describes the noble tradition of service that his final act exemplifies, a description cast in both working-class and masculine terms:

The run, it is finished, the shift's nearly ended,
So long, mates, so long; remember:
A man is a man, he must do what he can for his brothers.
By his deeds you shall know him,
By the work of his hands,
By the friends who shall mourn him,
By the love that he bore,
By the gift of his courage
And the life that he gave.[12]

The railwaymen's expressions of devoted service are reminiscent of a medieval squire pledging fealty to his liege or a courtly lover to his lady. Highly skilled and relatively well paid, railwaymen were among the aristocracy of the working class. They were not industrial workers bent on changing the world, but old-fashioned craftsmen proud of their work and relatively satisfied with their lot. In many ways, the valorization of John Axon's sacrifice was similar to wartime praise of the common soldier: both freely gave their lives for their countrymen, and a grateful nation saluted their courage. John Axon was, in other words, a working-class hero that a ruling class could love.

Praise for *John Axon* came from many quarters. In the *Sunday Times* of London, radio critic Robert Robinson called it "as remarkable piece of radio as [he had] ever listened to."[13] Tom Driberg, a Labour MP, wrote in the *New Statesman*, "A generation from now—I would even say centuries from now—listeners will surely still be moved by the recording of *John Axon*."[14] The BBC, despite its initial skepticism, was so pleased with the result that it submitted *John Axon* as its documentary entry for the Prix Italia.[15] Gladys Axon considered it "a very good and fine tribute to [her] husband's work."[16] Listeners were also strongly supportive. A particularly moving comment came from a locomotive driver: "Please *please* rebroadcast this programme. A magnificent tribute to John Axon and all his fellow locomen."[17]

Yet criticism accompanied the broadcast as well. Some objected to the fact that *John Axon*, a British story told by British people, had a musical accent that was distinctly American. Peggy had based much of the incidental music on jazz and blues; American instruments—including banjo, mandolin, and harmonica—predominated; and one of the most memorable songs was written in calypso style. But *John Axon* also drew on a large body of British folk traditions, starting with the ballad format itself. Ewan used traditional British folk tunes for several of the songs. "The Fireman's Not for Me" is similar to many traditional British songs in which women explain why certain men make inadequate husbands; the song even begins with the traditional opening words: "come all you." For a song that reconstructs John Axon's final moments, Ewan used many attributes of traditional British sailors' songs: dramatic action, humor in the face of death, internal rhyme, a repeated final line, and the words "brave boys." This creative combination of British and American musical traditions would become a hallmark of Ewan and Peggy's work together.

*The Ballad of John Axon* ended with a plummy voice saying that the program was the work of Ewan MacColl and Charles Parker. Ewan had asked for Peggy to be given equal billing, but she had declined, as she had not participated in the collection of actuality and had only been involved with the project since January. After the recording of *John Axon* was complete, Charles edited the tapes and made occasional requests for changes. Peggy was needed to make these changes—she was in charge of the entire musical aspect of the program—but her ability to remain in the UK was continually being threatened. In February, the American Embassy informed her that her passport would be invalidated for anything other than travel back to the United States. Through Charles Parker's lobbying and the BBC's intervention, her visa was extended until April, then May, so that she could continue to work on *John Axon*. But on May 17, there were no more extensions, and Peggy departed for Paris, still not knowing the precise legal condition of her passport.

If her legal status was confusing, her love life was even more tumultuous. Ewan had asked her to marry him (once he was divorced, that is). She considered him "the only heart's companion [she had] ever had," but she had her doubts about the feasibility of a long-term relationship.[18] In a letter to her father written on February 22, 1958, Peggy outlined her concerns: "The only time I am happy is when I am with him, and the thought of leaving is like dying right now. We talk and think a great deal of marrying, but there are a few serious problems, mostly based on a mythical but sometimes fairly tangible 'age difference.' . . . Everything would be perfect with us now, but 10, 20 years from now with physical differences and (worse), 'class' difference—not said with any condescension from either of us, just difference in outlook, reactions, etc."[19] She also worried that Ewan loved not the real flesh-and-blood Peggy but a vision he had of her, of a pure and perfect and stainless young maiden. Always sternly self-critical, she was afraid that this vision was partly of her own making. She had told him small lies and perpetrated minor deceptions in order to keep this image intact, and she became tortured with self-reproach.

While Peggy was in France, Ewan crossed the channel whenever possible for a few stolen days in the seaside town of Boulogne. In June, Peggy threw caution to the winds and boarded a boat headed for Dover. The British authorities refused to admit her and, since there were no more boats that evening, kept her in jail for the night. Weeping and emotionally exhausted, she telephoned Ewan, who traveled from London to Dover in a taxi, an extraordinary extravagance for one who had grown up in poverty. They talked until the morning came, and she headed back to France.

In June, her emotional uncertainty came to an end. In a small hotel on the Normandy coast, Peggy told Ewan that she wanted to marry and stay with him. Determined to destroy the false picture he had of her, she confessed her deceptions and inadequacies, and "at that moment began a really deep understanding and tolerance."[20] Impressed by her honesty and determined to be as candid himself, he took account of his own character in a letter to her:

> You mustn't love me for what I am not, Peggy, only for what I am. You must learn to criticise the bad things in me so that I can eradicate them. . . . I have many good qualities such as loyalty, brilliance, the capacity to feel deeply, the capacity to love. But I am also vain, selfish in some things, intolerant. . . . But, once again, I love you deeply and will love you till I die. I love everything about you, your ideas, your body, your voice, your skills, your warmth and understanding, the light in your eyes, the sweetness of your mouth . . . everything. And if you will bear with me, I will get better all the time.[21]

Summer brought increasingly passionate letters and the commitment to be together no matter what, but their practical problems had not been resolved. Ewan divided his time between Jean in London and Peggy in France, with occasional trips to Bulgaria and Germany, where his plays were being produced. Peggy moved between Paris and the French coast, with side trips to the Loire Valley and Mont-Saint-Michel and Berlin and an occasional radio gig in Geneva.

She had begun writing songs in China, and now, with plenty of time on her hands, she continued this pursuit, writing both political songs and love songs. Many of her early attempts are highly derivative, such as "Diplomacy Calypso," which describes the legal difficulties of traveling behind the Iron Curtain. "When I Was Young" takes the form of a traditional Anglo-American ballad and tells a story familiar to the genre: that of a young woman whose lover goes to war:

> When I was young I loved a lad and gaily we were wed;
> I knew no greater pleasure than to follow where he led;

But when he went away to war, O sorrow be to me,
For you cannot follow soldiers bearing guns across the sea.[22]

Peggy's heroine is far more passive than the bold protagonists of traditional ballads, who frequently did follow their lovers to war and whose greatest pleasures did not always consist of following the lead of someone else. In retrospect, Peggy is harsh in her judgment of "When I Was Young," describing it as filled with "cardboard-cutout characters who seem to have stepped straight out of a Hollywood B-movie: helpless, tragic figures who abdicate any responsibility for what happens to them."[23] Then in the autumn of 1958, she wrote a song that is still considered one of her best: "The Ballad of Springhill."

On October 23, 1958, a severe "bump" (underground earthquake) occurred near the Cumberland Mine in Springhill, Nova Scotia. Three shockwaves followed, and part of the mine collapsed, trapping more than 150 miners. Over the next eight days, rescuers were able to save most of the miners, though more than 70 men died, most of them crushed instantly when the mine collapsed. It was the worst bump in North American mining history, and though nearly forgotten today, it garnered worldwide attention at the time, in part because it was the first such disaster to be televised. Peggy's song is one of the reasons it is remembered at all, and it begins with some of the best lines she ever wrote:

In the town of Springhill, Nova Scotia,
Down in the dark of the Cumberland Mine;
There's blood on the coal and the miners lie
In the roads that never saw sun nor sky,
Roads that never saw sun nor sky.[24]

The song was later covered by the Dubliners and U2, it is still sung in the schools of Springhill, and it is sometimes mistaken for a traditional song. Paradoxically, "The Ballad of Springhill," with its modern story and industrial location, sounds more like a traditional ballad than the contrived "When I Was Young," with its archaic language and nameless fantasy people. The language of "The Ballad of Springhill" is like that of traditional ballads: objective, informative, and clear. Against this simple backdrop, the occasional poetic phrases shine like jewels. The melody for "The Ballad of Springhill" (which Peggy also wrote) is mournful and dignified, like a dirge, and it ends with a series of downward steps to an unresolved cadence, as though we are entering the mine, unsure of what we will find. Throughout her career, Peggy would return to the ballad format to write many of her best songs, finding in the ballad's narrative structure, specificity of detail, and understated yet poetic language the ideal framework for the stories she chose to tell.

Back in London, Ewan was busy writing songs and singing in concerts, clubs, and films. He and Charles had already begun work on the second Radio Ballad. Ewan missed Peggy desperately for both personal and professional reasons, but the British Home Office had not yet granted her permission to return to the UK. Across the channel, Peggy waited; weeks of waiting turned into months. But unplanned circumstances forced a decision: Peggy was pregnant.

Ewan was delighted by the pregnancy and full of plans for the future. "I thought of our baby in your belly and I felt terribly happy," he wrote. "Darling, boy or girl it's the fruit of our love and we are going to give him, or her, a good life. We are going to give each other a good life also."[25] He wrote that his mother, Betsy, was pleased with the prospect of a new grandchild and was knitting a blanket for the baby. Not everyone shared Betsy's outlook, however. Maud Karpeles, Bert Lloyd, and Charles Parker strongly disapproved of the relationship; Charles even threatened to withdraw from the new Radio Ballad if Ewan and Peggy continued their "immoral" behavior. Charles Seeger approved of the relationship with Ewan, but Peggy hesitated telling him about the pregnancy, worried that he might think ill of Ewan and concerned about Mar's reaction. She finally told him in December 1958.

In the autumn, Peggy moved into the Paris home of Lucienne Idoine, a friend of Ralph Rinzler, in the lively Saint-Germain-des-Prés neighborhood. Peggy called Lucienne "a godsend—a teacher, about 40, sprightly and sympathetic" who charged no rent and told Peggy that she could stay as long as she was "*utile et interessante*" (useful and interesting).[26] A highly political woman and a survivor of Ravensbrück, Lucienne became a friend and confidante to whom Peggy could speak candidly (in French) of her troubles with Ewan. Marriage to a British subject would solve her visa problems, so Ewan made urgent attempts to obtain a divorce. He could not divorce without Jean's consent, and Jean was vacillating—sometimes accepting divorce as inevitable, sometimes attempting to save her marriage for Hamish's sake, if not her own. Ewan had his moments of inconsistency as well. Jean and Hamish moved out of the family home in the early autumn but moved back in later in the year. Ewan cited the financial advantages of this arrangement as well as the need to provide stability for his son. He assured Peggy that the living situation was temporary: "I have told her [Jean] that nothing will ever make me change my mind about you and that we will be living together as soon as you land here.

. . . If you only knew how I love you and how unshakable my feelings for you are! . . . I only spark into life when I am with you. You are the sole reason for my existence and without you life would be one continual winter."[27] At the same time, he was tormented by doubt: "I feel bad about my son, I love him dearly, Peg, and cannot help feeling that I have betrayed him, abandoned him before he was old enough to form a vision of life. I hate to hurt Jean. . . . I am troubled because I have involved you in such misery. . . . I am, at the moment, haunted by the fear that I'm just a selfish bastard . . . marrying you for my own happiness and not thinking too much about yours."[28] "Ewan didn't find it easy to leave us," Jean recalled.[29] He told Peggy that living with Jean and Hamish was a temporary situation designed to simplify practical matters, but Jean saw it as a reconciliation attempt. Later events would show that hers was an entirely reasonable conclusion.

Near the close of 1958, the British Home Office told Peggy that she could not enter the UK without a valid passport, and the American Embassy told her that her passport was invalid for anything other than travel back to the United States. Marriage to a British subject seemed the only way she could legally enter and remain in Britain, but Ewan was still married to Jean. In an extraordinary display of friendship, the Scottish folksinger Alex Campbell offered to marry her. On January 22, 1959, after a flurry of legal paperwork, Peggy and Alex were married in Paris. The priest wore dirty sneakers and glared at Peggy's pregnant belly and Alex's unkempt hair and beard. The British embassy was still reluctant to admit Peggy, but as she later recounted to Charlie, Alex "took the indignant look-here-my-wife's-pregnant-and-about-to-drop-the-baby-any-minute attitude and, by gum, they telephoned to London, and we were told we could sail right through. Which we did."[30] They were in England in time to celebrate Ewan's birthday on January 25.[31] Ewan met them at Waterloo Station, where Alex handed off Peggy with a terse "here's your woman," as though she were a piece of valuable but contraband luggage. Within weeks, she had sworn her allegiance to Queen Elizabeth II and soon possessed a British passport in the name of Margaret Campbell. Her roving days were over, and her life as a permanent expatriate had begun.

# CHAPTER 9

# At Home Abroad

Songs of love, tales of grace,
Of flesh and blood and bone,
The first time ever I saw his face,
His heart became my own,
Then his heart became my home.

—Peggy Seeger, "Bring Me Home"

Ewan and Peggy's first home together was a small two-bedroom apartment at 55 Godstone Road, in the London suburb of Purley, not far from Hamish and Jean's home in Croydon. In a letter to her father, Peggy reported, "[Ewan] helps with everything he can, shopping, cooking, washing up etc.," though within weeks, Ewan's mother, Betsy, had moved in and was doing the bulk of the housework.[1] Peggy had mixed feelings about Betsy's presence: "Although I love her very much and she works like a Trojan I can see how in-laws change a household. . . . Ewan and I cannot talk quite so freely, our actions often have to take account of her idiosyncrasies. . . . In short, we're just not alone anymore."[2] But at least they were together, and Betsy's help allowed them time to work—a pattern that would continue for many years. They had been compiling a book of English and Scottish folk songs, and they now quickened the pace, hoping to finish the book before their child was born. On the afternoon of March 3, they delivered the manuscript of *The Singing Island: A Collection of English and Scots Folksongs* to their publisher. On the way home, Peggy had difficulty walking, with strange muscular twinges accompanying each step. The following morning, less than a month after the move to Purley, Neill MacColl was born.

Peggy had tried to reserve a bed at the Purley maternity hospital, but there was none left by the time she arrived in England, so Neill was born at home, with a midwife attending. This was common practice in the UK in those days, though uncommon in America, and Peggy was initially anxious about the prospect of a home birth. She ended up liking the midwife's constant attention and the fact that Ewan could be with her the entire time. Neill was a placid, healthy baby, and Peggy was absorbed in the minutiae of his care. "I have a complete physical identification with him," she wrote. "When he is hungry, I too feel hunger. When he is happy, you can't help but smile with him and play with him. Your body feels part of his."[3]

But all was not peaceful in Godstone Road. Peggy had never met anyone like Betsy and did not know how to deal with her. Betsy had lived in poverty most of her life; though her husband had been a skilled iron molder, ill health and political radicalism had kept him out of work for much of their life together. It was she who had provided the bulk of the family income by cleaning houses and office buildings. She had borne three children and buried two; she had also suffered two miscarriages before giving birth to Ewan, the one good thing that had not been taken from her. Betsy was hardworking, reliable, and a doting grandmother; she could also be wounding and sulky, angry at the world that had dealt her such a terrible hand. At times, she was warm and friendly, telling Peggy stories of Ewan's childhood and showing her how to cook his favorite foods. At other times, she lamented having to leave her beloved Hamish—for Jean no longer wanted Ewan's mother in her home. Sometimes Betsy lashed out unexpectedly, telling Peggy that Ewan would never leave his wife, and one particularly brutal day, told her why: Jean was pregnant.

Looking back from the vantage point of 2009, Peggy is remarkably understanding: "It was totally and completely forgivable. . . . It is possible to love two people at once."[4] But at the time, it hurt. It hurt to watch Betsy knitting a beautiful blanket for Ewan and Jean's child. Although Peggy forgave, she never forgot the pain of that year: "It was a very confusing time. I was very angry at him. I cried a lot."[5]

Peggy's anomalous social position hurt as well. She cared nothing for convention but was surprised to find that others did. Bert Lloyd and his wife snubbed her, even hiring another guitarist to accompany Ewan in a program that Bert had written. Hamish was not allowed to see Neill or visit the household in Purley, so Ewan made frequent trips to Croydon. Even her family seemed distant; when she sent photographs of Neill to America, only Charles and Pete wrote back. She had become a British subject on the condition of relinquishing her American citizenship, and it hurt to know that she could no longer freely visit the country of her birth.

On Christmas Eve 1958, when Ewan and Peggy were separated by circumstance, law, and the English Channel, Ewan had looked rapturously toward

1959. He wrote to her: "For my part, there's never been a new year which offered the possibility of so much joy, so much peace and so much happiness. This coming year belongs to us and we will face it together. . . . In 1959 we begin to live together; in 1959 our first child will be born; in 1959 we will stop writing letters to each other and start sharing every hour of the day."[6] The reality was less sublime. Despite the relief of being able to live in the same country and the joy of Neill's birth, 1959 was fraught with stress and confusion. When Ewan and Jean's daughter, Kirsty, was born on October 10, Ewan returned to Croydon to spend time with his children. He stayed in the apartment directly above Jean's, and Betsy went with him to help look after the baby. He continued in this fashion for the better part of a year, spending his nights in Croydon and returning to Purley while Hamish was in school, shepherding Betsy to wherever child care was needed most.

Work was plentiful throughout 1959, but it lacked some of the hectic luster of the previous year. Peggy accompanied Ewan on two collections of Scottish music: *Classic Scots Ballads* and *Songs of Robert Burns*, and they joined Ramblin' Jack Elliott and other artists on Topic Records' *Songs against the Bomb*. The peace movement had a special urgency in western Europe, located between the two opposing superpowers of the Cold War. "People are really getting scared over here now," she wrote to her father. "Reports of traces of radioactivity and strontium 90 are found in every newspaper . . . with the emphasis on how much it has increased in children's bones in the last few years."[7] Peggy's antinuclear song "There's Better Things to Do," based on an old gospel song, struck a chord with the British peace movement; it was sung in 1958 on the fifty-mile peace march from Trafalgar Square to the nascent nuclear weapons plant in Aldermaston, Berkshire. In the summer of 1959, Paul Robeson came to London to sing at a peace rally in Trafalgar Square, with Peggy accompanying him and singing a few songs on her own. Peggy found him warm, friendly, and very much in a hurry. After she introduced herself as "Pete Seeger's sister" and asked what he would like to sing, he replied, "Just follow me, honey." Peggy did, even though she found it difficult when he began "singing some song [she]'d never heard of in a key halfway between G and F sharp. . . . But the crowd went wild when he appeared."[8]

Robeson had spent a great deal of time in Europe, where he found racial prejudice less acute than in the United States. Peggy noticed a worsening of race relations in Britain in the late 1950s. During the August bank holiday of 1958, in the then-working-class neighborhood of Notting Hill (one of the few racially mixed areas of London), racial tensions exploded into violence, much of it targeting immigrant African and West Indian residents.[9] In response, Geoffrey Bridson wrote a ballad opera entitled *My People and Your People*, about a romance between Ian, a white man played by Ewan, and a Caribbean immigrant named Kathy, played by Nadia Cattouse, herself an immigrant from British Honduras (now Belize). Ewan and Peggy arranged the music, which drew on British and Caribbean folk traditions, and included Ian singing "The First Time Ever I Saw Your Face" to Kathy. The program was broadcast on July 22, 1959, on the BBC's Home Service but not recorded, and a television recording (which replaced Ewan with another actor) was never broadcast. The radio broadcast received good reviews but little attention; despite its timely theme and talented cast, *My People and Your People* lapsed into obscurity, its topic being too hot—and perhaps too painful—to touch.

The second Radio Ballad, *Song of a Road*, was already well under way by the time Peggy arrived in England in 1959. Charles Parker was eager to capitalize on the success of *John Axon* and create a Radio Ballad series. The topic for the second Radio Ballad was handed to him by his boss, Denis Morris: the building of the London–Yorkshire Highway, later called the M1. This was England's first motorway, what in the United States is called a "superhighway," and at first blush, it seemed an apt follow-up to *John Axon*. Cars had replaced trains as the primary means of transportation in Britain, so it made sense to investigate this phase in Britain's industrial development.

Yet practical problems dogged *Song of a Road* from the outset. The story behind *John Axon* was almost tailor-made for dramatic presentation, with its balladic focus on an individual protagonist and its dramatic action confined to one event in one day. By contrast, *Song of a Road* focused on a project that was still in the making, a process that lasted for years and involved more than nineteen thousand workers with a multitude of machines:

> There were tradesmen of all kinds: engineers, scaffolders, bridge-builders, bricklayers, carpenters, pavers, asphalters, cement-mill operators; there were labourers, the pick-and-shovel slingers, the ditchdiggers, the concreting gangs, the tea-nippers and the rest. There they were with their bulldozers and dumpers and Euclids, their caterpillar tractors, steam cranes and automatic shovels, their picks, rock-drills and nine-pound hammers. . . . In addition to the motley crew of Irish, Scots, Welsh, Indian, Pakistani, African, Greek, Turkish, Polish and English labourers, there were the designers, geologists, soil-chemists, archaeologists, planners, statisticians, contractors and sub-contractors.[10]

Morris wanted the program to include the managerial and professional staff as well as the workers, a task for which Ewan had undisguised contempt. Peggy and Ewan felt that the words of the middle-class staff were impersonal and somewhat boring: they spoke without emotion, in order to provide information. The workers, by contrast, spoke with dramatic feeling about the ways that the work affected them personally. "Charles wanted information," said Peggy. "Ewan wanted emotion and reaction to what work does to you."[11] This lack of agreement meant that the three were often working at cross-purposes as they collected actuality and organized the program.

Ewan and Charles began collecting actuality in late 1958 and continued with Peggy in 1959. She was struck by the contrast between the skill required by the work and the toll it took on the workers: "It's really fantastic to see this great beautiful wide stretch of road sweeping over the hills and then see the excruciating method by which it was done. The men have two breaks in the day for meals—10 minutes each, and 5 min. twice a day for tea. Winter and summer—they don't even get a hot meal in the mid-day in winters—no wonder they say the work breaks them. You talk to a man who looks about 60 and he turns out to be 35."[12] In the battle between men and machines, machines appeared to be winning.

After the actuality had been collected, Ewan and Peggy went through the thirty hours of tape to select the best portions and create a script for the program. As with *John Axon*, Ewan wrote the songs, and Peggy arranged the music. In early September, they sent a provisional script to Charles, who sent it back with instructions to include more about the work and less about the workers. Ewan and Peggy complied, though they felt that the choice was an artistic and political mistake. In future Radio Ballads, they insisted on having final say over the choice of actuality and stated frankly that the focus should be on the experience and mentality of the workers, rather than on the work process itself. Ewan's disappointment in *Song of a Road* is apparent in the liner notes:

> The building of the M1 provided us with a marvelous subject for a radio-ballad. Had we approached the subject with the daring and zest that it demanded, we might well have created one of the great programmes of all time. As it was, we fumbled the opportunity. We found ourselves asking questions about bridge-building, about running a concrete-batching plant, about prefabrication techniques. Worse, we found ourselves incorporating the answers in the programme itself. In short, we were behaving as though our intention was to create a programme which would inform the listeners how to build their own motorway.[13]

With such a strong condemnation coming from one of the creators, the freshness and vitality of *Song of a Road* comes as a pleasant surprise. Though Ewan and Peggy had no interest in presenting the viewpoint of management, they nonetheless did so in a way that is quite balanced. One consultant compared the machines to "prehistoric monsters digging up fossils that are millions and millions of years old."[14] There are few images in the program more striking than that of a modern monster digging up the bones of an ancient one.

The commentary of the workers varied enormously. Some expressed the same sort of attachment to their jobs found in *John Axon*. "I'd die if I was not in this work," said one laborer. "I still prefer the muck and the dirt and the grease and everything to being inside in a factory."[15] However, positive comments were far from universal. Many of the workers interviewed did not choose the work because of personal preference or job satisfaction; they chose it because nothing else was available. Unemployment throughout the British Isles, in many parts of Europe, and as far away as India brought together a multinational, polyglot workforce that worked until the job was finished and lived together in hostels and dormitories. Living away from home was one of the chief causes of complaint from the workers. One man described the bed he slept on as "like a camel's back" and the hostel as a "concentration camp," remarking, "All you want now is some gas chambers."[16] James Graham, one of the Irish workers interviewed for the program, aptly stated, "We're like soldiers, always away from home, only we don't know what we're fighting for."[17] Women are even more marginal in *Song of a Road* than they were in *John Axon*. There is no actuality from women at all, and relations with women are remembered as something sacrificed for the work that, paradoxically, supports them. "Come, Me Little Son," the one song sung by a woman, depicts a mother telling her small son about the father he barely knows, as she waits, steadfast as Penelope with Telemachus.

Peggy served as music director for *Song of a Road*; she also played banjo and autoharp. *Song of a Road* shows a growing sophistication in her use of music to create mood and highlight the text. She studied the speech patterns of the actuality, so that the incidental music would reflect the pace and tone of the spoken words, and she wove mechanical sounds into some of her accompaniments, creating a striking new kind of counterpoint. For "The Exile Song," a slow lament from the viewpoint of an Irish worker (and sung by Irish singer Seamus Ennis), she created a simple accompaniment for uilleann pipes, a quintessentially Irish instrument. The pipes sometimes mimic and sometimes harmonize with the tune, and they continue to play during the actuality that follows, underscoring the words that speak of exile from Ireland. "The Driver's Song," for which Ewan wrote both words and tune, is a labor anthem in the grand tradition of "Solidarity Forever." A steady banjo plays throughout, and Peggy has also incorporated the sounds of machines into the song, essentially using machines as musical instruments. The mechanical sounds weave in and out of Peggy's banjo ostinato and continue during the actuality that follows, alerting us to the musical qualities of industrial sound. In "Deep and Straight and Low," Ewan has created a modern song with the driving, insistent rhythm of a traditional work song. Peggy's banjo reinforces the unrelenting downbeat, while mechanical sounds add their own rhythms and melodies, creating a kind of dissonant counterpoint that her parents never dreamed of.

Looking back on *Song of a Road*, Peggy concluded that it "sometimes worked and sometimes didn't."[18] Critics of the time tended to agree. Paul Ferris called it "a near-triumph by *Axon* standards and an absolute marvel by any other."[19] Norman Corwin, who had produced *Lonesome Train*, liked it even better than *The Ballad of John Axon*. Others felt that the use of folk song, which had worked so well in *John Axon*, was inappropriate for the subject of *Song of a Road*. Robert Robinson had admired *John Axon*, but he felt that in *Song of a Road*, "the producers were guilty of . . . supplying a romance not inherent in the events."[20]

As Peggy cannily noted, "*John Axon* was not a political Radio Ballad; *Song of a Road* was."[21] The former told of individual heroism, while the latter depicted the historical trends that created the modern industrial system and modern politics. *Song of a Road* encompasses all the issues important to industrial development: the decline of agriculture and the rise of industry; the rise of new professions and the end of older ones; the reliance on wage labor and the concomitant marginalization of women's work; the growth of science and technology; the solidification of class divisions; the growth of wealth and freedom for some; the loss of stability and health for others. Where *Song of a Road* falters is in its lack of focus. It takes no clear political position on the political issues it raises. Calling it a "Radio Ballad" was simply an homage to the Radio Ballad form, for it has no story (an essential feature of ballads), and its dramatis personae are too numerous for us to get to know them. The disagreement on whether to focus on workers or work processes also contributed to the program's fragmentation, and its lurching from subject to subject can be confusing. Ewan dismissed it as a "debacle with a few bright spots."[22] Charles's boss approved of the work, but he did not enter it into the Prix Italia competition.

When *Song of a Road* was broadcast on November 5, 1959, Ewan and Peggy were in Canada on their first North American tour. They could not enter the United States because Ewan had been denied a visa, but they were able to see Peggy's father when he came to hear them play in Vancouver. Peggy thought the tour valuable for meeting new people and making contacts for future work, but she also found it exhausting and was relieved when she and Ewan returned to England. By December, they were at work on a series of television programs, sponsored by Newcastle's Tyne-Tees television, that focused on different industries. For each show, Ewan and Peggy spent three days in Newcastle, where they interviewed the workers, surveyed the work, recorded its sounds, and created a script with the producers. They then returned to London, where Ewan wrote the songs and Peggy created the arrangements.

The first of these programs focused on deep-sea trawling and provided the subject matter for the third Radio Ballad: herring fishing. In the winter of 1960, Ewan and Peggy met Sam Larner, an East Anglian herring fisherman who had first gone to sea as a cabin boy on a sailing vessel in 1892. Larner's career encompassed most of the major events in the East Anglian fishing industry: he had fished on boats powered by sail and steam and diesel; he had been a young man prior to World War I, when herring fishing was so prevalent that "you could walk across Yarmouth Harbor on the boats"; he had seen the industry's decline in the interwar years and had retired by the time of its resurgence during World War II.[23] He was a gifted singer and raconteur; at the age of eighty, he was "still full of the wonder of life."[24] After meeting Sam Larner, Ewan, Peggy, and Charles decided to make East Anglia one of the foci of their program, despite the fact that the East Anglian waters had been so overfished that herring no longer lived there. Their decision was finalized after meeting Ronnie Balls, a retired skipper from Great Yarmouth, who was twenty years Sam Larner's junior but full of the same eloquence and love for his craft. The program also focused on the northeast coast of Scotland, then the center of Britain's herring industry.

No subject could be better suited to folk song than seafaring, a source of many of Britain's greatest traditional songs. The island nation had sent men to sea for centuries, as part of the navy and the merchant marine as well as the fishing industry, and in the days before iPods and smartphones and the internet, the only entertainment on board was what the sailors could make for themselves, particularly songs and stories. In the days of sail, work songs (called "shanties") were used to coordinate tasks, and a good shantyman had pride of place on a sailing vessel. Sailors also had an extensive repertoire of entertainment songs (called "fo'c'sle songs" or "forebitters") about matters that concerned them: conditions on board, the joy of homecoming, the desire for women in port, and so on. To represent seafaring men in song was entirely appropriate, for they had long done so themselves, and the program was aptly titled *Singing the Fishing*.

Ewan's biographer, Ben Harker, has remarked that the third Radio Ballad "seemed charmed from the outset."[25] With *Singing the Fishing*, a set of principles was established that guided the Radio Ballads for the rest of the series. Ewan and Peggy decreed that they would choose the actuality, and the focus of the programs would be on workers and their responses to work, not on the work process itself. (Charles initially bristled at these demands but ultimately conceded that they were right.) Peggy also made an important change to the recording method. With *John Axon* and *Song of a Road*, the musicians had recorded their parts without hearing the actuality or sound effects, and Charles had cobbled the components together afterward. Beginning with *Singing the Fishing*, the taped actuality and sound effects were played while the musicians recorded, allowing them to respond to the recorded material as if to another musician. This required split-second timing, with Charles instructing his assistants to play the taped material at the appropriate times and Peggy directing the musicians, while playing four instruments herself. But the final product showed a coherent, interwoven tissue of sound that the first two programs had lacked. Ian Campbell, a singer on the program who later formed a popular folk group of his own, describes the process: "MacColl had isolated not only obvious elements such as vocabulary and phraseology, but subtler elements such as speech rhythms and vocal patterns. It was not possible to regard the actuality and songs as separate components which could be created independently and then assembled into a finished product; they were overlapped and intertwined. . . . Musical rhythm was synchronised with speech rhythm or sound effects, and songs took their tempo and pace from the preceding actuality."[26]

Peggy's influence on *Singing the Fishing* was greater than on the first two Radio Ballads, and she was involved with the project from the beginning. She collected actuality in Scotland and East Anglia, helped Ewan compose the script, wrote all the musical arrangements, acted as musical director (a far more complicated task with the new recording method), and played autoharp, guitar, mandolin, and banjo. However, she was not allowed on board the fishing boats, for the fishermen believed that a woman aboard would bring bad luck. Charles and Ewan went on board the *Honeydew*—and experienced a terrifying storm—without her.

*Singing the Fishing* was recorded in Birmingham from May 29 to June 10, 1960. It is a far more mature and fully realized work than its predecessors. Neither an elongated ballad like *John Axon* nor a patchwork like *Song of a Road*, *Singing the Fishing* is (as Charles Seeger noted) a ballad opera, in which the history of Britain's herring fishing industry unfolds through the words of the fishermen and songs based on their words.[27] Peggy's musical arrangements have become increasingly sophisticated, and the advantages of the new recording method are apparent from the beginning. In one of the earliest songs, "Cabin Boy," Ewan took a musical theme first introduced in *Song of a Road* and created a song about Sam Larner's early days at sea. Like many traditional sea songs, "Cabin Boy" contains both solo and choral singing; in between the sung portions, we hear the spoken words of Sam Larner. Peggy's arrangement of "Cabin Boy" is an elaborate and exciting tapestry of sound woven from singing, actuality, and instrumental music on pennywhistle, guitar, concertina, banjo, fiddle, and clarinet. In earlier Radio Ballads, the actuality had seemed an interruption of the music; here it is part of the music. On the "Net-Hauling Song," the texture is even more multilayered; Peggy has added the cry of gulls and the sounds of fishermen working to actuality, singing, and instrumental music.

Ewan hewed very closely to traditional models with *Singing the Fishing*, and some of the songs from this Radio Ballad are almost indistinguishable from their traditional ancestors. At the same time, the songs incorporate the words of the fishermen themselves. "The shoals of herring" is a phrase that frequently occurred in the fishermen's speech, and it became the title of the program's best-known song. The tune of "The Shoals of Herring" is based on the traditional ballad "The Famous Flower of Serving Men," and the words are drawn from interviews with Sam Larner. Larner's description of the rough conditions at sea introduces the song and interweaves throughout the verses, his harsh voice and harsher words in sharp contrast to this lyrical song, sung in an achingly pure tenor. When Ewan first played the song for Larner, the latter was delighted. "I've sung that song all my life," he said.

Women have a much more prominent role in *Singing the Fishing* than in the first two Radio Ballads, partially because women workers were important in the herring industry as they were not in either road building or engine driving. In addition, Peggy recorded much of the actuality and paid close attention to the women she interviewed. Two songs in *Singing the Fishing* are devoted entirely to the experiences of women. The "Fisherman's Wife" is similar to songs from the first two Radio Ballads, in which women lament being left behind while their men go to work. However, unlike the passive "Come, Me Little Son," the "Fisherman's Wife" is based on traditional fisherwomen's songs ("Who would be a fisherman's wife?") and on actuality gleaned from the fisherwomen themselves ("He's like a lodger—he just comes home to sleep"). As such, "Fisherman's Wife" has a sharpness and authenticity that the earlier songs had lacked. And for the first time in a Radio Ballad, there is a song that focuses on the work that women do. "The Fishgutters' Song" describes the golden days of the East Anglian fishing industry, when herring were so plentiful that extra hands were needed to gut and process the fish, and young women from Scotland came to Yarmouth in order to earn extra money.

*Singing the Fishing* is virtually apolitical. No distinction is made between fishermen who owned their vessels, such as Ronnie Balls, and those who did not, such as Sam Larner. The poverty-stricken fishermen of the interwar years and the prosperous fishermen of postwar Scotland are treated as part of the same brotherhood. *Singing the Fishing* is also tinged with nostalgia. The stars of the program are Sam Larner and Ronnie Balls, retired men of sail and steam, not the working fishermen of the Scottish coast, with their diesel boats, echolocation devices, and radiotelephones. We hear the words and stories of the modern-day Scottish fishermen, but we never learn their names.

The tightness and professionalism of *Singing the Fishing*, the beauty of its songs, the eloquence of Sam Larner and Ronnie Balls and the other fisherfolk, and (perhaps) the lack of controversy in its point of view pleased the BBC so much that it entered the program as its documentary selection for the Prix Italia.[28] This time, it won; and in October, Ewan and Charles traveled to Trieste to collect the award. At the time, no one questioned this relegation of Peggy to secondary status. Years later, Ewan recognized the injustice:

> Peggy had taken part in every stage of the work, had collected in the field, transcribed tapes, chosen actuality, planned sequences, suggested subjects for songs, arranged the music and directed its performance. It was grossly unfair that she should be credited with only the arrangements. . . . Peggy was definitely denied recognition as part creator of the radio-ballads. Was it naïvety or was I just another male chauvinist? I hope not, although it could have been that automatic attitude to women that also made Peggy and I call our joint company Ewan MacColl Ltd.[29]

Film and television work was important that year. For seven weeks, Peggy played banjo and guitar for a BBC children's series based on the work of

Mark Twain. She and Ewan did the music for a series of television films about people and places around Britain, and they wrote and played the music for monthly films produced by the National Coal Board. They produced a Tyne-Tees documentary about coal miners, entitled *Burning Light*, and found the miners fascinating: eloquent, politically astute, grimly ironic, and dedicated to working-class politics. The miners had created a legendary hero, a larger-than-life coal miner called "the big hewer," who would become the subject of the fourth Radio Ballad.

In 1960, Ewan was granted a visa to enter the United States, and Ewan and Peggy made their first tour of the country in the summer. They had a reunion with Pete and Mike at the Newport Folk Festival, where the lineup included Ed McCurdy, Cisco Houston, Flatt and Scruggs, Theodore Bikel, and John Lee Hooker. The tour also included several concerts in California and a visit with Charles Seeger, who had recently separated from Mar and, at the age of seventy-two, was living alone for the first time.

Though touring would always be an important part of her career, Peggy frequently found it stressful. She wrote to her father: "During the last year I have been getting fearfully out of practice on the guitar and banjo, due to housework and less lazing around the house, and working constantly with Ewan so that concert-giving gives me the biggest butterflies I've ever had in my life. I don't play well on the stage, especially compared to Mike and Pete, I play much less traditionally than I used to, due to the ties that are severed between me and America now."[30] She also worried about Neill, seven thousand miles away with Betsy, and the unresolved problem of Ewan's other family. Ewan and Jean were still legally married, and Hamish had yet to learn that he had a half-brother. The problem of balancing work and family was ameliorated by the fact that Ewan helped around the house, though it was tacitly understood that housework was Peggy's job, and Ewan was being kind and considerate by taking up a burden for which he had no responsibility. The problem of being an American folksinger who sang American songs while living in England was one she could never entirely resolve. Touring in the United States was one way of reinvigorating herself with the culture that she represented, and American audiences responded enthusiastically. In the autumn, she and Ewan returned to America with Neill and Betsy. The tour culminated in December with a concert at New York City's Carnegie Hall, before an audience of 1,200. A *New York Times* reviewer praised them both but clearly considered Ewan the senior partner:

Britain's leading folk singer, Ewan MacColl, strode on to the stage of Carnegie Hall Saturday night . . . and proceeded to give one of the most substantial and enjoyable folk concerts New York has had in several seasons. . . . Mr. MacColl's mastery of mood, scene and vocal control were evident everywhere. . . . Miss Seeger . . . obviously knows southern mountain banjo and vocal style inside out. . . . Her light soprano voice and her instrument made a formidable team. Her voice tends to get edgy and strident in the upper register, but when she was not pushing it too hard, it was handled with intelligence and skill.[31]

Traditional music held pride of place at their concerts, and they produced several albums in 1960 that concentrated on traditional British songs: *Popular Scottish Songs*, *Songs of Two Rebellions: The Jacobite Wars of 1715 and 1745*, and *Chorus from the Gallows*. Their songbook of traditional British music, *The Singing Island*, was also published that year. Peggy played guitar and banjo for Bert Lloyd on several recordings of Australian music, which were released as a compilation entitled *Outback Ballads*. She joined other artists on the Folkways recording *American History in Ballad and Song* and published her own banjo book, *The Five-String Banjo American Folk Styles*. Alan Lomax's anthology of traditional music, *The Folk Songs of North America*, for which she provided all the transcriptions, was also published in 1960.

To Ewan and Peggy, traditional music was the seedbed of the folk revival, not its culmination. They believed that contemporary folk songs could be based on traditional models but should not cling to the concerns of the past. In 1960, for the first time, Ewan and Peggy produced an album devoted entirely to modern songs composed in the folk idiom: *The New Briton Gazette*.[32] Most of the songs are political in nature, even those that deal with subjects not usually thought of in such terms. Ewan's Christmas song, "Ballad of the Carpenter," presents Jesus as a working-class hero; Peggy's New Year's song, "Come Fill Up Your Glasses," is a celebration of the working man. The songs are of uneven quality, in both their writing and their presentation. After the crisp professionalism and complex arrangements of the Radio Ballads, some of *The New Briton Gazette* seems almost amateurish. In "Come Fill Up Your Glasses," Peggy's voice sounds brassy and harsh compared with Ewan's velvety baritone; the harmony that they sing on the chorus is inconsistent and does not show either voice to advantage. They do a better job of blending their voices on "The Ballad of Springhill," but even here the harmony sometimes distracts from the melody and the story, and the accompaniment is so simple as to be virtually unnecessary.

Only a few songs are sung with real political conviction. One is Ewan's "Brother, Won't You Join in the Line?," which was written for the Campaign for Nuclear Disarmament (CND) march to Aldermaston in 1958. It is based on Uncle Dave Macon's labor song "Buddy, Won't You Roll down the Line?" and has the ironic tone, rollicking banjo accompaniment, and extremely singable chorus of its American ancestor. Peggy wrote "Crooked Cross" in response to Sir Oswald Mosley, leader of the British Union of Fascists in the interwar years, and his unsuccessful bid for Parliament in 1959. Though imprisoned and silenced during World War II, he was free to spout fascist rhetoric in 1959, and his followers drenched London with swastikas ("the crooked cross"). The melody is so simple as to be almost a chant, but the song has a drive and urgency that many others on the album lack. The lyrics are deceptively simple and fully utilize the irony embedded in the phrase "crooked cross." The first line of each stanza is repeated, almost shanty-like, after each ensuing line. The first stanza is particularly effective:

> Have you seen (Have you seen?)
> The butcher's sign, (Have you seen?)
> The killer's medal, (Have you seen?)
> The crooked cross? (Have you seen?)
> On that cross (Have you seen?)
> Millions died (Have you seen?)
> When the world (Have you seen?)
> Was crucified. (Have you seen?)[33]

The reflexive sexism of the day is apparent in the album. "Come Fill Up Your Glasses" praises the sort of workers who people the early Radio Ballads— fishermen, drivers, firemen, miners, and such—and who can be addressed as "lads." Ewan sings the only lines that mention women, "We'll drink a long life to our sweethearts and wives, / And the ladies, being willing, will greet us likewise," a curious point of view for a woman songwriter.[34] Ewan's "Come All You Gallant Colliers" ends with the lines: "And the men who built the old world, their kind will build the new, / For a world's not built by power alone but by men like me and you."[35] Women may be sturdy and dedicated helpmeets, but apparently they do not build worlds. Despite the working women that Ewan and Peggy had met during *Singing the Fishing*, despite the memory of the women who built airplanes and fought in the Resistance during World War II, despite the publication of Simone de Beauvoir's *The*

*Second Sex* in 1949 and its translation into English in 1952, despite the fact that Peggy worked as hard as Ewan and both had grown up in households where the mother was the primary breadwinner, the politics of gender was not yet on their radar.

The unevenness of *The New Briton Gazette* should not disguise its importance. Ewan and Peggy were attempting to answer the question of "whether traditional folk-song was capable of reflecting twentieth-century industrial society."[36] The 1960s would explode with political songwriting based on traditional models, but in the first year of that decade, it was a relatively rare phenomenon; the folk revival still concentrated on traditional material. Political songs based on traditional music were not new: Joe Hill and the IWW had remade hymns into labor songs in the early years of the twentieth century; Aunt Molly Jackson, Florence Reece, and Sarah Ogan Gunning did the same a generation later; during the Spanish Civil War, the soldiers of the International Brigades created antifascist songs from the folk songs of their home countries; and at that very moment, civil rights activists in the United States were fashioning freedom songs from the traditional music of the black church. Peggy's brother Pete had sung and written political folk songs since the 1930s and had kept this tradition alive with organizations such as People's Songs and *Sing Out!* magazine. Ewan's friend Hamish Henderson had used traditional Scottish music as the basis for his own songs about World War II. But none of this music was well known outside of a small circle of devotees and fellow activists. Most of these people treated political songwriting as a sideline, an adjunct to their real work. Hamish Henderson was primarily a scholar and a poet, Pete Seeger primarily a performer, though both had written some very fine songs. The labor and civil rights activists who used folk music did so mostly because it was well known to their constituencies, and though they created some wonderful songs, their main interest was in politics, not music.[37] Not since Woody Guthrie had anyone paid such close and concerted attention to both political activism and political songwriting. Ewan and Peggy's first album of new songs may have been a little rough around the edges, but it helped set the course of the folk revival during the 1960s, when political songwriting stepped out of its narrow and esoteric domain and became part of a worldwide popular movement. That popularity, of course, created its own problems.

# CHAPTER 10

# What Is a Folk Song?

Are my poems spoken in the factories and fields,
In the streets o' the toon?
Gin they're no', then I'm failin' to dae
What I ocht to ha' dune.

—Hugh MacDiarmid, "Second Hymn to Lenin"

"What is a folk song?" was the question that Ewan MacColl, Peter Kennedy, and Sean O'Boyle pondered on a BBC radio program on May 5, 1955. It was a question that had puzzled folklorists and musicians for centuries. MacColl, Kennedy, and O'Boyle reached no definitive conclusions, but they did mention many of the properties that their predecessors noted: oral transmission, communal acceptance, the existence of variants, and continuity with a received tradition. Kennedy felt that Cecil Sharp's definition "should satisfy anybody": "[Folk song] is the product of a race and reflects feelings and tastes that are communal rather than personal. . . . Its creation is never completed—while at every moment of its history it exists not in one form but in many."[1] Ewan concluded the program by stressing both the formal and the social aspects of folk song: "A folk song is a song written in the idiom of popular speech, the melody of which is a development of what the voice normally does in speech. It is current among the common people and reflects exactly their attitude to life, their dreams and aspirations, their fears and, above all, their hopes."[2]

The definition of folk song has been debated since the German philosopher Johann Gottfried Herder coined the term—and the concept of "the folk"—in the late eighteenth century. In Herder's view, each folk is molded by a common language and geography and possesses common cultural items, which he called "folklore." Folk songs, in this formulation, are those created by a particular folk group, and these songs represent the true spirit of the community that produced and nourished them. Herder would certainly have agreed with Ewan that a folk's songs reflect "exactly their attitude to life, their dreams and aspirations, their fears and, above all, their hopes."

The designation of "folk songs" as distinct from other kinds of songs has had, since its inception, a sense of imminent demise. Herder believed that German folklore was in danger, both from modernity and from foreign influence. Only the peasants, who were rooted in the soil and lived untouched by foreign ways, still possessed what Herder considered authentic German culture. But their way of life was threatened by a rapidly changing world, which was starting to encroach on the most isolated of communities. Herder called upon his fellow Germans to go out among the peasants and collect their lore before it was too late, and he practiced what he preached, publishing several volumes of folk poetry entitled *Volkslieder* (Folk songs) in the 1770s.[3] In his view, only authentic German folk material should provide the basis for German art and culture. His call to build the future on the lore of the past was answered by many of the major German musicians and writers of the nineteenth century, including the first major folklorists, the Brothers Grimm.

In the English-speaking world, the term *folk song* did not become common until much later; collectors and scholars referred to these materials as "popular songs" or "traditional songs" or simply "old songs."[4] However, the idea of collecting traditional songs before they disappeared had taken root even earlier. In 1765, Bishop Thomas Percy published *Reliques of Ancient English Poetry*, a collection of English ballads written by "our ancient English Bards and Minstrels."[5] In Scotland, collections of Scottish songs date from the beginning of the eighteenth century—an attempt to ensure that Scotland remained a culturally independent nation after its political union with England.

British folk-song collectors accepted Herder's dictum that folk songs were a precious component of the national patrimony, and like him, they were driven by a sense of urgency to collect and preserve the music before its traditional milieus were destroyed by industrialization, increased mobility, and growing literacy. By 1808, John Finlay lamented in his introduction to *Scottish Historical and Romantic Ballads*: "A very few years will carry into oblivion all that yet remains among the peasantry of our old hereditary song; for it is almost exclusively from the recitation of very old people, that the lately recovered pieces have been obtained."[6] Nearly a century later, Cecil Sharp, the most important and influential of the English folk-song collectors, expressed a similar sentiment: "It becomes . . . a matter of the highest importance that not only the songs, but that all things that relate to the art of folk-singing, should be accurately recorded while there is yet time and opportunity. They, one and all, form part and parcel of a great tradition that stretches back into the mists of the past in one long, unbroken chain, of which the last link is now, alas, being forged."[7]

Interest in folk music (sometimes called "the first folk revival") grew in England in the early decades of the twentieth century, spearheaded by the work of Sharp and his assistant, Maud Karpeles, and centered around organizations such as the Folk-Song Society and the English Folk Dance Society, which merged to form the English Folk Dance and Song Society (EFDSS) in 1932.[8] This folk revival concentrated on the collection and preservation of traditional songs and dances and the teaching of this material in schools. It was a primarily conservative folk revival, dedicated to the preservation of rural material that was in danger of being lost as England became a predominantly urban country. Sharp believed that the English character was decaying as it became unmoored from its rural past, and that the nation's children must be taught their rural—and hence quintessentially English—heritage. In his view, folk songs—rural products removed from the decadent immorality of the city—would inculcate a proper sense of Englishness, a love of country, and the love of one's fellow Englishmen.

By 1917, Cecil Sharp felt that song collecting in England was a closed project, but he was delighted to find that English folk songs thrived in the isolated hamlets of the American Appalachians, communities where young and old learned folk songs from birth. The Archive of American Folk Song, initially part of the Music Division of the Library of Congress, was founded in 1928 on principles similar to Sharp's. In 1928, Carl Engel, chief of the Music Division, noted:

> There is a pressing need for the formation of a great centralized collection of American folk-songs. . . . Countless individuals, numerous walks of life, several races have contributed to this treasure of songs and ballads. It is richer than that of any other country. Too much of it has remained scattered or unreported. The preservation of this material in remote haunts where it still flourishes is endangered by the spread of the radio and phonograph, which are diverting the attention of the people and their old heritage and are making them less dependent on it.[9]

John and Alan Lomax were among the collectors who sought "remote haunts" where folk songs still thrived. In the introduction to *American Ballads and Folk Songs*, they observe: "A life of isolation, without books or newspapers or telephone or radio, breeds songs and ballads."[10] When they collected African

American music in Texas, they sought "the Negro who had had the least contact with jazz, the radio, and with the white man" and reported, with no apparent sense of irony, that "in the prison farm camps . . . the conditions were practically ideal."[11] But isolation was a way of life that could not be sustained. In the preface to Cecil Sharp's 1932 edition of *English Folk Songs from the Southern Appalachians*, Maud Karpeles sadly notes the changes in the Appalachian communities where she and Sharp had found folk songs in abundance only a few decades previously: "It is surprising and sad to find how quickly the instinctive culture of the people will seem to disappear when once they have been brought into touch with modern civilization, and how soon they will imitate the manners and become imbued with the taste of 'polite Society' . . . And the singing of traditional songs is relegated almost immediately to that past life, which has not only been outgrown, but which has no apparent bearing on the present existence."[12]

Yet something unexpected happened in the middle of the twentieth century. The death of folk music, predicted for more than 150 years, had not occurred; to the contrary, folk music was enjoying a lively revival. The recording technology that had supplanted communal singing had also provided a way to preserve the songs. The folk-song collections that many had considered a dignified graveyard for dead songs had turned into the mechanism of their rebirth. In the preface to Cecil Sharp's 1952 collection, Maud Karpeles was fair-minded enough to admit that the changes in Appalachia had not gone quite as she had predicted: "To many a singer it was a great delight to be able to re-learn from these volumes a song that he had sung to Cecil Sharp over thirty years ago and had since forgotten. Thus, a song, originating in England and carried to America, lives there by oral tradition for some hundreds of years; it is written down and taken back to England by Cecil Sharp; then some thirty years later the song is carried back in printed form to the country of its adoption and takes on a new lease of life."[13]

That folk songs were taught in the schools—a practice championed by Cecil Sharp in England and by Charles and Ruth Crawford Seeger in the United States—was yet another factor that had kept such songs alive. Sharp and the Seegers believed that children should learn the folk songs of their home country as the first step in their musical education. But the Seegers, unlike antiquarians such as Sharp, had never believed that folk songs flourished only in pockets of isolation. They were convinced that new songs were being created even as old ones died, and that this process, far from being a cause for lamentation, was what kept folk music alive. In a letter dated April 6, 1937, Charles distinguished his approach from that of antiquarian collectors:

There never has been a time when "old" traditions and songs were not dying. What the collector almost invariably misses is the fact that new traditions and new songs are always being made, and that old ones are being modified. . . . At least two adventures into the field that have been made recently, lead me to believe not only that the traditional idiom is neither dying nor dead, but growing and producing new and startling mutations. I could show you one group consisting of 40 or 50 items from the industrial towns where songs are being made thick and fast—not as antiques, but as vital factors in contemporary life.[14]

Two decades later, his son Pete would make American folk music widely accessible by singing it to the young. Blacklisted because of his politics and his refusal to cooperate with HUAC, Pete found his primary employment singing for schools, camps, and colleges. He turned out dozens of recordings in the 1950s, many of them for children. His biographer, David Dunaway, estimates that "probably a few hundred thousand children first heard American folk music through these recordings."[15] By the late 1950s and early 1960s, these children were ready to sing, perform, and reinterpret folk music on their own.

The American folk revival provided inspiration to folk musicians in the British Isles, but by the end of the 1950s, many British and Irish musicians were turning away from American music and toward the musical traditions of their own communities. In Scotland and Ireland, musical attention to homegrown material was part of a broader based cultural nationalism, a reaction to the cultural dominance of England. In Ireland, musicians received institutional support from places such as the Irish Folklore Commission; since the founding of the Irish Free State, the government had encouraged the collection of traditional Irish lore as the basis of a national culture. In Scotland, musicians received encouragement and support from people such as Hamish Henderson, who was affiliated with the newly formed School of Scottish Studies at the University of Edinburgh. In England, where no sense of cultural suppression existed, less institutional support was forthcoming. The English Folk Dance and Song Society provided one of the few meeting places for people interested in folk music; it quickly became—almost without meaning to—a catalyst of the midcentury folk revival. But tensions developed between the antiquarians of the EFDSS, who considered folk music synonymous with traditional music, and younger musicians such as Alan Lomax, Ewan Mac-Coll, and Peggy Seeger, who believed that folk songs could be created anew. These tensions centered on the meaning of folk music itself.

Eighteenth- and nineteenth-century song collectors had been writers, printers, booksellers, and gentlemen of independent means. Their definition of "folk song" had been more intuitive than rigorous. By the twentieth century, however, folklore had become a professional field of study, with its own journals, learned societies, and university classes. Professional folklorists sought to maintain intellectual standards that would make folklore a respected academic discipline and to define their study object with scholarly rigor. Though no complete consensus was ever reached, Robert Winslow Gordon's 1938 definition provides a fair summary of the academic point of view: "Folk song is a body of song in the possession of the people, passed on by word of mouth from singer to singer, not learned from books or from print. . . . Genuine folk songs are not static, but are in a state of flux; they have been handed down through a fair period of time, and all sense of their authorship and origin has been lost."[16] In 1954, the International Folk Music Council defined folk music in similar fashion as "the product of a musical tradition that has been evolved through the process of oral transmission."[17] In both of these definitions, "folk music" is considered to be equivalent to traditional music; the IFMC changed its name to the International Council for Traditional Music in 1981. To many academics, only this music was genuine folk music; what the folk revivalists sang was, in Richard Dorson's derisive neologism, "fakelore." Pete Seeger remarked on the irony of this definition, which had little meaning for traditional musicians: "The real traditional folk singer, who lived in past centuries and learned and sang his songs within a small folk community, sang a song because he thought it was a good song, not because he thought it was old. . . . The person who beats his breast and says 'I will sing nothing but a folk song' is either fooling himself or trying to fool someone else."[18]

Throughout the midcentury folk revival, a battle raged among academics and musicians for the definition of the term *folk music*. Some academics, such as Hamish Henderson and Kenneth Goldstein, were friendly to the folk revival, but they were distinctly in the minority.[19] In 1953, John Greenway published *American Folksongs of Protest*, the first scholarly study of industrial and political folk songs. It received a stinging review from Stith Thompson, then head of the folklore program at Indiana University: "Here is a book called *American Folksongs* which contains not a single example of what a competent folklorist would call by that name. Folk songs are songs that are traditional, that are handed down from singer to listener and that are still alive. The songs in this collection are not anonymous and most of them are dead, preserved only in museums. They are not and never were folk songs."[20] But the songs had not been preserved in museums. Greenway had taken some examples from commercial recordings and others from folk-song books and field recordings. He utilized collections created by folklore scholars such as Frank

Dobie, George Korson, Vance Randolph, and Francis James Child. Indeed, the strictness of Thompson's definition would exclude many of the songs in Child's classic folk-song collection, *The English and Scottish Popular Ballads*. And Greenway was, by any academic definition, "a competent folklorist"; he had received his PhD from Indiana University's rival, the University of Pennsylvania, under the direction of folklorist MacEdward Leach.

Part of the hostility that academics felt toward the folk revival was the sense that revivalists were misleading the public about what folk music really was. In 1948, Wayland Hand lamented:

> It is distressing to note that much, if not most, activity in the entertainment aspects of folklore has been carried on quite independently of national and re- gional folklore societies and organizations, and without benefit of the research facilities of academic institutions and folklore depositories in our great librar- ies. . . . The American Folklore Society will abdicate one of its most important duties if it does not take positive action to combat the many negative forces at work in the field of the folk arts by insisting on greater fidelity to source materials, and by encouraging resort to them wherever found. Moreover, it should extend the hand of cooperation to local folk song, folk dance, and folk festival groups with a view toward a more scientific study of the materials.[21]

But there was more going on at midcentury than the desire for disciplinary control. In the McCarthy era, when Greenway's book was published, some feared that the field of folklore would be tainted by the left-wing associations of those in the folk-song revival. In their view, the best defense was to claim that the songs of the folk revival were not actually folk songs but self-conscious imitations of the real thing.

Richard Dorson, Stith Thompson's successor at Indiana University, de- spised the folk revival, but he despised all political uses of folklore. He was particularly horrified by the Nazis' emphasis on German folk culture and Ger- man folklorists' willingness to use their discipline to prop up Nazi ideology—a political use of folk culture so profound that it discredited the entire field of folklore in Germany for decades after the end of the war.[22] But the very distinction of folk culture from other forms of culture—and folk music from other kinds of music—was political from the outset. Herder called on his fellow Germans to collect folk songs not simply because he liked them but because he felt that German culture should be built on a German foundation. Herder believed that only the German peasantry possessed true German cul- ture—not because folklore was necessarily bound to this particular stratum of society, but because that was the way things had worked out in this historical instance. (He believed that the greatest Greek folk poet was Homer and the greatest English folk poet was Shakespeare, because they were the ones who had captured their nation's peculiar folk soul.) Nonetheless, folklorists and collectors tended to follow Herder's emphasis on the peasantry and to define folk culture as traditional, anonymous culture that had been handed down from generation to generation.

The identification of folk culture with one particular class of society was rife with political possibility, but it had no intrinsic political ideology. The liberal, democratic Herder believed that the peasantry possessed the soul of the German nation, but so did Adolf Hitler. Herder spoke of the German nation at a time when Germany was not a nation-state. Whether Herder was himself a German nationalist (and the subject is hotly debated), it is undeniable that German nationalists used his philosophy to foster the unification of Germany in 1871. The idea of the nation-state based on a common store of folk culture, a concept generally known as "romantic nationalism," swept Europe in the nineteenth and twentieth centuries, from Germany to Finland to Ireland. Thus the proper definition of folklore and the proper use of folk culture were political questions from the beginning.

In the United States, the connection of folk music with cultural tolerance and progressive politics is so strong that it seems natural. But this connection was carefully wrought in the early decades of the twentieth century, over and against other views of folk music as archaic survival or racial inheritance. Two of the most important advocates for this left-liberal view were Charles and Ruth Crawford Seeger. They argued against the racialist politics in the ideas of people such as John Powell, a composer and founder of the White Top Folk Festival in Virginia. Like the Seegers, Powell was tired of American music being compared unfavorably to European music, and he wanted to create a national music based on American folk song. The problem was deciding what kind of American folk music should represent the entire nation. In a 1927 article, Powell acknowledged composers of the "Red Indian School" and the "Negro School" (among others) while explaining why these musics could never be the basis for American music at large. He dismissed the "Red Indian School" by simply saying, "We Americans are not Red Indians; we are not even Americans; we are Europeans in race and language. And it could never be possible to express our European culture and psychology in terms of the musical idiom of an alien and primitive race."[23] He used the opposite argument to demolish the "Negro School." He acknowledged the beauty of African American music, particularly spirituals, but did not think them American enough to be the foundation for American music: "The negro [*sic*] spirituals . . . are . . . chiefly European in their origin, being merely negro [*sic*] adaptations of white camp-meeting and revival tunes of the last century. Most of these spirituals, when critically analyzed, show clearly in their melodic and harmonic structure their Caucasian origin."[24] In Powell's formulation, Native American music cannot serve as the basis for a national culture because it is not European; African American music cannot work because it is too European. After digesting this logic without even a gulp, Powell went on to tout "Anglo-Saxon folk-song" as the obvious basis for American music: "The beauty of Anglo-Saxon folk-music surpasses any other in the whole world. . . . Here, at last, we have a basic idiom thoroughly competent to express our national psychology. This music is not only marvelous in content but . . . often attains a perfection rarely achieved by even composers of the most surpassing genius. And this proves not only the innate musical gift of our race, but also the high plane of musical culture and taste that our forefathers . . . had reached, and which, consequently, is reattainable by us, their descendants."[25] Powell also suggested using Anglo-Saxon folk music to Americanize new immigrants and thought this cultural indoctrination far superior to asking immigrants to read the Declaration of Independence, the Constitution, or the Gettysburg Address. Here, Powell explicitly valorizes the mystic, romantic notion of folk as blood rather than the liberal, rationalist notion of citizen as legal entity.

The timing is significant; in the 1920s Powell was not alone in his racism and his nativism. In 1924, Powell's home state of Virginia passed the Racial Integrity Law, an antimiscegenation law that encoded the "one drop of blood" rule and remained on the books until 1967, when the Supreme Court struck it down in *Loving v. Virginia*. (The law had been vigorously promoted by the Anglo-Saxon Club, an organization that Powell had founded in 1922.) The Immigration Restriction Act of 1924 ended decades of open-door immigration policies and set national quotas to correspond with the percentage of national groups as they appeared in the census of 1890—the year in which immigrants from southern and eastern Europe began to predominate over immigrants from northern and western Europe. As northern European culture ceased to be the majority culture in the United States, Powell founded the White Top Folk Festival, which ran from 1931 to 1939. It was explicitly devoted to the preservation and valorization of Anglo-Saxon culture as the best, the purest, and, somewhat paradoxically, the most American of all cultures. In 1937, Powell's colleague Annabel Morris Buchanan wrote that the White Top Folk

Festival "[is important] not for the mountain people alone; not for one region alone; not for one class alone: the White Top activities, if they are to endure, must be wrought slowly, carefully, measure by measure, for a *race*. These native possessions—these songs and tunes and traditions—these are ours, to know, to love, and to build upon. For after all, the White Top Festival belongs to *the folk*. And we are *the folk*."[26] Like Cecil Sharp, Powell and Buchanan considered the folk songs of the southeastern Appalachians the high-water mark of American culture. Tucked away in the hills, cut off from the rest of the world by bad roads and harsh terrain, the Appalachians preserved a kind of Anglo-Saxon culture in amber, untouched by the influence of immigrants or even of African Americans. It took a curious mental leap to argue that isolated communities could most ably represent America precisely because they were cut off from most of the country.

All of this was anathema to Charles and Ruth Crawford Seeger. To the Seegers, the glory of folk songs lay not in their racial particularity but in their populist inclusiveness: they could be sung by anyone who had a mind to sing them. Charles had visited White Top as part of his work for the Resettlement Administration and considered the festival "reactionary to the core" and "really sinister."[27] He was revolted by the notion that true American folk music kept itself pure by having nothing to do with the vast majority of Americans. Instead, he believed that American folk music should be the basis of a national music precisely because it was grounded in the lives of the American people. To the Seegers, folk songs were living entities constantly subject to change, not museum pieces to be found and preserved in some pristine condition. In Ruth's introduction to *American Folk Songs for Children*, she explained her vision of American folk music, a vision in direct opposition to racialist antiquarians such as Powell and Buchanan: "This kind of traditional or folk music is thoroughly identified with the kind of people who made America as we know it. It is a music they liked and still like. They made it and are still making it. Some of it came with them from other countries and has been little changed. Some of it came with them from other countries and has been much changed. Some of it grew here. All of it has partaken of the making of America."[28] The Seegers shared this vision with Ben Botkin, director of the WPA folklore program. In Botkin's words, the WPA folklore program involved "the tremendous responsibility of studying folklore as a living culture and of understanding its meaning and function not only in its immediate setting but in progressive and democratic society as a whole."[29] Botkin and the Seegers saw these activities as ways to safeguard vital parts of American culture and to make this culture available to the nation whose provenance it was. In so doing, they argued for a vision of America more diverse and progressive than had heretofore been known, an America in which the cultures of rural and urban communities were valorized, the contributions of immigrants, workers, and minorities celebrated. Botkin's *Treasury of American Folklore*, for which Charles Seeger served as music consultant, contains a strongly worded denunciation of those who view folklore "in terms of the 'racial heritage' or insist that a particular folk group or body of tradition is 'superior' or 'pure.'"[30]

Botkin and the Seegers challenged the notion that folklore was an inherently conservative entity, rooted in the past and resistant to any change. Instead, they promoted folklore—and particularly folk music—as examples of the intelligence and creativity of ordinary Americans. In the 1930s, this left-liberal conception of folk music was embraced by several labor unions, certain branches of the Communist Party, and musicians such as Pete Seeger and Woody Guthrie.[31] Most academic folklorists strove to present folklore as politically neutral, but their work was little known by the general public. By the 1960s, the connection between folk music and left-liberal politics was so strong that when Pete Seeger sang in Los Angeles in 1963, a local organization demanded a congressional investigation of folk music as "an unidentified tool of Communist psychological or cybernetic warfare to ensnare and capture youthful minds."[32]

Peggy considered herself politically naive before she met Ewan. But she was born to parents who had considered music "a weapon in the class struggle," who saw folk music as the artistry of the powerless and the obscure.[33] She may not have been explicitly schooled in any political doctrine, but she could not have escaped her parents' dedication to the music of ordinary people, or her brother's demand for justice before HUAC, which turned down his request to sing "Wasn't That a Time?," a folk rendering of American history. Her radical-Puritan background, which demanded doing the right thing no matter what the consequences, easily joined Ewan's Marxist interpretation of folk music as the culture of the working class. Because they were two of the leaders of the midcentury folk revival, their conception of folk music had enormous influence. But like everyone else, they had to answer the question, "What is a folk song?" And not everyone agreed with their answer.

# CHAPTER 11

# High Noon

How soon the morning's over,
How soon the sun shines overhead,
But summer rain brings seedling trees,
And children were blessing our bed.

—Peggy Seeger, "New Spring Morning"


In the 1950s, when Peggy was still ensconced in France, Ewan had written despairingly of the poor quality of singing in the skiffle clubs. He complained of singers who sang with a mixture of "South London, stage-Irish and Bronx" and wondered:

> What is the answer? Training? Good models? To some extent but it is not the whole answer. You and I are the models that most young singers in this country are using. One of the most important factors in the whole business is this semi-professionalism. It's having the most awful effect on young singers. They learn half a dozen songs which they sing without style, feeling or understanding.... Whenever they sing a slow tempo song, their voices crawl with self-pity, if they sing in tempo they automatically surrender the text and adopt a spurious American accent.[1]

In June 1961, Ewan, Peggy, and several other folk artists attempted to rectify the situation when they founded the Singers Club in a union hall in Soho Square. The club was run by a committee of resident artists (Peggy, Ewan, Bert Lloyd, Fitzroy Coleman, Isla Cameron, and others), with occasional guest musicians, and an opportunity for lesser-known musicians to sing from the floor. The Singers Club embraced the musical diversity that had been part of the Ballads and Blues club but also introduced a radical new policy: "that singers do not sing anything but the songs of their own native tradition."[2]

The policy was not a sudden decision. Ewan had been mulling over the matter even before Peggy joined him in England. After an evening in a Glasgow folk club, he wrote her: "We must work and work for greater and greater purity of approach in singing. I have come to the conclusion that we cannot afford to be tolerant, we must bring the maximum of critical standards to our own work and to other people's. . . . Let us two work hard and consistently to perfect our skills so that we will be worthy to speak for our time."[3] The immediate catalyst for the policy was an incident that had occurred at the Ballads and Blues club. Peggy remembers:

> There's this guy singing, and he's doing Leadbelly . . . in a Cockney accent. I just started to laugh because it sounded so funny. . . . They had to take me out. . . . And it was discussed the next week about how it wasn't very polite of me to do that. And I said, "But it was very funny. Leadbelly used to visit our house, and I know what he's supposed to sound like." . . . And so then this French guy piped up; he said, "Well, when you sing French songs, I don't particularly like that either." And so I was offended . . . and I turned to Ewan, and I said, "And I wish you'd stop singing 'Sam Bass' [an American song]. It's dreadful." . . . Before it got to be a slanging match, we kind of decided that if you stood up on our stage, you sang songs from your own culture that you'd been brought up in, with the accent right.[4]

The policy had its defenders and its detractors. Ewan and Peggy believed that folksingers needed to learn more than texts and tunes; they needed to understand the singing style and performance practice of the songs they sang. No one would expect an opera singer to mount the stage at La Scala and sing "Un bel di" in a nasal Appalachian twang; why should the reverse practice be acceptable? In Ewan and Peggy's view, when people went to folk clubs, they deserved to hear genuine folk music, not bad imitations or ignorant portrayals of someone else's culture. Peggy and Ewan felt that the "anything goes" attitude common to many folksingers of the day was not only lazy but downright insulting; it implied that folk songs were so simple, so artless that anyone could perform them without taking too much trouble. A folk song, in their view, should be sung by a person who could honestly represent the culture from whence it came; if English folksingers didn't know English songs because they were too busy imitating Americans, then they needed to learn them, from books and recordings if necessary. The policy may also have had a certain amount of cultural defensiveness; before World War II, Britain had been the most powerful nation in the world but had since yielded this position to the United States. In retrospect, Ewan wrote: "We were also intent on proving that we had an indigenous folk-music that was as muscular, as varied and as beautiful as any music anywhere in the world. We felt it was necessary to explore our own music first, to distance ourselves from skiffle with its legions of quasi-Americans. The folk club should be a place where our native music should have pride of place and where the folk music of other nations would be treated with dignity and respect."[5]

On the other hand, traditional folksingers had never imposed such a policy on themselves. They sang songs because they liked them, not because they felt they were representing a particular culture. Folk songs have so many variants in part because they do leap linguistic and national boundaries; soldiers, sailors, traders, and immigrants leave songs in their wake and pick up new ones to carry on their journeys. Traditional singers do not typically learn songs from books; to some folklorists, only songs learned by oral transmission are truly folk songs. In addition, it is not always clear what culture a person is entitled to represent. Industrialization had ended forever a world in which most people were rooted in the soil of their ancestors. Ewan was reared by Scots parents in England; should he be able to sing both Scots and English songs? (He did.) Should Peggy, a white American of English extraction, sing only Anglo-American songs, or could she sing African American songs as well? (She did.) Should Americans who were not of English ancestry sing songs in English or songs in their ancestral tongues, whether they spoke those languages or not? These are complicated questions, not entirely addressed by the Singers Club policy.

The policy galvanized singers who wished to pay attention to the music of their own heritage; it alienated others who believed they should be able to sing whatever they chose. Folk music was immensely popular at this point, so the Singers Club grew, attracting a large and loyal following. At the same time, scores of other folk clubs sprang up around Britain (and the United States). Some enacted a policy similar to that of the Singers Club; others vigorously opposed any such limitation; others cheerfully avoided policy questions altogether. Some clubs were short-lived; others lasted for years. The Singers Club, with its policy intact, lasted for more than three decades.

At its core, the policy fastened on the questions, "What is a folk song?" and "Who should sing it?" In 1961, Sydney Carter investigated these questions in an issue of *English Dance and Song*, the newsletter of the English Folk Dance and Song Society:

> "Folk" has now become a prestige word. Records which no teen-ager would have bought ten years ago now sell briskly with this magic label. . . . It looks as if the dream of Cecil Sharp has now come true: people sing and play folk

music, not because it's educational, but because they actually like it! Up at Cecil Sharp House . . . you'd think they would be putting flags out. . . . But you also hear the sound of lamentation. The Song is getting out of hand. The wrong sort of people are singing it. Folk Song is going Commercial, going American, going (worst of all!) Political. Well, is it?[6]

Carter then interviewed several people involved with the folk revival. Folk guitarist Steve Benbow defined folk song as "any song that's sung by folk. What is a 'folk' if not a human being?"[7] Journalist Eric Winter, the editor of *Sing* magazine, described the essential character of folk song as "simplicity and directness. . . . A folk song tells a story, or describes something, in a straightforward way, without consciously aiming at an artistic or poetical effect. It is not contrived or 'composed.'"[8] To Peggy and Ewan, folk songs were representations of the cultures that created them. Peggy explained her reasons for concentrating on American songs: "As an American, the fact that the Americans have built up a culture which *is* American, which is absolutely unique, is valuable to me. And that's why I sing American songs. Because to me they represent the particular struggle of a particular people at a particular point of time. But when I hear a British person singing a folk song from America I feel that there's an anachronism—a spiritual anachronism, if you want to put it that way—there's something which is not quite right."[9] The definition of folk song had turned into a continuum, with the EFDSS definition of "traditional song" on one end, Steve Benbow's "any human song" on the other, and Ewan and Peggy somewhere in between.

Peggy and Ewan were not unaware of the contradictions embedded in the Singers Club policy. In *Two-Way Trip: American, Scots and English Folksongs Sung by Peggy Seeger and Ewan MacColl*, produced in 1961, Ewan and Peggy wrestle earnestly with the question of who should sing what. In the liner notes, Ewan speaks of growing up with Scots songs and learning English songs in adolescence, then becoming enamored of American songs as a young man. He stopped singing American songs when he felt he was doing violence to the songs themselves, when "the pseudo-American accent which [he] acquired . . . twisted the songs into mere parodies of themselves." Ewan states, "I returned to the songs I knew, the songs I had grown up with." However, he freely admits that he and Peggy were breaking Singers Club policy in this very album:

> At the hundreds of concerts and hootenannies where I have sung or acted as chairman I have made a point of insisting on the rule that singers do not sing anything but the songs of their own native tradition. . . . And now I am not

only singing American songs with Peggy but encouraging her to sing Scots and English songs with me! However, for the most part we confine ourselves to joining in the choruses of each other's songs. . . . There is a further point. When you work with someone over a period of several years, you begin to assimilate elements of their style and vocal habits. This need not mean that your approach to your own repertoire is affected but it does mean that you can stand on the edge of another musical tradition without feeling too conspicuous.[10]

For Peggy, an American singer living in England, the situation was even more complicated. In the same liner notes, she describes herself as living in a "cultural limbo" and remarks:

> I find myself in a double crisis: no oral sources from which to draw and no natural community with which to sing (for one can sing American folksongs *to* a group of non-Americans, but not *with* them, for the communication, the musical growth, is one-way. The group can neither reciprocate nor contribute, save with their appreciation . . . ). . . . It is obvious that new sources must be sought, new ties be established. For sources, I can go to the numerous excellent books and discs of American material. For a community, I must assimilate British habits, actions, inflections, usages of speech. In a word, I will become, consciously *and* unconsciously, less American and feel more and more in common not only with British people but also with British folk music. Under no circumstances, even were I to live here all my life would these feelings make me a "British folksinger," nor would they enable me to take anything but the supporting role in the performance of a Scots or English song.[11]

In *Two-Way Trip*, Ewan and Peggy attempted to work out these contradictions in ways that would show the songs to their best advantage. Yet because the questions, "What is a folk song?" and "Who can sing it?" can never be entirely resolved, contradictions remain. Her remark—that the musical communication involved in singing American songs to non-Americans is "one-way"—is a curious statement to make in an album entitled *Two-Way Trip*, particularly since she also mentions how much she has been influenced by British folk music. Even more importantly, the Anglo-American songs that she sings were initially English songs that Americans took and made their own—a prime example of what the Singers Club policy forbade. Indeed, the very skill with which Peggy and Ewan perform the songs on *Two-Way Trip* refutes the Singers Club policy. In "Waly, Waly" and "Richie Story," Peggy and Ewan sing together in beautiful and convincing Scots, which is the native dialect of neither. An unaccompanied, haunting version of "Old Lady All Skin and Bones" is sung by Peggy in her American accent and Ewan in his

English one, and because the song is in standard English, we never learn its provenance—nor do we need to in order to appreciate it. (The liner notes state that the song exists in English, American, and Scots versions—clear examples of traditional singers taking over the songs of other cultures.) And though the album was subtitled *American, Scots and English Folksongs*, some of the songs are in fact Canadian. Peggy sings an exquisite Newfoundland version of "Just as the Tide Was Flowing," an American singing a Canadian variant of an English song, and entirely doing it justice.

The musical score of the 1962 film *Whaler out of New Bedford* is another example of how violating the Singers Club policy could be appropriate to certain songs and musical traditions. Peggy arranged the music for the film and played guitar and banjo. The songs—traditional American sea songs of the whaling era—were sung by Peggy, Ewan, and Bert Lloyd, backed up by a chorus that included Louis Killen and Charles Parker, with instrumental accompaniment by Alf Edwards and Dave Swarbrick. There is nothing inauthentic or false about Englishmen singing American sea songs; many sailing vessels had international crews, all of whom would have sung each other's songs.

Thus the Singers Club policy was not cut in stone, nor did it apply to all singers or all occasions. Ewan and Peggy never attempted to implement it anywhere but the Singers Club and other venues where they were in charge. They might criticize musicians who sang the songs of someone else's tradition, but their sharpest arrows were focused on those who did so without bothering to learn the tradition in question. Peggy's brother Mike made a career out of playing the music of a milieu not his own and singing in an accent not his own—but only after making a careful and intensive study of the music. Indeed, the exact wording of the Singers Club policy was not always clear, and it may have changed over time. Ewan spoke of singing the songs of one's own "tradition" and Peggy of one's own "culture"; others recall that the policy required singing the songs of one's own country or one's own language.

Though the policy had been a group decision and the Singers Club was run by a resident committee, Ewan quickly became seen as the dominant member of the group and was singled out for censure and for praise. As the oldest and most experienced member of the group, he had the most clearly formulated ideas about folk music and was entirely comfortable acting as spokesperson. Peggy recalls that journalists who interviewed her and Ewan frequently spent most of their time talking to him and then asked, almost as an afterthought, if Peggy had anything to add. Charming, eloquent, intellectually impressive, Ewan became the public face of the Singers Club and the policy associated with it. English folksinger Brian Pearson recalls that when he walked into the Singers Club in its early days, he "fell immediately under Ewan's spell and became a regular audience member."[12] Others attacked Ewan as a man bent on controlling a popular artistic movement. In a 2006 television documentary entitled *Folk Britannia*, which began with the question, "What is a folk song?" Martin Carthy remarks: "Nowadays I have decidedly mixed feelings. When he [Ewan] stood up and he said, 'if you're English, you should sing an English song,' that irritated the hell out of me at the time. But then on the other hand, what it made people like me do, even though I didn't follow him, was go and look for it."[13]

Much of 1961 was spent creating *The Big Hewer*, the Radio Ballad about coal miners. Peggy, Ewan, and Charles had been collecting actuality since February and continued work until the program was broadcast on August 18. They chose three distinct areas in which to interview miners: the northeast of England, the English Midlands, and South Wales. In every area, they heard tales of a superhuman miner who was as strong as two men. In County Durham, he was called "Bob Towers"; in Yorkshire, he was "Jackie Torr"; in Staffordshire, his name was "Bob Temple"; in Wales, "Isaac Lewis." In some places, he was simply called "the big hewer." Ewan and Peggy chose to build the Radio Ballad around this legendary figure.

Coal mining was—and is—a difficult, dangerous occupation, a milieu in which only the strongest could survive. Peggy became increasingly impressed by the miners' strength and skill. She and Ewan visited miners' homes and went with them into the hellish, subterranean world of the mine. In June, Peggy wrote to her father about the miners' daily working conditions: "Going down mines, into seams 20″ high, into old old pits with the dust so thick in the air that you literally couldn't see, into old old pits where in a two-foot seam there is 9″ of water; where men have to crawl to their work two miles, work a whole day, then crawl back and still expected to act like humans—and they ARE humans, they are super humans."[14] Miners developed great pride in their ability to do work that would destroy lesser men, and they had a finely honed sense of gallows humor. Peggy recalls interviewing a miner in South Wales who was dying of black lung: "His cough would just frighten you; he sounded as if he had solid lungs. . . . He started chuckling, because our producer . . . said, 'Don't you call a doctor?' And the miner laughed; he said, 'Doctor? All I need is a plumber.' . . . They had so many jokes about death."[15]

When the director general of the BBC heard the subject of the fourth Radio Ballad, he allegedly responded, with some disdain, "another bloody working-class epic!"[16] But this was the first Radio Ballad—indeed, the only Radio Ballad—in which militant working-class politics appeared. In fact, for a series of working-class epics, the Radio Ballads were surprisingly pastoral, concentrating on small towns and byways away from Britain's industrial centers; they include virtually nothing about cities or factories or unions. *The Big Hewer* contains a section on political militancy—an essential feature of miners' character—but even here, the section is relatively short and somehow manages to avoid the word *union*.

The fourth Radio Ballad combined tales of the Big Hewer's legendary exploits with stories of real miners' accomplishments. The first song sets up the Big Hewer as a larger-than-life hero, like Hercules or Paul Bunyan:

> On the day that I was born, I was 6 foot tall, go down!
> And the very next day I learned the way to haul, go down!
> On the third day worked at board-and-pillar,
> Worked on the fourth as a long-wall filler,
> Getting me steam up, hewing the seam, go down![17]

Real miners may not have started work on the second day of life, but their job did require extraordinary strength of body and mind. One miner describes going down the mine: "The silence of the pit—it's like infinity. Or the bottom of the ocean. It's peaceful—and yet it's sometimes frightening. You can be driven to panic with it, I think. You've never known absolute blackness. Always there's stars at night, and there's always a moon. But there, there's nothing. And you can feel this pressing on you, the darkness, you can feel this darkness."[18]

Danger is the miner's constant companion. One song celebrates the Big Hewer's ability to cheat death:

> He knows how to tell when the roof's going to fall,
> Though the crack be as thin as a hair,
> When the odorless gas comes along in a mass,
> He can smell it before it is there.[19]

Real miners developed a similar ability to sense when danger was imminent. As they scraped in the belly of the earth, the earth sometimes fought back. One miner explains: "But down the pit, you've got to have that in you to sense hidden dangers. You know full well that she can be a nasty bitch when she likes. . . . She's just like an angry woman. She just throws her weight about. And if you're not sharp enough, and get out of the way of her, she'll kill you."[20]

Legends do not die; real men do. One of the most moving sections of the program intersperses a lament for a dead miner with actuality from a woman whose husband had died in the mine. The first stanza is sung by a man and is taken from "The Blantyre Explosion," a traditional song about a mining disaster in Scotland in 1877:

By Clyde's bonny banks where I sadly did wander
Among the pit heaps as evening drew nigh,
I spied a young woman all dressed in deep mourning,
A-weepin' and wailin' with many a sigh.[21]

The second stanza is sung by a woman, in the present tense and in the present time. It abandons the unnamed weeper of the first stanza and reflects the courageous stoicism of real miners' wives:

In from the mine in his pit dirt they bring him,
The neighbors, they stand by the door,
The fire will gang oot and the bairns will gang hungry,
He'll walk to the pit no more.[22]

Even more so than *Singing the Fishing*, *The Big Hewer* is a ballad opera in which all elements work together to tell a story of remarkable men in extraordinary working conditions. Peggy's instrumentation and scoring are extremely effective in creating and extending mood. In a section about going down the mine, Peggy's incidental music is as fear inducing as any Hollywood soundtrack, and it highlights the terror that the miners experience on a daily basis. In "Let the Cage Go Down," a song that praises the miners' ironic sense of humor, the lively rhythms and bright pennywhistle accompaniment show the miners' zest for life, even while death is near at hand. The music is so finely wrought that, paradoxically, it focuses attention away from itself and toward the courage and eloquence of the miners themselves.

*The Big Hewer* garnered favorable reviews and was immensely satisfying artistically, but radio programs did not provide much income. Record albums were slightly better in that regard, and there was an impressive crop that year, including *Bothy Ballads of Scotland*, *Two-Way Trip*, and *Ewan MacColl Sings British Industrial Ballads*. Peggy and Ewan produced two albums that focused on people they had met through the Radio Ballads: *Now Is the Time for Fishing* features the words and music of Sam Larner, and *The Elliotts of Birtley* focuses on a mining family from Durham. Ewan and Peggy also began to give lectures and workshops on folk music. In March 1961, Ewan, Peggy, and Charles Parker participated in a "Folk and Song" weekend sponsored by the East and South Shropshire Youth Committees. Ewan delivered the lecture "The Folk Music Tradition in Britain," while Peggy gave one titled "The American Scene." They also gave joint lectures, "Work Songs and Industrial Ballads" and "The Emerging Tradition," at this event. These lectures show an enduring concern: how to make contemporary folk song fit within the received tradition.

The year 1961 was a busy one both personally and professionally. Alex Campbell asked Peggy for a divorce, which she readily granted, and she legally changed her name back to "Peggy Seeger." Charles Seeger had also divorced and moved to a house near the UCLA campus, where he continued his ethnomusicology research. Pete had been convicted of contempt of Congress and sentenced to prison but was out on bail while his lawyer furiously worked on the appeal. A Pete Seeger Committee was established in England, with Paul Robeson as chairman and Ewan and Peggy as guiding members; supporters included Benjamin Britten, Sean O'Casey, and Doris Lessing. Peggy, Ewan, Bert Lloyd, and Dominic Behan (brother of the Irish writer Brendan Behan) gave a benefit concert for the committee in June, and Pete toured England in the autumn, drawing thousands at a concert in London's Royal Albert Hall.

The happiest change in 1961 was the purchase of a new home in August, the top two floors of a large Victorian house at 35 Stanley Avenue in the London suburb of Beckenham. The spacious rooms provided work space for Peggy and Ewan, and a large garden meant a ready-made playground for Neill. The largest room in the house was reserved for Betsy, who came to live there full-time, providing essential childcare for Neill. Ewan had been unable to obtain a divorce from Jean—and would not do so until the 1970s—but his daily commutes to Croydon were over. He would live the rest of his life at Stanley Avenue and would visit Hamish and Kirsty on Sundays.

The purchase of the house required going into debt, and Peggy and Ewan hoped that touring would provide sufficient income. They had been touring throughout Britain and booked an extensive North American tour for the autumn, beginning in Canada in October and concluding in the United States in December. A blow came when Ewan was denied a visa to enter the United States. The tour was an economic necessity, so Peggy went alone, crisscrossing the continent from Saskatoon to Vancouver, from Pennsylvania to California. She enjoyed visiting her father and giving several concerts with Pete and Mike, but for the most part, she disliked doing the tour without Ewan and found that many audience members felt the same: "I'd walk past the box office . . .

and people would be returning their tickets by droves when they discovered that Ewan wasn't there."[23]

The fifth Radio Ballad, *The Body Blow*, was inspired by a television film entitled *Four People*, for which Ewan and Peggy did the music in the spring of 1961. The film focused on four polio survivors, and the topic immediately ignited Peggy and Ewan's interest. The opportunity to do a Radio Ballad on the subject arose in the winter of 1962, when Charles Parker's boss, David Gretton, discovered that he had extra money that needed to be used before the fiscal year ended in April. The short amount of time available necessitated a pared-down Radio Ballad; Peggy refers to it as a "chamber ballad." This is the first Radio Ballad in which Peggy sang; indeed, she and Ewan were the only singers, and there were only four instrumentalists: Peggy on guitar and five-string banjo, Alf Edwards on ocarina and English concertina, Alfie Kahn on flute and harmonica, and Brian Daly on guitar. Charles Parker recorded the actuality in a few weeks, and *The Body Blow* was broadcast on March 27, 1962.

*The Body Blow* was very different from its predecessors. The first four Radio Ballads had large casts of active men and women at work; there was a sense of action and drama and noise. By contrast, the five people interviewed for *The Body Blow* lived in a world of enforced stillness. The workers in *Singing the Fishing* and *The Big Hewer* fought against raging seas and crumbling mines; the polio survivors showed a quieter courage by refusing to give up their dignity and their lives. It is a subject that could easily have become mawkish or sentimental; that it did not is a tribute to the sensitivity with which this Radio Ballad was done. There is neither pathos nor false cheer; the five survivors describe the pain and desperation of the disease with honesty and humor and without a trace of self-pity. *The Body Blow* requires us to discard shopworn prejudices about the ill and disabled; it also pays tribute to their intelligence and resourcefulness. Ewan remarked that "it has since been used in several large hospitals as training for nurses and hospital staff."[24] This Radio Ballad is also of enormous historical importance; recorded only seven years after the introduction of the Salk vaccine, it captures a moment in time that is, one hopes, gone forever.

Ironically, the depth and richness of the actuality completely overshadowed the music. Peggy herself criticizes the music as being "too soupy."[25] Her instrumental music, which had worked so effectively to create mood in *The Big Hewer*, sounds jarring here. Occasionally, the music seems an interruption of the deeply eloquent actuality, and the fragments of song lyrics never coalesce into songs. Like the hospital atmosphere that the interviewees describe, the music is gentle and encouraging, quiet and antiseptic. The subject clearly stirs Ewan and Peggy's compassion and respect but no deep personal or political connection. One wonders, ultimately, if the music was truly necessary.

Intense and eclectic musical activity filled 1962. There were tours throughout Britain—to Southhampton, Newcastle, Cambridge, Liverpool, Birmingham, and many other places. Monthly films for the Coal Board remained Ewan and Peggy's primary bread-and-butter activity. Their record albums included a two-volume set of broadside ballads and a second volume of *The New Briton Gazette*. Peggy also produced two short solo albums of traditional songs: *Troubled Love* and *Early in the Spring*. The Singers Club was doing so well that Bob Dylan made a point of singing there in December.

Traditional music continued to have pride of place at Ewan and Peggy's concerts, but political music was becoming increasingly common. In addition to her usual staple of traditional American songs, Peggy began to sing songs such as "In Contempt," written in 1950 as a condemnation of HUAC and surely more meaningful now that Pete had been convicted of being "in contempt" of Congress. Politics was becoming an essential part of Peggy's character, as it long had been for Ewan. Ewan's radicalism, rooted in working-class experience, made sense to her after spending time with miners and fishermen and men who built roads. Ewan's politics solidified and expanded the progressive stance with which she had been raised:

> I took Ewan's politics. . . . I parroted them. . . . I'd been brought up progressive as an optimistic, constructive way of making things better, without understanding that to make things better you really do need violence. . . . I'm not sure it can really be done peacefully. I would like to think it can. But the big lasting changes have mostly been violent ones, when things got so bad that people had to really do something about it. . . . I saw a strength in working-class people that I didn't see in the class that I came from. I saw a kind of unity of purpose.[26]

In a 1962 radio program entitled *Not Known in Denmark Street*, Charles Parker presented Ewan and Peggy as modern songwriters who took their inspiration from traditional music but also moved beyond it, deliberately employing the conventions of folk song to speak about contemporary concerns. Parker presented "The Ballad of Springhill" as a particularly successful example of this strategy. Peggy's compositions on the second volume of *The New Briton Gazette* show her increasing skill in using the formal features of traditional song to express modern political ideas. "The Ballad of Jimmy

Wilson" takes the ballad format to tell a story of racial injustice that occurred in Alabama in 1958. "March with Us Today," written for the 1958 peace march to Aldermaston, uses a traditional English melody that Peggy learned as a child. The structure of "Hey Ho, Cook and Rowe!," a protest against high rents in London, is based on "The Devil's Nine Questions" (Child 1) and has the question-and-answer format and internal refrain of its traditional ancestor. Ewan's contributions to this album display the same facility. His "Come Live with Me," an updating of Christopher Marlowe's "The Passionate Shepherd to His Love," uses several traditional ballad commonplaces, and never has the phrase "until the rocks melt in the sun" been used more effectively—or more literally.

The year ended with a television broadcast entitled *Sing in the New*. Ewan and Peggy wrote the script and sang on the program, along with Louis Killen, Bob Davenport, and Enoch Kent. The broadcast closed with Peggy's New Year's song, "Come Fill Up Your Glasses," looking critically but hopefully toward the new year:

> Let's drink to our children, and let us prepare,
> A world where they'll live free from sorrow and care,
> A world where goodwill among men is the law,
> A world without fallout, a world without war.[27]

These lines must have resonated deeply with Ewan and Peggy that New Year's Eve: Peggy was six months pregnant. As they interviewed young people for their sixth Radio Ballad, they were gathering information for their future.

*On the Edge*, a Radio Ballad about teenagers, was broadcast on February 13, 1963. Peggy, Ewan, and Charles had interviewed teenagers throughout Britain: "the sons and daughters of labourers and company directors, of professors and railway porters, miners, filing-clerks and factory hands. There were schoolgirls and boys, apprentices, mods and rockers, waged and unwaged."[28] The young people eloquently described their hopes, expectations, and fears as they began the journey into adulthood. As one young woman says, "It's all new and like an adventure which you've got to face. . . . It could be something really beautiful or it could be a cliff edge." In some portions of the program, there is a sense of breathless expectancy, of being on one side of a door just waiting to step through, a bud about to burst into flower, a chrysalis ready to open. Other portions are not so happy, as the young people talk about being "the first generation that's grown up with the bomb hanging over [it]." One girl says matter-of-factly, "I believe that unless the position changes radically for the better, that I've got about 10 years to live. I would like that 10 years to be as fruitful as possible in many ways."[29]

It was a fascinating time to look at the young, then the largest generation in history, a generation that believed—as previous generations had not—that it would be fundamentally different from the generation that came before it. The inability to speak meaningfully to parents—and the necessity to break from parents—was painful for both: parents wondered why their children needed to take a path so radically different from their own, and children were frightened because there was no beaten path before them. In "Parent and Child," Ewan pays homage to both points of view:

> PARENT: Where is the trust, the respect that is owed,
>     What of the plans and the schemes?
> CHILD: The dream, it was fine—it was yours, though, not mine.
>     Now let me find my own dreams.[30]

Like *Song of a Road*, *On the Edge* sometimes works and sometimes doesn't. Perhaps Peggy was slightly too old and Ewan a whole generation too old to truly understand—and represent—the young people's point of view. As a forty-seven-year-old parent (and soon to be the parent of a teenager, as Hamish would turn thirteen in July), Ewan seems to show a bit too much sympathy for the older generation. His voice is beautiful and expressive, but no one could take it for the voice of a teenager. Peggy does better in this regard; her voice is youthful and sweet, recalling the clear, pristine tones in *Songs of Courting and Complaint*. The nineteen-year-old Peggy would have been breathtaking in this role. But it is too late; her voice has matured and taken on a sound uniquely her own.

Nonetheless, when *On the Edge* works, it is illuminating and poignant. A section on romance is particularly moving. Ewan created a remarkable adaptation of the traditional song "Long a-Growing," which tells of a highborn young woman married to a boy much younger than she. When the woman, who apparently had no choice in the matter, complains to her father, he comforts her by saying that though the boy is young, he is growing—and, presumably, will soon be a man and a proper husband to her. Ewan's version has different referents and a different tune, but the sense of being on the threshold of sexual maturity is the same:

> HE: Why should you be lonely when your company I am craving?
> SHE: Come back in a year or two when you have started shaving.

HE: I know a dive where we can jive and do a spot of raving.
BOTH: No more waiting, hesitating, time that we were going,
Oh, we're young but we're a-growing.[31]

Peggy and Ewan's concern for the children of the future is expressed by the phrase "the children of a troubled world," which occurs several times in the program. Yet these children—particularly those of the working class—had a much easier time than people of Ewan's age, thanks to the postwar welfare state. Surprisingly, *On the Edge* does not address the postwar breakdown of the class system, which ended the expectation that everyone knew his or her place and would be like his or her parents. Perhaps this omission occurred because the program wished to capture the point of view of the young people, who were far more interested in the future than the past. And perhaps it was because Peggy and Ewan were concerned with their own future, as they looked forward to the birth of their second child.

Ewan and Peggy's second child had been joyfully planned. But the arrival of a new member to the Seeger-MacColl household naturally required disruption and change. When Peggy told Betsy that she was pregnant, Betsy replied, "I'll tak' care o' yen child, no' twa."[32] Though this announcement somewhat dampened Peggy's enthusiasm, she and Ewan agreed that it was unwise for a seventy-seven-year-old woman to look after a newborn and an active four-year-old. In March, they hired Sandra Kerr, a young English folksinger whom they had met at the Singers Club, to live in and help with housework and child care. In addition to room, board, and pocket money, Sandra received voice lessons, lessons in sight reading, and general instruction in the art of singing folk songs. Her entrée into the household came none too soon. Calum Mac-Coll was born early, on March 27, 1963, exactly seven years to the day after his parents had met.

Sandra's presence in the household solved many problems but created others. Neill fell in love with her immediately. Fed up with his father's pre-occupation with work, his mother's pregnancy, and his grandmother's age, Neill turned "to Sandra with zest." Peggy told Charlie, "For two weeks, he didn't look at the rest of us. Never any more did he come bursting into our room with the papers and the post every morning. No kisses for anybody but Sandra. Nothing but impudence and rudeness for Betsy."[33] Betsy was hurt and upset, and she took it out on Sandra. Harsh words and sharp criticism of Sandra's housekeeping skills were constant. The weeks after Calum's birth were chaotic. Neill came down with chicken pox when Calum was only two days old. Peggy, confined to bed on doctors' orders for ten days, was trying desperately to take care of a newborn, make sure that Neill was taken care of but kept away from the baby, soothe Betsy's feelings, keep Sandra from leaving, and discuss the seventh Radio Ballad with Ewan, who was hard at work and trying to avoid domestic matters as much as possible. "Those two weeks," Peggy wrote to her father. "May they never be repeated."[34]

By late spring, things had settled down. Peggy and Ewan toured English folk clubs in June. The seventh Radio Ballad was done and ready to be broadcast in July; they had already begun work on the eighth Radio Ballad, about gypsies and Travellers. Peggy and Ewan had sufficient money and leisure to take a holiday in Romania with Neill. They happily left Calum with Betsy and Sandra while they were away. Betsy had changed her mind about taking care of two children and had fallen in love with Calum, who looked very much like Ewan.

The first half of the 1960s was the golden high noon of the folk revival. Peggy and Ewan had sensed this in 1961, when they published *Songs for the Sixties*, a songbook for the growing number of people who loved and sang folk music. In 1963, at barely twenty-eight years of age, Peggy was one of the folk revival's acknowledged leaders, and her many recordings from the early 1960s show her versatility. On some albums, she took a secondary role to Ewan, particularly on those of British music, such as *Popular Scottish Songs* and *Chorus from the Gallows*. On others, such as *A Lover's Garland*, a collection of British and American love songs, they were complete equals. On still others, Peggy was alone, singing the American music she knew best: *Peggy Seeger Sings and Plays American Folksongs for Banjo*, *Popular Ballads*, *A Song for You and Me*, and *The Best of Peggy Seeger*. With two healthy children, a loving partner, a comfortable home, and scores of interesting musical projects to work on, Peggy had never been so happy. As summer approached, she wrote to her father, "Everything in our lives seems to be blooming."[35]

# CHAPTER 12

# Beginnings
# and Endings

Love will help us teach each other.
Teacher, pupil, all in one.
And then we'll start a chain reaction,
What you know, love, pass it on.
Adding two and two together,
Learning to explain the world,
Pooling all the knowledge gained
And using it to change the world.

—Ewan MacColl, "Love for Love"

On the closing night of the Singers Club in 1991, Peggy sang, "As Moses led the Israelites, we led the folk revival," words that she had added to Ewan's long retrospective song, "The Ballad of the Travels," about the many venues where the Singers Club had met.[1] But in 1963, it might have been more accurate to say, "We led part of the folk revival." The folk revival had grown so large that it had diverse and frequently quarreling factions. Ewan and Peggy had a large and intensely loyal following; they had also inspired fierce criticism and open anger. The questions, "What is a folk song?" and "Who should sing it?" were at the heart of the controversy.

When the Singers Club opened in the summer of 1961, Ewan fired off an opening salvo in the pages of *Sing* magazine. He ended his article "Why I Am Opening a New Club" with the words, "We need standards. Already the race for the quick pound note is on in the folk song world. 'Quaint' songs, risqué songs, poor instrumentation and no-better-then [*sic*]-average voices—coupled with a lack of respect for the material: against these we will fight."[2] In December of that year, Eric Winter fired back, accusing Ewan of "arrogance" and "isolation" and declaring: "MacColl sets out to be (and easily could be) a leader on the folk scene. . . . How can he lead a revolt effectively, if he insists on sitting on his throne?"[3] Bert Lloyd staunchly defended Ewan: "Let the critics do even half as much for the revival as Mr. MacColl, and the situation will be happier, and standards of performance and repertory will improve."[4] The battle lines had been drawn.

Though many in the folk revival had reservations about Ewan's theories and the Singers Club policy, few questioned his talent. Even Eric Winter's polemic in *Sing* (quoted above) spoke ungrudgingly of Ewan's "very considerable merits as a performer."[5] Peggy was also admired for her taste, her instrumental virtuosity, and her songwriting ability. But she was still finding her way as a musician; her singing—and sometimes her instrumentation—received criticism as well as praise. The pure, crystal-clear, and relatively anonymous voice of *Songs of Courting and Complaint* had all but disappeared by the 1960s. When singing traditional American songs, she frequently adopted aspects of the hard, nasal, and vibratoless style of the Appalachians, a strategy that sometimes succeeded and sometimes failed. The choice had practical advantages: few folk clubs had microphones, and the technique allowed Peggy's light soprano to be heard in venues where it otherwise would have been lost. In a 1962 review of her album *Popular Ballads*, John Makepeace remarks on the advantages and disadvantages of her singing: "Peggy Seeger can and often has done better than 'Popular Ballads' (Folk-lyric, FL 120). With the exception of one track, the singing is inclined to be harsh, shrill and unexpressive. The over-decoration comes between the singer and the song and, sad to say, the accompaniment is often in the way too. . . . However, the exception, a lovely and sensitive singing of *The Four Maries*, shows Peggy at her very best."[6]

To some, however, Peggy was the American folksinger par excellence. In the spring of 1963, Earl Robinson, a former member of the Composers Collective and author of the folk revival classic "Joe Hill," was putting together the *Young Folk Song Book*, which featured some of the most prominent American folksingers of the day. The first artist in the book is Joan Baez, and the last is Peggy Seeger. (Sandwiched in between are Bob Dylan, Ramblin' Jack Elliott, the Greenbriar Boys, and the New Lost City Ramblers.) Earl Robinson transcribed most of the songs from recordings, and he found Peggy "so damn creative" that some of her songs "gave [him] tremendous trouble." "It . . . took a tremendous time to assimilate what you did [and] are doing," he wrote her. "For me, you are far and away the most important person in the book."[7] In the book, Robinson praises Peggy's banjo playing by showing that she is her mother's daughter, noting, "Many things that Peggy does turn out to be compositions in their own right."[8] His greatest praise is for her rendition of "The First Time Ever I Saw Your Face": "This is more than just a sweet, modern love song with some baroque adornments. Peggy Seeger has enriched and deepened it not only with her singing, but with an incredibly lovely, subtle, deceptively simple and moving accompaniment. She uses constantly changing arabesques and dissonances, in such a way that you can never be sure where the chord change takes place. Peggy's guitar becomes a harp. Ewan's words and tune become, in the finest sense, an art song."[9]

It is fitting that Joan Baez and Peggy Seeger are the beginning and the end of the *Young Folk Song Book*. They were the preeminent American women folksingers of the day, yet they were very different artistically. Joan Baez's glorious, soaring voice had made her the best-known woman folksinger in the English-speaking world. Though she played guitar and occasionally wrote songs, her vocal prowess completely overshadowed her instrumental and songwriting abilities. Peggy, on the other hand, was a proficient instrumentalist and songwriter as well as a singer, and she never felt that her voice was as strong or as good as some of her contemporaries'. Her self-criticism does have some merit: her singing voice is rich, warm, and extremely supple, yet it lacks the full resonance that would earn admiration as an instrument in its own right. This is, perhaps, her intent. After listening to her early recordings, one wonders if she deliberately chose not to develop her voice in a way that would call attention to itself. In the retrospective film *A Kind of Exile*, Peggy remarks: "I could very easily have been a Judy Collins or Joan Baez, although not with as good voices as theirs. I could have done what they have done, which is to romanticize the music, take the edge off it, take the style away from the singing."[10] This is perhaps the fundamental difference between Joan Baez and Peggy Seeger. After listening to Joan Baez sing, one says, "What a beautiful voice." After listening to Peggy Seeger sing, one says, "What a beautiful song."

The seventh Radio Ballad, *The Fight Game*, was broadcast on July 3, 1963. Its subject was professional boxing, and in some ways, it was similar to the first four Radio Ballads. Like them, *The Fight Game* had a coherence and musical energy that the pared-down fifth and sixth Radio Ballads had lacked. "From a technical point of view," Ewan observes in the liner notes, "*The Fight Game* was the most successful of the radio ballads."[11] At the time, Peggy described her arrangements for the program as "by far the most complex ones that [she] had] ever done."[12] Charles Parker considered it "in some ways . . . the most exciting" of the Radio Ballads, and critics gave it lavish praise.[13]

It would be hard to find two groups with less overlap than fans of boxing and fans of folk music. Yet this tension was used to advantage in *The Fight Game*, and the most unlikely subjects were turned into vibrant and evocative songs. The "Skipping Song," its tune taken from the traditional Jacobite song "The Wee Wee German Lairdie," describes one phase of the boxer's training: skipping rope. Its buoyant rhythms, pizzicato accompaniment, and sounds of men skipping rope create an almost irresistible sense of movement; it is nearly impossible to stay still while listening to the song. "Punching Shanty" and "Speedball Song," based on traditional sea shanties, also describe the training process and incorporate the sounds of men hitting punching bags, like a syncopated percussion section. Perhaps the most remarkable song is "The Day of the Fight," which takes place entirely in the mind of the boxer. Sung to the traditional Irish tune "The Spanish Lady," "The Day of the Fight" describes the boxer's thoughts from the time he wakes in the morning until he goes into the ring. Only here, in thoughts unspoken and unexpressed, can the boxer's tough exterior be breached. The beautiful melody and Peggy's gentle accompaniment suggest that tenderness and even insecurity may lie behind the game's surface brutality:

> Wonder how the other bloke's feeling,
> Wonder if I'm in his class?
> Got those butterflies, can't stop yawning,
> It's murder waiting for time to pass.
> Wish I'd never left the foundry,
> Wish that I was there today;
> Wish I'd never put the gloves on,
> Wish that I was miles away.[14]

Some of the boxers saw fighting as an essential component of masculinity, even a basic part of human nature. In the song "Life Is a Battle," which takes its melody from the traditional ballad "Gil Morice," boxing emerges as a metaphor for life:

> You fight for health and wealth
> And everything that life can give;
> So what's the odds if some get hurt?
> You've got to fight to live.[15]

Some boxers defended the game as less brutal than other forms of sanctioned violence, such as war. Others praised boxing as one of the few ways in which a poor boy could become rich. One man said that he would probably have been in jail if he had not become a boxer; his desire to fight was channeled into a socially acceptable form.

Like the first four Radio Ballads, *The Fight Game* focuses on a working-class occupation, but with a difference. The railway workers, road builders, fishermen, and miners were celebrated for the useful and productive work that they did. By contrast, *The Fight Game* takes a distinctly ironic tone toward its subject. Despite the hard work, discipline, and courage of the boxers, it is hard to imagine what socially useful function their profession fulfills. One of the most thoughtful and damning comments on boxing comes from a boxer himself:

> I don't think you can call professional boxing a sport. More like a spectacle, like cock-fighting and stuff like that. . . . In football, if a man's injured he's immediately taken from the field and he's treated. The object is not to injure anybody but to achieve an aim, one team or one person against another. When there's an injury it's like a catastrophe. But in boxing when there's an injury it's good. . . . It's a terrific knockout! But that man may never get up again. It's brutal and callous. It's sort of going back to Roman times, really, with the gladiators and things like that. And yet I'm going into it. It sounds mad in a way, doesn't it?[16]

By the end of 1963, Peggy and Ewan had assembled a group of young folk-singers (Charles Parker was the middle-aged exception) who wanted training in the art of singing folk songs. Jim Carroll, who joined the group in 1969, describes the group's formation:

> The group . . . was first started . . . at the suggestion of a number of people . . . who were not happy with what was happening in the Revival at the time and felt that Ewan should start classes for singers in order to push up the standards. The main tendencies in the Revival then seemed to be the Joan Baez, Bob Dylan soundalikes, or the school of thought that suggested that folk singing required no particular talent and all that was needed was that you should get up and sing as long as you got the words and tune more or less right (even this didn't matter as long as you were armed with enough jokes). . . . The idea of the group was that singers should meet and, with mutual constructive criticism, should work on each other's singing under the direction of Ewan and taking advantage of his considerable knowledge and experience.[17]

Because of the focus on mutual constructive criticism and self-criticism, Charles Parker suggested that the group be called the Critics Group.

Ewan developed a number of ambitious objectives for the group: to raise the standards of performance in the folk revival; to understand the songs and the culture from whence they came; to develop individual expertise in singing; to expand the singers' repertoire of songs; and to learn how songs are made by actually writing them.[18] The first step was to learn a singing style appropriate to folk music. Brian Pearson, who was a member of the Critics Group from the beginning, recalls: "A basic premise of the group's work was that, although folksongs had survived in the British Isles, many of the elements that made up the style proper for their performance had been lost. By studying source singers from here and from around the world, we hoped to rescue or recreate a stylistic and technical basis for performing folk material."[19] The group listened to recordings of traditional singers from the British Isles, such as Harry Cox, Sam Larner, Joe Heaney, Maggie McDonagh, and Elisabeth Cronin, then moved on to recordings of traditional singers from Bulgaria, Italy, Azerbaijan, and other countries. According to Ewan, "The object of the exercise [was] to make the voice supple, able to do what you wanted it to do. The object was not to end up singing like McDonagh, Heaney, or Cronin. It was to develop the muscle of the voice and then move on to your own particular style."[20]

The group met on Tuesday evenings in Ewan and Peggy's home in Beckenham. Most members of the group had full-time jobs and had to travel a considerable distance to reach Beckenham, so the group required intense dedication. Brian Pearson remembers: "Ewan dominated the sessions. He was an astonishingly fluent and persuasive speaker, with, it seemed, an encyclopaedic knowledge of everything. And everything he didn't know, he made up. I'd been a voracious reader from an early age, but nobody among my family or friends was. Ewan was the first intellectual I'd ever come across— and a self-educated one at that! At last, someone interested in ideas: I was enthralled."[21] Ewan may have dominated the sessions, but Peggy did a great deal of the work. She did most of the behind-the-scenes organizing and took notes at the sessions. As coleader of the group, Peggy gave lectures on sight singing, vocal decoration, and instrumental accompaniment. "She was a better 'teacher' than Ewan—with more of a sense of true interaction and awareness of who she was talking to," recalls Frankie Armstrong, an English folksinger who joined the group in 1964 after an introduction from Louis Killen.[22] In addition, Peggy wrote a paper on the use of vocal decoration in traditional singing, which the Critics Group used as a guide. Yet despite the countless and varied tasks that she performed, she remained the second-in-command, willingly yielding prime leadership to Ewan. Frankie Armstrong recalls the dynamic: "Peggy . . . was vivacious and attractive with a driving energy that wouldn't let her be still. She would sit by Ewan while he expounded his ideas, always with a piece of crochet or needlework in her quick-moving fingers, until she was required to take up one of her many instruments to play and sing. Then we would realize what a gifted and knowledgeable woman she was."[23]

The Critics Group functioned as a master class. Each week, one singer would prepare a selection of songs and sing them as though he or she were performing in a folk club. Afterward, the group provided feedback. All aspects of the singer's performance were scrutinized: pitch, tone, demeanor, how the song was introduced, and so on. As coleaders of the group, Ewan and Peggy did not submit their own singing to the group's criticism. In retrospect, Peggy thinks this may have been a mistake, as it suggested that Ewan and she were beyond criticism.

Ewan also brought his vast theatrical experience to the Critics Group. Particularly important were the theories of the Russian theater director Constantine Stanislavski.[24] Stanislavski's major innovation was to require actors to find within themselves the emotional truth of what they were performing. Earlier directors had told actors to shake their fists and narrow their eyes to indicate anger; Stanislavski had his actors remember a time when they had been angry and then re-create that emotion while they acted. In similar fashion, Ewan instructed the Critics Group members to concentrate on the inner, rather than outer, aspects of performance. While they sang, they were to think about the content of the song and the emotions it encompassed, rather than concentrating on vocal prowess or wondering about the effect on the audience. Not only did this make the songs ring true to the listeners, it also kept the singers from becoming bored when singing the same song multiple times.

Knowing the subtext to the lines was also crucial to Stanislavski's theory and to Ewan's teaching. The application of "the idea of 'if'" required the singer to develop an imagined backstory for the song and then sing the song as if the story were true. Peggy recalls the effectiveness of this technique:

He did one extraordinary class with Sandra Kerr. I'll never forget. She said, "I just love the song . . . about the gypsies coming to take the rich man's wife ["The Gypsy Laddie"]. . . . But I'm getting tired of it." . . . So he asked her to sing it. And she sang it, and it was competent. But it was lacking something. So he said, "Suppose you're a woman brought up in a mining village. You marry a miner and have children. You spend your life in near poverty and the dirt and dust that coal bestows on all the miners. You have a beautiful daughter. You want her to have all the things you didn't have. She catches the eye of the son of a grocer, a class way above yours. She marries him, has a beautiful son. This reflects on you and your life becomes different, better. Then your daughter runs off with a gypsy. You are plunged into grief. If (and the operative word here is 'if') you were that woman how would you sing this song?" Sandra sang it and wow! . . . Never heard her sing like this. Sandra's got a good imagination. She responds very well to direction. . . . When you sing it, your brain is working. And somebody hearing it would not know that that was exactly the story. But they would know that you were thinking a truthful story that you utterly believe in. . . . And he ran her through three or four scenarios, and each time she sang it differently.[25]

The other method that Ewan brought from his theater days was the theory of efforts, taken from the work of Rudolf Laban. "All movement, and the voice is movement," explains Peggy, "has three facets: it has direction, . . . it has a weight, and it has a speed."[26] A direction can be categorized as either direct or indirect; weight is heavy or light; speed is either fast or slow. These three facets can be combined in eight possible ways (or "efforts"), each with a name: thrust, press, glide, float, dab, flick, slash, or wring. For example, a thrust is direct, heavy, and fast, while a press is direct, heavy, and slow. A vocal thrust is found in a marching or declaiming song; its tone is direct, its timbre heavy, and its tempo fast. "If I sing thrusting songs at you for ten minutes, you're going to feel as if you are being attacked," says Peggy. "And if I sang nothing but floating songs at you for twenty minutes, you'd soon be asleep."[27] So the theory of efforts was used to analyze and improve a singer's style and to vary the singer's repertoire.

Though all members of the Critics Group were expected to critique one another's performances, Ewan usually had the last word, and like many directors, he was not gentle with his criticism. "Theoretically, all were equal," recalls Brian Pearson. "In practice, Ewan was much more equal than the rest."[28] A recording from October 1964 shows the dynamic of the group. After one member had sung and been criticized by his fellow Critics Group members, Ewan took over:

> You might think I've been very hard with Charles. I have because you were too soft. . . . Tone is the problem. . . . He got it in the last song and he got much nearer to it than he's ever been before, but this doesn't mean that we have to kind of lay down on our backs and say what a brilliant performance as some of you did, because this does not help him. Charles is a grown man and capable of taking criticism, and if you don't criticise each other, you won't help each other, you're playing at it unless you criticise each other.[29]

How Ewan responded to criticism of his own work and ideas is the subject of some debate. "If ever one or more of us attempted to criticise him—however justifiably, he could be vitriolic and often wiped the floor with the person," remembers Frankie Armstrong.[30] By contrast, Jim Carroll and Pat Mackenzie recall: "There were several occasions where Ewan's ideas were challenged, sometimes strongly, without rancour. Ewan may not always have acted on them, but criticism within the Group went both ways—not every suggestion made by Ewan or the rest of the Group was taken up by the recipient. . . . Ewan was an extremely charismatic figure with a great deal of knowledge and Group members tended to defer to him voluntarily—perhaps one of the weaknesses of the work."[31] As coleader of the Critics Group, Peggy was free to challenge Ewan's dicta, but she did so only in the gentlest fashion while in the presence of others; serious criticism was saved for private discussion. Brian Pearson remarks:

> Ewan and Peggy had very clear ideas of what folk music was all about and how it should be performed. No other approach was tolerated. . . . At the time, I felt Peggy to be even more of an ultra-Orthodox MacCollite than Ewan himself. She came across at times as rather severe and dogmatic and was fiercely protective of him and the "party line.". . . Looking back, I can see that she must have been in a very difficult position. She was not much older than the rest of us and the strength of her relationship with Ewan was palpable. Underneath his bravura exterior Ewan was deeply vulnerable and Peggy was very good at protecting him.[32]

Ultimately, resentment over the dynamics of the Critics Group would prove its undoing, but that was many years in the future. In the early years, most Critics Group members accepted its strict discipline; those who did not left. "There was so much to be gained from the group," recalls Brian Pearson. "A lot of the time it was a brilliant place to be."[33]

Peggy fully agreed with Ewan that folk music is a product of the class not in power: peasants in an agricultural society, the working class in an industrial one. The political context of folk music was another factor explored by the Critics Group, and for Peggy it deepened her understanding of the music she had always loved. In a letter to her father, she remarked:

> I don't ever remember feeling sorry for Barbara Allen in the way I do now, ever really grasping her predicament emotionally. The songs were lovely toys, a family toy I suppose. . . . But there was never a continuity of feeling leading from one to the other song, never an identity with the characters in the songs.

I was born into the wrong class for that kind of feeling—I feel sure, at least from my experiences with the two folk scenes (here and in America) that the only people who do make this identity with the folksongs are working people. . . . I can see how folk music proper is the weapon of a class, I can see who "the folk" really are. And to me, this is where the American revival seems to have gone off the track.[34]

Not all working-class people agreed that folk songs were political expressions. In the retrospective film *Folk Britannia*, Shirley Collins remarks, "I had always thought that MacColl was just hijacking English or British folk music for his own political ends, and I minded that. It didn't belong to him; it belonged to ordinary working-class people, of which I was one."[35] The battle over the political use of folk song, which had raged since the eighteenth century, would not end during the golden days of the folk revival.

On April 17, 1964, the final Radio Ballad, *The Travelling People*, was broadcast. The Radio Ballads were expensive to produce, and the BBC had decided that it could no longer afford them. Radio was losing ground to television: in 1954 more people had radios than televisions; the reverse was true a decade later. The left-wing orientation of the Radio Ballads also made them unpopular with some BBC decision makers. Though deeply disappointed, Charles, Ewan, and Peggy knew that *The Travelling People* would be the Radio Ballads' swansong.

In many ways, *The Travelling People* is the best of the Radio Ballads. It has no false notes, no places where the music or the actuality drags. It contains some of the best songs in the entire series. Its subject is perfect for a program filled with folk songs, for the Travellers of Britain and Ireland still sang many traditional songs in 1964, including the great ballads collected by Francis James Child. The singers for *The Travelling People* included Peggy, Ewan, the traditional Irish singer Joe Heaney, the young English folksinger (and Critics Group member) John Faulkner, and the Travellers Belle and Jane Stewart.[36]

In the early 1960s, there were many nomadic and seminomadic groups of people in Britain and Ireland. Some claimed kinship with the pan-European Roma, while others considered themselves ethnically and linguistically distinct. Some used the much-romanticized, much-maligned word *gypsy*, a term usually reserved for Roma but sometimes applied to British and Irish Travellers as well. Some felt that the word *tinker*, a term virtually never applied to Roma, was derogatory, while others used it to refer to themselves. Ewan and Peggy always used the term *Traveller*, since the people whom they knew used it for themselves. In their song collection *Travellers' Songs from England and*

*Scotland*, Ewan and Peggy write: "The continuing debate among gypsiologists as to which group of people should, or should not, be awarded the title of *true Gypsies* is one in which we have no desire to participate. For the purpose of this collection of songs, we have chosen to designate our informants as Travellers."[37]

The gypsy, with the Jew, is the quintessential European Other, a fact of which the Travellers were keenly aware.[38] *The Travelling People* is as much a study of prejudice as it is an examination of the lives of traveling people. The program begins with British folklore that is distinctly anti-Traveller, including the children's rhyme, "My mother said I never should / play with the gypsies in the wood." Ewan's "There's No Place for Me" uses images of nature to suggest that all living creatures should have a place in the world; to deny such a place to Travellers is unnatural:

> On a rock on the shore is the cormorant's dwelling,
> The wild warbling blackbird has its nest in the tree—
> The birds of the sky and the fish of the ocean,
> Each has its own place—but there's no place for me.[39]

Others use natural imagery with less sympathy. Non-Travellers interviewed for the program compare Travellers to starlings that arrive with the seasons "and they're making a mess." One man refers to Travellers as "the maggots of society."[40]

Travellers have a rich store of tales, including origin stories about themselves. One woman links British Travellers to the Battle of Culloden; one man goes back to the Bible and casts the Travellers as children of Ishmael. "Our Savior traveled," says one traveling woman. "He was born in a manger among straw. His mother carried him on a little donkey's back."[41] She is not the only person to present Jesus as a traveling man. Ewan uses this image to great effect in "Moving on Song," inspired by the actuality of a traveling woman whose family was forced to leave its encampment even though she was in labor:

> The winter sky was hung with stars
> And one shone brighter than the rest;
> The wise men came, so stern and strict,
> And brought the order to evict.
> "You'd better get born in someplace else,
> So move along, get along!
> Move along, get along!
> Go! Move! Shift!"[42]

Many of the songs have a sweet nostalgia for bygone days. In 1964, traveling seemed a dying way of life, due to restrictive legislation, the loss of traditional campsites, and the inconvenience and harassment that Travellers endured. "Freeborn Man" ends on a word of farewell:

> All you freeborn men of the travelling people,
> Every tinker, rolling stone and Gypsy rover:
> Winds of change are blowing, old ways are going,
> Your travelling days will soon be over.[43]

But folkways, like folk songs, may prove to be surprisingly hardy, even when they seem to be dying out. In 2001, Peggy reported that Travellers had begun to sing "Freeborn Man" with a different final line: "Your travelling days will never be over." Peggy and Ewan thought they were recording the final days of Britain's nomads; decades later, nomadism is on an upswing. "The despair of the sixties has been replaced by a mood of optimism," Peggy notes.[44] Travellers are still traveling.

Prejudice, discrimination, and persecution of Travellers are the subjects of the final portion of the program. One Traveller compares the treatment of Travellers in Britain to the treatment of African Americans in the southern United States. "We're hounded the same as Hitler hounded the Jews," says another.[45] Gypsies were also victims of the Nazis' death machine, a fact that Ewan uses in a bone-chilling song near the end of the program:

> Some o' them were gassed at Belsen,
> Some at Buchenwald did fa',
> Ithers kenned the Auschwitz ovens,
> Men and women, bairns and a'.[46]

The use of Scots words for a distinctly non-Scottish experience draws a parallel between the treatment of British Travellers and the fate of their Continental counterparts—the Roma, Jews, and other Others who perished in the death camps. At first, this seems an exaggeration. As Peter Cox says, "You hear this and think: Come on, Ewan, you're going too far here, this is England. Then you hear the last words of this last Radio Ballad, and the complaint dies in your throat."[47] The final words come from an interview with Harry Watton, a Birmingham alderman, who remarks, "How far does it come in your mind before you say I have done everything I possibly can and I will help the broad mass of these people. But there are some I can do nothing with whatever. Doesn't the time arise in one's mind when one has to say, all right, one has to exterminate the impossibles. I know all that leads to in one's mind, Nazi-ism, who is it next: the Gypsies, the tinkers, the Jews, the colored man. I don't accept that really on these particular people."[48] Next we hear the soft voice of Charles Parker (the only time in the entire series when an interviewer's voice is heard), confused, sure that there has been some mistake, giving Watton every opportunity to take back the frightful thing he has said: "Exterminate's a terrible word—you can't really mean that." "Why not?" asks Watton.[49] Thus the Radio Ballad series ended.

Though the Radio Ballad series was over, Peggy and Ewan continued to write and perform for the mass media throughout 1964. They wrote music for the radio series *Landmarks*, produced by Charles Parker, which told the history of humanity in six broadcasts and began with Ewan's stirring song "The Ballad of Accounting." They wrote and performed in the television program *An Impression of Love*, which ended with Peggy singing "The First Time Ever I Saw Your Face." They worked with Charles Parker on the twelve-part radio series *The Song Carriers*, which featured traditional singers and showcased Ewan's theories about folk music. They also focused much creative energy on live performance. This focus would lead Peggy in a direction totally new to her, though utterly familiar to Ewan: theater.

# CHAPTER 13

# Different Stages

Each new development in the theatre, however
slight that development may be, makes it necessary
to evaluate and re-evaluate the immediate past.
—Ewan MacColl, "The Evolution of a
   Revolutionary Theatre Style"

For art to be "unpolitical" means only to ally itself
with the "ruling" group.
—Bertolt Brecht, *A Short Organum for the Theatre*

Peggy's meticulously detailed program book for 1964 shows an impressive number of activities at a large number of venues. Ewan and Peggy toured extensively throughout Britain and sang at the Singers Club nearly every week. Peggy particularly enjoyed performing in folk clubs, where "the audience knows what it's getting, there is a lot of backchat and informality and, most important, the audiences are critical. . . . Wonderful atmosphere in these clubs, and you can literally sing anything."[1] In addition, they frequently gave lectures, performances, and classes on folk music. They tried to schedule a tour of the United States, but Ewan was denied a visa. Peggy was only mildly disappointed, as she explained to her father: "To tell you the truth, you are the only thing that makes me want to come at all. I am beginning to hate leaving home and the children. I am beginning to love working in one place, learning one milieu, working constantly with one group of dedicated people. To travel around singing is not really rewarding artistically."[2]

By the early 1960s, most of the organizational work of the Singers Club was done by the London Co-operative Society. The English Co-operative Society was deeply involved in political and cultural work, and its democratic, egalitarian philosophy was completely in line with Ewan and Peggy's principles. In 1964, the Co-operative Society celebrated its 150th anniversary. To honor this milestone, Ewan wrote *Ours the Fruit*, a play—with music—about the history of the Co-operative Society. Directed by Ewan, with musical direction and arrangement by Peggy, *Ours the Fruit* was staged on a Sunday afternoon at the Theatre Royal, Drury Lane. Musicians from the Critics Group and the Radio Ballads participated as singers and instrumentalists. Peggy conducted the orchestra and the singers while simultaneously playing the banjo.

Theater was a new experience for most Critics Group members. Brian Pearson recalls: "This was, I think, the first time that any of us had trod a proper stage and the Drury Lane one is enormous."[3] It was the first time that Ewan had written and directed a play since leaving Theatre Workshop. Encouraged and inspired by the success of *Ours the Fruit*, Ewan and Peggy decided to form a folk theater with the Critics Group. Their second theatrical venture was an updated mumming play titled *St. George and the Dragon*. Mumming plays have been performed in the British Isles since the Middle Ages, typically at Christmas time. Like much folk drama, these plays are frequently performed in private homes and on the streets rather than in theaters. The dramatis personae are stock characters, such as the hero, the doctor, and the fool, and the actors present their lines in rhyme and in song. Usually the hero fights several foes before he is killed and then brought back to life.[4] In England, the hero of the mumming play is often the English patron saint, St. George, and his foe is the legendary Dragon.

Peggy and Ewan's updated mumming play was a protest against the Vietnam War. The St. George character was presented as a tough motorcyclist clad in leather (played by Ted Culver, a London butcher who really did ride a motorcycle), and his foe was a warmongering American general. Ewan wrote the script and directed the play; Peggy was musical director, and she and Ewan wrote the songs. Frankie Armstrong and Peggy played Billy and Jack, the two fools who introduce the play and sing narrative portions throughout the performance. Frankie remembers, "We were very physical and playful and that was a joy. I have an image of a great wide vivacious grin on Peggy's face as we ran around singing and acting."[5] The play began with Peggy's song "Billy and George," which praises both the hero and the Everymen who support him:

> When David faced Goliath
> We were standing there to guide him;
> When Georgie killed the dragon
> It was us that stood beside him.[6]

*St. George and the Dragon* was initially performed at the Singers Club in the spring of 1965, then at folk clubs and street performances throughout England. As is common in folk drama, the line between performers and audience sometimes became blurred. At the first performance, the audience cheered the hero, booed the villain, and cried out, "Come on, George, you can whip him" during the fight.[7] Peggy recalls a performance at "a very tough club" in Wolverhampton, a place frequented by motorcyclists who typically jeered at folksingers. At this performance, however, the motorcyclists were mesmerized "because one of them was the hero."[8] As the American general prepared to attack St. George, one of the motorcyclists in the audience called out, "He's behind you! Turn round!" (His friends were able to keep him from charging the stage.) Brian Pearson recalls a performance that took place "outdoors in one of those 1960s developments somewhere near Tower Bridge—all high-rise concrete building and 'piazzas' that probably looked like a modernist dream on the architect's drawings, but turned out to be grim windswept desolations of chip papers and dog shit. Across the square there was a group of policemen with German shepherds. Every time St. George fought (which was frequently, this being a mumming play) the dogs went crazy, barking hysterically and trying to attack the actors."[9] The mumming play was so successful that Ewan wrote a second version in Lowland Scots.

As Ewan and Peggy began to concentrate on theater, their film work lessened. The BBC considered them too political to employ on a regular basis, though occasionally Peggy—considered the less political member of the duo—was offered BBC gigs on her own. The National Coal Board underwent new management, which no longer wanted Ewan and Peggy to provide music to accompany its monthly films. They continued to tour throughout Britain, primarily in folk clubs, so much so that Neill and Calum began to complain about their frequent absences from home. Touring now provided the majority of their income. It also solidified Ewan and Peggy's reputation, as Peggy noted in a letter to her father: "Due to our travelling so much and exerting so much influence we are at last considered the two main folksingers in the country and we can draw a packed-hall wherever we go. And when you think that we put the emphasis on ballads and serious music, this is a feat."[10] They had planned to tour the United States in 1965 and went to the U.S. embassy, traversing lines of protesters against the Vietnam War, to fill out the necessary paperwork. But while doing so, Ewan suddenly said, "I'm not going." American policy in Vietnam so appalled them that they chose to boycott the United States. "We threw the forms away and went out and joined the picket line," Peggy wrote to her father. Peggy felt that her home country had become "enemy territory," and it would be years before she would return.[11]

Peggy and Ewan had developed such a complete symbiosis that she could remark, "People rarely say our names apart because we are considered a unit, for better or for worse."[12] The *Ewan MacColl- Peggy Seeger Songbook*, published in 1963, presented just such a partnership: each was given equal billing, and the book contained songs by Ewan, songs by Peggy, and songs by both. But sometimes, Peggy displayed a slight deference to her beloved mentor—reminiscent of the deference that Heloïse paid to Abelard, or Beauvoir to Sartre, or Ruth Crawford to Charles Seeger. As Peggy explained in a letter to her father, "His talents are so diverse that he can tackle almost anything in the musical, literary or theatre world. And of course, my work complements his perfectly—he has the large ideas, I can type them up, correct the spelling! He writes the songs, but cannot accompany them, notate them or arrange them, which I can do. He hates writing letters, I don't mind writing letters. And so on—in the small things that create a partnership."[13] This deference is apparent in their 1965 publication *Folk Songs and Ballads of Scotland*. Though Peggy transcribed and edited all the songs, only Ewan's name appears on the front cover and title page, where he is listed as compiler and editor. A photograph of Ewan and a biographical paragraph about him appear on the copyright page. Peggy is listed as music editor, and her name appears briefly in Ewan's biographical paragraph, but there is no picture of her, though the picture of Ewan originally contained both of them and has been cropped so that only Ewan appears.

Despite Ewan and Peggy's status as musical unit, Peggy continued to do projects on her own. In 1964, she published the songbook *Folk Songs of Peggy Seeger*. Most of the chosen pieces are traditional Anglo-American songs, while a few, such as Sarah Ogan Gunning's "Girl of Constant Sorrow," are twentieth-century compositions based on traditional models. (Interestingly, the songbook contains no songs *by* Peggy Seeger.) In the introduction, Peggy writes, "A folk song belongs to no one in particular. It is the creation of no one person any more than history is the creation of one general. . . . The singer is but one link in the chain and if this is a book of 'my' songs that means that this is the way one singer has treated the common heritage before handing it on."[14] She suggests that revival singers listen to traditional singers in order to learn vocal and instrumental technique but not try to imitate them slavishly: "Observe the processes with which they create and imitate the processes rather than the final creation. In this way the non-ethnic singer can create within the folk sphere, without overstepping the disciplines of the folk idiom."[15]

Peggy also worked with other American folk artists. In 1964, she recorded an album with Tom Paley, who, with Mike Seeger and John Cohen, had been an original member of the New Lost City Ramblers, though by this time he had been replaced by Tracy Schwarz. The album, *Who's Going to Shoe Your Pretty Little Foot?*, received a glowing review in *Sing* magazine:

> This is the true voice of Peggy, which has somehow not quite shone through many of the records she has done in recent years, but which is here, really HERE, on this disc. . . . The result shows as clearly as any folk record ever could THAT A GOOD RECORD DOESN'T NEED TO BE FILLED WITH SMART-ALEC GIMMICKRY TO BE ENTERTAINING—THAT GOOD HONEST SINGING AND PLAYING NEEDS NO FACETIOUS INTRODUCTIONS TO "APOLOGISE" TO AND PREPARE THE AUDIENCE FOR WHAT IS TO FOLLOW. ON THE CONTRARY, A JOB DONE AS WELL AS THIS IS IT'S [*sic*] OWN JUSTIFICATION.[16]

In 1965, her brother Mike came to England, and Peggy and he gave a sold-out concert at Cecil Sharp House, headquarters of the English Folk Dance and Song Society.

The success of Peggy and Ewan's updated mumming play solidified their plans to form a theater company with the Critics Group. "After all," explained Peggy, "a ballad is a dramatic form and one's identification with a ballad is, it seems to me, similar to that of an actor with his role."[17] In the autumn of 1965, Ewan was inspired by another midwinter tradition, the Festival of Fools. A medieval descendent of the Roman Saturnalia, the Festival of Fools was a pan-European inversion festival in which those in power were criticized and mocked by their social inferiors. Herbert Thurston has called it "a brief social revolution, in which power, dignity or impunity is conferred for a few hours upon those ordinarily in a subordinate position."[18] Bawdy, irreverent, filled with music and wordplay, the Festival of Fools was a challenge to the powerful from the powerless.[19]

During the Middle Ages, the prime seat of power had been the Catholic Church, and hence it was the prime target of the Festival of Fools' mockery and criticism. During the Renaissance, the reins of power had passed to the state, where it had remained. Therefore, Peggy and Ewan's Festival of Fools involved political, rather than religious, criticism and satire. Their first production ran for the twelve days of Christmas, from December 26, 1965 (Boxing Day), to January 6, 1966 (Epiphany or Old Christmas). The play chronicled and lampooned the news of the preceding year, one month at a time. Each month was introduced by a traditional rhyme or folk saying, such as "The blackest month of all the year / Is the month of Janiveer."[20] Though Ewan wrote the script, the entire group was involved in choosing the news items on which it was based: "All the class went through newspapers of the year, cutting out political, economic, curious bits of information, and Ewan sat down for six weeks and put together a play, THE FESTIVAL OF FOOLS. . . . It is held together by weather lore and a recital of old customs taking us from month to month and could best be called a political satire based on folklore."[21] The festival lampooned events that had been reported with great seriousness in the press and shone a cold light on matters that had been underreported and neglected. In the late autumn, Ewan closeted himself in his study, chain-smoking and drinking myriad cups of coffee, while he wrote the script; Peggy and he wrote the songs that were an integral part of the production. Ewan directed the Festival of Fools, while Peggy served as musical director and performer.

The Festival of Fools was initially performed in the New Merlin's Cave, then home of the Singers Club, in a room that had a stage at one end and seating for 170 people. The group added two temporary stages and set up a lighting and sound console in the unused bar area. Charles Parker, utilizing the skills that had served him so well in the Radio Ballads, was in charge of sound effects. The play began with the actors singing a wassail song. Then they elected a king of the revels (traditionally called the "Lord of Misrule" in England and the "Abbott of Unreason" in Scotland) and crowned their king with a wassail bowl. A press release for the 1965–66 Festival of Fools describes some of the topics in that year's production: "The criticism of circumcision, a survey of Bedfordshire public lavoratories, the furore over Senegal's bare breasts and the Dublin gravediggers' strike, form a core for the jesting, whilst bitter and direct statement of fact on the 'democratic' activities of President Johnson, and the escalation of the war in Vietnam provide the trenchant and sobering comment. Similarly, the expedient and erratic activities of the British Government over the past year do not escape MacColl's scalpel."[22]

Using techniques similar to the ones he had used in Theatre Workshop, Ewan turned his band of young singers into athletic and musically adept actors. He was very proud of their accomplishments: "These singers became absolutely first class and could have earned their living in any theatre in the country."[23] Brian Pearson, who played the narrator in all but the final Festival of Fools, recalls the process: "The Festival of Fools was a big commitment. We rehearsed several evenings a week and all of us had full-time jobs. But we were young and committed and, when we weren't cold, tired, bored, hungry or demoralised by Ewan's outbursts, the whole thing was a blast. Ewan was a brilliant but dictatorial director. It was fascinating to watch him working. He turned us, a bunch of theatrical amateurs, into very respectable actors very quickly."[24] Audiences were enthusiastic, and the Festival of Fools received glowing reviews from the press. "Even Tory journalists have reported it favourably as a professional and unique show," remarked Peggy.[25]

The Critics Group would present a Festival of Fools each year through the winter of 1972. "Each year's show was better than the last," writes Brian Pearson, "but all would have benefited from cutting. . . . At its best, his [Ewan's] writing was terrific: pointed, funny, moving. At its worst it was long-winded, turgid and hectoring."[26] While Ewan raced against time to finish the script, Peggy organized the rehearsals, informed Critics Group members of the schedule, and kept track of endless script revisions. She sent periodic newsletters to the cast, covering every conceivable part of the rehearsal and production process: casting, scripts, costumes, rehearsal schedules, rehearsal venues (usually with directions and sometimes with train schedules), publicity, voice and movement classes, and so on. She color-coded the blizzard of paper she generated (white for the script, yellow for casting information, green for address lists, blue for newsletters, and pink for rehearsal schedules) and issued directives that were alternately brusque and charming (and sometimes both at the same time). For example, she addressed the first newsletter of 1971 "to all fools in the Festival," ordered those in need of vocal training to take lessons from Sandra (and baldly stated who "those in need" were), and reminded the cast that changes to the script would be frequent: "Please alter your script AS THESE CUTS COME IN, otherwise you will find yourself in a state of unparalleled confusion."[27] She was solicitous and protective of Ewan's time, warning the cast, "It is unsafe to give messages to Ewan during production. Call Peggy for this—do not give him little slips of paper for her, or ask him to bring anything, etc. His mind is too full of production."[28] Like Ewan, she delighted in lush wordplay: in the newsletter for December 7, 1971, she noted that certain scenes had been "cut, slashed, to be omitted, deleted, rejected, ejected, banished, vanished, struck out, chucked out, ousted, boosted, eliminated, evacuated, expelled, (see Roget's Thesaurus, no. 300) unconditionally."[29]

The festivals' topics varied from year to year. Peggy's song "It's All Happening Now" opened the 1968 festival and lists some of the subjects that came under the Critics Group's microscope that year:

In Greece, the colonels are holding fast and they won't let go.
Rhodesia hangs black civilians, who says No?
South Africa, Malaysia, America, Spain,
It'll keep on going till we break the chain, for
It's all happening now,
It's still happening now.[30]

A highly acclaimed sketch from 1968 was "The Shithouse Saga," about a hostile takeover in the toilet paper industry. The sketch explained and critiqued the nature of monopoly capitalism and took place in a men's lavatory. The actors wore bowler hats and faced imaginary urinals, their backs to the audience, singing their lines in operatic fashion. The 1967 festival included a sketch about the German National Democratic Party, a far-right political party that had many former Nazis in positions of leadership and had won several local elections in 1965 and 1967. The sketch is primarily a conversation between an unnamed British journalist and the leader of the National Democratic Party, Adolf von Thadden (with some assistance from his underlings, Gottfried, Baldur, and Eva). Using fractured German and referencing Germany's Romantic folklore tradition (which had been used with deadly intent by the Nazis), Ewan deals satire with a savage hand:

> REPORTER: A number of statements made by you appear to correspond almost
>     word for word with passages from "Mein Kampf".
> VON THADDEN: "Mein Kampf?" Vass iss "Mein Kampf?" Eva! Diss "Mein
>     Kampf"—has it for you significance?
> EVA: Nein, kleine fader.
> REPORTER: O, come sir, you must be familiar with Hitler's notorious bible.
> VON THADDEN: Ah-h-h-h! DASS iss der Mein Kampf—for ein moment it had
>     mein mind verloren. You must forgiff me. Mein kopf iss of plans full for
>     starting a wood-working class in Vest-phalia. To make der vooden toys,
>     you know.
> REPORTER: There's a great feeling of unease generally, Herr von Thadden.
>     For example, your insistent demand that Germany should be allowed to
>     develop nuclear weapons . . .
> VON THADDEN: But . . . ! Would you leave us poor peace-loving people of the
>     West-Faderland-unt-Marching Society absolutely defenceless?[31]

There is no humor in an equally effective sketch from the same year: a trial of the ancient Greek playwrights for subversion. This sketch was inspired by a news item from June: the Greek government had in fact banned production of classical plays on the grounds that they were subversive.

While many of the sketches focused on topical incidents, the festivals did not ignore larger themes. A monologue from 1971 describes the nature and history of British colonialism, written in a jargon that sounds as if it had been jointly composed by Karl Marx, James Joyce, Jonathan Swift, and Rabelais. In this sketch, Ewan mangles the names of several prominent Conservative politicians: Reginald Maudling; Robert Carr; and Quintin Hogg, Lord Hailsham:

> As a notion, we, the Brutish peep-hole have long been famous intrepid eggs-ploders and colonists. The secret of our success lay in our ability to divide and roll; they divided and we rolled—over them. The effectiveness of this policy has been nowhere more apparent than in Northern Ireland, or (as we prefer to call it) ANCIENT OLDSTER. . . .
> Even the most brilliant of our statesmen—and let us be quite clear that no other period in the history of mankind (or any other kind) has produced such giants of intellect—even THEY have failed to clarify the position in Ancient Oldster. It is, of course, true that they have been busy with more important affairs. . . . The Supra-Tory of Steak for Home Affairs, Original Muddling, has been minding his own business, or businesses; while the Lord Chinchilla—Lord Hailscum—better known as Rintin Hogg the Wonder Dogg, has been hard at it memorising extempore witticisms for the next general erection; the Right Gonorrheal Robber Carr has, of course, been toiling away at his Unemployment Productivity Program.[32]

The youth movement received both censure and praise in the festivals. The middle-aged Ewan criticized the nonpolitical hippie culture, with its emphasis on sex, drugs, and personal satisfaction:

> Go, man, go, shake your bells and count your beads,
> It's what you feel, not what you do, quiescence is the creed,
> The problems of the universe could drive you round the bend,
> So contemplate your navel and you'll find peace in the end.[33]

On the other hand, the much younger Peggy had respect for the youthful militants who tore up the streets of Paris and protested the Vietnam War on American college campuses. The 1971 Festival showcased her song "We Are the Young Ones," which was later taken up and sung by young people throughout Britain. The song concludes with words that challenge the older generation and reflect Peggy and Ewan's Maoist phase:

> We don't believe in profits. We don't believe in shares.
> We don't believe in magic. We don't believe in prayers.

Turn around and face us! The future has begun—
From you we learned that power grows from the barrel of a gun.[34]

Ewan and Peggy also integrated the Critics Group into several projects for the mass media. Critics Group members worked with Ewan and Peggy on *Landmarks*, *An Impression of Love*, and *The Song Carriers*. In 1966, Charles Parker commissioned an updated, shortened radio version of *Romeo and Juliet*. Ewan was the director and Peggy the musical director of the production, which was broadcast in May of that year. They set the play in East London, with the rival families having competing automobile businesses. There was no set script; the Critics Group improvised the entire production, with all the actors providing their own lines. They rehearsed and recorded the production in the Seeger-MacColl home in Beckenham. They staged the fight scene in which Tybalt is killed on the back porch and were so effective that the neighbors called the police.

Peggy, Ewan, and the Critics Group also developed "feature evenings": evenings of songs dedicated to specific topics. Several of the feature evenings led to recordings. *Sweet Thames Flow Softly* and *A Merry Progress to London*, released in 1966, celebrate songs about London. *The Female Frolic* (women's songs), *The Angry Muse* (political songs), and *Waterloo-Peterloo* (songs of the Industrial Revolution) were recorded in 1968. *The Female Frolic* was one of the first expressions of what would become a lifelong passion of Peggy's: women's issues. Peggy, Frankie Armstrong, and Sandra Kerr are the only singers in *The Female Frolic*, and they are in particularly good form. Their voices blend beautifully in the Irish work song "The Doffin Mistress," while each singer shines in her own solos. *The Angry Muse* shows Ewan and Peggy together at their very best, and the diversity of songs showcases Peggy's versatility. In Aunt Molly Jackson's "I Am a Union Woman," her voice has the hard, nasal quality reminiscent of Jackson's own. In "Grey October," for which she also wrote the tune (the lyrics were written jointly by the Critics Group), her voice is relaxed, simple, and clear. She and Ewan sing "In Contempt" with dignified passion, and their version of Ewan's anti–Vietnam War song "Brother Did You Weep?" ends with a high, chilling harmony, reminiscent of the style of the Appalachians.

The Critics Group also worked with Ewan and Peggy on the fourteen-volume series *Poetry and Song*, which was released in 1967 and 1968 and was done in conjunction with a series of books for secondary school children. In 1968, Critics Group members joined Peggy and Ewan in another educational project: the six-volume *Voices* series, a compendium of music and literature that came with three accompanying books. The 1968 album *The Paper Stage* is a two-volume set of Renaissance broadside ballads that tell the stories of Elizabethan plays, including some by Shakespeare. Produced and sung by Ewan and Peggy, with accompaniment by Critics Group members, *The Paper Stage* is an astringent critical corrective to anyone who thinks that all folk songs have noble sentiments or that the Renaissance was an age of enlightenment. The violence, misogyny, and bigotry of these songs are shocking; the dispassionate vocal delivery and simple accompaniment highlight the casual way that Renaissance artists accepted these evils. The 1968 album *The Wanton Muse*, a collection of traditional songs about love and lust, was yet another joint production of Peggy, Ewan, and the Critics Group.

Peggy and Ewan also made recordings without the Critics Group in the late 1960s. *Manchester Angel*, a collection of traditional English songs that Ewan sang and Peggy accompanied, came out in 1966. In 1968, they recorded *The Amorous Muse*, a collection of traditional love songs from England, Scotland, and North America. Peggy's voice is especially strong and supple on this album, and she also provided the instrumental accompaniment on guitar, banjo, autoharp, English concertina, and Appalachian dulcimer. Their most ambitious recording project was *The Long Harvest*, a ten-volume set of traditional ballads culled from commercial records, field recordings, and books (particularly the Child collection).[35] Accompanied by detailed notes and bibliography, *The Long Harvest* was designed for the ballad scholar as well as the folk music fan. The ballad remained Peggy's favorite musical form, as she noted in a letter to her father: "I really feel in my element with ballads and I think my singing is getting better. . . . When everything falls into place, the understanding of the ballad, the relating of it to other versions, and the vocal technique, it is about the most stimulating experience I think I know."[36]

Peggy also produced two albums of Anglo-American music, one done with her brother and called *Peggy 'n' Mike*, the other called simply *Peggy Alone*. *Peggy Alone* is composed entirely of traditional Anglo-American songs and showcases Peggy's versatility as a singer and an instrumentalist. She shows superb vocal flexibility and control in her recordings from the late 1960s; the tentative quality and the occasional shrillness of her earlier recordings has all but disappeared. In "The Mermaid" (Child 289), Peggy's voice is as soft and alluring as the voice of a mermaid might be, and the flowing guitar accompaniment mimics the waters of the sea. In "Henry Lee" (Child 68), a dark tale of jealousy and murder, her voice takes on the quality of keening, with a highly effective use of vocal decoration. She expertly captures the weird melody of "American Land" and backs this strange story with an eerie banjo accompaniment. Her unaccompanied version of "Mathie Groves" (Child 81) is twenty stanzas long, but she presents the story so clearly and dramatically that our attention never flags. The only flaw in *Peggy Alone* is the occasional overuse of decoration.

In 1968, Peggy launched the *New City Songster*, a monthly magazine that was sold at the Singers Club and other folk clubs. The *New City Songster* was devoted to new songs: "songs for tomorrow, today and possibly yesterday, but no further back."[37] Though her name never appeared on the masthead, Peggy did all the editing, layout, and transcriptions of songs. Dave Scott, a young artist, provided the graphics. The first issue was composed entirely of songs by Ewan and Peggy, with one exception: "Grey October," a song composed collectively by the Critics Group. For the next eighteen years, Peggy solicited songs from the English-speaking world, resulting in twenty-one issues with hundreds of songs.

Peggy and Ewan continued their extensive touring schedule, primarily though not exclusively throughout the British Isles. At a festival in Turin in 1966, she was completely flummoxed by the Mediterranean sense of time:

> You turn up at 10:45 for an 11:00 rehearsal (which in England is expected. You must be tuned up and READY by the time the rehearsal is called.) You sit and sit and sit and the director of the rehearsal turns up at 12:30, looks at you in surprise and says, "O, you're early!" At which you say accusingly, "The rehearsal *was* called for 11." At which he gives an airy little laugh and looks a little confused (I think because no one has ever turned up so "early" as to be on time in his experience). The rest of the cast turns up on time. At 2:00.[38]

Two years later, the Italian ethnomusicologist Roberto Leydi sponsored their return to Italy, when Peggy, Ewan, and five members of the Critics Group gave concerts of Anglo-American songs at the Piccolo Teatro in Milan. In the summer of 1967, several Critics Group members joined Ewan and Peggy on a trip to Havana, Cuba, where they performed at a festival of left-wing musicians and activists. "It was thrilling and boiling hot," recalls Peggy. "They didn't make much of our music—too many words, not enough atmosphere and dancing rhythms."[39]

By this time, Peggy and Ewan were among the best-known political song-writers in Britain. Peggy's politics hardened during these years, as she accepted Ewan's class analysis and the European perspective of those around her. In a letter to her father, she admitted feeling a bit guilty about being "un-family minded" and then remarked, "This is possibly my political development, in which I agree with Marx that the family in capitalist society is a retarding force."[40] Though she continued to specialize in American music, America was becoming strange to her politically and personally. "I don't think I've ever met anything more ignorant than the average American that comes over here," she remarked to her father in 1966. "We had a lot of them this summer come to the club and really, they are like children as far as awareness of what is really happening is concerned."[41] When she sang "Hitler Ain't Dead" (written by the American expatriate Jack Warshaw), a song that compared Lyndon Johnson to Adolf Hitler, many Americans criticized the comparison, citing Johnson's relatively progressive stance on race. Peggy dismissed this argument, seeing Americans' concern for racial politics as yet another sign of their political immaturity: "After all, black man against white man is not a basic issue. It stems from an economic and politic issue which goes back two hundred years."[42] The dismissal of race is surprising for an American leftist, especially one who had written so eloquently about the murderous effects of racism in "The Ballad of Jimmy Wilson." Indeed, Ewan and Peggy would devote much energy to criticism of the apartheid regime in South Africa: Ewan had written "The Ballad of Sharpeville" back in 1960; and Peggy had written "I Support the Boycott," about the ways an ordinary housewife could strike at apartheid, in 1963.

Peggy's politics were still developing, but she had become—and would remain—a fundamentally political person. "Politics is like a background to everything we do," she wrote to her father in 1969.[43] They were active in demonstrations against the Vietnam War, including one in July 1968 that resulted in violent confrontations between the police and the demonstrators. Their criticisms of the Vietnam War were far to the left of the American peace movement, which concentrated simply on ending the war. By contrast, Ewan and Peggy actively supported the North Vietnamese, and Ewan's song "The Ballad of Ho Chi Minh," written in 1954, was frequently sung at demonstrations. (In 1968, "The Ballad of Ho Chi Minh" was translated into Vietnamese, and Ewan reported receiving a message of thanks from Ho himself.) Brian Pearson remembers:

> There was a kind of religious quality to the left at this time. We attended a meeting in a room over a pub in Tottenham Court Road to discuss a forthcoming demonstration. A furious argument ensued between the Trotskyist (the Vietnam Solidarity Front) and the Maoist faction (The Front for Solidarity

with Vietnam, I think) as to the precise wording of the slogans for the march. . . . I caught the expression on the face of Nguyen Van Sao, the North Vietnamese representative in London, a man who had lost several children in the course of the war, and felt ashamed.[44]

The British Left had fractured into multiple factions, with Ewan and Peggy supporting the "anti-revisionist" (Maoist) position. This stance resulted in Ewan, Peggy, and several members of the Critics Group being invited to the Chinese legation in London, where Brian Pearson remembers the food being "stunningly good, well worth having to watch propaganda films which invariably started with a shot of Mao's head with rays of light radiating from it."[45] The Maoist position is reflected in one song from *The Angry Muse*, which praises the youth of China while criticizing the young people of Great Britain. Written by Sandra Kerr, with small additions by Peggy and Ewan, the song has the improbable title of "The Freedom-Loving Peoples of the West Will Not Be Overtaken by the Revolutionary Hordes of the People's Republic of China—Rag." The chorus fondly addresses the nation as "China, me old China"—a pun on Cockney rhyming slang, where "China" or "China plate" means "mate" (British slang for "friend").

The frenetic pace of the 1960s could not continue. "When I look back on it, I get tired just thinking about it," recalls Peggy.[46] By the end of the decade, Ewan's health was suffering, the Critics Group was showing signs of internal dissent, and the folk club movement was declining, with some folk clubs disappearing and others splintering into clubs so small that they could not afford Ewan and Peggy's fees. Peggy was suffering from severe headaches and noticed, with some distress, that thirty-four years of living had left their mark on her face. Peggy had grown up with the folk revival, and both were still strong and healthy. But the folk revival was past its prime, and Peggy had lost the quality of invincibility that is the perquisite of extreme youth.

Peggy, Mike, Barbara, and Penny Seeger, Dallas Avenue, shortly after Penny's birth. Photograph courtesy of Sonya Cramer, Seeger Family Collection.

Peggy, Barbara, and Pete during World War II. Photograph courtesy of Sonya Cramer, Seeger Family Collection.

Peggy and Penny, mid-1940s. Photograph courtesy of Sonya Cramer, Seeger Family Collection.

Penny, Ruth, Barbara, Charles, Mike, and Peggy Seeger at home in Chevy Chase. Photograph courtesy of Sonya Cramer, Seeger Family Collection.

Peggy in Boston, 1954. Photograph courtesy of Peggy Seeger.

Peggy with students from the University of Louvain (Belgium), winter 1956. Photograph courtesy of Maurice Van de Putte.

Peggy and children in Belgium, winter 1956. Photograph courtesy of Maurice Van de Putte.

Peggy and Ralph Rinzler, Ballads and Blues Club, 1956. Photograph courtesy of Peggy Seeger.

Peggy and Guy Carawan, Moscow, 1957. Photograph courtesy of Peggy Seeger.

Peggy in China, 1957. Photograph courtesy of Peggy Seeger.

Peggy and Paul Robeson, Trafalgar Square, 1959. Photograph courtesy of Peggy Seeger.

Peggy and Ewan, Newport Folk Festival, 1960. Photograph courtesy of
Peggy Seeger.

Ewan and Kitty, 1970s. Photograph by Peggy Seeger.

Ewan, Peggy, Neill, and Calum at the Singers Club, 1979. Photograph courtesy of Peggy Seeger.

Calum, Neill, and Peggy, 1992. Photograph courtesy of Peggy Seeger.

Peggy and Irene. Photograph © by Marc Marnie.

Kitty, London, August 2009. Photograph by Jean R. Freedman.

Peggy at the wedding
of Neill MacColl
and Kate St. John,
Italy, August 2014.
Photograph by Kitty
MacColl.

Jean Freedman and Peggy Seeger, Chevy Chase, 2015. Photograph by
Jonathan D. Pollock.

# CHAPTER 14

# Things Fall Apart

I've learned to be angry, I've learned to be lonely,
I've learned to be many, I've learned to be one.
I've earned all my friends, even foes will commend me,
I stand with the many, I am not alone.

—Peggy Seeger, "Song of Myself"

The winter of 1969 was a hard one. Ewan suffered ill health after the Festival of Fools and took to his bed for weeks. "He came very near to a nervous breakdown," Peggy told her father.[1] In March, he suffered a slipped disc and was in constant pain until an osteopath provided some relief. The burden of his care fell on Peggy, and she was also doing extra work that Ewan, in his weakened state, was unable to manage. For more than a year, she had experienced intense headaches accompanied by nausea and double vision—all the symptoms of migraine. Her doctor assured her that they were merely tension headaches caused by, in Peggy's words, burning "one candle at four ends."[2]

Work was steady, but not at the frenetic pace of the previous years. Ewan and Peggy toured folk clubs and gave concerts throughout Britain, but there were fewer large folk clubs now, and many of the smaller ones could not afford their fees. They continued to teach and give workshops; in February a ballad-making workshop for London schoolteachers produced several songs good enough to be published in the *New City Songster*. Offers of work from the mass media were less frequent, but they did write the music for a film about Scottish racecar driver Jackie Stewart. Their disdain for pop music remained undiminished, and the 1968–69 Festival of Fools closed with a parody of pop musicians. Thus it is ironic that in 1969 several pop musicians recorded Ewan's songs and brought them to a wider audience than Ewan had. British rocker Rod Stewart recorded "Dirty Old Town," his gravelly voice embracing both the tenderness and the harshness of the lyrics. Roberta Flack, a young American soul singer, recorded a slow and lushly sensual version of "The

First Time Ever I Saw Your Face," her beautiful voice, with its perfect diction, lingering on every note and every word. The recording was little noticed at the time, but a few years later, it would make the song known throughout the English-speaking world.

Domestically, things were going well; as Peggy put it, "The family is close-knit despite our crazy way of life."[3] Neill and Calum shared a bedroom and were close friends, though they had markedly different personalities: Neill was gentle and pensive, like the Seegers; Calum was a feisty and energetic Mac-Coll. Both were already adept singers and critics of folk music; music was as much a part of their childhood as it had been for Peggy. "It was always there," remembers Calum. "People were always singing, playing instruments, writing songs, discussing politics."[4] They frequently accompanied their parents to the Singers Club on Saturday nights. Neill remembers

> a room above a pub that smelled of stale beer. I just absolutely loved it. And the place was always completely packed and the atmosphere very reverential towards them. They were fantastic performers. And the music that they played felt incredibly alive and vibrant. . . . There was something about that combination of my mum as an instrumentalist and my dad as a songwriter, which is where I think they were always at their best. I always thought her banjo playing was one of the most exciting sounds on Earth, really. Because she didn't play it like anybody else I've ever heard since.[5]

Because Peggy and Ewan were away from home so frequently, one of her tasks was making sure that the household ran smoothly in her absence. In addition to seeing that the housework was done and the boys' physical needs were met, Peggy was careful to reassure the children that they had not been abandoned. Once, when Calum was a small boy, Peggy gave him a record before going on tour and told him to play it when he missed them; by doing so, she explained, they would always be there. She felt that Calum would be comforted by hearing his parents' voices, but she had not taken into account how literal children can be. Calum played the record eagerly, looking for Ewan and Peggy in the orange light that indicated that the record player was on; he remembered, "I'd put my eye right up to the little orange light and stare into it, so that I could see them. And I did."[6] Betsy remained a stable presence but was becoming increasingly frail, and though she insisted on helping, it was necessary to hire people to do most of the housework and child care. Since Betsy had earned her living doing housework, her standards were high, and she could be bitingly critical, resulting in a high turnover of housekeepers who simply did not wish to deal with her. On the other hand, some of the people whom Peggy hired were genuinely inadequate. Calum recalls, "They [Ewan and Peggy] had this knack of hiring extremely dysfunctional, inappropriate people . . . alcoholics, a paranoid schizophrenic. . . . It wasn't through neglect; it was just through . . . juggling loads of things. . . . Everything was done really quickly."[7] By June 1968, they had found a stable housekeeper, Mary, who was able to "take Betsy with a pinch of salt" and who got on well with the whole family.[8]

By 1970, things seemed to be back to normal. Peggy's headaches disappeared after she went off the pill, a solution she chose when her doctors' treatment did not help. She and Ewan produced three albums, two of them with the Critics Group: *As We Were a-Sailing* was a collection of sea songs; *Living Folk* was a recording of the concert they had given two years previously in Milan. *The World of Ewan MacColl and Peggy Seeger* was a compilation of some of their favorite songs, ranging from "Peggy Gordon" to "The Shoals of Herring" to "The First Time Ever I Saw Your Face." They appeared in the documentary *Sweet Thames*, which interspersed their singing with images of the river, beginning with traditional songs and culminating with "Sweet Thames, Flow Softly," Ewan's love song to London.

In April, they traveled to America. It was Peggy's first visit since 1961 and Ewan's since 1960. As they prepared for the tour, she realized how alienated she felt from her native land. She wrote to her father: "I am really becoming very British, or at least, very European. I feel this especially when I meet and hear Americans, when I read the news and when we contemplate coming to America. . . . I begin to look on the U.S. as a European does—as a mad, many-armed monster that is heading for destruction."[9] The United States seemed strange to Peggy after so many years away. A family dinner in Washington, which included Mamie and Libba, left her so emotionally drained that she had little energy for the concert that she and Ewan gave that evening. Ewan hated Washington, the seat of American power, and barricaded himself in Mike's apartment as much as possible. But in an odd way, the visit to the States left them feeling optimistic. Things were so bad, Peggy concluded, that revolution must surely be around the corner:

> Everyone talked about revolution, even taxi-drivers and women in shops and beauty parlors. . . . The Americans know their country is falling apart and face it with a stoicism and sense of reality that is quite amazing to the European and (myself) the Europeanised. . . . Awareness . . . this is something we didn't

hit at all in 1960 and it gave both of us a boost. Everyone was talking about serious things. Sure, a lot of them are going to fall on the wrong side of the fence when the crunch comes, but at least the people are getting involved in what's happening in their country.[10]

In the wake of the American tour, she tried to sort out her feelings for the working class, people she admired but with whom she never felt entirely comfortable, the class that she and Ewan trusted to be in the vanguard of the coming revolution. She recognized that many working-class Americans were devoted to the status quo; they voted for Richard Nixon and supported the Vietnam War. Nonetheless, like Ewan, she retained hope for a working-class revolution: "When the crunch comes, they'll soon know who they are. Some of them may go fascist, maybe even the majority of them. But their kids won't, after the revolution. That is, if the country doesn't revert to savagery."[11] In her 1968 "Song of Myself," she had praised workers: "people who labour, people without whom life cannot go on, people whose function it is to change society, the only class who can change society."[12] The song (its title borrowed from the American radical poet Walt Whitman) chronicled her life and her developing political consciousness. It is the first song in which she wrote about her own experience and her own political ideas. She struggles with the fact of living a comfortable, middle-class life while protesting the inequity around her: "But to live amid plenty can only torment me / When the wealth of the country belongs to the few."[13] In her previous songs, she had been a spectator and commentator; in "Song of Myself," she presents herself as a revolutionary political actor. The exact form her political actions will take is unclear, for the future is uncertain:

> For I fear the fate of the rebels and fighters
> Who ransom the future with torture and pain.
> As the trial comes near if I find I can dare it,
> I'll willingly share it, no longer afraid.[14]

Most of her previous songs had been ballads or political songs written for specific events. With "Song of Myself," she began to branch out, to develop new kinds of songs, and to weave together the personal and the political. "Che Guevara," also written in 1968, is less the story of Che's life than a paean to his memory. It is more a lyric than a ballad, with its appeal to emotion, exquisite melody, and poetic language: "Stars are lost in the fields of darkness, / Hunter's moon stalks the empty night."[15] "Hello Friend," written in 1969, is a warm welcome to nonwhite immigrants to Britain. It was written as a riposte to Enoch Powell's 1968 speech in which he predicted that "rivers of blood" would accompany immigrants of color. In the final stanza, Peggy reminds us that she too is an immigrant:

> Hello friend, all of us are strangers in this green and pleasant land.
> Once again battle ranks are forming and we need a friendly hand.
> Yours the fear and ours the shame, but our goal is just the same,
> In the end this will be *our* native land.[16]

Her 1970 composition "My Son," the first song she wrote about her children, is a poignant testimony to the inevitable separation between parent and child: "Are we becoming strangers, that once did breathe as one? / Who are you now, my son?"[17]

In the summer of 1970, their housekeeper Mary left, and they decided to do without housekeepers for a while. Ewan, Peggy, and the boys (including Hamish, who had been living in the house since March) did the housework, with Betsy helping as much as she could. Ewan and Peggy curtailed their touring schedule until a new housekeeper could be found; their only foreign trip that summer was to Lugano with the Critics Group to tape five shows for Swiss television. In October, they returned to the United States for a tour of California and a visit with Charles. Manny Greenhill, who managed the tour, noted that "press notices [had] been universally ecstatic."[18] Barry Olivier, an organizer of the Berkeley Folk Music Festival wrote to them: "You two were absolutely magnificent in the Festival! . . . As always, your singing and discussions were without peer and your great artistic integrity and deep feeling for folk music added immeasurably to the Festival."[19] Then it was back home in time to get ready for the Festival of Fools.

Perhaps no issue that the festivals explored was more important—or more unexpected—than the burgeoning women's movement. Concurrent with similar movements in France and the United States, the second wave of British feminism had brought about an increased awareness of women's second-class status and had led to important legislation, such as the 1967 Abortion Act, which allowed abortion under certain circumstances, and the 1970 Equal Pay Act, which forbade different pay scales for men and women doing the same work (though it was not enforced until 1975 in order to give employers time to prepare). The Critics Group began to recognize the beams in their own eyes. Festival of Fools scripts referred to "men" and "girls." Publicity material from 1968 described Frankie Armstrong's voice as having "unusual depth and fullness for a woman."[20] Ewan chose to write several sketches about the women's movement for the 1970/1971 Festival, and he charged Peggy with writing a woman's song. (Brian Pearson remembers the "Pregnant Man" sketch—based on a family-planning poster that showed a pregnant man and asked, "Would you be more careful if it was you that got pregnant?"—as "the funniest Festival of Fools scene of all.")[21] Peggy had written some mildly feminist songs, such as "Darling Annie," about an equal partnership between a man and a woman, and "Nightshift," about a woman's sexual stamina exceeding a man's, but none had been very pointed or even overtly political. Overworked, harassed, and mildly annoyed that she had to write a song on demand, Peggy came up with the song that would be her most famous: "I'm Gonna Be an Engineer." She recalls, "'Engineer' appeared so fast on the page that it almost seemed to write itself—you'd think I'd been brooding on discrimination and prejudice all my life. Not so. I had been encouraged personally, academically, musically, and sartorially to do whatever I wanted. And I never wanted to be a boy or an engineer . . . or operate a turret-lathe."[22]

The song was a departure for Peggy in terms of subject matter and musical style. With its syncopated rhythms, wide vocal range, and melody that occasionally departs from the primary key, "I'm Gonna Be an Engineer" does not sound like a folk song. Yet it retains several characteristics of traditional music: the narrative structure is reminiscent of the ballad, and like many traditional songs, it presents two clearly articulated and diametrically opposed points of view. In a traditional song, these two points of view would probably be of a man and a woman for whom arguing is a form of courtship and who resolve their disagreement in the course of the song. In "I'm Gonna Be an Engineer," there is no resolution between the unnamed woman who wants to be an engineer and the opposing voice—or voices—of a social order that urges her to abandon her ambition and become a "lady." Amber Good points out that the two voices are differentiated in the tune as well as the words: "A range of only a fourth—perhaps underscoring the narrowness of thinking—characterizes society's voice, while the heroine's melodic range is quite wide, with leaps and skips dominating the melody. Seeger likewise differentiates the two voices harmonically, casting the protagonist in major and the antagonist in minor."[23] A line of miniskirted women sang "I'm Gonna Be an Engineer" during the 1970–71 Festival of Fools. It quickly became popular and remains her best-known song to this day. Frankie Armstrong recalls:

Peggy came into her own as a brilliant songwriter with "I'm Gonna Be an Engineer." She had written many fine songs before but this one was so fine.

(It was my most requested song for decades after I learned and recorded it.) Ironically I did overhear a snippet of conversation at around this time which points up how Peggy wasn't fully aware of her "inner" feminist. One of the women asked her if she plucked her eyebrows to which she replied, "oh no, Ewan wouldn't let me." It seems very funny now.[24]

Perhaps Peggy's interest in feminism was not just a desire to make the world a better place for others. Despite her insistence that she had always been encouraged to do what she wanted, perhaps she had a need for feminism, too.

The 1970–71 Festival of Fools was the most successful yet. The show had full houses almost every night of its twenty-night run. Radical documentary filmmaker Felix Greene proposed making a film of it. American folklorist Kenneth Goldstein suggested bringing it to the United States on tour. It impressed many theater professionals, some of whom suggested transferring the show to the West End. Peggy dismissed the possibility of taking it either to the West End or the United States, sure that its radical content would not be allowed in either place. Journalists were reluctant to write about it; one said to Ewan, "I was gripped! But I daren't write it up! My editor wouldn't let me."[25] But even those who disagreed with its politics were impressed; one audience member said to Peggy, "I hated every minute of it, but it was brilliant."[26] It also impressed Joan Littlewood. Brian Pearson remembers her sitting "in the front row, clutching her handbag and looking inscrutable." He admits, "Delivering those monologues with Joan sitting about three feet away was one of the scariest things I've ever done."[27] She joined the cast members for a meal afterward. Sandra Kerr, from a working-class family in the East End of London, was disappointed by the formerly radical Littlewood. Kerr explained, "The comments she made about people in the East End of London I found quite anti-working class, and I got angry when she talked about schoolchildren there being completely out of control. . . . Ewan said afterwards to me that he particularly wanted me to see how reactionary Joan had become."[28]

The success of the 1970–71 Festival of Fools gave Ewan hope that he could once again build a workers' theater like the ones he had known in his youth. Peggy described him as "almost euphoric" as he embarked on this new project.[29] But he was no longer a young man. In January 1971, he became ill with the heart trouble that would plague him the rest of his life. The sight of the reaper in the wings spurred him to make plans for his new theater troupe before it was too late. It also caused him to reflect on his role in the Critics Group and to acknowledge where he had gone wrong. Brian Pearson recalls:

"He realised that his practice had been at odds with his rhetoric and beliefs and that he recognised the group needed to be democratised. We were going to form a touring theatre company. Sandra, Jim O'Connor and I would be directors. The group would write the material."[30]

Peggy was enthusiastic about the new venture, and she eagerly described their plans to her father: "We're going, at the end of two years, to have a company of 12 people who can all act, produce, do lighting, sound rigging, singing and writing! The possibilities are enormous. . . . I only know that a revolutionary theatre group would be absolutely in its element even now—a group of a dozen people who really know what we're doing could have a fantastic effect."[31] She recognized that relinquishing—or at least sharing—leadership was essential to the success of the theater group. She remarked that Ewan had "gained an insight into . . . his failures as a leader, as well as his successes, and started to be less of a tyrant, more a friend, to members of the group."[32] Sharing the work would also give Ewan and Peggy time to do other projects. And Peggy recognized that Ewan's health would no longer permit him to shoulder all the burdens of writing, directing, and producing.

In May, Ewan suffered a nervous breakdown and "just dissolved as a person for about four months. It was the swing of the pendulum from the euphoria to utter depression."[33] Both withdrew from the Critics Group and the proposed theater troupe, turning the reins over to Sandra Kerr, Brian Pearson, Jim O'Connor, and Mike Rosen. The group worked on scenes from Sartre and Lorca, Ben Jonson and Aristophanes. "We were given scenes from a variety of plays, for members to direct," recalls Frankie Armstrong. "I remember enjoying these rehearsals enormously—feeling a freedom I'd never felt while in the group before."[34]

Despite Ewan's fragile health, he and Peggy continued their punishing touring schedule, giving more than one hundred concerts throughout the British Isles in 1971. They had found a new housekeeper, an Italian woman named Bianca, who filled the house with laughter and bawdy jokes. Their record output was slight that year, though they did put out a collection of sea songs entitled *Ye Mariners All* with the Critics Group, and their work appeared in several collections with other folk artists.

With Ewan keeping a low profile during 1971, Peggy stepped into the limelight. A television documentary entitled *A Kind of Exile*, filmed in the spring and broadcast in the summer, focused on Peggy and her experience as an American folksinger living in England. It began with one of the first songs she recorded, "When First unto This Country a Stranger I Came." When she recorded the song back in 1955, she had no idea how appropriate it would be to her own life. Despite the title of the film, she declared, "I haven't been exiled; I've immigrated. Now I think as a European person."[35] Unlike most Europeans, however, she specialized in American music. Ewan supported this choice: "I think that the first big lesson that Peggy learned was that the greatest impact she could make would be through the songs of her native country, the songs of America and particularly through the songs of that part of America that she knew best, that is, what I suppose we might call white Anglo-Saxon America, that part of America which had been settled by Scots-Irish and English who brought the songs with them from the seventeenth century onward."[36] Because these songs were in English, they could easily be understood and appreciated by an English audience. The question of how to adequately present American music while living in England, however, remained a problem as long as she lived there. As she explains in *A Kind of Exile*, "I'm not trying to be a museum piece, singing American songs 14 years after I left America. I'm really trying to create the best I can out of the knowledge I have of American folk music, classical music, and my observation of England. Most of the songs that I have made up have been about my own self as being part of England. I'm not yet British and probably never will be."[37] Of course, the categories of "British" and "American" folk songs are not mutually exclusive. As Ewan pointed out, many of the traditional songs that Peggy sang came from British people who had immigrated to America. Like many immigrants, Peggy continued to sing the songs of her homeland, while collecting new songs and new ideas from her adopted country.

In *A Kind of Exile*, Peggy presents herself as staunchly political, sometimes dogmatically so: "What Ewan has done is literally make me see what folk song is all about—a direct expression of social antagonism, of social struggle and conflict."[38] She sensed this conflict even as a child, living a comfortable middle-class existence while listening to the songs of people whose daily lives were filled with struggle. While Peggy implicitly understood the social and political aspects of folk songs, Ewan made this understanding explicit. His memories of poverty and his anger over class inequity did not disappear when his own life became easier. Peggy accepted Ewan's political analysis intellectually, but she did not feel it in her bones as he did: "The fire was his; the anger was his." She compared her own politics to "warming your hands at someone else's fire."[39]

Some statements that Peggy made in *A Kind of Exile* she would modify if she could. "I've repudiated America," strikes her in retrospect as "badly phrased":

"'I've repudiated what America is doing' is what I probably should have said."[40] In 1971, the United States was mired in the Vietnam War, governed by Richard Nixon, and still dragging its heels on civil rights. She despised U.S. politics of this era, but she did not despise the American people, who had created the songs that formed the basis of her musical identity and repertoire. "I was brought up with those songs," she remembers. "And because I listened to them as a child, something of the truth of them must have come through. And the need to bring that truth forward."[41] This was the America she treasured, but it was an America that sometimes seemed more theoretical than real. "I was so sunk into living in England," she recalls, "that, other than writing to my father and to Penny and occasionally to Mike, America had vanished for me."[42]

As the autumn of 1971 approached, it was time to start thinking about the Festival of Fools. Ewan was feeling better, and in August he "began to take the reins again."[43] Peggy and Ewan were unaware of the mounting tensions that existed among several members of the Critics Group. Many had enjoyed the unwonted freedom of Ewan's absence and were less than pleased to be relegated, once again, to the position of followers. "We were all in our 30s, with artistic and political ideas of our own, growing increasingly frustrated at Ewan's seeming inability to 'let go' the reins," remembers Sandra.[44] Ewan was highly critical of the work done by the leaders he had appointed, and he reasserted control, choosing the subject for the upcoming Festival of Fools (money) and assigning six Critics Group members to write the script. Frankie Armstrong and Brian Pearson, who were living together at the time, decided to leave the group. Frankie remembers, "Brian and I could see that this change in dynamics of the group was causing Ewan to feel unsafe and out of control. We feared it would all end in tears, as it indeed did, and so we left before this happened."[45] Because it was an "amicable parting," they remained on good terms with everyone in the group.[46] Others were not so lucky.

Ewan rejected the script that the Critics Group wrote, and as there was no time to write a completely new one, he suggested that the upcoming festival be a collection of scenes from past festivals. The group acquiesced but without enthusiasm: "Its [the Festival of Fools'] strength had always been that it was topical, and instead the show was a retrospective—re-cycling material from previous shows," recalls Sandra.[47] Ewan wrote several new scenes and directed the show as he had in the past. It seemed to many in the group that Ewan's talk about sharing responsibility was not reflected in his actions. "He couldn't really let go," recalls Brian. "At the time, I remarked that it was asking a lot of a man of 55 to change his ways so radically. Looking back today (I'm 71) that seems a bit ageist."[48]

Shortly before the festival, Ewan called a meeting with six members of the group to discuss plans for the upcoming theater troupe. Reluctantly, they agreed to the meeting but completely rejected the idea of the troupe. "It all felt absurd and inappropriate and unrealistic, and compounded our unhappiness," recalls Sandra.[49] The dynamics of the group, with Ewan as leader and the other members as followers, were no longer working. Ewan and Peggy were shocked. Peggy wrote to her father of her hurt and disappointment:

> This was the final blow for us, for Ewan in particular, as he seems to be a compulsive theatre-former and really had his hopes pinned on this one. But the real shock was not that the group didn't want to go on—it was their attitude toward us. We had been friends with this small group for nearly six years, with Sandra for nearly 9 years, and they hadn't even bothered to let us know they had changed their minds. The sense of strain during the rest of the rehearsals and the performance of the festival is indescribable. . . . Sandra, Jim, John and the others would come into a rehearsal or a performance, not even say good evening to us, would never mention us by name or allow their eyes to meet ours, they went into little cliques of conversation hushed in a corner, and resisted direction in the play itself.[50]

Sandra, on the other side, was equally unhappy: "The whole run was a fairly dismal affair (though audiences were still good) punctuated by clandestine meetings and rumblings of discontent."[51]

In the middle of the run, several members of the group asked Ewan and Peggy to come to a meeting of their own. Six members of the group wanted to break away from the Critics Group and form a separate organization. They asked Ewan and Peggy if they could divide the equipment (lighting, microphones, speakers, props, etc.) between the Critics Group and the new breakaway organization. Ewan and Peggy refused: "We felt that since there [*sic*] were not going to form a theatre company as such they had no right to take the equipment out, especially as three out of the six had never paid subscriptions into the group anyway, due to unemployment and hard-up circumstances. This meeting broke up bitterly."[52]

In the midst of this turmoil, the Festival of Fools was going surprisingly well. "They were troupers," remembers Peggy. "They worked so hard."[53] A film made that year shows crisp professionalism, excellent singing, and fine comic timing—a tribute both to Ewan's direction and to the talent of the Critics Group members. Sandra and John Faulkner (who were married at the time) performed a hilarious sketch about a couple in which the husband was in love with his work—he made springs in a factory—to the distress of his amorous young wife. Peggy delivered a moving speech about a former Singers Club member who had died in a South African prison. The cast performed a chilling scene about torture in a Greek prison, interspersed with a song about the ignorance and apathy of tourists who lounged on the beaches just a few miles away. The women's singing was particularly good; a chorus of women provided moving renditions of "Love for Love" and "I'm Gonna Be an Engineer." Reviews were positive, and audiences were appreciative. No outsider could have guessed the discontent seething in the wings.

Peggy, as usual, was fulfilling many roles in the festival. In addition to acting, singing, and playing guitar, she served as musical director and production secretary. Though no one is credited for writing the program notes, some of them bear her unmistakable comic stamp: "Do keep your feet out of the aisles unless you want them flattened. Do keep your belongings out of the aisles—if you do not they may be re-distributed thru [*sic*] the hall (or used as props)."[54] The program contained advertisements for the Singers Club, the *New City Songster*, and Ewan and Peggy's most recent records. There was also a form for people to fill out if they were interested in joining a new traveling theater company—a company that would never exist.

On the final night of the run, Ewan and Peggy lingered after the performance, chatting with a group of trade unionists who had enjoyed the show. Meanwhile, six members of the cast "quietly and with more efficiency than they had ever shown before, stripped the hall of £1500 worth of microphones, speakers, tape machines, lights, cable, props, etc., got them into vans and were away." Peggy wrote her father, "It has been a bitter experience, and we have no way of retrieving the stuff."[55] What hurt most was the fact that these six people were among the Critics Group members who had worked with Ewan and Peggy the longest and, in many ways, had known them the best. Peggy was stunned that night when she confronted Sandra: "When we turned around on that last performance night and saw the hall stripped, I went and asked her [Sandra] where they had put the stuff—she rounded on me like a wolf at bay, and literally snarled, 'Where *you'll* never find it!'"[56]

Not all members of the Critics Group defected, and those who remained continued to meet for several months. But the heart had gone out of it. There would be no more talk of a traveling theater company. Peggy was angry and hurt, but Ewan was heartbroken. The group he had nurtured, the people he had trusted to continue the work he loved, had cast him out. He and Sandra never spoke again. For the last time, his hopes for a revolutionary theater had been destroyed. King Lear watched the departing Cordelia with less grief.

# CHAPTER 15

# Late in the Day

From noon to early evening,
Always together yet drifting apart;
Hold fast the bonds that bind us,
Companion of my heart.

—Peggy Seeger, "New Spring Morning"

In the years to come, there would be reconciliations with some members of the Critics Group, and Peggy would reconcile with still others after Ewan's death in 1989. Frankie Armstrong, who remains a respected folksinger and teacher, was grateful that Brian and she did not have to deal with the aftermath of the group's painful ending. She remarked, "I'm so glad we weren't part of that horrid bust up—nobody came out of it very well and for years, indeed decades afterwards, some of the group involved still hadn't let go of their anger and resentment. It was great to see Peggy some years after and not have any of that hanging over us."[1] Sandra Kerr, who became one of the leading folksingers and teachers of folk song in England, credits Ewan and Peggy with providing her with "an extraordinary education . . . a knowledge of literature, politics, folk song studies, performance techniques (many of which [she uses] to this day with [her] students and choirs), songwriting skills, musicianship, theatre training—it goes on!"[2] Yet she had no contact with Peggy until after Ewan died. From the vantage point of nearly four decades later, Peggy remarks, "We ran the group too tyrannically—what Ewan wanted to do, and I followed Ewan absolutely."[3] Peggy and Sandra would eventually sing together again, the old wounds forgotten—or at least unmentioned. But in the winter of 1972, the pain was fierce and raw. Peggy recalls, "It was a watershed in his life, where I think he realized his days of theater were over. The Critics Group broke up; it broke him; it broke something very vital in him. It broke his trust in people. . . . He took such pleasure in them. He was so proud of them when they did a good show. . . . It was like being kicked in the teeth by your children."[4]

Ewan would continue his career as one of the major figures in the folk revival; he would also return to writing plays, though he would never again act or direct. But things were never quite the same. Neill recalls, "The breakup of the Critics Group . . . changed them forever, really. . . . I don't think he ever regained that absolute belief back. Maybe belief in himself. . . . A bit of that dynamism went."[5] Ewan and Peggy continued to meet with the remaining members of the Critics Group, but the numbers were so small and the pain so recent that nothing came of it. The group that had departed sent a letter to Ewan and Peggy saying that the equipment had been "fairly distributed," and the Critics Group ended officially at a meeting of the London Co-operative Society in November 1972.[6]

Peggy and Ewan continued to sing frequently at the Singers Club and gave concerts throughout Britain, but their pace of life had slowed considerably. In June, Peggy wrote to her father: "For now, we are living a slightly distracted life. We cannot seem to concentrate on anything. We go to bed late, sleep late, watch television a little too much, go out to do club dates, play chess and canasta, have a class meeting once a week, go to the movies. . . . Our incentive to be involved with people has, quite naturally, diminished noticeably. We are both optimistic about this period, recognize it is a period of reaction to an extreme emotional shock, and hope it will go soon."[7] Fortunately, 1972 offered great gifts. Clint Eastwood's 1971 film *Play Misty for Me* had prominently featured Roberta Flack's version of "The First Time Ever I Saw Your Face." This exposure sent the song to the top of the pop charts; *Billboard* listed it as the top song of the year in 1972. Suddenly, money poured in. Ewan and Peggy were still much in demand, but now they had the luxury of taking only the jobs that they wanted. In the coming years, they would use part of the money to expand the Beckenham house and buy a holiday cottage in Scotland. They were also solvent enough to have a third child.

For years, Peggy had wanted another child, but they had lacked sufficient money and time for a larger family. Now they had enough of both, and it was Ewan who suggested adding to the family. "We were sitting in a café in Bromley," remembers Peggy, "and he said, 'Let's have another child.' . . . He'd lost his Critics Group children, and he wanted another baby."[8] Calum, after ten years of being the baby brother, wanted a baby brother of his own. As autumn approached, he showed the characteristic MacColl wit, as Peggy recounts in a letter to her father: "Calum, who (after putting his head on my stomach and getting a lusty kick,) gave forth the priceless remark, 'I wonder if he'll mind that your insides have been used twice already! Never mind, at least we didn't hang anything on the walls.' This was in regard to our constant comments to Neill (who is in his pop music stage now) on the ridiculous posters of pop-singers on his half of their room wall."[9]

With her first two children, Peggy had had relatively easy home births. This time, there were complications, and she was taken to a nearby hospital. The umbilical cord was wrapped around the baby's neck, and "she was navy blue—it was terrifying."[10] Fortunately, the danger was short-lived. Ewan and Peggy's daughter was born on December 2, 1972, and like her brothers, she received a Scottish name: Catriona. Like her mother, she was immediately called by a nickname: Kitty.

Shortly before Kitty's birth, Alice Dawson joined the household and remained until Kitty was in her early teens. Calum remembers Alice as "the salt of the earth" after "a succession of bonkers housekeepers": "Alice was completely grounded . . . bright. . . . She could deal with me. . . . She was great with kids. And she was great at curbing, in a sense, Mum and Dad's excesses or pointing out when she thought they should be doing stuff. . . . She wasn't afraid of them. . . . She was kind of like the nanny from heaven."[11] Peggy concurs, calling Alice "Kitty's second mother." Kitty had severe asthma as a child and needed the steady presence that Alice could give. Peggy remembers, "Alice was my lifesaver. . . . She adored Kitty from the moment she was born. . . . She gave Kitty the conservative, regular motherhood that I didn't give her. She was with her all the time. . . . I was the irregular mother, the crazy one."[12]

Yet the household was less crazy than it had been during Neill and Calum's early years, when Peggy and Ewan were away from home so frequently. Now they had no need to be gone so often, and when it was necessary, they had the comfort of knowing that Alice was in charge. They continued to tour throughout the British Isles and occasionally ventured farther afield: in 1973, they sang at the Como Music Festival in Italy; in 1974, they added a German tour; and in 1975, they toured Sweden. Even when they were away, an invisible tether connected them with home. On a holiday in the Scottish island of Mull in 1973, Peggy wrote to her father:

> I miss the baby very much. . . . My arms need her. . . . We've left Kitty three times now, twice on work and this time for a holiday, and each time I've felt it a solace to take photographs with me. Ewan's the same. . . . We'll be walking over the mountain and he'll say, "Well, Kitty will just be waking up for her juice now"—or just starting the concert and he'll say "She'll just be having her bedtime bottle—" Funny, isn't it? Ewan says that it's knowing that this one is our last makes her babyhood more precious.[13]

There was a mellowness to life in the mid-1970s. "Dad softened a whole lot," recalls Calum. "Kitty was really the apple of his eye."[14] In the spring of 1974, Peggy wrote to her father about the relationship between Calum and Kitty: "He is a master at parent psychology. If I say I haven't time to give him a bed-time talk, he puts on a sulk and says, 'You haven't time for *[me]*. Only Kitty.' Then he gives a sunny, humorous smile and says, 'Never mind. I had you a long time before Kitty did.' . . . He worships Kitty absolutely."[15] Kitty was the subject of Peggy's second song about her children, "Lullabye for a Very New Baby." The tune is gentle and slow, deliberately soporific, while the words describe that mix of emotions that accompany the early months of a child's life—exhaustion, wonder, worry, and delight:

> But my back is broke and my belly sore,
> Your daddy can't come near me,
> And it's up all night to walk the floor—
> Hushabye, my dearie.
>
> Though you keep me waking night and day
> And your crying makes me weary,
> You're welcome as a flower in May—
> Hushabye, my dearie.[16]

In 1973, "The First Time Ever I Saw Your Face" won two Grammy awards: Ewan received the Grammy for Song of the Year, while Roberta Flack was awarded Record of the Year for her version of the song. The recognition and the concomitant royalty checks came at an ideal time. In 1974, Ewan had a series of respiratory infections, and Peggy had surgery for a nonmalignant lump in her breast. Both chose to take a much-needed break. In a letter to her father, Peggy wrote, "[Ewan] seems more and more to just want to stay at home, something which is new to him. He is happy to garden, make shelves and decorate, read and go to an occasional film. I reckon that he is doing now what he should have done just following his breakdown."[17] The slower pace of life suited her as well:

> I am happier than I have ever been before. . . . Our whole home life seems to have crystallized. We actually have a home routine, which we never had when we had the group or when we were out on tour so much. The children expect to find us home and that makes them happy, more content and, in a way, more comradely. . . . Whenever I pick Kitty up for a cuddle or go down to the garden, or so many other little things, I am really and truly happy into my bones. What luck that THE FIRST TIME EVER bought us this breathing space.[18]

Their record output for the mid-1970s was relatively modest. In 1972, they produced two albums that had been recorded with several members of the Critics Group: *The World of Ewan MacColl and Peggy Seeger, Volume 2* contained songs from the Radio Ballads, while *Solo Flight* featured traditional songs and a few of Ewan and Peggy's compositions. In 1973, Peggy and Ewan produced two albums of their own songs: *At the Present Moment* and *Folkways Record of Contemporary Songs*. Their music also appeared in several television documentaries produced by Philip Donnellan, the distinguished BBC producer with whom they had worked since the 1950s. In 1971, Donnellan produced *Before the Mast*, a film about the days of sail, which featured the music of Ewan, Peggy, and the Critics Group. The film's theme song was Ewan's "Shellback Song," which was based on interviews that Peggy and he conducted with Ben Bright, a seventy-six-year-old sailor who began work on sailing ships and was still going strong in the 1970s. "Shellback Song" ends with the kind of valediction found in "Freeborn Man," a tribute to a way of life that is gone:

> Goodbye, you square-riggers, your voyaging's done, farewell to the
>     days of sail—
> Goodbye, you Cape Horners and every tall ship that ever defied a gale—
> Goodbye to the shellbacks who rode the winds through a world of
>     sea and sky—
> Your roving is ended, your seafaring's over. You mariners all, goodbye.[19]

Donnellan also adapted several of the Radio Ballads for television: *The Shoals of Herring* in 1972, *The Fight Game* in 1973, and *The Big Hewer* in 1974.

Peggy remembers the mid-1970s as "a political limbo . . . a feeling of utter apathy."[20] The Vietnam War began to decline in 1973 and finally ended in 1975. No other political cause seemed to have the same immediacy and weight, though Peggy and Ewan remained loyal to the trade union movement and the fight against apartheid in South Africa. Peggy was just beginning to be involved in the women's movement. She had received requests for permission to publish "I'm Gonna Be an Engineer" in women's songbooks, and she began to get invitations to sing at women's events. Peggy recalls:

> I didn't have anything else that was in any way feminist. . . . I had to start think-
> ing about what feminism really was. I started reading up about it and going to
> meetings that had to do with feminism and consciousness-raising. . . . I also
> began looking at my own home life. We'd come in from a concert, and we
> both bring the instruments up; I put them away. I make the list of what we've

sung. I bring him a cup of tea in bed. And I am still cooking and shopping and running this house, and we are both going out singing.[21]

She also served as the duo's business manager: keeping the accounts, taking care of correspondence, booking gigs, and making sure that contracts were in order.

Peggy began to write avowedly feminist songs. "Emily" (written in 1977) and "Winnie and Sam" (written in 1978) are about domestic violence. They were inspired by women whom Peggy interviewed at a shelter for battered women in South London. Other songs deal with issues closer to home and were based, at least in part, on her own experience. "Nine-Month Blues" (1976) discusses family planning, contraceptive failure, the difficulty of getting a safe abortion, and the toll that pregnancy and childbearing take on women's bodies—yet the song remains lighthearted and affectionate toward men and family. "Housewife's Alphabet" (1976), "Talking Matrimony Blues" (1978), and "Lady, What Do You Do All Day?" (1978) describe the massive amounts of unacknowledged and unpaid labor that is the housewife's lot. She concludes "Talking Matrimony Blues" with a classic socialist-feminist critique of marriage:

> So marriage is really to safeguard the boss,
> 'Cause without a workforce he'd make a loss,
> And how could he rob 'em and screw 'em and twist 'em
> Unless he had marriage to uphold the system
> That supports the class
> That exploits the man
> Who exploits the wife
> Who bears the kids
> Who live in the house that Jack built . . .
> AND JILL CLEANS.[22]

This is the musical expression of the argument that Engels put forth in *The Origin of the Family, Private Property, and the State*: "The first class oppression [is] that of the female sex by the male."[23]

Peggy amassed more than fifty tapes of interviews and hoped that she and Ewan would create a Radio Ballad about women. Ewan was uncomfortable with the subject. He supported the women's movement intellectually; how could he not support a movement for human rights and dignity? But the material that Peggy was collecting troubled him. The tapes were filled with women discussing unhappy marriages, describing domestic violence, complaining about how their husbands treated their children. "I was coming home with a stack of stuff that was not very man-friendly," remembers Peggy, "and Ewan began to feel bad about that."[24] In many ways, Ewan's attitude was that of the Old Left, focusing on the economic rather than the cultural aspects of feminism. Peggy explains, "He thought it [feminism] was a very good thing. But he saw it more as getting women into the workplace and getting them equal wages. Neither of us realized that there was so much bad behavior among men. And women allowed it. And the whole system courted it. It was part of the system. . . . I think he kind of felt it was a bit divisive. But he encouraged me in it."[25]

The first inkling of a political division between Ewan and Peggy appears in a recording from 1975. The recording was produced by the Amalgamated Union of Engineering Workers (AUEW) and consists of just two songs. On the first side is Ewan's "We Are the Engineers," a song that the AUEW had commissioned for a film of the same name. The song is stirring and heroic; in Peggy's words, "the tune is magnificent and the language is in the style of nineteenth-century panegyrical poetry."[26] On the 1975 recording, Ewan sings the lead, while Peggy plays English concertina and comes in on choruses, such as the following:

> But they fought the cruel laws and when
> They lost they rose to fight again,
> For the right to work and live like men,
> They were the engineers![27]

On the second side is Peggy's song about the second sex, "I'm Gonna Be an Engineer." It is a telling contrast to Ewan's song and ends with lines that are practically a direct riposte: "But I'll fight them as a woman, not a lady, / Fight them as an engineer!"[28]

If Peggy was subtly challenging Ewan's entrenched political ideas, Neill and Calum were doing so explicitly. Neill became aware of "glaring contradictions that were being ignored," such as Ewan's uncritical admiration of Stalin and Mao, despite the mass murders committed during their regimes.[29] Neill also wondered at his father's continuing identification with the working class, though he had lived a middle-class life for many years. Neill rarely challenged his father directly. He recalls, "I have a vague memory of once just taking the alternative view and saying, 'People are naturally greedy; capitalism is an obvious result of people's natural desires.' I only did that once."[30] Neill was not confrontational by nature; instead, he rebelled by playing electric guitar:

I know, to an extent, that my dad was very disappointed. I think he was so certain that we would pick up acoustic guitars, paint "this guitar kills fascists" on it, and go out and join the class struggle. Which was kind of ironic because they brought us up very middle-class in suburbia, in South London. You don't go to fight the class war there, really. Not in Beckenham. Not when your parents are earning a lot of money off one of the songs that they've written and having four lovely holidays abroad a year—it's just not going to work. You're not going to feel the rage, really.[31]

Whereas Neill disliked direct confrontation, Calum was a natural fighter. Peggy paid tribute to this quality in "Song for Calum," written when he was twelve years old:

> Son of my youth, so honest and open,
> I'm proud of your will, your compulsion to fight,
> Keep raising your voice, insist that you're counted,
> And if you're wrong, the world sets you aright.[32]

Ewan was also a natural fighter, and he and Calum were often at loggerheads, in part because they were so much alike. Calum remembers, "I'm fiery like my dad. . . . My brother, because of his temperament, his natural reaction was to run away and hide. My natural reaction was to stand up and fight. . . . It got quite adversarial by the time I reached my midteens, and Mum would be very much a peacemaker. And it upset her a lot; she hated all that. She doesn't like that kind of confrontation."[33] Though Ewan and Calum frequently argued, they intuitively understood the other's temperament. Ewan found Neill much more of a puzzle. Neill recalls:

> I don't think he really understood me particularly. I was a bit more like her [Peggy]. . . . Slightly more female, for want of a better word. And he didn't like seeing that in a man. . . . Gentler, less feisty than Calum. I mean, my dad could relate to Calum because Calum would kind of fight. . . . His [Ewan's] whole thing was, "Come on, be confrontational," and I just went, "No, I'm not gonna." He didn't like that particularly, but he also didn't understand it. He didn't understand why one of his male children would behave so oddly, I think. Whereas my mum, I think she understood instinctively why I would be like that.[34]

Though Peggy was the family peacemaker, she did not shy away from direct confrontation. As a political activist, confrontation was an inevitable part of what she did. Though not a natural fighter, she had learned to fight in order to achieve ends that she considered important. "Making enemies is important," she says, "because it means you're taking a stance and there's a kind of perverse purity about what you're doing."[35] If Ewan taught her to fight politically, Betsy taught her to fight personally. In May 1974, Peggy wrote to her father about her fraught relationship with Betsy:

> Sometimes I love her and sometimes I hate her. I never like her, because she is impossible to get on with. After her last quarrel with Alice, about a year ago, in which she called Alice every filthy name she could lay her tongue to, I did something I hope I never have to do again. I was ashamed afterward—you wouldn't have recognized your gentle daughter, Charlie. I shut her door and shouted her down until she was too weary to counter me. Then I told her, putting every ounce of assumed hatred into it—because I am afraid that that dear little old lady has taught me to hate—that if I had a choice between Alice going and Betsy going it would be Betsy.[36]

Betsy remained for several months, but so did the uneasy undercurrents between her and Peggy. She finally left after a quarrel with Alice. Betsy was eighty-eight years old at this time, frail and barely able to walk, yet she tried to lift her granddaughter (who was not quite two years old) out of her playpen. Alice was afraid that Betsy would drop Kitty and injure them both. Alice offered to pick Kitty up and take her to her grandmother but asked Betsy not to lift Kitty by herself. Betsy refused, and Alice told Peggy that she could not remain under the circumstances. The choice between Alice and Betsy had been theoretical a few months earlier; now it was real. Peggy told Betsy that she would have to promise not to lift Kitty or leave. Betsy left—but it was up to Peggy to find her a place to go. Relations between Betsy and Peggy improved greatly once they were no longer living together. "All our contacts now are good ones," Peggy wrote to her father. "She talks to me again, eats like a horse, has regained her colour."[37] By 1975, Betsy found permanent accommodation in a retirement home just a few blocks from Ewan and Peggy. "For an old people's home, [it] is really quite nice," remarked Peggy. "Betsy says she doesn't like it, but she seems happier to me than she has in ages. . . . She sees us nearly every day. . . . We get along fine now."[38] Though Betsy was Ewan's mother, it was Peggy who visited her daily, who took her shopping and to cafés, and who brought her to Stanley Avenue to play with Kitty.

Ewan was starting to feel his age. In 1975, he turned sixty, and his health was declining. In the past, he had dealt with illness by ignoring it or stoically enduring it, but this was getting harder to do. He suffered from diverticulitis, gout, chronic bronchitis, and a slipped disc. The mid-1970s continued to be a time of a lingering malaise, both personally and culturally. "We haven't done any really important work, although we are singing better than we ever have," Peggy wrote in 1975. "Everyone over here feels a sense of WAITING for something to happen."[39] The golden days of the folk revival were long gone. Though Ewan and Peggy were still much in demand, they were no longer the center of a vibrant cultural movement. They spent less time working and more time at home and with the family—acting out Shakespeare's plays and reading *The Communist Manifesto* with the children, taking long walks, improving the Beckenham house, and fixing up the cottage in Scotland.

By 1976, the period of shock and apathy following the breakup of the Critics Group seemed to be over. Ewan and Peggy began several new ventures. They started their own record company, Blackthorne Records, in order to have complete artistic control over their recordings. The first record that the label produced was groundbreaking. *Penelope Isn't Waiting Any More* is composed entirely of women's songs. The album (like Peggy's youngest sister) was named after the wife of Odysseus, who patiently waited twenty years for her husband to return from the Trojan War. Peggy's liner notes provide an ingenious reorientation of the Greek classic. Rather than focusing on the adventures of Odysseus, the *Odyssey* itself, she pays attention to the woman left behind: "Even allowing for inadequate travel facilities it is difficult to escape the conclusion that the hero had been dragging his feet. His loving spouse, Penelope, had (in the meantime) occupied herself in doing the household chores, spinning, and bringing up the kids."[40] Peggy continues with a socialist-feminist analysis of high culture, arguing that both classical literature and classical music have constructed an image of women as passive, brainless, and completely controlled by their lovers. In contrast to these unrealistic and condescending images, she celebrates the women found in folk music:

> It is only when we turn to traditional song that a recognisable woman begins to emerge. The female protagonists of the folk songs have their feet (real feet) on real ground. They work and sweat at harvesting—they bleach clothes on the banks of the Kelvin, herd sheep and cows, spin cotton and flax. . . . Above all, they are prepared to argue and fight for what they want. . . . It is this realistic and positive attitude in folk song which I, a woman singer, find most compelling. It is through these songs, made up and sung by generations of working people, that I first became conscious of the nature of the class struggle. In them, I discerned signals sharp and clear, showing how songs could play an

important role in women's struggle to be recognised as the other important half of the human race.[41]

The songs on *Penelope Isn't Waiting Any More* discuss housework, factory work, marriage, and childbirth. Many are traditional; some were composed by Peggy and other women songwriters. "You Didn't Do No Wrong" is a union song from the 1930s. "Jenny Bell," a painfully realistic song about a woman seduced and abandoned by her lover, was written by Mahala Nice during a ballad-writing workshop that Ewan and Peggy gave in 1969. Peggy is the lead singer on all the songs, with Ewan, Neill, and Kirsty (among others) providing additional singing and accompaniment.

In February and September 1976, Ewan and Peggy served as consultants to the Stantonbury Campus Drama Group, a community theater group associated with Stantonbury Campus, a school in Milton Keynes. The group was creating a documentary play based on local history and wanted to include original songs in the production. In workshops and seminars, Ewan and Peggy described their method of songwriting and oversaw the creation of songs for the group's production, *All Change*. In autumn of that year, they toured Australia for the first time. The Australian tour was sponsored by the Amalgamated Metal Workers' Union, which also produced *Songs of Struggle*, a recording of a concert that Ewan and Peggy gave in Sydney. After their return to England, a union official wrote an appreciative letter:

> One of the things for which I am truly indebted to you is that you made me aware that folksongs can arouse far deeper and lasting passion than the fiery speeches given at lunch hour meetings. Through the songs one can really experience the epochs during which they were written. The joy and sorrows, the happiness and pathos is so beautifully reflected through the authors' souls. I came to realise that one simple song can express the class conflict in the society in such a simple way, a task which writers can not accomplish in a whole book.[42]

In the same year, Ewan and Peggy produced *No Tyme Lyke the Present*, an album of traditional and modern folk songs, with the Australian label Larrikin.

Peggy and Ewan had been collecting music from Gypsies and Travellers since the early 1960s, and the 1970s afforded them the leisure to continue this work. Their respectful behavior and keen interest in the music earned the trust of Travellers throughout Britain. They had developed a particularly warm relationship with the Stewart family of Blairgowrie, Scotland. "It was always fun with them," remembers Peggy. "You get together and spend the whole evening just singing and talking."[43] In 1977, Peggy and Ewan published *Travellers' Songs from England and Scotland*, a compendium of songs collected from more than fifteen Travellers. The repertoire of songs was so rich that Ewan and Peggy called the Travellers "the real custodians of English and Scots traditional song."[44] The Stewarts were not included in this collection; their repertoire was so extensive that it was saved for a book of their own, entitled *Till Doomsday in the Afternoon*, published in 1986.

The late 1970s saw personal as well as professional changes. Changes to the tax law meant that Ewan and Peggy would benefit financially if they were legally wed. So on January 25, 1977 (Ewan's birthday), with Alice and Calum as witnesses, Peggy and Ewan went to a registry office in Bromley and married. (Kitty was sick, so Neill stayed home with her.) Telling the children about the upcoming nuptials was an interesting exercise, since they had (quite naturally) thought that their parents were married already. "You mean I'm a bastard?" asked Calum. "Good! When they call me a little bastard at school, I'll say, 'Yes, that's what I am.'"[45]

Despite Neill and Calum's interest in rock and popular music, they continued to play folk music with their parents—at home, on stage, and on recordings. By the late 1970s, the MacColl brothers had mastered an impressive array of instruments: Neill played guitar (classical and folk), autoharp, and mandolin; Calum played guitar, Appalachian dulcimer, psaltery, bongo drums, tin whistle, and kalimba. In 1977, Blackthorne Records produced two albums that featured Ewan, Peggy, and the boys: *Cold Snap* and *Saturday Night at the Bull & Mouth*. (The Bull & Mouth pub was then the home of the Singers Club.) The albums contained both traditional and contemporary folk songs. While Ewan's compositions tended to be political, Peggy's songs were personal. "Song for Calum" is a lighthearted tribute to her middle child, written in response to Calum's complaint that she had written a song for Neill and Kitty but not for him. "Thoughts of Time" is a poignant reflection on the age gap between Ewan and Peggy. With its haunting melody and its spare, pointed language, "Thoughts of Time" captures the concerns that Peggy would face for the rest of Ewan's life:

> We've been through every weather, you and me,
> Forever twining ourselves together till death will us part;
> But death seems nearer than it used to be—
>     Thoughts of time will break my heart.

We know our children will take wing and fly,
Ties will be broken and a circle torn apart;
But to know our children will grow old and die—
    Thoughts of time will break my heart.[46]

Ewan was beginning to weary of touring, but Peggy still enjoyed seeing new places and meeting new people. They continued to tour throughout Britain and in 1977 added a tour of the Netherlands. A highlight of the Dutch tour was a reunion with Peggy's old *vereeniging* from the University of Leiden. In the late summer, she traveled alone to the United States to attend a celebration of her father's life at the University of California at Berkeley. The Charles Seeger celebration, organized by ethnomusicologist Bonnie Wade (a Berkeley faculty member) and historian Ann Pescatello (who was writing his biography), attracted scholars and musicians alike. A university publication reported: "He [Charles Seeger] played music, attended conferences, and went to parties. Photographs from the event showed an able-bodied man with a gleam in his eye, ready to live another 90 years."[47]

In the same year, Peggy and Mike put out a three-cassette recording of songs culled from their mother's songbook *American Folk Songs for Children.* In the liner notes, Peggy and Mike write: "The book is a documentary about communication, with music as the medium. . . . Children make and sing songs in the same way, and for the same purpose, as they play games: to prepare themselves for the adult world. They see that world all around them in its true violence, with all its bewildering contradictions. . . . Children *are* violent, passionate, innocent, knowing and utterly involved in life. . . . Adults who ignore this or suppress a child's interest are asking for trouble."[48] This earnestness pervades much of the recording, which, like the book, is really designed for adults who wish to teach the songs to children. The album showcases the enormous diversity of traditional American songs: there are ballads, play-party songs, hymns, lullabies, and work songs. Some of the songs are mere fragments; others have lyrics that show little artistry or imagination, but Peggy and Mike bring them all to life with exciting instrumentation and a wide variety of singing styles. They enliven the undistinguished lyrics in "Jim along Josie" by varying the rhythm and tempo to suit the words: "Run, Jim along, Jim along Josie" is sung quickly, while "Hop, Jim along, Jim along Josie" has a bouncing rhythm. This variation is exactly the sort of game a child might devise for this song. "As I Walked Out One Holiday," a variant of the Child ballad "Sir Hugh" (Child 155), has the gripping story and spare, poetic lyrics that characterize the best of Anglo-American folk music. (This version does not have the anti-Semitism found in many variants of "Sir Hugh.") Peggy and Mike's matter-of-fact vocal delivery is especially effective in conveying the everyday horror of the story—a child killed by a neighbor when he goes to retrieve his ball from her yard. "I'm Going to Join the Army" is one of the many Anglo-American folk songs in which a woman follows her sweetheart to war. In this version, just three stanzas long, the lovers agree to go to war together and to marry as soon as the battle is over. Mike sings the words with simple dignity, while Peggy's beautiful and lighthearted banjo accompaniment reinforces the naive hope expressed in the story.

If *American Folksongs for Children* showcased traditional music at its most basic, Peggy's next recording, *Hot Blast*, presented folk revival songs at their most complex. Produced by Blackthorne in 1978, *Hot Blast* contains Ewan and Peggy's most recent songs. Ewan's "Blast against Blackguards" and "Legal Illegal" are stringent (and hilarious) critiques of British politics, filled with wit, wordplay, topical references, and Marxist analysis. While they use certain features of folk style (acoustic accompaniment, repeated final lines, etc.), their modern referents and ironic tone make them very different from traditional folk songs. "The Tenant Farmer," based on a man who lived near their cottage in Scotland, is much closer to traditional models; it tells the story of a farmer who can no longer afford to work the land he does not own. "White Wind," a self-styled "folk cantata" written for the anti-apartheid movement, is composed of five different songs with different foci and different musical styles. "White Wind" is somewhat reminiscent of the work of the Composers Collective: a complex and politically conscious musical creation that uses folk music as a foundation.

Peggy wrote only two of the ten songs on *Hot Blast*. These two songs reflect the causes that would engage her for many years to come: the women's movement and the environmental movement. "Emily" is a realistic, painfully detailed story of one woman's violent marriage and her eventual escape from her attacker. Like a traditional ballad, "Emily" addresses a social problem by focusing on the story of a single person. "The Invader," by contrast, protests nuclear power by addressing the grand sweep of human history, beginning with a mythic golden age:

> On the first six days we lived in trees,
> We hunted, farmed, made bread and cheese;
> We forged and built, white, black and brown,
> The kingdom of man in Eden's ground—

And when we'd made our heaven and hell,
On the seventh day we killed ourselves . . .[49]

The 1970s were a fruitful time for writing and scholarship. Ewan and Peggy found an intellectual ally in Raphael Samuel, the prominent social historian and leader of the History Workshop movement, which grew out of the workshops that Samuel developed as a tutor at Ruskin College. History Workshop championed the study of people and subjects that conventional, elite history had neglected; "history from below" was a term frequently used to describe the movement's focus. In the 1970s, History Workshop published a pamphlet based on Ewan and Peggy's interviews with Ben Bright, entitled *Shellback: Reminiscences of Ben Bright, Mariner*. Ewan also began collaborating with Samuel on a book about the history of radical theater, a project that would absorb him for years. Ewan's health began to limit how much they could travel, though they continued to tour throughout the British Isles and in 1978 added a tour of Belgium. In August 1978, Peggy wrote to her father, "Ewan remains well, but has caught every ailment possible in the last four months—gout, bronchitis, diverticulitis, slip-disc, sore throats galore. When I say 'he remains well,' I meant in spirit."[50]

Peggy's father had always been an important part of her life. He was the person who approved of everything she did, the person to whom she could say anything. Charles traveled to England every few years, and his visits were eagerly anticipated by the entire family. But when he said good-bye after a visit in 1978, Peggy sensed a seriousness that had not been there previously. Charles was ninety-two at the time, still writing, still working on the "Principia Musicologica," which he hoped would be his magnum opus, healthy and strong enough to make a transatlantic journey and return to the house where he lived alone. But he had been experiencing heart tremors, and Peggy remembers, "I got a different kind of hug from him when he left."[51]

Charles Louis Seeger Jr. died on February 7, 1979, at his home in Bridgewater, Connecticut. Accolades from friends and colleagues poured in from around the world. Composer Henry Cowell said, "Charles Seeger is the greatest musical explorer in intellectual fields which America has produced."[52] Ethnomusicologist and music historian Gilbert Chase asserted, "In the realm of logic and theory he stands on a par with such thinkers as Russell, Whitehead, and Wittgenstein; in the social sciences, with Durkheim, Kroeber, Parsons, and Weber; in musicology, with Adler, Helmholtz, and Sachs."[53] And ethnomusicologist Mantle Hood counseled students and colleagues alike, "*Read all Charles Seeger has had to say before claiming to have a new idea.*"[54] Peggy knew that her father had lived a rich and productive life, filled with work and love and friends. But his death left a gap that could not be filled. In the summer, she returned to the United States to help her family sort through his belongings. At the airport, waiting for the plane that would take her back to England, Peggy "howl[ed] at him with anger for leaving [her]." She remembers, "Shaking my fist at the sky like something in a Greek tragedy. Howling at him, 'You have no right to do this. You have no right to leave me.'"[55]

In 1979, Blackthorne Records produced two albums that showed the two sides of the folk revival: the traditional and the contemporary. The traditional album, *Blood and Roses* volume 1, was the first of a five-volume set devoted to the classic English and Scottish ballads, primarily from the Child collection. The contemporary album, *Different Therefore Equal*, was Peggy's second album of women's songs. While *Penelope Isn't Waiting Any More* is largely composed of traditional songs, *Different Therefore Equal* has only contemporary songs—all but one written by Peggy. As such, it is more hard-hitting and politically focused than its comparatively gentle predecessor: many traditional songs complain about a woman's lot, but few offer practical solutions. The songs on *Different Therefore Equal* vary widely in style and subject matter. The perennial favorite "I'm Gonna Be an Engineer" tells the story of a woman who tries to balance work and family and finds herself a second-class citizen in both. Its lyrics are sophisticated yet easy to understand, and the tune—with its Scots snaps, wide range, and variations in key—is difficult to sing yet rests comfortably on the ear. "Union Woman," based on the testimony of union activist Mrs. Jayaben Desai, is both a defense of unionism and an indictment of an entrenched labor movement that does not aid women of color. "Winnie and Sam," about domestic violence, is that rare song that uses humor to heighten, rather than mute, the seriousness of its theme. "Reclaim the Night" has a haunting tune and beautifully crafted lyrics; it is one of the first songs to treat rape as a political problem:

> Though Eve was made from Adam's rib, nine months he lay within
>    her crib;
> How can a man of woman born thereafter use her sex with scorn?
> For though we bear the human race, to us is given but second place;
> And some men place us lower still by using us against our will.[56]

The year 1979 was filled with travel. In addition to tours throughout Britain, Ewan and Peggy toured Australia in the winter and the United States in the autumn. In the spring, they traveled to their cottage in Scotland for a holiday.

Ewan was in the barn chopping wood when he felt the violent pain that signaled his first major angina attack. His recovery required major changes in the way he lived. He gave up smoking. He cut down on red meat and rich cheeses. He made sure to get sufficient rest and exercise. He would have another productive decade, filled with singing, writing, and spending time with friends and family, but the specter of death would never be far from his peripheral vision. In his autobiography, he wrote, "I have been able to deal with illness, with gout for example, . . . with diverticular disease, with hiatus hernia. But heart malfunction—that is a different kettle of fish. You feel so vulnerable, such a pawn in the game played by your body."[57]

In the summer, Ewan, Peggy, Calum, Kitty, and Alice set out for a vacation in the Scottish islands. (Neill stayed behind to spend time with his girlfriend.) Ewan was at the wheel when he suddenly began to drive erratically. Peggy remembers:

> He was going around curves on the wrong side of the road. . . . And Calum was saying, "Dad, stop!" . . . Alice is white as a sheet. . . . And I said, "Ewan, I don't like the way you're driving." He said, "Close your eyes." Now that wasn't Ewan. . . . And the only thing I knew to do—I said, "Ewan, I'm going to be sick. You don't want me to be sick in the car, do you?" I wasn't going to be sick, but he stopped the car. It was an absolute wonder that we weren't killed, that we didn't hit somebody head-on coming the other way.[58]

Peggy drove the rest of the way, but she could not drive the return journey; she was flying directly from Scotland to the United States. She called Neill and asked him to come to Scotland and drive the family home, which he did. Peggy was terrified and furious; she left Ewan a letter saying that if he did something like that again, she would leave him. She was even more frightened when Ewan told her he had no memory of the event. She had noticed, when she stepped into the driver's seat, that Ewan's face was slightly askew. The lapse of memory, the erratic behavior, and the alteration in Ewan's appearance led Peggy to the conclusion that he had had a minor stroke.

That year foreshadowed the decade that was to follow. The 1980s were a time of exploration and discovery, when Ewan and Peggy produced some of their best albums and wrote some of their finest songs. It was a decade when Peggy began to work on projects of her own, to travel down roads where Ewan could not follow. It was also a time of illness, uncertainty, and loss.

# CHAPTER 16

# The Day Is Ending

Can it be the day is ending,
Our harvest gathered, our fledglings have flown;
Would you leave me in the autumn, love,
To live out my winter alone?

—Peggy Seeger, "New Spring Morning"

"The eighties were not like anything that happened before," recalls Peggy. "It was a shift in power."[1] Ewan's many illnesses were taking their toll. On tour in Seattle, mock malaria sent him to bed with a high fever and delirium, which resulted in Ewan creating a Joycean stream-of-consciousness monologue that kept him and ten-year-old Kitty convulsed with laughter. Two days later, he was back on tour. He retained a gallant stoicism with regard to his ailments, never complaining even when he collapsed at the airport and spent the next few days at home in bed rather than on the holiday he had planned with Peggy and Kitty. Perhaps he felt, wordsmith that he was, that the dangers within him could be held at bay if he never gave them voice. But his autobiography, written in the final decade of his life, shows that he accepted their reality: "All through the thirties, forties, fifties, sixties and early seventies, I plunged headlong into each day like a swimmer intent on racing the tide. So many interesting things to do, so much work to be done; so many people to meet, friends to be made, enemies to be fought.... I have reached the point in my life when I am ... frequently halted in my tracks by the thought of leaving so much work unfinished (and unstarted) and so many things left unsaid."[2]

Ewan and Peggy cut down on touring, though they continued to travel to the United States (occasionally with Neill and Calum) and in 1982 sang in Milan. A holiday in Venice ended in disaster: Ewan suffered his second major heart attack and spent three days in intensive care. Ewan and Peggy continued to tour throughout the British Isles, though sometimes he had to cancel because of illness, leaving Peggy to perform alone. Neill and Calum joined them on a tour of Germany in 1984, and Ewan gave his final foreign performance in 1988 at a festival of political songs in East Berlin, where Peggy says they were "totally out of place. . . . It was mostly young rockers."[3] By 1988, political music and political causes were different from what Ewan and Peggy were used to. She recalls, "We met some amazing activists there. . . . By that time, I think our politics were beginning to be old-fashioned. The old movement politics were moving into nuclear power politics, into feminism. . . . A number of the activists who came there were from places where you were shot if you sang a song like what we sang. . . . Some of our songs were too intellectual, which separated them, brought them back to the realm of theory."[4] After many years of raging against the complacent and comfortable, they found they were a bit too comfortable themselves to completely understand the raw urgency of the singer/activists from Chile and El Salvador.

The 1980s were a decade of looking forward and looking back, of reflection and engagement. The folk revival was much smaller than it had been in its heyday, and some suggested that pop and rock music had supplanted folk music as the preferred musical form of modern life, for the working class as well as the middle class. Was folk music still a valid means of expression for the people it purported to represent? In a 1980 column in the *Lark* (the newsletter of the Singers Club), Jim Carroll wrote:

> It cannot have failed to come to the notice of anybody involved in the folk song movement that the revival is in a pretty poor condition. Club attendances are on the wane, record sales have plummeted and magazines have disappeared. . . . For over twenty years The Singers Club has concerned itself with presenting folk song and music, contemporary song (mainly in the folk idiom), theatre, poetry and storytelling to a standard that enables an audience to come, listen and enjoy without wondering if they have come to the right place on the right night. The accusation that we are politically biased is one that most of us involved in the club would happily plead guilty to. . . . We believe that the songs and music came into being and proliferated to supply a need in the lives of "ordinary" people. Despite the fact that the tradition has declined, we are of the opinion that what has now replaced folk music in working people's culture does not supply that need and that folk song still has a part to play in modern society.[5]

Ewan and Peggy continued to pay homage to traditional music and to use it as a foundation of their work; they also continued to write topical songs that pushed the boundaries of the folk tradition. In 1980, they appeared in the BBC television production *Stories and Songs of a Scots Family Group*, about the

Stewart family of Blairgowrie. The Stewarts had become well known to folk revival audiences—largely through Ewan and Peggy's promotion—for their starkly beautiful renditions of traditional Scots songs. By contrast, Ewan and Peggy's one album from 1980, *Kilroy Was Here*, features no traditional songs. Taking the slogan attributed to American servicemen during World War II, the album treats Kilroy as a twentieth-century Everyman, the subject and creator of modern folk culture. The liner notes, unattributed but showing Ewan's unmistakable stamp, blast the modern enemies of Kilroy—the politicians who control Kilroy's life without caring about it:

> The windy rhetoric of politicians . . . the gobbledygook that issues nightly from the talking heads which occupy ten million illuminated screens throughout this island. . . . The voices . . . unctuous, avuncular, pompous and patronising . . . scarcely bothering to conceal the contempt they feel for clods like us. . . . And Kilroy, who has heard it all before and who is accustomed to getting the shitty end of the stick begins to wonder whether the world wouldn't be a safer place without all those talking heads and this shrill pantomime dame whose verbal diarrhoea threatens his world with imminent inundation.
>
> Almost all the bands on this disc are made about this or that aspect of Kilroy's condition: Kilroy old, Kilroy young, Kilroy male, Kilroy female, Kilroy hoping, Kilroy despairing. Above all it is about the terrifying dangers that confront Kilroy now, NOW, NOW![6]

Margaret Thatcher, the Conservative prime minister elected in 1979, is the "shrill pantomime dame" who became the special target of Peggy and Ewan's hatred during the 1980s.

*Kilroy Was Here* is an eclectic collection. Peggy's song for Kitty, "Lullabye for a Very New Baby," is featured on the album, and for the first time Ewan has songs about personal, rather than political, topics. "Nobody Knew She Was There" is a tribute to his mother, who spent her life cleaning houses and office buildings but was scarcely noticed by the people for whom she worked—not the office workers, not the families whose houses she cleaned, not even the husband and son she supported. "My Old Man" is an achingly beautiful song about Ewan's father, a skilled iron molder who lost his sense of purpose when he lost his job and died many years before his wife.

The title song and "Seven Days of the Week" are more typical of Ewan's oeuvre—heroic songs in praise of the workers (the Kilroys) who built the world but did not share in its riches. "Seven Days of the Week" shows a worker (significantly called "my old man") who rises each morning to create wonders—from Monday to Friday, he builds the pyramids, Nineveh, Babylon,

Rome, and the Suez Canal. On Saturday he is fired, but on Sunday he begins to create revolution:

> My old man got up on Sunday morning,
> Went and gave the boss this little warning:
> "You've sat on your arse and played at God,
> And watched me sweat and carry the hod—
> But now that caper's over, chum, you're leaving!"[7]

Most of Ewan's political music had been written in relatively masculinist terms—both the heroes and the villains are men. The 1980s provided a powerful woman—Margaret Thatcher—whose politics were diametrically opposed to everything that Ewan and Peggy believed. "In Praise of Famous Men (and Women)," "The Androids," and "Get Rid of It" are hate letters to Margaret Thatcher, songs that feature Ewan's familiar combination of humor, wordplay, and biting political commentary.

Peggy has fewer songs on this album than Ewan, but hers are the ones that point toward new political directions. "The Plutonium Factor" has a simple, almost chant-like melody and remarkably sophisticated lyrics; it discusses the scientific and political aspects of nuclear power. Without minimizing the complexity of her subject, Peggy makes it comprehensible to the ordinary person:

> The problem is elemental, easy to understand:
> Uranium's incidental, lying beneath the land.
> Find it, mine it,
> Enrich and refine it—
> No matter its use,
> A demon is loose,
> Plutonium's left, long after the death of man.[8]

"The Plutonium Factor" discusses the dangers that occur with even the most benign intentions for nuclear power. "Four-Minute Warning," by contrast, shows the devastation that nuclear weapons would cause. Written to last exactly four minutes—the amount of time that the British government had allotted to give warning in case of a nuclear attack—the song invites us to imagine a nuclear bomb landing on London:

> The rulers are sheltered, but God has gone under,
> Victim perhaps of a technical blunder.
> The vermin survive disease and starvation,
> To witness the end of a civilisation.[9]

Though Peggy wrote relatively few songs for *Kilroy Was Here*, her influence was everywhere. She arranged all the songs, sang on most of them, and played guitar, concertina, banjo, autoharp, and dulcimer. Her musical choices heightened the effectiveness of the songs' messages—from the gentle guitar on "Lullabye for a Very New Baby" to the taut banjo on "Kilroy Was Here" to the starkly unaccompanied "Four-Minute Warning."

1981 was a relatively quiet year. Ewan and Peggy toured the United States and the British Isles, but their concert dates were fewer now. Peggy gave a series of women's concerts with Neill in Ireland, and Ewan and Peggy did an increasing number of performances for the Campaign for Nuclear Disarmament (CND). The second volume of their *Blood and Roses* series, which features traditional ballads, was produced that year. They joined other folk artists in Philip Donnellan's television documentary *The Other Music*, which chronicled the folk revival from 1945 to 1981. The program featured interviews and performances with traditional singers, such as Harry Cox and Sam Larner, and with folk revival artists, including Frankie Armstrong, Martin Carthy, Alan Lomax, A. L. Lloyd, and Louis Killen. Charles Parker was a researcher on the production, but he did not live to see the broadcast. He died on December 10, 1980, at the age of sixty-one. In "Song for Charles Parker," Peggy pays homage to the man she called "one of my dearest friends":

> Time, tide me over a few more years,
> Please allow my comrade's friends to thrive;
> We're part of all that he held dear—
> We keep our friend alive.[10]

Charles Parker's death and the waning of the folk revival were both unwelcome signs of the passage of time. The suggestion that pop and rock music had replaced folk music, particularly in the hearts of the young, was not new, but by the early 1980s the reality of this phenomenon appeared on Ewan and Peggy's doorstep. Neill and Calum had played folk music with their parents for years, but now they were leaving home both literally and figuratively: their music of choice was rock, and both formed rock bands. Ewan disliked and dismissed rock, but Peggy was quietly intrigued. Calum remembers, "Mum had this sneaking, kind of quiet, secret admiration for other types of music. . . . I remember her saying to me when I was about six or seven that she really liked 'Eleanor Rigby.' . . . If she had said to Dad, 'Actually, I think the Beatles are really good,' it would have sparked off this huge intellectual argument discussion, and it would have created sulks and rifts, and so she just didn't. It was easier not to."[11] From the vantage point of more than three decades after the fact, Peggy offers a similar point of view: "It's one of the great regrets of my life that we didn't allow them [Neill and Calum] to educate us in the music they were doing. . . . They would listen to things in their room that . . . Ewan called trash. I listened to some of it. . . . I kind of followed Ewan too much on these things without thinking. I should have listened more closely, because some of what they were listening to was excellent."[12]

Both Neill and Calum became successful professional musicians, but the MacColl who became the best known was their half-sister, Kirsty. Kirsty Mac-Coll was unapologetically a pop singer who considered folk music passé. "I wasn't really into folk music," she said. "It wasn't particularly because I had anything to prove against my dad, or anything. It was just because I was a different generation."[13] Though one can find folk influences in Kirsty's music, the influences of pop, rock, and even American country music are stronger. In 1981, her country-infused single "There's a Guy Works down the Chip Shop Swears He's Elvis" reached the top of the pop charts. Her music is similar to Ewan's in its nonconformist stance and clever lyrics, but her style of musical expression was quite different.

Though the folk revival was on the downswing, Ewan and Peggy were still much in demand. Unfortunately, Ewan's failing health required them to turn down many requests to sing. After Ewan's heart attack in Italy in 1982, the Singers Club closed for a year. Ewan's doctors forbade him to do any heavy lifting, so Peggy hauled the instruments and the boxes of records. "He was not invincible anymore," recalls Peggy.[14] A further sign of time's inevitability occurred on September 1, 1982, when Betsy Miller died at the age of ninety-six. Despite their fraught relationship, Peggy recognized Betsy's strength and worth. And they had gotten on well after Betsy left the house, eight years earlier. "When I first met her," recalls Peggy, "it seemed as if she'd just last forever. She was one of those people that would survive anything. . . . She was born to hardship; she lived in hardship. . . . She died without any self-pity. She worked like a dog. . . . She never asked for thanks for anything she did; she just did it."[15] Still another blow came on September 29, when Ewan and Peggy's old friend and coworker A. L. Lloyd died.

Ewan wrote few songs that year and participated in only one album: the third volume of the *Blood and Roses* series. As Ewan's energy and musical output decreased, Peggy stepped into the breach. "Mum became the person in charge," recalls Kitty, "because she had to."[16] Peggy produced a solo album, *From Where I Stand*, a collection of new songs by some of the best American singer-songwriters, including Don Lange, Hazel Dickens, Charlie King, and Si Kahn. The songs reflect Peggy's position as an American folksinger who lived in England, a choice that needed continual renegotiation and updating:

> The crisis didn't really hit me until the mid-1970's when I discovered that there were a number of my favorite indigenous American songs that I just never seemed to sing any more: Old Joe Clark, Cindy, and many of the banjo tunes. I was definitely leaning towards that section of American music which had originated in Britain, and indeed I became a fine ballad-singer. But I was a prime case of cultural displacement and disorientation. I had always been interested in industrial and protest songs and I now became interested in contemporary American topical music. . . . I need these musical ties that make me feel as if I am still part of the action of the land of my birth. They make it possible for me to continue singing the folksongs on stage. . . . I have included three of my own songs on this album because this is where I stand, where I live, with one foot in each country and a perspective that is mid-Atlantic.[17]

Most of the songs on *From Where I Stand* fall into two categories: songs about the environment and songs about workers' rights. Muriel Hogan wrote about both topics: "Third Shift" is about a factory worker on the night shift, while "Agent Orange Song" is about a soldier who fought in Vietnam and suffered the poisonous effects of Agent Orange. Some of the songs are relatively well known, such as Si Kahn's "Aragon Mill," about the closure of a textile plant, and Hazel Dickens's "Black Lung." Others are less familiar, such as Deborah Silverstein's haunting "Draglines," about the dangers of strip-mining, or Don Lange's exquisitely written "Cargo of Dread," about the dangers of radioactivity. Peggy's two political songs, "Please, Mr. Reagan" and "Enough Is Enough," are stylistically reminiscent of Ewan's work: humorous, tongue-in-cheek songs about serious subjects. Peggy wrote "Enough Is Enough," about the dangers of nuclear power, after interviewing friends, family, and complete strangers. She spoke to people on buses, in doctors' waiting rooms, and after gigs, telling them of her project and asking them to contribute ideas. The method, reminiscent of the Radio Ballads, "worked beautifully," she says. "They came up with ideas and ways of expressing them that I would never have hit upon."[18] With its rollicking tune and clever wordplay, "Enough Is Enough" manages to be lighthearted and amusing until the final lines: "Just remember that the nuclear way may any day turn out to be a / Very Final Solution."[19]

In many ways, the categories in *From Where I Stand* represent both the politics of the Old Left, which Peggy learned from Ewan, and the politics of the New Left, which Peggy discovered on her own. Starting in the late 1970s, Peggy became a staunch environmental and antinuclear activist. The catalyst for her antinuclear activism was a newspaper article that described how nuclear waste traveled by rail through Beckenham Junction Station en route to a reprocessing plant in the Lake District. The trains ran on ordinary railway lines, close to suburban houses and less than a mile from Kitty's school. Peggy began a discussion group to study nuclear power, relying heavily on the 1979 publication *No Nukes: Everyone's Guide to Nuclear Power* by Anna Gyorgy and friends. The dangers described in Gyorgy's book, from the hardships of uranium mining to the possibility of an accident or collision with a train carrying radioactive material, quickly led the study group to become a political organization: the Beckenham Anti-Nuclear Group (BANG). BANG was initially composed of mothers whose children attended school with Kitty, but other Beckenham residents joined as well, including a few men.

BANG members lectured on the subject of nuclear power, passed out leaflets near the Beckenham railway tracks, canvassed passersby in communities near the railway line, and organized meetings in Beckenham Town Hall. Peggy also withheld 11 percent of her electricity bill, since 11 percent of British electricity was provided by nuclear power. When she was threatened with having her electricity cut off, she relented and wrote a check—but in a way that made redeeming the money as inconvenient as possible. British law did not require that checks be written in checkbooks; so long as all the appropriate information was supplied, any method could be used, a policy that Peggy exploited with wicked humor: "I would write the cheque out on a door, on a rotten egg, on a cake, or on a small coffin-shaped dulcimer case. . . . All cheques have to go through a system of checking, stamping, filing, and being sent back to the originator. My 'cheques' came back to me by courier. The egg was *very* gently presented to me on my doorstep. The cake never came back. I had sent a note with it, requesting the bank staff to eat it."[20] Kitty sometimes joined in her mother's antinuclear activities. As a child, she helped her mother run a CND stall on Beckenham High Street on Saturdays, which Kitty remembers as "the worst place to have that sort of thing. . . . Beckenham is a very right-wing suburb."[21] She also accompanied Peggy when she delivered her unconventional checks to the Lewisham Electricity Board. "I remember it being quite fun when I was really young," recalls Kitty.[22]

At the same time that BANG developed as an antinuclear organization on the local level, the women's peace camp at Greenham Common emerged on the national level. Greenham Common, near the town of Newbury, was (as its name implies) technically common land, but the British and the Americans had used it as a military base since World War II. In 1979, NATO decided to house nuclear missiles at the Greenham Common airbase, and in 1981 preparations began to send ninety-six American Tomahawk cruise missiles—each four times more powerful than the atomic bomb at Hiroshima—to Greenham Common. Concerned about the destructive capabilities of the missiles, a small group in Wales called Women for Life on Earth chose to publicize their concern with a 120-mile walk from Cardiff to Greenham Common. (The original marchers included four men as well as thirty-six women.) Upon their arrival at Greenham on September 5, the marchers sent a message to the base commander stating their opposition to the cruise missiles and asking for a peaceful debate on the subject. Their request was denied, and the base commander reportedly said that "they could stay as long as they liked as far as he was concerned. So they did."[23]

For nineteen years, the Women's Peace Camp maintained a presence at Greenham Common. The original marchers were soon joined by antinuclear activists from around the country, then the world. Donations poured in: tents, food, water, firewood, blankets. A fire burned continually, but living outdoors with primitive cooking, washing, and toilet facilities was not easy, particularly considering the characteristically cold and damp English weather. Supporters came and went; some stayed for years. Initially, men were involved, but it soon became a women's initiative, and men were not allowed to participate. The women insisted that the protest remain peaceful but not necessarily legal; they engaged in civil disobedience when construction began on the silos that would house the nuclear missiles, and several women broke into the airbase itself. The camp was well organized but had relatively little hierarchy. Peggy recalls, "The press . . . would come and virtually say TAKE US TO YOUR LEADER. When it became obvious that there WAS no leader, they would ask, say, Genevieve, 'Why are you all here?' The drill was to say, 'well, I'M HERE because . . . But you might want to ask Anne/Maisie/Samantha, etc., why SHE'S here.' The press was baffled by this. . . . The place was noticeably lacking in the usual concept of 'leader.'"[24]

Both supporters and detractors showed a canny ability to exploit the images of a "proper" woman's place. The protesters frequently presented themselves as mothers concerned about their children's future. Their adversaries excoriated them as witches and "bedraggled lesbians" and asked if they were so concerned about their children, why weren't they at home with them?[25] In December 1982, the protesters organized a demonstration to "embrace the base"—to join hands around the nine-mile perimeter of Greenham Common airbase. More than thirty thousand women took part, enough to form two circles around the wire fence that surrounded the airbase. To promote their image as loving family members, the women decorated the fence with photographs, children's clothes, teddy bears, and other bits of family memorabilia. But they violated the conventional image of femininity by refusing to be soft or self-effacing. The human chain became a human blockade that resulted in hundreds of women being arrested and removed by the police.

Peggy drove to the "embrace the base" demonstration with Ewan and Kitty, but only Peggy participated: "men were not welcome at the demonstrations and it was dangerous for children."[26] Afterward, she wrote "Carry Greenham Home," which quickly became one of the main anthems of the Greenham Common peace camp. Here she captures the image of women as simultaneously loving and strong, practicing politics in a uniquely feminine way:

> Woman tiger, woman dove,
> Help to save the world we love,
> Velvet fist in iron glove,
> Bring the message home.[27]

In November 1983, the cruise missiles arrived at Greenham, a fact that energized the peace movement. On November 15, thousands of protesters demonstrated outside the Houses of Parliament. When told to disperse, they sat down in Parliament Square, and hundreds were arrested, Peggy Seeger among them. For her trial in February 1984, she wrote a song to sing in her defense. The song, "Tomorrow," describes the fear of living under the threat of nuclear oblivion:

> I know where my pleasures lie, for pleasures I have many,
> Hopes and dreams that carry me through daily care and worry;
> But every pleasure's touched with grief, every hope blighted with sorrow,
> Nightmare overtakes the dream—I fear I've lost tomorrow.[28]

The judge cited her for contempt of court before she had finished these four lines. "But she got what she wanted—it got into all the papers," recalls Kitty.[29] Kitty was a young teenager at the time, and her reaction to her mother is reminiscent of the young Peggy's reaction to Ruth—pride mixed with embarrassment. Recalling her mother's singing defense, Kitty says, "That was quite mortifying, but a great thing to do. I was just like, 'No, Mum, no. Be a normal mother. Go and cook or something.'"[30]

Peggy went to Greenham more than a dozen times, sometimes alone, sometimes with other members of BANG. One of the most dedicated BANG members was Irene Scott. Peggy had known Irene for years; they originally met in the mid-1960s in Belfast (Irene's hometown) when both sang at a benefit concert for Dave Kitson, an anti-apartheid activist who was then imprisoned in South Africa. In the late 1960s, twenty-one-year-old Irene moved to Beckenham to be near her brother, Dave, who was a friend of Ewan and Peggy and did most of the artwork for the *New City Songster*. Peggy and Irene became reacquainted during this time, and they frequently found themselves at the same place: at the Singers Club, at the Festival of Fools, at an anti-apartheid demonstration outside of South Africa House, on a bus going to Greenham Common.

For years, Peggy and Irene were casual acquaintances, but when Irene joined BANG, the two became friends. By this time, Irene was married to a local veterinarian and administered his practice. Peggy had few close friends; her energies were focused on her music, her politics, and her family. Ewan was the confidant to whom she had always turned, but as his health declined, he was no longer the bulwark of strength on which she could lean. In addition, her politics were developing in ways that Ewan respected but did not entirely understand. Calum remembers the political complexities that emerged in the late 1970s and 1980s:

> Feminism . . . sits in a very weird place in Britain with the whole history of the Left. A lot of the lefties . . . that were Dad's friends and I saw when I was growing up; a lot of them were male chauvinist pigs. . . . So it was Mum's kind of way, "Right, you believe in this politics. You believe in democracy and true egalitarianism. Here we go. Apply it to women." Oh yeah. They'd all very much agree in principle. But it was slightly uncomfortable. . . . He supported her on it and he was very proud of her. . . . But I think he was a bit taken aback because it was something suddenly for the first time politically—it was something that she was leading.[31]

Increasingly, Peggy turned to Irene, who wholeheartedly shared her enthusiasm for feminism and environmentalism.

By the mid-1980s, some of Ewan's work had taken on a valedictory air, a sense of examining the legacy that he would leave behind. In 1983, Blackthorne Records produced *Freeborn Man*, which, while not billed as a "greatest hits" record, was essentially that; it presented "some of the most frequently requested songs in [Ewan and Peggy's] joint repertoire."[32] In the same year, Ewan and Peggy were featured in Philip Donnellan's television documentary

*The Good Old Way.* They discussed the history of the folk revival, reminisced about its early days and the changes that had occurred, and discussed their own vision of folk music's style and purpose. "Folk music is not something that you do if you can't do anything else musically," said Peggy. "It is a discipline all on its own."[33] In 1984, Mary Orr and Michael O'Rourke began interviewing them for a radio documentary, entitled *Parsley, Sage and Politics: The Lives and Music of Peggy Seeger and Ewan MacColl,* which broadcast in 1986 on National Public Radio and later was released as a three-CD set. *Parsley, Sage and Politics* covers Ewan and Peggy's childhoods, Ewan's early years in the theater, the Ballads and Blues clubs, the Radio Ballads, the Festival of Fools, and their contemporary political work. If much of this work had a slight valedictory edge, both Ewan and Peggy made it clear that nostalgia was not their aim. In the film *Ewan MacColl and Peggy Seeger,* made by Seattle filmmaker Jane Muir, Ewan said, "I hate the idea of music as antiquarian. I think it's the death of folk music."[34] Even more pointedly, Peggy spoke about the necessity to connect to both the past and the future: "It's not only the function of the folksinger to sing the songs from the past and make people realize their roots or to reaffirm the sense of identity. You have to point a way to the future. This is the function of art. Not just to be a museum piece, but to see that what we have now and what we are making now comes out of what used to be."[35]

The twin aims of honoring the past and working toward the future became more urgent in light of Ewan's failing health. During a 1984 tour of the United States, he suffered another heart attack. In the same year, a national crisis galvanized Ewan and Peggy politically. In March, Great Britain's National Coal Board announced its intention to close twenty mines, which would result in the loss of twenty thousand jobs. The National Union of Mineworkers (NUM), led by Arthur Scargill, called for a national strike of all mineworkers. Some unions struck in solidarity, while others did not, and not all miners participated in the strike. There were violent confrontations between the strikers and the police, with many arrests and even a few deaths. Margaret Thatcher was determined to defeat the strike (and eventually did so) and referred to the striking miners as "the enemy within."[36]

No industry had been more important to Britain's industrial development than coal, and no union was more militant than the NUM. It was no coincidence that as the coal industry declined, so did Britain's position as the world's preeminent industrial and military nation. The difficult work and dangerous working conditions in the mines had created a long tradition of militant trade unionism, and British dependency on coal had given the miners a strong bargaining position. In the 1950s, the demand for British coal declined drastically, due to the low cost of imported oil, a decline in heavy industry, the development of nuclear power, and attempts to control air pollution following "the great smog of 1952," which resulted in the death of more than four thousand people. Mines closed, and hundreds of thousands of miners found other ways to earn a living. These trends had accelerated by the 1980s. The Thatcher government cast the issue as one of necessary cost-cutting measures in a declining industry; the miners saw it as an assault on their ability to make a living.

The 1984 miners' strike polarized the country. Ewan and Peggy were firmly on the side of the striking miners. In collaboration with the NUM, they put out a cassette entitled *Daddy, What Did You Do in the Strike?* Unlike their recent albums of traditional songs and old favorites, this one has an up-to-the-minute freshness and urgency. In many ways, it is similar to the Radio Ballads: six songs are interspersed with testimony from the miners and their families, and the whole album has an energy, passion, and coherency reminiscent of those earlier works. For Peggy, one of the highlights of making *Daddy, What Did You Do in the Strike?* was Calum's participation. He produced the album, played on all the accompanied songs, and toured with his parents when they sang to the miners. As in *The Big Hewer*, the miners speak thoughtfully and with great eloquence on this album. A miner gives the rationale for the strike: "Basically, it started when it was suddenly announced that my colliery was to close. Five-year reserves: we were given five weeks' notice. In five years' time, you've time to plan, you've time to get ready, you've time to prepare. In five weeks, you've not got time to spit."[37]

The songs show a mixture of humor and seriousness, and they are unabashedly partisan. Ewan's song "The Media" shows how news media create as well as present public opinion; a guitar throbs in the background like an angry heartbeat. The police, as agents of the government and enemies of the strikers, are targeted in several songs. Ewan's "Only Doing Their Job" takes a phrase reminiscent of the Nazis' defense at the Nuremberg trials and applies it with cold sarcasm:

> There are shortsighted folks who insist that these blokes are just
> uniformed masters of thuggery;
> There can be no dispute, if they didn't put the boot in the country would
> all go to buggery.

So try and keep calm when they're twisting your arm or planting a fist in
    your gob;
When they're giving you hell in a cold prison cell, they're only just doing
    their job.[38]

Peggy's "The Villains' Chorus" also targets the police. It is a tongue-in-cheek
song told from the point of view of a professional criminal, who proclaims
that crime can now run rampant because the police are busy attacking the
miners and their supporters. The chorus takes the familiar stereotype of British policemen—kindhearted public servants who return lost children to their
parents and escort old ladies across the street—and turns it on its head by
having *criminals* praise the police:

> I think our police are wonderful, wonderful, wonderful,
> So join us in the chorus.
> We don't have to pay 'em to stay away ...
> The government does it for us.[39]

The title song focuses on the villainy of scabs (also called "blacklegs"),
miners who do not support the strike and cross picket lines to go back to
work. The title is a play on a World War I recruiting poster, which shows a
man with his daughter on his knee and his son playing with toy soldiers at
his feet. The legend reads "Daddy, what did *YOU* do in the Great War?" and
the man looks sadly ahead, apparently having shirked his duty at a time of
crisis. The song targets Ian MacGregor, head of the National Coal Board, and
echoes the antifascist rallying cry of the Spanish Civil War, *no pasaran* (they
shall not pass):

> Well, the battle it is joined at last, the forces they are massed:
> On their side, the press, the telly, all the weapons of their class,
> Plus MacGregor and his blacklegs, but we'll never let them pass,
> For the NUM's the weapon of the miners.
> > Daddy, what did you do in the strike?
> > Did you scab and let your workmates wage the fight?
> > How the neighbours stood and booed us,
> > Said we had the stink of Judas,
> > Daddy, what did you do in the strike?[40]

Both men and women were interviewed for the album, and there is a song
titled "Miner's Wife," as there was in *The Big Hewer*. But the 1984 "Miner's

Wife" shows both an activism and a tension not present in the earlier work. One miner's wife describes the situation: "I was involved in the '72 strike and the '74 strike. '84 is different. It's the involvement of the whole community. The women, not behind their men; they're beside them. And this is how we feel here—that we're really beside each other. Their fight is our fight."[41] Her words are echoed in the song, which Ewan wrote and Peggy sings:

> I've always stood behind him, but I swear
> From this time on you'll see me standing right beside him . . .
> On the picket line.[42]

*Daddy, What Did You Do in the Strike?* ends with a miner's wife saying, "The strike will go on till we win."[43] Yet the strike ended in March 1985, when the miners, worn out by nearly a year of poverty and hardship, voted to return to work without achieving their demands. The defeat of the NUM was a serious blow to Britain's trade union movement. Peggy's song "Forty-Five, Eighty-Five," written after the end of the miners' strike, links the New Left's current battles with the Old Left's past triumphs: she compares the postwar building of the welfare state with Thatcher's determination to dismantle it. In her description of the song and the era that gave birth to it, Peggy notes, "The fact that the opposing sides were coming out so violently against one another clarified and restated once more the history of class warfare in Marxist terms."[44] The final stanza is a call to arms:

> In '85, the time is ripe, the war has never stopped;
> The enemy's in the open now, the velvet glove has dropped.
> Every gain is dearly bought,
> Every issue must be fought—
> If we give an inch they'll take a mile—and then the bloody lot![45]

However, the politics of the 1980s could not be reduced simply to class antagonism or to the forces of progressivism versus the forces of reaction. The Old Left's focus on industrial unionism had begun to collide with the New Left's focus on environmentalism. Environmentalists challenged Britain's traditional dependence on coal, a fuel destructive to the environment and to the miners' own health, and began to champion cleaner sources of energy. (During the 1984 miners' strike, the environmental costs of coal were not at issue. The Thatcher government's solutions to a decreased use of British coal were an increased use of foreign coal and an increased dependence on nuclear power. Neither solution appealed to environmentalists.) Peggy, more so than

Ewan, was able to grapple with the complexity of the issues involved. Calum recalls: "The problem, in a sense, of the last ten years of Dad's life was the creeping realization that a lot of the politics that he'd sworn by his whole life didn't square up with each other completely. . . . For instance, green issues and unionization and protecting industrial jobs at all costs. When it's strip-mining—which one's going to win? It's a moral maze; there's moral mazes to everything. And those started to unravel a little bit toward the end."[46]

In navigating the moral mazes of the 1980s, Peggy took the lead. She wrote more than forty songs during the 1980s, covering a wide range of subjects: apartheid, the miners' strike, environmentalism, nuclear weapons, feminism, Latin American dictatorships, domestic violence, and abortion, among others. The songs that Ewan wrote during the 1980s were, with very few exceptions, about subjects he had addressed for many years: workers' rights, apartheid, and Tory politicians. He did branch out somewhat in the directions where Peggy led: his 1980 "What the Poet Called Her" is a gently feminist song that targets men's lazy romanticism, and he began writing songs about his own life and family, as Peggy had done for years. He also wrote a few songs about the environment: his 1986 "The Vandals" is a bleak description of a post-nuclear-holocaust future, and his 1988 "Nuclear Means Jobs" demolishes the argument that nuclear power is a boon to the working class. The environment was not an entirely new subject for him: his play *Uranium 235*, originally produced by Theatre Workshop in 1946, was about the danger of nuclear weapons.[47] He had written songs for the CND since the 1960s, and his 1970 song "Nightmare" is a dystopian fantasy of a ruined earth. But it was Peggy who wrote song after song about the new subjects and who pushed the issue of environmentalism beyond the dangers of nuclear power.

In 1986, Ewan and Peggy produced four albums: the fourth and fifth in their *Blood and Roses* series and two albums of topical songs, *White Wind, Black Tide* and *Items of News*. *White Wind, Black Tide* contains songs about apartheid, all but two of which were written by Ewan and Peggy. *Items of News* is Ewan and Peggy's first joint album that takes its title from a song that Peggy wrote—a piece, with both spoken and sung portions, about the violent history of twentieth-century El Salvador. The final song on *Items of News* is Ewan's "The Joy of Living." He wrote the song, using the melody of a traditional Sicilian folk song, during a walking holiday in Scotland. He set out for a day of mountain climbing with Peggy and Kitty but found he could not keep up with them and sat down to wait as they climbed to heights he could no longer reach. "The Joy of Living" is actually about the nearness of dying, but the title is not ironic; it is, instead, a tender valediction to a life well lived. The stanza about Peggy is particularly moving:

> Farewell to you, my love, my time is almost done.
> Lie in my arms once more until the darkness comes.
> You filled all my days, held the night at bay, dearest companion.
> Years pass by and are gone with the speed of birds in flight,
> Our life like the verse of a song heard in the mountains.
> Give me your hand then, love, and join your voice with mine—
> We'll sing of the hurt and the pain and the joy of living.[48]

Goaded by thoughts of death, and by Alan Lomax's persistent urging, Ewan started writing his autobiography. He was the elder statesman of the folk revival, and awards began to pour in. In 1986, he received an honorary Doctor of Letters from the University of Exeter, and a symposium in honor of his seventieth birthday was held at County Hall in London. Peggy was frequently included in these honors: both received a brass engraving of a ship from the Workers Music Co-Operative in Dublin in 1986, and both received the English Folk Dance and Song Society's gold badge for service to folk music in 1987. But Peggy was no elder stateswoman looking back on her life while preparing for death. She was writing more songs than ever, becoming ever more politically involved, and singing frequently, even when Ewan was too ill to join her. The age difference between them mattered as it never had before. Neill remembers, "It was a massive strain on her still being essentially a young woman in her early fifties nursing an old man. Him being jealous about her going out on tour without him, when they'd done everything together. And her trying to placate him to a degree but still feeling . . . , 'I have to go out and sing. It's what I do. It's where we get money from.'"[49] "The eighties was a period when I was learning to lead," Peggy recalls.[50] She wrote many feminist songs and frequently sang at women's events—as a solo act. She wrote and sang the songs for *Needs Must When the Devil Drives*, a film about women in the British trade union movement. She formed a women's singing group, Jade, with Irene and three women she knew from the Singers Club.

By the late 1980s, Ewan's angina attacks and sudden bouts of illness were so frequent that Peggy had to play many of their concert dates without him. She asked Irene to sing with her on some of these bookings. Irene was delighted. Though somewhat shy about singing, she had a beautiful, crystal-clear voice and a rich store of Irish songs. Peggy and Irene were frequently in one another's company—as members of Jade and BANG, as participants at Greenham Common—and were becoming increasingly close. One cold Saturday morning, BANG set up a table at a school in southeast London, hoping to interest people in the issue of nuclear power. Ewan had had an attack that morning, and Peggy was in particularly low spirits. After a brief time, she excused herself and left. "I was sitting in the car, and I was crying," remembers Peggy. "And she [Irene] came and knocked on the window. She got in the front, and she just put her arms around me and said, 'You need a hug.' . . . She said, 'You can talk to me anytime you want.'"[51]

Peggy was unused to female affection. Her mother had died before they had the chance to develop an adult relationship; her sisters were thousands of miles away. She had no close women friends. But she had been involved with the women's movement for more than a decade and was deeply interested in women's lives and experiences. Her one album from 1988, *Familiar Faces*, covers many different topics, but almost all the songs are about women. "Carry Greenham Home" and "Woman on Wheels" are about the Women's Peace Camp; the self-described "woman on wheels" is activist Jennifer Jones, an architect and headmistress of a school in suburban London, who moved about Greenham Common in her wheelchair. "Women's Union" is about the part that women played in the miners' strike. "Missing" (also called "Murielita") is based on an interview with the mother of a young woman who "disappeared" in Chile during the Pinochet regime. "I Support the Boycott" shows how an ordinary housewife can help defeat apartheid. Perhaps the most interesting song on *Familiar Faces* is "Different Tunes," a folk cantata about mothers and daughters. Based on Peggy's relationship with Ruth and Kitty and on interviews with other mothers and daughters, "Different Tunes" consists of two distinct voices: a mother and daughter who speak eloquently but find it hard to make the other understand. With its frequent changes of key and rhythm, its many different melodies punctuated by a tense recitative ("where are you going, when will you be back?"), "Different Tunes" does not sound like a folk song.[52] It is reminiscent of the work of Peggy's own mother—a complex musical piece that shows the influence of both classical and folk music.

Two songs on *Familiar Faces* refer to Peggy and Ewan's relationship. "New Spring Morning" charts the course of their life together and, in Peggy's words, "was my realisation that within a decade he would be gone."[53] "That's How the World Goes On" is a more generalized song about growing old, yet it speaks directly to the situation that Peggy faced:

When a lover grows old, he's tempted to spurn
The knowledge that took him a lifetime to learn;
But a woman is more than a mine or a ship—
My lover's grown old and I won't let him quit.[54]

Irene's friendship came at a crucial time, when the specter of Ewan's death was constantly in Peggy's peripheral vision. In November 1988, Peggy and Irene went walking in the Derbyshire hills. To break up the long drive home, they stopped for coffee at a roadside pub. Peggy remembers, "I looked at her, and I thought, 'Oh my God, I love her.' Just like that."[55] Peggy was stunned by the realization but said nothing. "All of December, I wrestled with it," recalls Peggy. "That was a hell of a month. . . . You're in love with somebody, and you can't tell them. And you're horrified by the whole idea. And you're married to a man who's ill, and you love him."[56]

Irene left on Christmas Day for a month-long trip to Australia. In early January, Peggy spent a week at a health spa in the English countryside. She told Ewan—truthfully enough—that she was exhausted and needed a rest, away from home and chores and the constantly ringing telephone. She spent the week in abundant quiet, taking long walks, doing exercises, and figuring out how to explain her feelings to Irene. Back home, she wrote "Love Unbidden," her first song for Irene, hiding the words as though they were a classified document:

Love: unbidden, unwelcome friend,
Wild bird in my hand—
I hold you, trembling, terror-bound,
Yet am at your command.

Love: new-bidden, welcome foe,
Bird forever wild—
Love: one moment loose your hold,
Let me rest a while.

Love: though I be one of those
That dare not come to claim thee—
Hold me till my heartbeat slows,
Wild bird, you have tamed me.[57]

These deceptively simple lyrics are filled with powerful, densely textured allusions. Lydia Hamessley points out that, in its language and its imagery, Peggy's first love song to Irene echoes Ewan's first love song to Peggy:

The first time ever I kissed your mouth,
I felt the earth move in my hand—
Like the trembling heart of a captive bird
That was there at my command, my love,
That was there at my command.[58]

Hamessley also notes that Peggy's characterization of herself as "one of those / That dare not come to claim thee" recalls Lord Alfred Douglas's phrase "the love that dare not speak its name," made famous at Oscar Wilde's trial for homosexuality.[59] "Love Unbidden" also has structural similarities to "The First Time Ever": both songs have three stanzas and begin each stanza in the same way. But "Love Unbidden" does more than mimic its antecedents. By using language and imagery reminiscent of "The First Time Ever," Peggy shows subtle but important differences in the beginnings of her two major love affairs. The bird in "The First Time Ever" is captive, while in "Love Unbidden" it is wild (a Wilde bird, perhaps). Ewan's song shows the lover with almost godlike control: he holds the whole world in his hand; he is the one who commands the trembling, captive bird. Peggy's song shows the lover fearfully out of control; it is she who trembles; it is she who is at the command of the wild bird she holds. Ewan's song is one of joyful expectation; Peggy speaks of a love unbidden and unknown.

Irene returned to Beckenham on February 1. For Christmas, Irene had given Peggy a voucher for a day at a women's spa in London, and the two women planned to go there together upon Irene's return. Irene recalls that when Peggy picked her up that morning, "she seemed so delighted that [Irene] was back."[60] During a moment of privacy at the spa, Peggy—mortified and embarrassed—declared her love. Irene replied that she would have to think about it. The next day, she told Peggy that the feeling was mutual. "Then life got very confusing," recalls Irene.[61]

For Peggy, it was the beginning of nine months of lies and deceptions, of "racketing between heaven and hell."[62] There were stolen minutes and stolen hours, secret meetings when Peggy told Ewan she was going shopping or taking a walk. There were days when she returned home, flushed with the happiness of her newfound passion, feeling "like your skin isn't big enough to hold you," and had to force herself to adopt a calm demeanor as soon as she crossed her threshold.[63] If the stealth and uncertainty reminded her of the beginning of her relationship with Ewan, she recognized important differences as well. She never considered leaving Ewan. For more than thirty years, their lives had been so intertwined that leaving him would have been like tearing off a piece of herself. She could not abandon him at the close of his life. Nor could she stop loving Irene.

Several days after Peggy and Irene's mutual recognition of love, Mike and Penny arrived in England to record *American Folk Songs for Christmas* with Peggy, Ewan, Calum, and Kitty. Mike's son Kim and Penny's daughter Sonya would later provide additional vocals and instrumental accompaniment. The result was a much more professional rendition than the one that the Seeger Sisters had recorded more than thirty years earlier. For Peggy, the recording represented both a return to her roots and a departure into something new. For the first time since the original *American Folk Songs for Christmas*, Peggy played piano on a recording—as well as guitar, concertina, and banjo. It was the first album that involved Peggy's English and American families, and it has the warmth of a family reunion combined with the crisp professionalism of highly skilled musicians. A wide variety of instruments was used: some typically American (mandolin, spoons, Appalachian dulcimer, banjo, auto-harp, harmonica, and quills), some typically British (bowed psaltery, English concertina, and pennywhistle), and others with more universal provenance (piano, guitar, and fiddle). The use of both English and American instruments provides exciting and unusual musical textures—Calum's bowed psaltery paired with Mike's autoharp on "Cradle Hymn" is particularly effective—and such combinations would not have been unknown among America's many immigrant families. The instrumentation is effective and enjoyable, but singing is the real focus of the album. Some of the best songs are unaccompanied, such as Calum, Ewan, and Mike's stirring rendition of "Star in the East," or Sonya and Penny's lovely harmony in "A Virgin Most Pure." As in a family gathering, no musician dominated; most of the singers led at least one song. Indeed, the whole recording has the quality of a family Christmas, and Peggy makes clear that this was their intent:

> One of the natural habitats, the intimate family room, was almost duplicated as we arranged and re-arranged microphones and singing positions in an attempt to get separation of voices and instruments, for we wanted to sing together, make music together, not impose and superimpose one track upon another. . . . The basis of our approach was spontaneity and enjoyment. . . . We have tried to communicate this enjoyment, to communicate the excitement which our mother felt in locating and arranging the songs. We feel that they take us back to a time when Christmas was a total involvement—a time for a good time to be had by all.[64]

Ewan and Peggy's final album together, *Naming of Names*, was recorded in 1989 and released in 1990. This recording shows the transitional period that Peggy was in, both in her life and in her work. She sang several songs with Ewan, others with Irene and Jade. Ewan wrote eight of the thirteen songs on the album and sang most of them with Peggy. His voice was still beautiful, but it seemed tired, lacking in the power it once had. Many of Ewan's songs cover familiar territory: "Economic Miracle," "Nuclear Means Jobs," "House Hungry Blues," and "Rogues' Gallery" are attacks on Tory policies and politicians; "The Grocer" and "Dracumag" target Margaret Thatcher in particular. "The Island," with a tune adapted from a Sicilian folk song, is a rare song about the British colonization of Ireland; it is a history lesson in poetry.

Some of Peggy's songs on *Naming of Names* are similar to Ewan's: "Just the Tax for Me" and "Maggie Went Green" are attacks on Thatcher's policies. But Ewan did not sing on her songs, as she did on his; instead, Peggy was joined by Irene and Jade. The most remarkable song on the album was jointly created by Ewan and Peggy: the ten-minute cantata "Bring the Summer Home," which tells the story of the Peasants' Revolt of 1381. Written for antiphonal men's and women's choruses and for several sections sung in unison, "Bring the Summer Home" is less a history lesson than a musical reenactment, a kind of secular oratorio. The Peasants' Revolt, led by Wat Tyler and John Ball, arose in response to restrictive laws that followed a period of relative freedom after the Black Death. The spark that lit the fire of rebellion was the introduction of a poll tax, a flat tax paid by everyone, peasants and landowners alike. A similar tax, also called a poll tax, was introduced by the Thatcher government in 1989. The final stanza is a call to arms:

> Nineteen hundred eighty-nine,
> Against the new poll-tax combine,
> Join the men of '81,
> Finish what John Ball began.[65]

"Bring the Summer Home" was the flowering of Ewan and Peggy's long musical collaboration: Ewan wrote the words, and Peggy wrote the music, basing the melodies on traditional Sicilian folk songs. It combines their long-standing interest in history and politics, their commitment to creating new music based on traditional models, and their belief in honoring the past while pointing the way to the future.

Though Ewan's songs predominate on the album, the last word—and the title song—is Peggy's. "Naming of Names," also called "We Remember," is an elegiac listing of twentieth-century activists, a text that Peggy describes as, "one of those songs that can be constantly updated."[66] The list is international and heavily weighted toward revolutionaries who died or were imprisoned for their acts: Ernst Thaelmann, Joe Hill, James Connolly, Patrice Lumumba, Victor Jara, Nelson Mandela, César Sandino, Karen Silkwood, Rosa Luxemburg. Ewan was no doubt proud of the list, but he did not sing it on the recording. Peggy and Jade sang "Naming of Names" in a stately call-and-response style, and the leading voice was not Peggy's but Irene's.[67]

Peggy never told Ewan of her relationship with Irene, and Ewan never confronted her, but Peggy believed that he guessed. How could he not notice the change in her behavior? She was away from home so frequently—with BANG, with Jade, with her own political activities—and when she was at home, her mind seemed elsewhere. She spent much time practicing and doing other activities that precluded conversation. That Ewan never expressed his suspicion was, Peggy believes, a wise choice—it enabled them to continue living together companionably. In September 1989, Ewan and Peggy celebrated the birth of their first grandchild: Neill's son James Alexander MacColl (Jamie). (Ewan had two grandchildren already, as Kirsty had two young sons.)[68] Peggy and Ewan continued to sing together, though frequently Ewan had to cancel because of ill health, and Irene usually sang in his place. But he never lost his joy in their musical partnership. When they recorded *Naming of Names*, Ewan remarked, "It's wonderful recording again like we used to."[69]

By the autumn of 1989, Ewan's attacks were becoming so frequent that scarcely a day passed without one, and some days had more than one. Singing, making plans, and even the normal activities of daily life were difficult. His doctors suggested that angioplasty might provide some relief. He went into the hospital on October 21 feeling cautiously optimistic, but told Peggy that he did not wish to live if nothing could be done to improve his health. Sadly, the operation was not a success. "I am of the opinion that he willed himself to die," says Peggy.[70] She and his five children were with him on his final day, singing to him throughout his last hours. Jean came to say good-bye but got lost on the way to the hospital and arrived minutes too late; she sat quietly with him in the moments following his death. Ewan MacColl was a fighter all his life, but on that day he met the enemy who will always win. He died on October 22, 1989.

# CHAPTER 17

# The Long Road Home

The reaper left an empty chair,
An endless silent song.
I sat and cried on the topmost stair,
And lost the way back home.
I lost my way back home.

A woman's hand took hold of mine
In comradeship until
We poured a glass of sweeter wine
And learned to drink our fill.
Oh, we drank our fill.

—Peggy Seeger, "Bring Me Home"

Ewan had been working with the BBC on a television documentary about his life until the day before he went into the hospital. It became a posthumous celebration: *The Ballad of Ewan MacColl* aired on BBC 2 in 1990. The music of Vivaldi, the most joyous and life-affirming of composers, played at his funeral. Ewan's body was cremated, and his family scattered his ashes in the Derbyshire moors the following spring. Phone calls and letters of condolence poured in from around the world. Some were from well-known people such as Hamish Henderson, Billy Bragg, Alan Lomax, Sydney Cowell, and Louis Killen. Others were from his many friends and admirers, some of whom had never met him but whose lives had been touched by his music. While it was gratifying to know how profound Ewan's influence had been, it occasionally intruded on the family's private mourning. Calum recalls a well-meaning but tactless fan who telephoned shortly after Ewan's death and commiserated by saying, "He was like a father to me." "Well, he was my father!" Calum snapped.[1]

Ten years of illness had prepared Peggy for Ewan's death, but nothing had prepared her for the horror of its aftermath. She felt no relief that her burden of caretaking had been lifted. She found it hard to enjoy the freedom of being with Irene openly. She was mired in guilt and grief. "I felt a child had been put into my hands—Ewan when he was ill—and I'd let the child die," she said.[2] Irene's presence was crucial to her. "I felt that I could help," recalls Irene. "Her family had their own grieving."[3] "Irene saved me," says Peggy. "I would have gone nuts."[4]

Peggy and Irene sang at most of the gigs that Peggy and Ewan had booked. "It was a mercy to be able to go out and sing," recalls Peggy.[5] Performing was difficult and absorbing enough to take her, if only briefly, away from her sorrow. In early 1990, she tried to find an agent who would book her as a solo act and also book gigs for her and Irene as a duo. On a dreary February night, they traveled to a pub "on the other end of nowhere" to meet an agent who seemed unfamiliar with Peggy's work and who referred to her as "a remnant of a dead duo."[6] Peggy recalls, "He said, 'I really need a demo.' I'd been singing in that country for thirty years, and he wanted a demo. That was too much for me. I was just ready to fold up. So I got up and went to the loo. And while I was in there, he told Irene, 'She's no spring chicken. And she's not really commercially viable.'"[7]

Irene took over. She decided that her partner had endured enough disrespect for one evening; she collected Peggy from the ladies' room, and they left. Irene had the gift of finding humor in adversity, and she suggested a project that gave Peggy focus and hope: making an album. Irene proposed that they call themselves "No Spring Chickens" and their first album "Almost Commercially Viable."

Peggy had been writing steadily and well, and now, with the prospect of a new recording on the horizon, she redoubled her efforts. Despite the turmoil in her personal life, the songs that Peggy wrote between 1988 and 1990 are numerous, varied, and among her very best. There are love songs to Ewan and to Irene; songs about the poll tax, about Margaret Thatcher and her political confreres; about unions, family relationships, abortion, domestic abuse, the environment, war, and the beauty of the French countryside. Some of the songs, like the folk cantata "Different Tunes," show a stretching of her musical muscles, an exploration of new subjects and new genres. Other songs represent the culmination of decades of songwriting based on traditional models. "My Friend Pat," the song about domestic abuse, is a well-nigh perfect example of a twentieth-century ballad. Like its traditional ancestors, "My Friend Pat" tells its story with carefully crafted and deliberately understated lyrics; it has a touch of bitter humor and a complete absence of self-pity. It is unflinchingly truthful, and its attention to detail can be heartbreaking:

We couldn't afford to live apart, for years we lived in silence;
He never laid a hand on me, they call it "mental violence";
He stripped our joint account and turned our daughter dead against me;
Sold my rings and the china tea-set that my mother left me.

Smashed the pictures, spiked the mixer, slashed my little sofa;
Looked like Ali Baba and his boys had done us over;
Telly, hi-fi, pots and pans, the fixtures and the fittings;
Then it finally dawned on me: my Pete was splitting.

> My friend Pat says, "That's that! Possessions? You don't need 'em.
> You're going Dutch, and that ain't much to pay to get your freedom."[8]

No Spring Chickens toured the British Isles, Australia, and New Zealand, but Peggy's mental distress did not lessen. She had frequent intense headaches. Home was almost unendurable without Ewan. Her relationship with Kitty was strained and filled with the misunderstandings that frequently occur between mothers and teenage daughters. "I had headaches because I couldn't bear to live with myself," recalls Peggy. "I felt guilty for everything, guilty for not getting on with Kitty, guilty for Ewan's last year, guilty for having lied to him."[9] Since Ruth's death in 1953, Peggy had been the strong one, the capable one, the one who rolled with the punches and could deal with everything. Finally, she had reached the limits of her strength. "I had a black hole inside me," said Peggy.[10] And that black hole remained with her for two long years.

"When it's a close family," recalls Calum, "and somebody dies, it's like an abacus where everything is set in a particular pattern, and then somebody takes two bottom rows away, and the whole pattern changes. So everyone becomes somebody else; they have to. Mum kind of became a little sister. Kitty became a big sister to Mum. Neill assumed this head-of-the-family thing. . . . And Mum completely fell to pieces for two years."[11] Neill and Calum grieved deeply for their father, but they had not lived with him for years. Both were busy with their own work and relationships; they never ignored or neglected the family in Beckenham, but it was not their primary focus. Kitty, however, was a schoolgirl still living at home, a home that had irrevocably changed. Her father was gone, and her mother was frequently absent, on tour or the occasional holiday with Irene. When Peggy was at home, she and Kitty quarreled and rarely understood each other. The relationship eventually became so strained that they agreed that Kitty should move out for a while. For the better part of a year, Kitty stayed with friends and with Kirsty, and years passed before Kitty and Peggy could talk about their differences.

Shortly after Ewan died, Peggy told her children that she was romantically involved with Irene. "We just laughed and said, 'Yeah, we already know,'" remembers Calum.[12] They expressed no disapproval or anger, as she had feared. "She seemed happy," recalls Neill. "What is there to be angry about?"[13] They were serenely unconcerned that Peggy had chosen a woman partner. "The only person who ever had a problem with that was Mum," says Kitty.[14]

In 1990, the final Seeger-MacColl productions were released. *Naming of Names* was the final album that Ewan and Peggy had worked on together. *Black and White: The Definitive Ewan MacColl Collection* is a compendium of songs (primarily Ewan's compositions and a few traditional songs) that Peggy, Neill, and Calum chose to represent the best of Ewan's work. *Black and White* includes songs from the Radio Ballads and from Ewan's theater work, political songs about Vietnam and apartheid and the despair of the working class, personal songs about Peggy and his parents, and his painfully sweet swansong, "The Joy of Living." *Journeyman*, Ewan's autobiography, was published early in 1990, with an introduction written by Peggy.[15] In the final words of the introduction, Peggy shows how intimately the past remains embedded in the present: "The El Salvadorean guerrillas say, 'We bring our dead forward with us,' never forgetting, always mentioning them, honouring them. Comrade Ewan MacColl, I salute you. I love you and miss you. You seem to be in every corner of the house we shared, in every corner of my being. You come forward with me and it will always give me pleasure to hear about you, sing your songs, remember our life together. Who speaks to me will speak to you."[16]

But the past could be a prison cell as well as a comforting haven. In June 1991, Peggy wrote in her diary: "I talk to Ewan quite a bit in the house, telling him I miss him. I still feel he's out there somewhere. The absolute finality of death just doesn't make sense to me, the complete and utter absence of someone who was so completely and utterly present for so long. . . . I cannot imagine the nothingness of not being, the absence of feeling, seeing, touching and individuality. I suppose it's because I am so trapped in my own head these days."[17] She did not wish to forget the past; she wanted to remember it without pain. In her diary, she wrote about her early days with Ewan, the birth of her children, the days of her youth when "life seemed endless."[18] "They were good days. Please, memory, bring them back to help me with my loss, to help me connect with a part of myself that I have lost. If I forget them, Ewan dies all the more completely. I am the person with the memories now, the rich one, the repository. I must learn to want to remember without the wrong sort of grief."[19] Living in a house cluttered with shards of the past was becoming too painful, so she donated the bulk of the Seeger-MacColl materials (papers, tapes, awards, etc.) to Ruskin College in Oxford. On the last day of June 1991, she wrote:

> I hope I have been right in my choice. The house is beginning to look less crowded. When it was all in the van I began to panic and feel that Ewan was dying yet again as if I had betrayed him further for pushing him out again. When the van drew out of the drive I wanted to ask them to drive slowly down the street while I walked beside them. I remembered Charlie walking down West Kirke Street slowly after Dio's hearse—Then I walked slowly around the block talking to Ewan and myself. . . . The day got normal and good again when Irene turned up and we ran over all the tracks carefully. I am really enjoying and admiring her thoroughness—she listens so carefully and is so pleased when the singing is good. The evening passed very quickly. . . . Goodnight, Ewan—you don't have to suffer any more.[20]

Peggy found great pleasure in working on the album with Irene. Kitty returned home. With Irene, Peggy toured Britain, Australia, and the United States. She reached out to former members of the Critics Group and restored contact with Brian Pearson, Frankie Armstrong, Sandra Kerr, Jim O'Connor, and others. "I wasn't apologizing for anything that had happened; I just said, 'It would be nice to be in touch again.' They were all very pleased."[21] But the headaches and the grief did not disappear. The Singers Club "lost its heart when Ewan died" and formally ended in 1991.[22] Her relationship with Kitty, while improving, continued to be strained. The headaches became so severe that Peggy chose to be sedated for six weeks: "I just wanted to sleep. . . . A protracted sleep because the tension had gotten so bad. . . . I said, 'I want to be out of this world for a month or two; I can't handle living anymore.'"[23] Kitty and Irene kept guard, waking Peggy only to feed her or to help her to the toilet. A nurse came regularly to check on her and give her sponge baths. When the sedation was over, Peggy required two months of physical therapy to restore muscle tone and to bring her, once again, to the land of the living.

In 1992, Peggy produced three very different albums: *Peggy Seeger, The Folkways Years 1955–1992: Songs of Love and Politics*; *Animal Folk Songs for Children*; and *Almost Commercially Viable*. The first album is a compendium taken from earlier recordings, primarily from Folkways but a few from live performances and some from Rounder Records. In the liner notes, Peggy describes the process of choosing twenty-one songs to represent a career of more than thirty-five years: "What was it like, listening to thirty-five years of my own recordings? At worst it was like going to a class reunion and seeing as grown-ups all those kids you liked and loathed; like meeting all your old lovers thirty-five years on. At best it was like leafing through a photograph album, pointing at this one and laughing, saying, 'did I really look like that?'"[24] The choice of songs is eclectic and in some places surprising. There are the expected classics, such as "The First Time Ever I Saw Your Face" and "I'm Gonna Be an Engineer," but also some little-known gems, such as Fred Small's "Talking Wheelchair Blues" and the then-unreleased "Garden of Flowers." Nearly half the album (nine songs) is composed of traditional songs; there are also nine songs by Peggy, two songs by Ewan, and Libba Cotten's "Freight Train." Eight of the songs (including both of Ewan's and six of Peggy's) are personal: "Song of Myself," "The First Time Ever I Saw Your Face," "My Son," "Song for Calum," "Little Girl Child," "Nobody Knew She Was There," "Thoughts of Time," and "Garden of Flowers." Despite the subtitle, few of the songs are overtly political, though many of the personal songs have a political dimension. Surprisingly, considering the time when the folk revival was at its height and the popular association of folk music with the 1960s, there are no songs at all from that decade.

The last two songs on the album are "Thoughts of Time" and "Garden of Flowers," and they provide a telling contrast. "Thoughts of Time," written in 1976, looks to a future when Ewan and Peggy must part and when their family will die, but that future is too far away to cause any real distress; the song is poignant rather than painful. Peggy's voice is confident and strong, warm and supple, with the occasional well-controlled decoration. The accompaniment (Peggy on autoharp and Neill on guitar) is lively, fast, and relatively simple. The tune is upbeat and cheerful except for the third line of each stanza, which ends with a minor second, the mediant reaching up to the subdominant. This minor interval gives the melody a quality of yearning, a suggestion that sorrow may be hidden within joy.

In the liner notes, Peggy states that she wrote the words to "Garden of Flowers" for Ewan; later, she said that it was in fact inspired by her love for Irene. The tune is a traditional Sicilian folk melody. Whereas "Thoughts of Time" is straightforward and fairly simple, "Garden of Flowers" is mysterious and musically complex. The words are impressionistic and somewhat unsettling; we never know why the woman weeps as she holds her sleeping lover, nor why she turns away from him when he awakes. Musically, the song is far more multilayered than "Thoughts of Time": Peggy and Irene sing in close harmony, while three guitars add additional melodies, weaving an almost contrapuntal tapestry of sound. Irene and Peggy are in exceptionally good voice, but their singing has a tentative quality, quite unlike the serene confidence Peggy shows in "Thoughts of Time." We know exactly what Peggy is saying in "Thoughts of Time," but there is something hidden in "Garden of Flowers," perhaps the love that dare not speak—or sing—its name.

For *Animal Folk Songs for Children*, Peggy was joined by Irene, Neill, Calum, Kitty, her brother Mike, her sisters Barbara and Penny, Mike's son Kim, and Penny's children Sonya and Rufus. Like her 1989 recording of *American Folk Songs for Christmas*, the 1992 *Animal Folk Songs for Children* is a much more professional version of an album, based on her mother's songbook, that she had originally done in the 1950s. The final album of the year, *Almost Commercially Viable*, shows a break with the past and a focus on new directions for the future.

Highly original and meticulously crafted, *Almost Commercially Viable* remains one of Peggy's favorite albums. The seventeen cuts are a mix of love songs, political songs, and humorous songs; most were written by Peggy, and most were recent compositions. Peggy and Irene are the only singers on the album, and both show considerable vocal versatility. Peggy sings "New Spring Morning," one of two songs on this album about Ewan, in an utterly simple fashion, the tenderness and poignancy of the words highlighted by her complete lack of histrionics. Irene's pure, clear soprano is particularly striking in Ian Davidson's love song "My Joy of You," the sweetness of the words reflected in the timbre of her voice and the precision with which she sings. "You Don't Know How Lucky You Are" is a tongue-in-cheek monologue from the viewpoint of a woman who is telling a potential lover exactly how things will proceed in a romantic relationship. Peggy wrote the song in blues style, with the syncopated rhythms and blue notes typical of the genre, and she sounds like a blueswoman as she sings it, her voice taking on the timbre and tone of blueswomen such as Ida Cox, Billie Holiday, and Mary Dixon, whose songs told men that they would put up with no nonsense.

Neill and Calum suggest that Peggy felt freer to experiment with new musical styles after Ewan's death, to write songs that were not in the folk idiom and to present folk songs in nontraditional ways. Irene was also instrumental in encouraging Peggy to explore new musical directions. "She sensed my abilities in genres other than folk and encouraged me endlessly to exploit them," recalls Peggy.[25] In *Almost Commercially Viable*, several of Peggy's compositions are not in folk style, and the instrumentation contains frequent elements of jazz, pop, and classical music—choices Ewan might not have sanctioned. "Sweet Heroin" is an updated version of "Miss Heroin," which Peggy had previously sung a cappella; the new version has a blues-inspired accompaniment of jazz piano, trumpet, and drums. A traditional singer would probably have sung "My Joy of You" without accompaniment, but this version contains piano, cello, and zither, creating a complex and sophisticated musical arrangement for this relatively simple song.

Despite the pleasure that *Almost Commercially Viable* gave her, the headaches and the grief did not disappear. In January 1992, Peggy wrote, "I can tell you what grief is like. Can you vomit up your soul, the dry heaves of the heart? The hole inside is wide, black—it throbs and the walls of it are bruised."[26] As long as Peggy was in the house in Beckenham, she sensed the presence—and absence—of Ewan. One of her New Year's resolutions for 1992 was to move to a new home, but she did not know exactly where this home would be. Irene suggested Ireland, though at the time, she was still living with her husband, Philip. Peggy, on the other hand, was thinking about the United States: "I desperately wanted to come back to the States and see what the States was like. I was American; I was still an American in England."[27] The songs she sang, the culture she represented was becoming increasingly separate from her own experience. How could she continue to be a singer of American songs if her knowledge of America was so tenuous and so out-of-date?

In 1993, an amnesty on political exiles allowed Peggy to regain her U.S. passport. This gave her the option of living in the United States or visiting whenever she chose, rather than applying for visas as a British citizen, as she had done since 1959. Getting work in England was much more difficult than it had been when she was with Ewan—another factor that spurred her decision to leave. She also "needed to discover [her] own self separate from anybody else" and compared this voyage of discovery to her mother's choice to return to composing shortly before she died.[28] After years of taking care of her family—including transcribing and teaching to support them—Ruth had declared, "I want to see if Ruth Crawford still exists." In similar fashion, Peggy needed to know if Peggy Seeger existed on her own, not the "daughter of," "sister of," "partner of" that she had always been.

Nonetheless, the leave-taking came slowly. She remained in England throughout 1993 except when on tour; she and Irene toured the British Isles, the United States, Canada, Australia, and New Zealand. Peggy also began assembling two anthologies, one of Ewan's songs and one of her own. In the latter part of the year, she found it virtually impossible to work in Beckenham: "the emotional impact of it was just too much for [her]."[29] With her work materials, instruments, and a few suitcases of clothes, Peggy rented a refurbished stable ten miles from the city of York. It was one more step away from Beckenham and toward a new home.

Perhaps it was also personal loss that sealed Peggy's decision to return to the United States. In the autumn of 1993, her sister Penny died of cancer. Peggy returned to the States to be with Penny during her final days. Penny's daughter, Sonya, remembers, "My mother really wanted to see her and Mike, so they came. . . . They came with their instruments to the hospital, and they played the songs that she requested. . . . From when she could remember, they had always been playing music together and playing beautiful, beautiful songs. . . . So those were old childhood memories for her, and she wanted to hear them. . . . That was really important to her. There was a lot of lovely singing in the hospital room."[30] In the summer of 1994, Peggy's old friend Ralph Rinzler died. Once again, she returned to the United States to say good-bye. With the death of two people to whom she had once been close, she remembered all the things she had left behind in America: friends, family, a musical culture that formed the basis of her life's work. It was time to reconnect with her distant past, to see if her homeland could once again be her home.

# CHAPTER 18

# Heading for Home

My face to the sky, my back to the wind,
Winter is entering my bones.
The day has been long, and night's drawing in,
And I'm thinking of heading for home,
And I'm thinking of heading for home.

—Peggy Seeger, "Heading for Home"

Peggy's decision to return to the United States was the result of several factors. As long as she remained in England, she was continually reminded of her life with Ewan. Eventually, she would be able to recall that part of her life without distress, but at the time she was locked in the habit of grief. On the positive side was Peggy's desire to reconnect with her American family and friends and to explore the part of the world that had produced the traditional songs she sang.

Despite her teenage remarks about disliking the South, the region had long held a mystique for her as the place that had produced an important body of American folk music. She recalls, "Certain names rang in my head from my childhood. Mike and my father went away to Galax. I thought, 'Galax! That sounds fascinating.' ... My father went down to Asheville to a conference there. ... Libba came from Chapel Hill."[1] She asked Mike, who lived in Virginia, to recommend a place for her: "I said, 'I want a town that is kind of civilized à la Europe. ... Where it's known to have music. I'd like to be in the mountains. And I'd like it to be small. Minimum of industry.' Without hesitation, he said, 'Asheville.'"[2] Asheville, in the mountains of North Carolina, was also close enough to Mike's home in Lexington, Virginia, to make frequent visits possible.

Peggy's father had traveled to Asheville as part of his work for the Resettlement Administration, and it was there that Pete first heard the five-string banjo in 1936. A longtime commercial center and popular tourist destination, Asheville in 1994 was a growing city, with beautiful mountain scenery and a branch of the University of North Carolina. Peggy was initially unable to find housing that she liked in Asheville proper and rented the top floor of a house in nearby Montreat. The cathedral ceiling gave a sense of space and light, and the windows offered stunning views of the Appalachians. After thirty-five years in the UK, the American South seemed an alien culture, in which Peggy moved warily, hoping to fit in. The fact that nothing was familiar meant that there were no painful reminders of her life with Ewan. She was able to open a bank account immediately and without references because the bank manager was an avid Pete Seeger fan. She went into Asheville several times a week and went square dancing for the first time since the 1950s. She found an American agent, Josh Dunson, and began extensive tours of the United States.

In the summer of 1995, Peggy moved to a rented house in West Asheville and then set off for several months of traveling with Irene. They traveled throughout the South, headed west across the Great Plains, visited Yosemite National Park, and came back through Wyoming and Montana. Philip joined them in Chicago. In August, they went to Mike's home in Lexington to celebrate his wedding to Alexia Smith. For this occasion, they cowrote the tender love song "Autumn Wedding." By the end of the summer, however, Irene had to leave; as a British citizen, she could not remain in the United States longer than ninety days per year.

For years, Peggy and Irene continued as long-distance lovers. When she was in America, Irene frequently went on tour with Peggy, although she found the touring life wearing. During one visit, she did the editing and layout of *The Peggy Seeger Songbook* (published in 1998) and *The Essential Ewan MacColl Songbook* (published in 2001). Peggy made frequent trips to England to visit, tour, and record. Her 1996 album *An Odd Collection* reflects her transatlantic existence: it was recorded partially in England and partially in the United States. Calum produced the album, and he, Kitty, and Neill were among the musicians. Irene cowrote several of the songs but did not sing on the album. *An Odd Collection* shows Peggy's new musical developments while simultaneously reflecting patterns that had continued for decades.

Despite its title, *An Odd Collection* has three relatively coherent themes: women, relationships, and the earth. "Housewife's Alphabet," originally recorded for *Penelope Isn't Waiting Any More* in 1976, has been rerecorded with more emphasis on instrumentation. Freyda Epstein's lovely fiddle playing, with its touches of American country and old-time music, gives this recording a distinctly American accent, despite the fact that Peggy pronounces the last letter of the alphabet as "zed." The union song "If You Want a Better

Life" is accompanied only by backup vocals, vigorous hand clapping, and foot stomping. The lack of instrumentation makes it sound as though it were actually being sung in a union hall, and Peggy's vocal timbre is occasionally reminiscent of Aunt Molly Jackson. "The Judge's Chair," the story of a woman who dies after an illegal abortion, was cowritten with Irene and sounds very much like a traditional song:

> I don't want the boy with the long brown hair,
> I don't want the one with the curls.
> I want Jimmy with the devil-may-care,
> Jimmy's good with the girls.[3]

The story of a woman seduced and abandoned after becoming pregnant is a familiar one in Anglo-American balladry, and often—though not always—the consequences are tragic. "The Judge's Chair" follows the woman (named Annie, a common name for a ballad heroine) through her brief love affair, the discovery of her pregnancy and her lover's subsequent desertion, her unsuccessful attempt to obtain a legal abortion, and the illegal abortion that kills her. For the most part, the song adheres to ballad style, with its spare lyrics, quatrain format, and repetition of important words. The final stanza, however, has a different melody and a different point of view; it seems almost to belong to a different song. Here, the song departs from its detailed focus on an individual person and takes a God's-eye view:

> Men sit in the judge's chair—
> We are up on trial.
> Woman, if you conceive
> You must bear your child.[4]

Kitty provides a trenchant critique of the song: "In the last verse, she patronizes the audience by going, 'Oh, and this is what the song's about.' I think we knew that. You don't need to patronize the audience like that. . . . All the way through, it's great, and then at the end it's like 'the men do this, and the women do that.' Why? Why do that? It was great up until then, and I've played it to people who aren't into folk, and they're totally with it up until then, and then they're lost on the last verse."[5] Kitty has identified precisely where "The Judge's Chair" departs from its traditional models. No traditional song would contain those final lines; it would have ended with the previous stanza, trusting that it had made its point. Looking back from the vantage point of 2014, Peggy remarks:

I put the final verse there because the paucity of women in Parliament makes it obvious that it is actually *men* who make the laws that govern abortion. It is a very important point to make. Kitty may be right—perhaps this was not the place to make it. . . . The jump from the detailed personal story to the general, direct political statement *does* come very suddenly—but then it was *meant* to shock. Feeling pity and sorrow for Annie is not enough. . . . Annie's personal plight is the political plight of all women in her situation directly because of laws made by *men* which deny women access to safe abortion. However: when analysed carefully, the final two lines can be taken as either pro-choice *or* anti-choice. So these days, depending on who the audience is, I will either include or dispense with that verse.[6]

Many of the songs on *An Odd Collection* reflect Peggy's eco-feminist philosophy. "A Wonderful World," cowritten with Irene in 1995, retells the biblical creation story, with God ultimately rescinding man's dominion over the earth and giving it instead to the other animals. The unusually clever lyrics adapt familiar commonplaces ("Paradise lost? We don't give a toss!") and provide a savage critique of humanity's pollution of the earth:

> When we've drained the marshes, cleared the trees, levelled the hills
> and mountains,
> Choked the rivers and killed the seas, put frames around the falls
> and fountains,
> Then we'll add the finishing touch: a rocket aimed at heaven,
> And we'll head for the moon while humming this tune as the wheels
> go round.[7]

The bitterly ironic words are sung to a lively melody, with a bright vocal tone; the bouncy instrumentation adds layers of musical irony by pairing cheerful music to horrifying words. "You Men out There," also cowritten with Irene, is a poem that takes the mythology of a golden age ruled by women and uses it to suggest a pathway to gender equality. (Written for the seventy-fifth anniversary of women's suffrage in the United States, it is oddly lukewarm toward the vote.) Perhaps the loveliest song on the album is "Old Friend," Peggy's tribute to Ralph Rinzler. In words that are simple but deeply affecting and with a tune of surpassing beauty, Peggy describes a forty-year friendship:

> Your life and mine entwined with the music and the songs—
> Our future was set from the moment that we met we were old,
> old friends;

> The work that was our play carried us away then brought us home,
> Brought us home again.[8]

In the summer of 1997, Peggy bought a house on Woodlawn Avenue in downtown Asheville. She described her new home in a letter to her friend Ann McKay:

> It is square. Externally in excellent condition. A very pretty garden, all laid out by flower-conscious people. Not a lot of lawn. Cozy porch on the front, huge long porch on the back. An excellent new outbuilding, built as a workshop. . . . Four bedrooms, each with ENORMOUS closets. . . . Although the decor of the inside leaves a lot of wanting, it has received care and love. We stand there in the garden, looking out on green trees which, when they lose their leaves will allow me to see the opposite hills. . . . While we were cogitating and discussing the pros and cons we hear the church bells from the cathedral in Asheville! So many pros.[9]

Peggy moved into the house in the autumn, and Irene returned to England. At last, Asheville felt like home. Peggy became involved in local politics, writing a campaign song for left-liberal mayoral candidate Leni Sitnick. (Sitnick won, becoming the first woman and the second Jew to be mayor of Asheville.) Peggy made close friends with her neighbors, a group of women who called themselves the "Woodlawn witches." And Irene decided to move to Asheville and live with her.

Irene had lived a peripatetic existence for years. But now, she and Philip were divorcing, and their house was being sold. She was ready to move to America, but not being an American citizen meant that she had no legal right to stay. She was unable to get a green card, which would have enabled her to work in the United States and would have set her on the path toward citizenship. Ultimately, she solved the problem by realizing a long-time dream: opening a coffeehouse. As a business owner, she was able to obtain a visa that allowed her to remain in the United States. After years of remodeling and meticulous care and preparation, Irene's coffeehouse, Pyper's Place, opened on Valentine's Day 2003. Irene chose the name to honor her mother, whose maiden name was Pyper.

In 1998, *The Peggy Seeger Songbook: Forty Years of Songmaking* was published; it contains most of the songs that Peggy had written from 1956 to 1997. Peggy wrote a long introduction describing her family and musical upbringing, her thoughts about folk music and songwriting, and the political ideas that informed her work. The songbook is filled with photographs and personal reminiscences and the lively, sharp-tongued cartoons of Jacky Fleming. Peggy introduces each song by describing the circumstances of its creation, and she criticizes some songs that she feels have not aged well, such as "When I Was Young," about which she says, "It sings well enough, but I hope you don't like it."[10] Not surprisingly, *The Peggy Seeger Songbook* received glowing reviews from folk-music and women's publications. What is equally interesting are the positive reviews from people who were not particularly friendly either to folk music or to Peggy's politics. Helen Brown's review in England's conservative *Daily Telegraph* is a case in point:

> We tend to think of the folk movement as wilfully anachronistic and cosily crafty. . . . Seeger, as she admits, can at her worst be over-wordy, musically frilly and preachy. But at her best, she produced such feminist classics as I Want to be an Engineer and she caricatured John Major's sinister smiling response to on-screen criticism—like a "slow, slow velociraptor." My favourite aspect of folk music, though, is the way its narrative nature can mark in our minds the small stories that make up the bigger picture, as in the song Seeger wrote for the miners who were killed in the 1965 Cambrian Colliery disaster:
>
> > Thirty-one voices cried out in the darkness
> > Thirty-one lamps blew out in the gale;
> > Thirty-one check discs are left in the lamp room
> > Thirty-one miners lie low in the vale.
>
> By singing these songs, we remember those men, and MacColl and Seeger too.[11]

In 1998, Peggy released *Period Pieces*, an album of songs that she had written or cowritten with Irene. All the songs on this album are about women, and all but one (the little-known "Turncoat") were written before 1990. Neill produced, directed, and played on the album; Calum provided research and accompaniment; Kitty sang and helped with the design. Irene sang on several of the songs, as did the other members of Jade. Though most of the songs were not new, putting them together on one album showed how thoroughly Peggy had dealt with many different aspects of women's existence. One song describes a woman's struggle to control her fertility ("Nine-Month Blues"), while other songs discuss the joys ("Lullabye for a Very New Baby") and challenges ("Different Tunes") of motherhood. "Twenty Years" details the process by which women are taught appropriate feminine behavior, while "I'm Gonna Be an Engineer" pays tribute to a woman who ultimately rejects this socialization. "Winnie and Sam" describes the experience of a battered wife, while "Darling Annie" celebrates a loving relationship between a man and a woman. Several songs are about individual women activists ("Missing," "Union Woman II," and "Woman on Wheels"), while other songs describe groups of women involved in political movements ("Reclaim the Night," "R. S. I.," and "Carry Greenham Home"). *Period Pieces* does not address every feminist issue of its day, but it does provide a compelling glimpse into the rich variety of women's experiences.

As the century drew to a close, Peggy found herself becoming an icon of folk music, the elder stateswoman of the American folk revival. She was the featured singer at the 2000 Smithsonian Folklife Festival in Washington, D.C., the event founded by her friend Ralph Rinzler. With Irene, Neill, Calum, Kitty, and a variety of other folksingers, she performed her music and recited her poems in the Festival's Annual Ralph Rinzler Memorial Concert. While it was gratifying to be recognized for her own merits (as opposed to being "Pete Seeger's sister" or "Ewan MacColl's partner"), Peggy found the experience of becoming an icon somewhat unsettling. At a gathering of folk musicians in New Hampshire in July 2000, she wrote in her diary:

> The organisers treat me like an "equal" but there is often a restrained hero(ine) worship atmosphere. Am I really a revered figure or a leftover from a past that many people here regard as ancient history? . . . Part of me loves this adulation—it's often quite thoughtful respect, admiration, comradeship. . . . But it's almost as if I don't know what to do with it. Have I really *earned* this? After all, I have been doing something I was not only compelled by my nature to do but which I really enjoyed! . . . Maybe I have a sneaking feeling that I'm not as good as "they" think I am.[12]

Paradoxically, it was this relentless self-criticism, this drive for perfection that kept her music at a consistently high level and made it worthy of the praise it received.

Another factor that kept Peggy's music on a consistently high plane was her refusal to rest on her laurels, her need to constantly push herself to experiment with new musical styles. Her 2000 album *Love Will Linger On*, a collection of love songs, shows the many different ways that Peggy handles the same theme. Some songs on the album are familiar, such as "The First Time Ever I Saw Your Face" and "My Joy of You." Others are new arrangements of old songs. "Down by the Flowing River" is a traditional American song, which Peggy sings in a simple, traditional style. The accompaniment, however, is anything but simple and traditional. Peggy plays the melody on English concertina, but most of the accompaniment is a mix of synthesized and engineered sound. It is a distinctly modern accompaniment that would have been impossible for a traditional musician—it could only have been created in a recording studio. Yet it works well: the accompaniment creates a rich and exciting countermelody that highlights the tune and never obscures the words. This unusual accompaniment demonstrates that an old song can be elegantly adapted for the modern world.

Nearly half the songs on the album are Peggy's compositions, and many are love songs for Irene. "Primrose Hill" has particularly strong lyrics:

> I used to think that love was blind,
> But love can surely see—
> Among the flowers of the field
> I found one for me,
> I found one for me.[13]

This new song is sung in a much simpler fashion then was the traditional "Down by the Flowing River." The instrumentation on "Primrose Hill" is also simple and uses traditional folk instruments: Peggy accompanies herself on guitar, while Calum adds breaks on pennywhistle. "Call on Your Name" is reminiscent of Protestant hymnody in melody and singing style. Peggy sings the lead, while a large group joins her on the chorus. The piano and autoharp accompaniment reinforces the similarities with Protestant hymns, as does the use of phrases such as "days gone by" and "the story that has no end." "Birds of a Feather" sounds less like a folk song than a popular song of an earlier era; "love is cream on your apple pie" is the kind of line that Cole Porter would have enjoyed.[14] Perhaps the most interesting song on this album is the title song. It is a simple, eloquent song about the joys of love and the recognition that these joys will one day end:

> Now—now as a flower turns to the sun,
> So now I turn to you;
> The song sung by the living soon to be dead and gone.
> CHORUS:
> Dawn will follow dawn,
> Love will linger on
> And on and on
> Till the end.[15]

This is the same theme that Peggy addressed in "Thoughts of Time," and she even uses the same melodic cluster at the end of the third line that she used in the third line of "Thoughts of Time," with the achingly poignant reach of the mediant to the subdominant. But whereas the melody of "Thoughts of Time" resolves in fairly conventional fashion to the tonic, the melody of "Love Will Linger On" does not really resolve. Instead, it ends by lingering on the dominant, as though reminding us that love will indeed linger on. *Love Will Linger On* was particularly satisfying because it gave Peggy the opportunity to work with all three of her children; in the liner notes, she explains, "Working with my sons is always special, but when my daughter Kitty joined us it was special-plus."[16] Calum produced and directed the album, with help from Neill; Neill, Calum, Kitty, and Irene were among the musicians.

Peggy saw little of her stepdaughter Kirsty but had become a quiet admirer of Kirsty's music. In December 2000, Kirsty went on vacation to Mexico with her boyfriend and two young sons. A week before Christmas, she and her children were scuba diving near Cozumel when a powerboat sped into the water, heading directly toward them. Kirsty was able to push her children to safety before the powerboat struck and killed her. She was forty-one years old. Her many friends and fans reacted with shock and grief. Jean was heartbroken.[17] *The Essential Ewan MacColl Songbook*, published in 2001, ends with Peggy's tribute to Kirsty:

> Her songs were intelligent, humorous, quirky, listener-friendly and savvy. She made an indelible impact on all who knew her and those who knew *of* her. Because Ewan often spoke slightingly (and sometimes in ignorance!) of "pop" music, Kirsty (like her musical siblings) never knew how deeply proud her father was not only of her and her work but also of her ability to deal with the Music Establishment. Her two teenage sons lost a loving and caring mother and her lover lost a life-partner. She leaves a mother who lost her only daughter and who acknowledged her at the memorial service as "my best friend." She leaves a legion of fans, of whom (unbeknownst to her) I am one. In the music world, she leaves friends and comrades whose respect and friendship will stand as a lasting tribute to her.[18]

*The Essential Ewan MacColl Songbook: Sixty Years of Songmaking* contains most of the songs that Ewan wrote, a list of his published and recorded works, and a long introduction in which Peggy describes Ewan's life, ideas, politics, and approach to songwriting. She admits that her love for Ewan does not allow her to be objective, but she nonetheless provides intelligent criticism of his songs and ideas, and she candidly describes their life together. *The Essential Ewan MacColl Songbook* is filled with photographs and personal reminiscences, but it lacks the lively, tongue-in-cheek cartoons that gave Peggy's songbook an up-to-the-minute freshness and reminded us that Peggy Seeger's work was still in progress. There is a slight museum quality to *The Essential Ewan MacColl Songbook*, a recognition that this book represents the closing of a door. Peggy ends her introduction by saying:

> I love Ewan MacColl and I miss him daily, even though it's twelve years since he died and I now have a new partner. Writing this book has been hard for me. I shared so many of my best days with him. He filled my life and our house with ideas and singing and if there is anything about him that I miss more than anything else it is the sound of that dark chocolate tenor. . . .
>
> Ewan: This book is my last material gift to you, from your *compañera* who wants it to be known that whoever, whatever you really were, you did manage to become the best part of what you wanted to be.[19]

Peggy continued to enjoy living in Asheville but found that the music scene there was not exactly what she had imagined. While many talented instrumentalists lived in the Asheville area, relatively few local singers sang the traditional ballads that had come from the region. When she held singing sessions at her house, most participants sang sentimental love songs or gospel. Peggy had occasionally sung gospel music in her youth but had given it up under the force of Ewan's disapproval and her own political stance. A staunch secularist, she felt somewhat uncomfortable with religious music, but one can see its influence in many of the songs that she wrote during her Asheville years: the biblical theme in "A Wonderful World," the hymnlike structure of "Call on Your Name." Nowhere is this influence more pronounced than in her song "Love Call Me Home."

Peggy wrote "Love Call Me Home" for Christine Lassiter, a friend in Asheville who died of cancer in the winter of 2001.[20] Christine had organized her friends into a "love schedule," a group of people who made sure she was never without companionship or support. Peggy frequently kept her company in the evenings. A few nights before Christine's death, Peggy wrote: "I am learning things from this. . . . That there *is* something 'out there' to go to and be part of. It may be a cloud of light where the individual becomes a particle in the ether—it may be a clamor of thoughts but it doesn't feel frightening."[21] Peggy put this perspective into her song, using the word *home* to signify death, as is common in Protestant hymns:

When the waters are deep,
Friends carry me over
When I cry in my sleep

Love call me home.
CHORUS:
Time, ferry me down the river,
Friends carry me safely over
Life, tend me on my journey
Love call me home.[22]

The song struck a chord with people of liberal religious beliefs and with the hospice movement. Hospice choirs adopted it as a theme song. On May 2, 2010, Peggy was the featured performer on the radio program *Song of the Soul*, which explored music and social justice from a Quaker perspective. Just as her mother had presented a secular Christmas, Peggy had envisioned a secular heaven.

Religious music abounded in Asheville, but political music did not, and Peggy missed it intensely. Political music continued to be a cornerstone of her work. In June 2001, she traveled to Northampton, Massachusetts, to interview peace and antinuclear activist Frances Crowe. Crowe had become a peace activist in 1945, following the bombing of Hiroshima. Since the 1960s, she had been active in organizations such as the American Friends Service Committee and the Women's International League for Peace and Freedom. Crowe has been arrested multiple times for her activism, the first time in 1972 at a protest against the Vietnam War. In 2011, she was arrested outside a nuclear power plant in Vermont, when she was ninety-three years old. In the summer of 2001, Crowe was protesting sanctions against Iraqi civilians. Peggy wrote a song in her honor, "Peaceful Woman, Fighting Hard," which became the title song of a small album released in 2002. This album was the first of Peggy's Timely series, relatively short, informally produced recordings of topical songs.

The five songs on *Peaceful Woman, Fighting Hard* all address the theme of war. The first song, the traditional "Soldier's Farewell" (also called "I'm Going to Join the Army"), was featured on Peggy and Mike's album *American Folksongs for Children*. Peggy and Mike play the song together on both recordings, and they even use the same exuberant, rippling banjo accompaniment. But the two versions are very different. Mike sings the version on *American Folksongs for Children*, and it is very short: just three stanzas in which a man expresses his intention to join the army, his sweetheart asks if she might join him, and he says yes. The version that Peggy sings on *Peaceful Woman, Fighting Hard* is much longer. It describes the dangers of wartime ("Hear the cannon roaring, see the bullets fly / Hear the drum a-beating to drown the soldier's cry") and expresses the woman's fear that her lover will not return to her. Initially, the woman begs her lover not to go, and only as a second choice does she ask if she can go with him. In this version, he refuses her request and is killed in battle. The last stanza could serve as the leitmotif for the album:

> I'm weary of the fighting, weary of the war,
> Fare well, my Johnny, I'll never see you no more.[23]

The differences between these two versions illustrate the flexibility of the traditional form; two variants of what is purportedly the same song present diametrically opposed points of view. Peggy added several verses to the song, but she does not remember which ones, so perhaps she has caused this change in point of view. The seamless grafting of new verses on to old songs is a time-honored part of traditional music. Robert Burns did the same thing when he collected Scottish songs for James Johnson's *Scots Musical Museum*. He altered the words of traditional songs and created lyrics for tunes that had no words, and he did not always indicate which lines were traditional and which were of his own making.[24]

The other songs on *Peaceful Woman, Fighting Hard* were written by Peggy or Ewan. Ewan wrote "The War Game" in 1953, in the shadow of the Cold War. The song describes how war—with its emphasis on competition, uniforms, and team loyalty—is frequently made to seem like a sport. Peggy rewrote the final stanza "to suit the new political times, replacing the labor movement/ class-action terminology and themes with those involving life, liberty and responsibility."[25] Ewan's final stanza speaks the language of masculinity and class warfare:

> So Johnnie lad, get wise, wipe the sweat out of your eyes,
> It's time to cut the enemy down to size, man.
> With their statesmen and their banks, their bombers, guns and tanks,
> You've got to kick 'em out to take the prize, lad.[26]

Peggy's final stanza takes a much broader perspective, reminding us that war has the power to destroy the human race and not just the working class:

> So Johnnie, while you train, remember war is not a game,
> Not something you return that you've borrowed,
> It'll decimate your team, destroy your hopes and dreams,
> It'll rob you of today—and tomorrow.[27]

Peggy wrote the title song, an eight-minute explication of Frances Crowe's life and politics. In many ways, the song is reminiscent of the Radio Ballads: it is based on personal interviews, has both sung and spoken portions, and is as much a musical performance piece as a song. For most of the song, the only instrumentation is a simple, unobtrusive guitar backup. However, when the song discusses the things that Crowe is fighting against, Peggy plays harsh and dissonant guitar chords. This dissonance highlights the tension and struggle in Crowe's life—a technique Peggy's mother had used many years earlier.

In September 2002, Peggy and her sons rented a cottage in Norfolk, England, and turned it into a recording studio. For several weeks, they recorded the songs that would form the basis of three new albums, which they dubbed the Home Trilogy. Most of the songs were traditional, a focus her sons had strongly encouraged. They did not want her to forget her musical roots as she wrote new songs and explored new musical styles. Neill remarks: "It was Calum and I who actively encouraged her to do a series of albums that were entirely traditional. Because actually, we do love it. . . . But she's steered further and further away from that. I think she almost wants to leave it behind now. It's just that she's lived with those songs all her life; she's done it."[28] Calum adds that, though she had recorded many traditional songs in her youth, she could do them differently now:

> Neill and I . . . wanted her to make those three albums of fiercely traditional things because we thought that she'd never recorded them . . . in the kind of mature way that she could then do them. . . . We wanted to make it three very purist kind of American murder ballads, the big songs. . . . She insisted, and I understand completely why, that on each album there was a song that she wrote but that was in that style. . . . That was her way . . . of stamping herself on it.[29]

As with most Peggy Seeger productions, the trilogy was a family affair, with Neill and Calum producing the albums, Kitty designing the cover and booklet and editing the content, and all three children—as well as Irene—among the musicians. In the liner notes of *Heading for Home*, Peggy writes, "For the first time in my life, a studio felt like home."[30] Yet political differences with her children came to the fore during the recording process. Calum recalls a disagreement that began when he was editing Peggy's recording of "Bad Bad Girl":

> I just thought she could do it better. . . . So she agrees; we rerecord the song; I get about three or four versions of it up; . . . I sit for two or three hours, doing

a lot of cutting, and play it to her. She agrees; she loves it; it's much better. . . . And that evening, we were going to go out with my little sister to have dinner; it was her birthday dinner. . . . I'm a very firm believer that I don't attach weight to certain words in this culture that don't have weight attached to them. . . . I said, "Yeah, it's a much better take, Mum. It's really got balls." And she kind of looks at me a bit funny, doesn't say anything. And we're at the restaurant, and we're half a bottle of wine down, and she turns to me and says, "I took real offense at what you said." . . . And it just escalated. . . . She said, "I think you should be able to find some other word for it." And I said, ". . . In this culture, it doesn't have gender attached to it. It might've come from that, but it's meaningless." My point was that the whole PC thing by arguing those tiny little points, it's a smokescreen for the Right, it's a smokescreen for everyone else to poke fun at us and to go, "See? See how stupid they are?" . . . It's not the point. The point is domestic violence, the point is women not having a glass ceiling in society; the point is all the other stuff, not this. She said, "Perhaps we can find another word," at which point Kitty roars at the top of her voice, "Oh, for God's sake, Mum, you can't say 'that's got real clit,' can you?" . . . It only ever got resolved about nine months later, and it didn't really get resolved. . . . She brought it up and said, "I think it's better if you and me don't talk about feminism."[31]

In response, Peggy writes:

For me, the crux of the argument was the importance of language and how laden and subtle it can be with gender assumptions. I already felt that for men to herald their balls as a sign of strength is odd as those little globes are probably *the most vulnerable part of a man's body and can bring him to his knees if you kick them.* So why think that saying a woman (or a man for that matter?) has *balls* is complimentary? . . . There are a number of people (but more men than women) who don't seem to understand how touchy many females actually are about words and concepts that are in common parlance. One word can actually make a huge difference: witness using "mankind" and "he" when actually referring to the whole human race.[32]

Despite—or perhaps because of—Peggy and Calum's differences, their musical partnership was very successful. Calum's wife, Kerry Harvey-Piper, suggests that the "creative tension" between Calum and Peggy can actually be beneficial to the finished product, with their differences pushing each to consider choices that they otherwise might not have made.[33] The first album in the trilogy, *Heading for Home*, was released in the summer of 2003. The album consists entirely of traditional American songs, with two exceptions:

the first song, Peggy's "Heading for Home," and the last song, Sarah Ogan Gunning's "Girl of Constant Sorrow," which is so old and so thoroughly grounded in traditional music that it sounds like a traditional song—and many think that it is. All three albums have the word *home* in the title, a word that frequently appears in Peggy's writing during the Asheville years, when home had to be actively sought and created, not taken for granted as it had been in her childhood or during her years with Ewan. "Home is wherever you rest," she says.[34]

In many ways, this collection is Peggy's musical resting place—songs that she has known most of her life, entities that are utterly familiar and entirely beloved. For the Peggy Seeger fan, these songs also provide a kind of home-coming; they are well-known classics such as "Dear Companion," "Oma Wise," and "Henry Lee." In most cases, Peggy presents these songs in a classic traditional style, using simple accompaniments and arrangements. On "John Riley," she is the only vocalist, using well-controlled vocal decoration, while her dulcimer provides a simple harmony that highlights the beauty of the tune. On "Henry Lee," she provides a stirring, driving banjo accompaniment that aptly accompanies this unsettling tale but never overshadows her voice. "Jenny's Gone Away" might have been recorded in the MacColl living room. Kitty joins in on the vocal refrain, while Neill provides guitar accompaniment—an utterly simple presentation, well within the parameters of the folk tradition, but done with the skill of professional musicians.

There is a museum quality to much of this album: the songs are presented to their best advantage, with their beauty in full view, but nothing here startles or astonishes. As Calum predicted, Peggy performs these songs with a maturity and sureness of touch that comes from long and intimate association. *Heading for Home* represents the perfection of a familiar style, not musical innovation or the exploration of something new. The one exception to this generalization is, significantly, the one new song on the album. "Heading for Home" has a freshness and urgency that the traditional songs, with their well-worn sounds and old-fashioned settings, do not. In this song, Peggy's multilayered use of the word *home* is richly apparent; she uses the word to mean love and death, as well as a literal dwelling place. There is a sense of taking stock of the past while simultaneously looking ahead:

> As time's my old friend, and death's my new kin,
> I'm not taking the journey alone,
> I am old, I am young, I am all that I've been,

And I'm thinking of heading for home.
And I'm thinking of heading for home.[35]

Peggy was frequently heading for home because, paradoxically, she was so often away from it. Asheville provided a familiar lodestar, particularly now that Irene (now known as Irene Pyper-Scott) lived there. Pyper's Place opened in the winter of 2003 and became a popular Asheville landmark: it featured high-quality vegetarian food, a roaring fireplace, and live music four nights a week. Irene worked long hours to keep the business going, and Peggy helped out by performing, booking the musical acts, even washing dishes on a busy night. But she was frequently away from home, playing at a wide variety of venues. In March, somewhat bemused by the vast distances she traveled, she wrote, "Yesterday I drove five hours to get from Minneapolis (Minnesota) to Bemidji (Minnesota). After another three hours of driving north, still in Minnesota, I would reach Canadian border. Two hours south of Minneapolis is the southern border of Minnesota. That's a lot of Minnesota."[36] She continued to travel long distances throughout the year. In April, she had a weeklong residency at Dartmouth College in New Hampshire. In May, she gave a concert at the Carl Sandburg House in western North Carolina, attended by Sandburg's daughter Helga, who, many years earlier, had been Ruth Crawford's piano student. In September, Peggy spent three days in Boston, singing and lecturing at MIT. In October, she sang at the Santa Barbara Music Festival and enjoyed a reunion with Mar's daughter, Edith.

In March 2003, the United States went to war with Iraq, after years of economic sanctions and failed diplomatic missions. Peggy became deeply involved in the peace movement. In 2004, she produced the second of her Timely CDs, *Songs for October 2004*, which contains six songs about war, peace, and feminism. The next CD of the series, released in 2005, has only one song: the beautifully written "Ballad of Jimmy Massey." Once again, Peggy shows how skillfully she can use the ballad format and how the balladic focus on one person can effectively highlight a political issue.

Jimmy Massey is a real person, an Iraq war veteran whom Peggy interviewed when he returned to his Waynesville, North Carolina, home after twelve years in the Marine Corps. He became a highly controversial figure after reporting that he and other Marines had killed Iraqi civilians. Some hailed him as a truth-telling hero; others derided him as a liar or a madman. Peggy's song makes clear that she is on his side and completely believes his accounts. Nonetheless, she presents him as a complex figure, a troubled but ultimately decent and courageous man. He is not a pacifist, like Frances Crowe, nor is he an objective reporter of facts. He is simply telling his own story, and in Peggy's hands, his story becomes art:

> We became barbarian warriors, princes in our prime,
> Lived the life of emperors—women, food, and wine,
> Took away my love of beauty, gave me a love of war,
> Turned me into a killer; that's what the training's for.
> Some of the boys went crazy, some went crazy mean,
> I woke up, a fall guy in someone else's dream.
> I went to my lieutenant, I told him, "Sir, I'm done,
> This isn't what I came to do. Can't do it, sir, I'm done."[37]

Peggy turned seventy on June 17, 2005. "None of the decades I've hit was hard," she wrote, "but 70 is different."[38] Loved ones were gone: Alan Lomax had died in 2002, Charles Seeger III in 2003. Her voice was thinner and less resonant than it had been in youth and middle age, and years of playing many instruments had resulted in carpal tunnel syndrome, for which she had a successful operation in March 2005. But Peggy did not complain about age; instead, she celebrated it as a gift: "My prime years were from 30–60. . . . I've come to the conclusion that the manner in which you mature is a matter of fate, fortune, attitude, lifestyle, diet, genetic input and colonic output. My father's family have lived well into their nineties. My mother's family generally died in their 50s and 60s. So floating about at nearly 70 in the human ocean, observing my place and purpose, is a luxury for which I am grateful."[39]

On May 29, Peggy celebrated her seventy years with a concert in London's Queen Elizabeth Hall. One thousand people came to her musical birthday party. She was joined onstage by Billy Bragg, Martin and Eliza Carthy, Norma Waterson, Mike and Pete Seeger, her three children, and Irene, among others. The concert resulted in a two-disc set entitled *Three Score and Ten*. In the liner notes, she states: "I felt born again when I walked out on that stage and knew that so many of the people who had touched my life were there, ready to touch again and bawl the choruses out. It began with a wish and ended with a wish: that I might do it, like my life, all over again."[40]

*Three Score and Ten* provides a condensed history of the Anglo-American folk revival. Peggy and her guests played British and American ballads, instrumental tunes, love songs, old-time music, children's songs, labor songs, and political songs both old and new. Peggy and Mike sang their childhood favorites "When First unto This Country" and "Soldier's Farewell," while Pete joined them on "Cindy." Billy Bragg sang with Peggy on "Darling Annie," and the two provided witty, off-the-cuff repartee between stanzas. Some of the most effective songs featured only Peggy and her guitar, such as "The First Time Ever I Saw Your Face" and "I'm Gonna Be an Engineer." But the concert did not depend entirely on old favorites. Pete got the entire audience to sing on the chorus of his ever-hopeful 2002 composition "Take It from Dr. King," a tribute to the nonviolent political activism practiced by Martin Luther King Jr. "Sing about These Hard Times" sounds like a labor song from the 1930s—and Peggy's autoharp accompaniment reinforces this association—but she wrote it in 2004. One has to listen very closely to realize that it is, in fact, a modern protest song:

> They moved my job to Mexico,
> Where children slave and the pay is low,
> How I'm gonna live, I just don't know,
> When will the good times roll?[41]

The most recent song at the concert was only a few months old: "Home Sweet Home." With its weird melody and chilling lyrics, the song compares the post-9/11 United States to a zoo with unfriendly keepers:

> The big corporations are making your laws,
> Yanking your chains, clipping your claws,
> Removing your choice, stifling our voice
> In our home sweet home.[42]

The concert ended on a slightly subdued note, with Peggy's tribute to Christine Lassiter, "Love Call Me Home." This became the title song on the second album in Peggy's Home Trilogy, which was released in 2005. *Love Call Me Home*, like its predecessor *Heading for Home*, consists of traditional American songs, with two contemporary songs in the folk idiom at the beginning and the end. The first song, "Sing about These Hard Times," was inspired by the Depression-era photographs and artwork of Ben Shahn, and Peggy based the tune and structure of the song on the traditional hymn "Down to the River to Pray."[43] Both influences are apparent in the song: the word choice and subject matter give the song a distinctly 1930s feel, and the religious association is heightened by the timbre of Peggy's voice, the mandolin and autoharp accompaniment, and the large group that joins her on the chorus. All these factors make the song sound much older than it actually is, and it fits seamlessly into an album of traditional songs. Only the final song, "Love Call Me Home," with its modern sensibilities and original tune, sounds like a new song.

*Love Call Me Home* contains ballads, love songs, play party songs, and songs of complaint. There is little that is surprising or unusual in the album, but the tradition has enough inherent variety to prevent one from getting bored. Peggy sings "Hangman," a traditional ballad about a man condemned to death because no one will pay his fine, with a simple guitar accompaniment. She varies her voice to show the different characters in the drama but introduces no pathos or sentimentality; her voice remains steady and calm in the face of the staggering indifference of the condemned man's family. On "Rynerdine," Calum's psaltery and Peggy's dulcimer provide an appropriately eerie accompaniment for this strange tale. One has to look very hard to find anything wrong in this album. Peggy's voice is pitched a bit too high in "Poor Ellen Smith," and "Careless Love" could do with a little less instrumentation, but these are quibbles. *Love Call Me Home* is as fine a collection of traditional American music as one could hope to find.

Peggy continued her extensive touring schedule throughout 2005, touring the United States, Canada, Britain, Australia, and New Zealand. Living in North Carolina had drawbacks for a traveling folksinger; most of the North American venues that hired her were located north of Washington, D.C. The southeastern United States may have been the seedbed for the songs she sang, but folk music fans were primarily located in the North. Her friend Judith Tick, a professor of music at Northeastern University and Ruth Crawford Seeger's biographer, suggested that Peggy move to the area where most of her concert venues were located. In 2005, Peggy was offered a job teaching songwriting at Northeastern. She chose to accept the offer and relocate to Boston.

Asheville had grown considerably since Peggy first moved there, becoming busier, noisier, more sophisticated, and more expensive. Peggy had enjoyed living there, but it made sense to move to Boston, in the thick of the folk revival circuit. In the winter of 2006, she and Irene toured Australia and New Zealand; she also released *Enough Is Enough*, the next CD in her Timely series. In April, she found an apartment in the lively Jamaica Plain area of Boston. On April 22, she sang and played at a farewell concert in Asheville, despite having fractured her wrist only two days earlier. For the concert, she wrote "North Carolina Home," a tribute to the complexities that make up Asheville's quirky charm:

Asheville is our town,
A honey-sweet and sour town,
A northern-southern flower town
In the North Carolina mountains.
CHORUS:
Roads run straight or round the bend
Or up and down but in the end
All roads lead to Asheville,
North Carolina home.[44]

"I hate to say good-bye," she sang at the concert. She would miss the good friends she had made, the beauty of the mountains, the big front porches where passersby stopped to chat on the long summer evenings. For the rest of the spring, she and Irene sorted through their belongings and sold the house and Pyper's Place. With a mixture of excitement and nostalgia, Peggy did as she had done fifty years earlier: she packed her essential belongings, said good-bye to a home she had loved, and headed to Boston.

# CHAPTER 19

# Old New England

Rolling home, rolling home,
Rolling home across the sea,
Rolling home to old New England,
Rolling home, dear land, to thee.

—Traditional sailor's song

Peggy and Irene moved to the Jamaica Plain section of Boston in June 2006. Their apartment was the first floor of a house in a neighborhood of handsome old homes, some of them still single-family dwellings, others divided into flats. By Boston standards, the apartment was relatively spacious, with a living room, dining room, kitchen, office, and bedroom. Nonetheless, it was only 1,200 square feet, as opposed to the 2,200 square feet they had had in Asheville. As Irene put it, "It was an apartment, really, for one."[1] Living in Boston would mean both compromise and change.

Asheville had initially seemed an alien culture to Peggy. Boston did not. Peggy had lived there during her college years, and she had family and friends in the city and nearby. The area was politically progressive and musically vibrant; a folksinger with a same-sex partner was no oddity in Jamaica Plain. Unfortunately, Irene could not remain a permanent resident of the United States. After selling Pyper's Place, she lost her status as a business owner and was able to stay in the country for only ninety days per year. At this point, she decided to move to New Zealand. She had fallen in love with the Marlborough Sounds area when she and Peggy had visited New Zealand early that year. Marlborough Sounds was quiet and peaceful and filled with the natural beauty that Irene loved. Peggy and Irene had seen a house they liked in the area and decided to buy it. Irene moved there in February 2007.

Since separation was imminent, Peggy and Irene decided to have a civil union ceremony in England. The Civil Partnership Act of 2004 had granted same-sex couples virtually all the rights of marriage in the UK, as opposed to the far more restricted rights in the United States, even in states where same-sex marriage was legal.[2] "To me, it was a declaration of sharing everything," said Peggy. "It was a declaration of intention and solidarity."[3] On December 15, 2006, they registered a civil partnership in England, making clear their intent to stay together even if they were half a world apart.

Peggy did not teach during the 2006–7 academic year and instead spent the time touring and recording. In March, she attended the "How Can I Keep from Singing?" conference, a tribute to the Seeger family, held at the Library of Congress. The title was taken from an old hymn that Pete had made famous, and it so exemplified the Seeger family ethos that David King Dunaway chose it as the title of his biography of Pete. In the keynote address, folklorist Neil Rosenberg identified several core "Seeger family values" that informed the Seegers' work, including an intellectual fascination with folk music and a belief that this music could and should be used to further progressive political causes.[4] Music historian Judith Tick and music theorist Taylor Aitken Greer spoke about this duality in the work of Ruth Crawford Seeger and Charles Seeger respectively, the tension between the world of the scholar-thinker and the artist-activist. Mike Seeger discussed his extensive experience learning, performing, and recording old-time southern music. American studies professor Robert Cantwell cast the Seegers as part of a long progressive trend and compared Pete to Tolstoy as a person who embodied the ideas he espoused. Pete traced his political activism to his father's insistence on speaking out against injustice, a trait that Pete described as "old New England." Folklorist Millie Rahn summed up the 1960s folk revival as a life-changing experience for many participants: "The revival helped to change notions about the nature of American culture and raised questions about to whom it belonged, as well as to create new models of social and political action where the prevailing ethos can be, as it was in the 1960s, inspired and united by music."[5] The event ended with a sold-out concert featuring three generations of Seegers. "Only time I've seen more Seegers together in one place is at the family reunions," Peggy said.[6]

As much as the symposium showed the common threads in the Seegers' work, it also showed the distinctive niche that each Seeger had created. Charles Seeger was a major scholar of folk music, an important theorist, and a pathbreaking collector. Ruth Crawford Seeger was one of the first modernist composers to use folk music in her compositions, and she was the consummate folk music transcriptionist and anthologist. Mike Seeger was an instrumental virtuoso and one of the few revival musicians to completely master a traditional idiom. Pete had politicized folk music and brought it to the attention of the world. Peggy was the one who wove together the many strands of her family's musical heritage; she was simultaneously a collector, songwriter, singer, instrumentalist, and political activist. She was the best ballad singer in the Seeger family and the one with the best sense of the dramatic—possibly because of her long association with Ewan. She was the only Seeger to foreground the importance of women's lives and women's voices, and she had a unique position as one of the leading figures in both the American and the English folk revivals.

In the autumn of 2007, Professor Peggy Seeger began her first classes, entitled "Some Perspectives on the Art of Songwriting." The students wrote one song per week and sang it a cappella to the class, who (with Peggy) provided feedback. The students were required to write songs on various themes and in various styles; they wrote songs about love, about war, about money, songs in dialogue form, and so on. One class was spent writing a song together, as the Critics Group had done many years earlier. The course ended with a class concert in which each student sang one of his or her compositions. Peggy also had her students read two books: Ernst Fischer's *The Necessity of Art* (a Marxist analysis of the role of art) and Barry Sanders's *A Is for Ox*, which explores the relationship between oral and literate music. "Art is not just art," says Peggy. "It is totally dependent on the society it exists in."[7] This statement could serve as the musical credo of the Seeger family, the recognition that art is the product of social and political conditions, the opposite of the "ivory tower" conception of art as a rarefied and untouchable entity that exists above the mundane.

Peggy showed her students that the songwriter's craft exists within the discipline of a received tradition. Each week, Peggy provided a selection of tunes for the class to use; some tunes were traditional, while others had been written by Peggy, Ewan, and other contemporary songwriters. For some students, this technique freed them from the relentless pressure to be constantly innovative. Elias Bouquillon, then a Northeastern music major, recalls, "People wanted to have their own perfectly unique and isolated, in-a-vacuum, aesthetically-better-than-all-else kind of vibe, and she [Peggy] would always kind of shed that off and say, 'Start with where you are and move forward and just do something.'"[8] By showing that tradition and innovation are inextricably intertwined, Peggy gave her students a foundation for their own creativity and ideas. Elias recalls writing a song based on Ewan's "Dirty Old Town." At first, Elias's song seemed highly derivative, but the more he worked on it, the more it became his own. By the time he recorded it with his band, Eli Whitney Houston & the

Cotton Gin and Tonics, the song was very different from "Dirty Old Town," yet the band members felt a sense of familiarity with it. Elias remarks:

> As a songwriter, that's the ideal—to make somebody think they've heard the song before when they've never heard it before in their lives. . . . It was a wonderful experience to see how first you take one step away from the original, and then let time pass and let your memory do its thing and then it's two steps away, and without telling anybody where you came from, you're now taking three, four, five steps away from that original. . . . People are going to manipulate something by performing it; there's no perfect transmission, and if you embrace that, then you start to see the joy of this passing on and the borrowing that happens. . . . [There is a] whole cultural and community aspect behind sound.[9]

Peggy loved teaching and was very proud of her students. "They came up with some stunning songs," she says.[10] Peggy taught for three hours on Mondays and Thursdays; other days were reserved for concerts or small tours. Health problems plagued her throughout 2007, but they did not slow her down. A knee injury kept her on crutches for much of the winter, but she continued to tour, doing physical therapy exercises in hotel rooms and friends' houses, using wheelchairs to transport her in airports. She was diagnosed with advanced osteoporosis, and in November, she had an operation on her right shoulder, which had been troubling her for years. Six weeks after her surgery, she was able to play all her instruments and was well enough to fly to England for Christmas and to New Zealand for New Year's.

Irene and Peggy spoke on the phone nearly every day, but they had not seen each other since the preceding April. It was their longest period of separation in the nearly two decades they had been together. After five years of living together, each had to get used to living alone. "It has good aspects and bad aspects," says Irene. "It allows Peggy complete freedom to work. . . . It allows me a great amount of peace of mind."[11] Peggy concurs: "I can get an awful lot done when I live on my own. I write songs, I practice much more. . . . On the other hand, I really miss being with her. . . . I miss seeing the things that she sees, because she sees things I don't see."[12]

Peggy spent the early weeks of 2008 in New Zealand. In February and March, she and Irene toured Australia, after which Irene returned to New Zealand and Peggy to Boston. In May, they toured England with Martin Carthy and the Watersons, then traveled to France. The trip included a visit to Belloy-en-Santerre, where Alan Seeger died during World War I. The town council greeted Peggy and Irene as honored guests. Peggy recalls, "Members of the council took us into the church, which was rebuilt from the ground up in the 1920s. They took us into the *mairie* [town hall] for champagne. They presented me with a beautifully bound set of his poems, letters and diaries. They took us to the spot where my uncle's body had been found. They took us to the ossuary where he is buried with his companions. The Somme is filled with such ossuaries, cemeteries and memories—and people like the council of Belloy-en-Santerre. May we never forget."[13]

Peggy produced three albums in 2008, including the last in her Home Trilogy. *Bring Me Home* follows the same pattern as the other albums in the trilogy: traditional American songs are sandwiched between a modern Peggy Seeger song and a song that is not traditional but sounds as if it is (in this case, Aunt Molly Jackson's "Peacock Street"). For this album, Peggy chose some of the most beautiful and varied songs in the American tradition. In some of her recent albums, her voice had shown signs of age; here it does not but is as strong and supple as it ever was. Instrumentation is used effectively but kept to a minimum. "Napoleon" is a song that pairs an unusually beautiful melody with exquisite lines of folk poetry:

> Old Boney is away from his warring and his fighting,
> He has gone to the place that he ne'er can take delight in,
> He may sit down and tell of the battles he has been in,
> While forlorn he does mourn on the Isle of St. Helena.

Peggy sings with such concentration that we imagine every detail in the lyrics' splendid description; we feel the despair of the old warrior who will never again see the people and places he loved. Against these anguished words, Peggy's steady guitar continuo has the inevitability of time and death. "Home, Dearie, Home" has an equally beautiful melody but is completely different in content and mood. It is a bawdy, lighthearted tale of a one-night stand between a sailor and a young woman he meets in port—a fairly typical theme in Anglo-American folk song. Most such songs end in disaster for the woman, particularly if she is left pregnant, as may be the case here. This song, however, is told from the woman's point of view and features a plucky heroine who is quite capable of taking care of herself—with the help of the money that the sailor has left behind.[14] Peggy's warm singing, John Herrmann's exuberant banjo playing, and the lively harmony of the backup singers assure us that the heroine will land on her feet.

Many of the songs on this album have British ancestors. Others are more distinctly American. "Let Them Wear Their Watches Fine" draws on the experience of American factory workers, particularly women. The song discusses the hardships of factory work, including long hours, low pay, and child labor. The final lines feature that brilliant political doublespeak that enables songs about controversial issues to be sung in full hearing of the singer's adversaries, because the words are ambiguous.[15] "Let Them Wear Their Watches Fine" ends with the following lines:

> Let them wear their watches fine,
> Their rings and pearly strings,
> But when the day of judgment comes,
> We'll make them share their pretty things.

Is this a song of religious resignation or political revolution? It is impossible to say—and therein lies its genius.

Peggy ended the album with the autobiographical "Bring Me Home." Here, "home" means not a place but a person so beloved that his or her mere presence brings contentment. The song tells the story of Peggy's life with an emphasis on the people whose love could make a home for her: her parents, her brothers, Ewan, Irene. The graceful, poetic lyrics show Peggy's ability to use a deeply personal commonplace:

> Songs of love, tales of grace,
> Of flesh and blood and bone,
> The first time ever I saw his face,
> His heart became my own,
> Then his heart became my home.[16]

*Crazy Quilt*, the next album in the Timely series, was also released in 2008. (A crazy quilt is made of randomly sewn pieces of cloth, often embellished with embroidery. The tradition began when thrifty housewives found creative ways to recycle old fabrics.) The album contains fifteen songs on a wide variety of topics. The religious influence is apparent in several songs. "Tree of Love," a simple and moving love song, uses a tune drawn from the hymn "Amazing Grace" and even has some of the same words:

> I did not plant the seeds of love,
> They sprang when first I saw you,
> I was lost, lost and found,
> On my knees before you.[17]

"Then God Made Adam" is an intriguing retelling of the biblical creation story. In this version, which is partly spoken and partly sung, Eve is created first, and God creates Adam (out of "spare parts") only after Eve complains of being lonely. "Dick and the Devil" is an ingeniously written, bitingly funny song about the devil seeking new recruits among contemporary American politicians. If Jonathan Swift had written songs, they would sound something like this:

> The devil is a perfectionist, and he never makes mistakes,
> He cannot fill Inferno up 'cause he's careful who he takes,
> The sinners line up at the gate, and even if you got there first,
> He might not take you in because he only wants the worst.[18]

"Shadow Prisoners," by contrast, is a deadly serious condemnation of evil; it talks about prisoners who are held without trial, without rights, without mercy, and without hope. It is less a song than a performed poem; dissonant piano chords effectively accompany the chilling words. "One Plus One" is not overtly political but celebrates the sort of collective action that can lead to political change. With its lively tune, vivacious banjo accompaniment, and extremely singable chorus, it is reminiscent of the clear-eyed optimism of many of Pete's songs:

> One plus one is two,
> 2+2 is four,
> 4+4 is eight, for sure
> 8+8 is many more,
> One plus one is great,
> 2+2 is better,
> 1+2+4+8,
> That's all of us together.[19]

The autumn of 2008 was a time of intense political activity. The United States was in the midst of a presidential election, and Peggy was campaigning for the Democratic candidate, Barack Obama. Her next Timely CD contained only one song: "Obama Is the One for Me," in which she praises the young senator from Illinois with a bluesy melody and his own campaign slogan ("Yes, we can!"):

> Obama is the one for me,
> Got the youth, the energy,
> He knows the ropes and how to steer,
> States the issues loud and clear.
> Can he win? Yes, he can.

Can he win? Yes, he can.
He's a member of the team and a one-man band,
Obama is the one for me.[20]

On November 4, 2008, Barack Obama became the first African American to be elected president of the United States. Peggy rejoiced at the success. But November brought bad news as well: Peggy was diagnosed with breast cancer. On November 25, she had a successful lumpectomy and afterward said, "As far as I'm concerned, I no longer have cancer."[21] She was well enough to continue teaching and called the class concert in December her "high spot of the year."[22] On December 15, she flew to New Zealand and stayed for the winter.

In 2009, *Bring Me Home* was nominated for a Grammy Award in the Best Traditional Folk Album category. Both Peggy and Pete were nominated in this category, and Pete ultimately won for his album *At 89*. In the spring, Peggy and Irene flew to the United States for Pete's ninetieth birthday. On May 3, eighteen thousand people gathered in New York's Madison Square Garden for a four-and-a-half-hour concert to celebrate Pete's ninety years. The lineup included major folk artists (Tom Paxton, Bernice Johnson Reagon, Joan Baez, Arlo Guthrie, and Ramblin' Jack Elliott, among others), as well as musicians from many other genres (John Mellencamp, Billy Bragg, Bruce Springsteen, Emmylou Harris, Kris Kristofferson, and Richie Havens, to name a few). Bruce Springsteen described the nonagenarian as someone who looks "like your granddad, if your granddad could kick your ass." Peggy chose not to sing and instead read a letter, which ended with the words: "Brother . . . You didn't change my life—you were a deep, formative part of it, a guiding force. You helped set me on a good path and walked a good part of it beside me. You are what brothers should be. I'm proud to be your sister, privileged to have been part of YOUR life and to help carry the message on. I love you, Pete. I love you. The glorious indelible memories are my thanks."[23]

Peggy spent the spring and early summer touring the United States. Irene joined her in July, and they planned a few months of traveling. They were looking forward to a visit with Mike, who was fighting cancer. Mike had been diagnosed with chronic lymphocytic leukemia (CLL) in 2001. While any cancer diagnosis is serious, Mike's type of CLL was slow growing, with a typical life expectancy of five to twenty years or more. Following treatment, Mike's CLL had gone into remission, and he had lived a busy and productive life. But in the summer of 2009, he began to experience pain and fatigue. He discovered that he had multiple myeloma, an aggressive form of blood cancer unrelated to CLL. Mike continued to play and travel until late July, when his condition worsened so much that he had to be hospitalized. Unfortunately, chemotherapy and radiation had virtually no effect on the cancer. Mike rejected further treatment and chose to go home. Peggy was with him for his last days, along with his wife, Alexia, and his children, Kim, Chris, and Jeremy. Mike's biographer Bill Malone writes, "Mike's life had been consumed with music, but in his last days, he wanted only quiet. He took great pleasure in the sounds of nature. If he felt pain, he did not express it. He even preserved his sense of humor: at one point when Alexia asked if he was comfortable, Mike responded that he felt 'fair to middlin'.'"[24]

Mike Seeger died on August 7, 2009. He left behind an impressive body of work and a thriving old-time music revival that he had helped bring into being. Through videos, albums, and numberless concerts, through solo performance and collaboration with other musicians, Mike had combined musical virtuosity with dedication to traditional performance style. He had championed the work of traditional musicians and promoted the careers of performers such as Dock Boggs, Hazel Dickens, and Libba Cotten. In a profession known for egos, jealousy, and emotional drama, no one had a harsh word for Mike Seeger. Bill Malone observes, "Everywhere, Mike was remembered for his musical versatility, his generosity, his patience and willingness to help anyone who sought his counsel on a musical question, and his sense of humor."[25] It would no doubt have pleased him that the old-time music revival he had midwifed into existence could survive without him.

For Peggy, Mike's death was the deepest personal loss she had experienced since Ewan had died twenty years earlier. Mike had been her close friend and musical companion since the day she was born. At his memorial gathering in December, she sang "I Remember," her musical tribute to her brother:

> Down the years, you took care of me,
> You were everything I thought an older brother ought to be,
> I hope you know, I'm sure you know.
> When you died on that warm summer evening,
> It was hard, so hard, to let you go.
> I remember, I remember,
> Once upon a time, we'd both remember.
> Now you're gone, I will remember for you,
> I will remember.

Peggy had been thinking about returning to England for some time. She missed her children and grandchildren; and Irene, a British citizen, could remain indefinitely in the UK, as she could not in the United States. With Mike gone, Peggy felt adrift in America. She did not teach in the autumn of 2009, preferring to tour extensively. She flew to New Zealand for Christmas and remained there for several months. While in New Zealand, she received yet another blow: John Seeger died at the age of ninety-five. Of Charles Seeger's seven children, only Pete, Peggy, and Barbara were left.

The decision to leave America was not an easy one. She had made close friends in Boston and enjoyed her lively, urban neighborhood. In the spring of 2010, as she planned her final months in the United States, she reflected: "When I walk around Jamaica Pond, I think: how can I do without this? . . . I will really, really miss the United States. . . . The informality of the people, the wide-open spaces, the predictable weather, more or less. You can pretty much be sure of getting a summer here."[26] She would continue to tour in the United States and would spend part of each year with Irene in New Zealand. But England, she decided, was home.

# CHAPTER 20

# Everything Changes

That was then,
Now it's now,
Everything changes
Somehow,
The house I lived in,
The town I lived in,
Everything changes,
Everything.

—Peggy Seeger, "Everything Changes"

In September 2010, Peggy set down new roots in a rented house on the outskirts of Oxford, England. A small city of beautiful architecture and immense cultural attractions, Oxford had the sophistication of a major metropolis without the attendant bustle and high costs. Since the thirteenth century, it has been the site of one of the world's great universities. It is also the home of Ruskin College, an independent institution designed for working-class adults, where Peggy deposited the artifacts (papers, letters, albums, photographs, awards, mementos, etc.) that became the Ewan Mac-Coll/Peggy Seeger Archive. London, where Peggy's three children lived, was only an hour away. Peggy and Irene, both British citizens, could come and go as they pleased.

Though resettled in England, Peggy continued to make American music her specialty. In 2011, *Fly Down Little Bird* was released, an album of traditional American music that Peggy had recorded with her brother Mike. *Fly Down Little Bird* consists of the songs that Peggy and Mike had learned in childhood, which she described as "songs of disappointed love, incarceration, murder and mayhem, cowboy and coal-miners songs, testimonies to courage in the face of poverty, misery and social injustice that wove a tapestry that is on the walls of my conscious mind to this day."[1] The album drew from the same well as Peggy's Home Trilogy but is very different in presentation and choice of songs. There are almost no ballads on *Fly Down Little Bird*, nor are there any songs with the magnificent folk poetry so prominently featured in the Home Trilogy. All these albums have a museum quality, but they seem to come from different museums. The Home Trilogy is reminiscent of an art museum, in which beautiful songs were polished and presented in arrangements that functioned like carefully crafted frames. *Fly Down Little Bird* is more like a history museum, concerned with preserving the songs and performance practice of a bygone age. Whereas Peggy's Home Trilogy presented new songs and incorporated innovative recording techniques, *Fly Down Little Bird* resists newness and attempts to re-create a time-honored tradition:

> Mike and I took up the instruments in our early teens but our paths diverged over the decades. . . . Our styles differed hugely, but we each still sang the songs in our own way. When Mike suggested that we record some of them as closely as possible to the way in which we originally heard them, I wondered if it was possible. Once we got together, it was like old times. He used his usual recording method: no overdubbing, little or no cutting between takes, singing the song all the way through. We enjoyed the sessions tremendously—it was the first time in 50 years that we had taken time to just *sit back and sing*.[2]

The resultant album has the quality of an informal singing session with extremely talented participants. The accompaniments are skillfully done but not complex or showy: instrumentation primarily backs up and repeats the melody, as is common in folk-song accompaniment the world over. On most songs, Peggy and Mike sing solo or in unison; even when harmony does exist, as in "Poor Little Turtle Dove," it is very simple. There is mild social criticism in a few of the songs but nothing overtly political. Mike and Peggy have equal billing and do equal amounts of singing and playing, but Mike's vision predominates.

Mike had never made his politics part of his music. Pete, by contrast, had made political music the backbone of his career. Peggy is equally comfortable in the purist world of traditional songs and in the activist world of political songs, seeing them as two sides of the same coin—the artistic expressions of people who are not in power. In 2011, a challenge from the powerless to the powerful arose in the "Occupy Wall Street" movement in New York. Its foundational document, the "Declaration of the Occupation of New York City," had echoes of the Declaration of Independence and the Paris Commune, but with a distinctly modern point of view:

As one people, united, we acknowledge the reality: that the future of the human race requires the cooperation of its members; that our system must protect our rights, and upon corruption of that system, it is up to the individuals to protect their own rights, and those of their neighbors; that a democratic government derives its just power from the people, but corporations do not seek consent to extract wealth from the people and the Earth; and that no true democracy is attainable when the process is determined by economic power. We come to you at a time when corporations, which place profit over people, self-interest over justice, and oppression over equality, run our governments.[3]

Within months, the Occupy Wall Street movement had inspired similar movements around the world. In England, the Occupy St. Paul movement set up camp outside St. Paul's Cathedral, the iconic London landmark in the heart of the financial district. Peggy wrote three songs for the Occupy movements, all of them based on earlier songs. "Sit Down Occupation: USA" and "Sit Down Occupation: UK" have identical tunes and practically identical words. Both are based on a labor song written by Maurice Sugar for a 1937 sit-down strike in Flint, Michigan, which ended in a major victory for the American labor movement. In using this song as her foundation, Peggy links contemporary political movements with the Left's past successes:

When the rich get richer and the poor stay poor,
Sit down! Sit down!
When there's always cash for another war,
Sit down! Sit down!
When 1% is running the show,
Sit down! Sit down!
Then 99% say, "No!"
Sit down! Sit down! [4]
CHORUS:
Sit down; just take a seat,
Sit down, and rest your feet,
Sit down on Wall Street (USA)/Sit down on the concrete (UK),
Sit down! Sit down!

"Doggone, Occupation Is On" is also based on an American labor song from the 1930s. Hezekiah Jenkins wrote the blues-styled "The Panic Is On" in 1931, taking as his title a phrase that had described economic depression since the late nineteenth century. In 2011, the American songwriter Dave Lippman rewrote Jenkins's song for Occupy Wall Street, and Peggy adapted Lippman's words to reflect the Occupy St. Paul movement in England. By using American music and American vernacular yet writing from an English perspective, she highlights the global nature of the Occupy movements:

> I reckon those bankers shoulda never been bailed,
> They should be sitting tonight in jail.
> No use waiting for the by-and-by,
> Let's go to St. Paul's and occupy.
> Doggone, occupation is on.
> The top 1% are feeling fine,
> We're here to represent the other 99.
> We may be sitting down, but we're standing tall,
> After the Arab Spring comes the European Fall.
> Doggone, occupation is on.

Peggy sang "Doggone, Occupation Is On" on the 2012 CD *Celebrating Subversion*, produced by the Anti-Capitalist Roadshow, a collective of progressive performers in the UK. Her principles were utterly in line with those of the Anti-Capitalist Roadshow, as described on its website: "We are part of the resistance to a capitalism that functions only on behalf of the wealthy, that aims to shrink the public sphere and privatise public services, including the NHS [National Health Service], and that is destructive to the planet. We are part of another way of looking at the world."[5] The inspiration for the Anti-Capitalist Roadshow came from folk revival stalwart Leon Rosselson. Frankie Armstrong, also a member of the group, writes: "He sent a number of singers with whom he's worked over the years an email at the time of the St. Paul's Occupation against the excesses of the banks and finance industry. He suggested we might put together a loose group of those willing to take part in concerts wherever we're offered the chance to perform. . . . Each concert lineup will be different according to who's available and willing—and there's normally been six performers per event."[6] In addition to folk revival artists such as Sandra Kerr, Frankie Armstrong, Leon Rosselson, and Peggy Seeger, the Anti-Capitalist Roadshow featured younger musicians such as Grace Petrie and the self-described "socialist magician" Ian Saville, the only nonmusician in the group. Peggy enjoyed working with the Anti-Capitalist Roadshow immensely. In addition to performing, she was in charge of creating the document that specified the group's technical requirements. "This document regularises backstage protocol and food, sets standards of accommodation, arranges sales of CDs etc.," explains Peggy. "In short, it puts performers and organisers on the same page."[7]

Peggy's major album for 2012 was *Peggy Seeger Live*, which was recorded at a concert in Nelson, New Zealand, in 2010. The album has twenty-three tracks and is more than an hour long, but it is so varied that it holds our interest from beginning to end. There are ballads, laments, blues songs, political songs, love songs, humorous songs, and the beginning of Beethoven's "Moonlight Sonata." Peggy also recites some of her poems and reads bits of humorous commentary that she has collected from various sources. Many musical styles are featured in the concert, and Peggy skillfully varies her singing to the needs of the song. In "I Been a Bad Bad Girl," her voice takes on the vibrato and harsh timbre that were in the original field recording of prison inmate Ozella Jones. In "Mountaineer's Courtship," a traditional two-part courting song, Peggy sings the two parts in styles so different that it is always clear which person is talking. Her voice takes on slight Spanish inflections in "Missing," her 1987 song about a woman who "disappeared" in Chile during the Pinochet regime; she and local musician Nathan Torvik also provide a Latin-inspired guitar accompaniment. After this harrowing song, she goes immediately into two lighthearted traditional songs, "Sally Goodin" and "Sourwood Mountain." The lively accompaniment (Peggy on banjo, Irene on spoons, and Nathan Torvik on mandolin) and cheerful words completely change the mood from one of despair to one of joy. Irene edited the concert and turned it into an album, Peggy's only live album to date.

Peggy's next album, *Folksploitation*, was completely different. She calls it "an outrageous dance album . . . an apt project for the magic year of seventy-seven years old."[8] *Folksploitation* was produced by the English musician Broadcaster and Peggy's son Calum. It was Peggy's second collaboration with Broadcaster. In 2007, Broadcaster and Calum produced *Primary Transmission*, a rock-inspired remixing and reworking of several cuts from the Radio Ballads. Peggy had given her consent to the project but did not rerecord any of the music. For *Folksploitation*, Peggy recorded seven songs (some traditional, some written by her or Ewan) that were then remixed and rearranged, with insistent drum beats, sampled instrumentation, and synthesized effects. The transformation of folk songs (with their emphasis on words and singing) into rock songs (with their emphasis on rhythm, instrumentation, and complex recording processes) took many people by delighted surprise. Nick Dent-Robinson proclaimed the *Folksploitation* version of "The First Time Ever I Saw Your Face" as "the year's best dance track" and wrote, "The track bravely fuses Peggy's still rich and potent voice with the heavily-rhythmic, multi-layered, many-sampled sounds and electronic wizardry that is Broadcaster's trade-mark."[9] A review in *Q Magazine* remarked, "With her weathered, steadfast voice filtered and edited, there's steel in her performance"; the *Daily Telegraph* called the album "a daring and uncompromising dance record that hurtles at you in a blazing barrage of offbeats, loops and samples"; while Folk Radio.com commented that "Broadcaster has done for Peggy Seeger what the likes of Martyn Bennett did for Lizzie Higgins, he has brought Peggy into greater prominence for a new generation."[10]

Peggy also released a two-hour DVD in 2012: *Peggy Seeger Teaches Guitar Accompaniment for Folk Songs, Ballads, and Originals*, in which she demonstrates the guitar styles and techniques that she uses to accompany songs. In the autumn, she became involved in Oxford's local politics. An ardent swimmer, Peggy discovered that her local leisure facility—the Temple Cowley Pools and Fitness Centre—was slated for closure. Peggy became active in the campaign to keep the Temple Cowley Pools open; she wrote a song and made a video for the campaign. Local swimmers and singers, ranging in age from four to eighty, took part in the video, which had to be shot in another location (a private boys' school), as the Oxford City Council did not grant permission to film in the Temple Cowley Pools.

Making the video brought an unexpected disaster. The pool at the boys' school was well appointed and boasted two diving boards. Peggy easily dove off the low board and decided to jump off the high one. It was a serious mistake. She landed on her back and was in such pain that she could not get out of the water without help. Her chiropractor diagnosed "compressed lumbar and fractured thoracic vertebrae and stupidity on the part of his patient."[11] She spent most of the next six weeks lying on her back, taking painkillers and cursing herself, occasionally getting up to work on her next album.

The year 2013 was a quiet one. Peggy performed at several concerts with the Anti-Capitalist Roadshow, gave a benefit concert for Oxford's Pegasus Theatre, and spent a week teaching at the Wren Music School in Devon. She had only one gig in the United States that year: on May 12, she and Pete gave a concert in Schenectady, New York, a benefit for Camp Killooleet. "It wasn't just a concert," noted Greg Haymes. "It was a bona fide sing-along hootenanny, nearly all night long."[12] At the concert, Peggy sang "It's Pete," the song she had written for Pete's ninety-fourth birthday, a song that celebrates his matchless ability to get people singing:

> Raise your voice, loud and sweet,
> Feel that rhythm and tap your feet,

Turn, turn, hear the banjo ring,
The whole wide world begins to sing.
St. Peter will smile when Pete comes along,
And God Himself will be singing those songs.
CHORUS:
It's Pete, it's Pete,
Strumming his banjo, stamping his feet,
That lanky man comes down your street.
Then whaddaya know? You're singing.

Summer brought the enemy that no one can fight: time. On July 9, Toshi Seeger, Pete's wife for nearly seventy years, died at the age of ninety-one. "She was the brains of the family," said Pete. "I'd get an idea and wouldn't know how to make it work, and she'd figure out how to make it work."[13] In June, Peggy fell down a flight of stairs and injured her spine. She spent the next month lying on her back and remarked: "Poor little set of vertebrae . . . they will never be the same again. BUT—I'm walking, swimming, still self-motivating. For that I am thankful."[14] The same lack of self-pity governed her reaction to the news that her breast cancer had returned. In August, she had a mastectomy and informed her family and friends, "Three months ago I was told I was not clear. NOW I AM. . . . It's done and dusted and life (other than the English weather) looks really good."[15]

The beginning of 2014 was peaceful. Peggy was in New Zealand with Irene. Pete's daughter Tinya called to say that Pete was in the hospital, but the prognosis looked good. Peggy had a long telephone conversation with her big brother, perhaps the longest conversation of their lives. Then in late January, Peggy received another call telling her that Pete was dying. She and Irene were on the next plane. Family and close friends gathered in Pete's room at Columbia-Presbyterian Hospital in New York City, filling his last hours with music. Peggy arrived four hours too late to say good-bye. "I take solace from our last phone calls where much was said but unspoken," she remarked.[16]

Pete's death was front-page news. Every major American news outlet ran an obituary, often a lengthy one, as did many foreign news organizations. Dorian Lynskey, writing in the *Guardian*, describes Pete's genius in an article called "The Man Who Brought Politics to Music":

Pete Seeger was a good man. There aren't many musicians you can say that about without seeming simplistic. Music is often progressed by flawed, volatile, glamorous egotists, and thank God for them. But Seeger carved out his place in history with a quieter, rarer set of qualities: nobility, generosity, humility and, when things got rough, breathtaking courage. Perhaps uniquely, he became one of the most important singers in America without ever being a star, because he believed in the song rather than the singer.[17]

Millions of friends, fans, and admirers grieved for the man who had always looked for the best in people and had always fought against the worst. Peggy recalls an outpouring of grief and love at the funeral home two days after Pete's death:

I stood at the door for six hours greeting people. . . . Between 2,000 and 3,000 people filed through: people in tears, people hugging. There was music going on, his ashes were in the urn on the side. There were people of all ages: the oldest was 95, the youngest could barely walk. So I knew the effect that Pete had. I had been Pete Seeger's sister for all my life. And it's an honored position to hold. Not only honored because of him, but because what he did made it possible for me.[18]

Pete had been the de facto leader of the folk revival for decades, the only American folksinger who was a household word. This position made him uncomfortable, for he disliked the cult of personality, but it gave him a powerful platform from which to express his ideas and to effect social change. "A real revolution," he said, "is not achieved with guns. It's achieved with arts. The arts can leap over barriers of words, barriers of religion, barriers of politics."[19] He was not naive; he had seen evil too often and too closely to believe that the arts were sufficient unto themselves. But they were the weapons that he knew best. Like Peggy, he always had hope for the future, even in the midst of tragedy or disaster. Two days after Pete's death, Peggy addressed her friends on Facebook, acknowledging the deep sorrow within her but refusing to succumb to despair: "I know many of you will be saddened by Pete's death but we must remember that he led a very full and productive life. He leaves a prodigious body of work for us to enjoy, a legacy . . . which will continue to grow. He touched so many people's lives, from children to the golden oldies like myself. As for me, I have lost the last person who has known me from birth and who has always been there for me. I cannot express how heavy losing Pete lies with me."[20]

Peggy continued to tour and perform until mid-April, when she underwent major emergency surgery, an ileostomy that required a long convalescence. Irene came from New Zealand the day after the surgery and, with Peggy's family, insisted that she cancel all work until the end of the year. Peggy spent the summer resting and regaining her strength, emerging from seclusion only to attend Neill's wedding to Kate St. John in Italy.

Her most recent album, *Everything Changes*, was officially launched on September 1, 2014. Its title is fitting, for it is unlike any other album she has made. "It's much more of a singer-songwriter album rather than a folk album," says Peggy's daughter-in-law Kerry Harvey-Piper.[21] Kerry is correct. It is *not* a folk album. There are no traditional songs on *Everything Changes*, nor are there any songs written in traditional style. Peggy had always considered instrumentation to be secondary to singing in folk music, but in this album, instrumentation is essential to the songs. The instrumentation goes far beyond mere accompaniment; it has a life and a voice of its own. Many of the instruments used are not folk ones: there are drums, pianos, and synthesized effects but no banjos, dulcimers, autoharps, or mandolins. And many of the folk instruments used are not Western ones, such as the sentir from Morocco (a distant relative of the banjo), the kalimba from Africa, and the bapang from India.

Yet *Everything Changes* does not have the shock of Bob Dylan going electric at the 1965 Newport Folk Festival. Peggy has been singing songs like these for years; one of them, "Miss Heroin," is decades old. None of these songs, put by itself in an album of folk music, would be startling. Only when all of these songs are put together do we realize how much Peggy's style has changed. The changes do not shock because they have been gradual, building on the foundation of tradition rather than rejecting it. In this way, Peggy is acting like a traditional folk artist (even if she is not singing traditional folk songs), taking aspects of traditional practice and altering them to fit contemporary concerns. Each step has been a logical movement away from the step before. If you take enough steps, however, you find yourself in a foreign land, and in this album, Peggy is no longer in the world of folk music.

And yet this album is vintage Peggy Seeger. Her voice has lost some of the hard edge it had in youth and middle age, but it sounds stronger than ever, as though she had cut away a hard shell to reveal the pure voice within. Thanks to Calum's skillful production and direction, the sound quality of the recording is crystal-clear, giving it a sense of intimacy and immediacy, as though Peggy were sitting nearby and singing directly to us. Lyrics have always been one of her strengths, and the words on this album are particularly inventive and multilayered. For the past twenty-five years, Irene has been an invaluable part of Peggy's songwriting, providing what Peggy calls "ex post facto honing—trimming in both ideas and text."[22] The first song, "Swim to the Star," coauthored by Peggy and Calum and honed by Irene, shows the success of this collaboration. "Swim to the Star" commemorates the sinking of the *Titanic*, and though not a folk song, it shows the folk poet's clarity, detail, and sparseness of expression:

> The ship went down in calm water,
> The band played on.
> Women and children float away
> Nearer, my God, to Thee.[23]

Every word in the stanza is necessary to tell the story, and each line has multiple meanings. "The ship went down in calm water" is a simple statement of fact, but on reflection, it is a surprising one; usually, ships are threatened by stormy waters, not calm ones. "The band played on" is, again, a statement of historical fact, but it is also the name of a popular song from the 1890s, a song that many *Titanic* passengers would have known. "Women and children first" is the rule of the lifeboat; women and children did float away as the *Titanic* sank—some to safety, others to death. "Nearer My God to Thee" is, by some accounts, the song that the band played while the ship went down. In 2015, "Swim to the Star" was named Best Original Song in the BBC Radio 2 Folk Awards.

"Go to Sleep," the second song, transports us to the sleepy warmth of a child's bedroom. It is, in Peggy's words, "a love song, a lullaby and a plea."[24] The song was written by Peggy's sons when they had small children of their own and features the vivid and comforting imagery common in lullabies:

> Gray houses covered in roses in the rain,
> Dreams that sat and played around the window pane.
> Go to sleep, go to sleep,
> Your mother is sleeping.[25]

With its kalimba accompaniment and syncopated rhythm, the song shows a definite African influence, highlighting the universality of its theme. Peggy sings the lead, while Neill and Calum join her on the chorus. Rarely can a mother sing with her children a lullaby that they have written.

Possibly the best song on the album is "Nero's Children," a protest song with words far more complex and oblique than the typically straightforward lyrics of a folk song:

> Nero's children play with matches,
> Noah's children cannot swim,
> Adam's children kill each other
> And sing of love and money.

Tune the fiddle, build the ark,
Dance in the dark,
Ashes to dust, in God we trust,
And dream of love and money.[26]

The mythical and the historical are skillfully intertwined in this song. In the Bible, ashes and dust are listed as the components from which human beings are made and to which we will return. By pairing the biblically inspired "ashes to dust" with the motto found on U.S. money ("in God we trust"), she suggests that human-made evils are caused by "love of money," which the New Testament calls "the root of all evil." In this song, instruments as well as words make eloquent statements. An unobtrusive guitar plays in the early part of the song, but in the middle an insistent drumbeat begins, along with unsettling guitar and piano parts. This strident, somewhat dissonant instrumentation continues as Peggy sings about war, which destroys life yet must be fueled by love and money. But the song ends with hope, as most Peggy Seeger songs do. The discordant instrumentation fades, and the light, harmonious instrumentation returns, bringing soothing reassurance and gentle advice. The lyrics end with yet another biblical reference:

Strike the match, light the candle,
Head for land and swim.
Save each other, save your mother,
And sing of love, of love, of love,
Sing of milk and honey.[27]

At the very end, we hear the drumbeat, but the tempo has slowed, and the sound is very faint and far away. As Peggy says, "The track fades not to settled chord sequences but to slightly unsettling improvisation and thence to silence. It is hopeful but with reservations."[28]

Ironically, the song that sounds most familiar is entitled "Everything Changes." With its clear, straightforward lyrics, blues-inspired melody, and simple jazz accompaniment, "Everything Changes" sounds, in many respects, like the contemporary folk songs that Peggy has been writing for decades:

The house I lived in, when I was a child,
Had woods, we all ran wild,
You could hide, then come home after a while.
The town I lived in when I was young,
Everybody knew my name,

The world was my own,
Safe in the dark, playing games,
Till Mama called me home.
But that was then,
Now it's now,
Everything changes
Somehow,
The house I lived in,
The town I lived in,
Everything changes,
Everything.
Oh, you been gone so long,
Memories fade,
It's dark and I'm afraid,
I'm your little girl child, your own,
Your very own.
Mama, it's late,
Time to call me home.[29]

Initially, the song appears to be nostalgia for the joys of youth in a simpler era, a lament for today's children, whose "world's on a screen / They play games alone." And indeed that may well be part of the song's intended message. Peggy says, "I got the idea from Susan Forbes Hansen, the well-known U.S. folk DJ, who was lamenting the diabolical changes wreaked upon her family house/hometown by Prince Progress and Duke Developer."[30] Peggy had a happy childhood climbing trees and playing games in the dark, secure in the knowledge that her mother would call her home when the time was right. But if this song is in part sincere nostalgia, it is also nostalgia stylized, set on view. Neither Silver Spring nor Chevy Chase was small enough for everyone to know her name, and she never called her mother "Mama." As David Lowenthal writes in his classic *The Past Is a Foreign Country*, "Nostalgia is memory with the pain removed."[31] The grand trees and gracious houses of Chevy Chase hid a world of racial segregation, restrictive covenants, class ignorance, and parents who (unlike Peggy's) told their daughters to "be a lady." For a person who has spent her life agitating for social change, the notion that "everything changes" may be no bad thing.

Perhaps the real object of nostalgia is not the joys of childhood without smartphones nor even youth itself but the person for whom the song was written: Ruth Crawford Seeger. It was Ruth who called Peggy home when things became dark and frightening; it was Ruth who taught her to love folk music and showed her how to combine work and family. The line "I'm your little girl child" recalls a song that Peggy wrote for Kitty many years ago. In "Little Girl Child," Peggy spells out the lessons that she wants her young daughter to learn but also recognizes that Kitty will develop a point of view independent of her mother. In the same way, Peggy developed a musical style that was very different from Ruth's, and not until years after Ruth's death did Peggy realize how much they had in common.

In her youth, Peggy was close to both parents, but Charles was her confidant, the person to whom she could tell anything and to whom she wrote detailed letters; Ruth's early death prevented such a relationship from being possible. Charles made the major decisions in the Seeger household; it was he who introduced Ruth to politics and insisted on fighting the good fight, no matter the personal cost. Charles's decision to take on unpopular causes was all the more noble because he did not have to; life was set up very nicely for the Charles Seegers of the world. Again and again, Charles took political stances that limited his reputation, freedom of movement, and ability to make a living. Yet he was not an angry person—he was a fighter with no rancor toward his enemies.

Like her father, Peggy took firm political positions and would not change them for personal gain. Like him, she fought without personal anger. But as she grew older, Peggy turned more and more to her mother for inspiration, forging in imagination bonds with Ruth that had not been forged in life. Ruth was an angrier person than Charles; whereas Charles chose to fight, Ruth had to. As a young woman, she fought for the education she needed to develop her talent. As a composer, she fought for recognition as "a composer of genius . . . though a woman," to use the words of one admirer.[32] As a working mother, Ruth fought to balance work and family in a world where feminism was virtually forgotten. And at the age of fifty-two, newly inspired to compose and receiving fresh recognition for her efforts, she fought the cancer that struck her down in what should have been the prime of her life. Though Peggy would always miss her father's gentle presence and piercing intellect, it is Ruth who haunts this unique new album. Ruth's creative dissonance, her blending of folk and other forms of music, her restless insistence on pushing boundaries as far as they would go, her refusal to rest on her laurels or to give up no matter what her age or physical condition—all these are gifts that Ruth bequeathed to Peggy, and that Peggy has used in ways that Ruth could not have imagined.

Ruth's musical accomplishments are the subject of a recent book, *Ruth Crawford Seeger's Worlds: Innovation and Tradition in Twentieth-Century American Music*.[33] The twin concepts of innovation and tradition are vitally important to both scholars and artists, and few artists exemplified their interweaving better than Ruth Crawford Seeger. Judith Tick, Ruth's biographer and Peggy's close friend, points out that Charles wrote about innovation and tradition in music, but Ruth put these ideas into practice. Peggy's musical and intellectual world was deeply influenced by both parents, but Ruth provided a working model: "[Peggy's] mother was a brilliant composer. . . . She was always pushing the limits of technique and style in her own music. . . . So this notion that you keep on exploring through art is very much a part of Ruth Seeger's legacy. . . . Peggy is very aware of tradition. . . . On the other hand, she's also aware that, as a singer-songwriter, she has new things to say that speak to the folk tradition of talking about contemporary issues."[34]

This interplay between tradition and innovation has always driven Peggy's music, making it seem both familiar and surprising, comprised of parts old and new bound together. Peggy has lived a life of creative contradictions: a gentle fighter, an intellectual college dropout, an American folksinger who sings the songs of her own country but prefers to live in another. She is an artist dedicated to preserving traditional music and to writing new songs that focus on the present and incorporate new musical styles; she is someone who can look forward and backward at the same time. Her incorporation of innovation and tradition is so complete that she sees in them no contradiction; they are partners, not adversaries, and are present in every work of art. Traditional musicians *are* innovative: they create new words to old songs and change old melodies to fit the changing times; by its very definition, a traditional song has more than one variant. And even the most innovative artist uses the tools—words, instruments, keys, and such—of an earlier generation.

In *Everything Changes*, Peggy takes the lessons of the past and uses them to suggest guidelines for the future: don't follow the path of Nero; save the poor as well as the rich when the ship of state begins to sink. Her messages are not always simple. When she sings, "Mama, it's late, / Please call me home," what does she mean? A religious interpretation might suggest that, for a person nearing eighty years of age, death may seem a pathway to peace, a final home and a reuniting with loved ones. This nod to Protestant hymnody gives the lines a familiar sound, a secure anchor in the world of tradition. But Peggy's secular worldview suggests that such an interpretation may not cover all possibilities. For a peripatetic artist like Peggy, "home" might be a set of guiding principles for living, principles that Ruth taught her in the first home she knew. From Ruth, Peggy learned to strive for perfection in her work, to make family a cornerstone of her life, to make the world a better place. In an increasingly mobile world, perhaps the stability of home is found not in a single place but in an idea, an adherence to personal conviction. As Heraclitus remarked 2,500 years ago, perhaps the only constancy in life is the recognition that everything changes.

In assessing her legacy, Peggy is modest. "I'd like to be remembered as having been useful," she says, "and for having written some good songs. My legacy is my songs, my children, and my grandchildren."[35] She is deeply gratified when people come to her after a concert and say, "I (or my daughter or granddaughter) became an engineer because of you." In a 1990 interview, Peggy spoke about the effects her songs have had: "A person comes up to you to say, 'You were responsible for my doing this,' and then mentioning something fantastic that they've done: changing their lives or taking a course in education or maybe not going home and battering their wife. . . . Because I've had that happen; I've had men come to me after singing the song 'Emily' and say, 'I didn't know what I was doing.' . . . You have reached them. . . . You've changed the world."[36]

Many people have commented on the power of Peggy's songs and performances. In a review of *An Odd Collection*, Ken Hunt of *Q* magazine observed: "The muse who inspired Ewan MacColl's 'First Time Ever I Saw Your Face' has produced a body of work that is unparalleled in its vehemence and remains a fountain of inspiration in a sea of bogus political correctness. Many of her songs are genuinely, uncomfortably, challenging. . . . Easy listening this is not but, if difficult, it is difficult only in a stirring sense."[37] Neil Johnston, reviewing a concert in Belfast in 2002, wrote: "Peggy Seeger: She must be one of the most complete artists around today. Peggy Seeger's tongue-in-cheek look at life comes accompanied by music from all sorts of sources. Alongside the piano, the guitar, the Appalachian dulcimer, the concertina and the banjo, she set the lot aside for a moment or two last night and just simply created rhythm and music by tapping the side of her guitar. For her it spelt out a sort of rhythm of life."[38] Equally moving are the letters she has received from listeners and concertgoers: the (male) engineer who sent "I'm Gonna Be an Engineer" to his friends and made sure that women were hired at his firm; the wife of a math teacher who uses "One Plus One" to teach advanced mathematics; the musician who bought his first banjo while a student in 1964 and received an impromptu lesson from Peggy after a concert; the man whose deep despair lifted when he heard "the joy and passion and belief and strength" in Ewan and Peggy's singing. Many women see her as a role model; an admirer from Australia wrote: "It was great to see you live, for the wonderful range of music, but also for the pleasure of seeing a woman who is so clearly at ease in her own skin. You were funny, smart, feisty, warm and wise, and managed to be very assertive without getting anyone offside, and very intelligent without making anyone feel stupid. It's a combination I hope I'll get close to someday!"[39]

Part of Peggy's appeal is her willingness to engage with her audience and her listeners. At concerts, she might bring dinner for the stage crew or play banjo with the soundman. She sells her own CDs at intermission and after the show; she greets old friends and makes new ones. The line between artist and audience blurs, as she instructs the audience to sing along and makes clear that they have an important role to play. Julian Owen, reviewing a concert in Bath, puts it well: "For a sold-out gig, the intimate sense of communality is a wonder, a matriarch leading her extended brood through a family songbook they never knew they had."[40]

At the close of her eighth decade, Peggy looks both backward and forward. Her accomplishments are legion: she has produced a myriad of recordings, given countless concerts, written books, taught workshops and classes, helped create the Festival of Fools and the Radio Ballads, created and played music for film and radio and television, and written songs that will be sung long after she is gone. In 2011, she was awarded an honorary Doctor of Arts from the University of Salford, the town where Ewan was born and raised. In 2014, *Music Week* named her the first winner of the Women in Music Inspirational Artist award. In 2015, the Folk Alliance honored her with its Lifetime Achievement Award. But the restless perfectionist cannot be satisfied. There is still so much to do. Her desires are simple yet monumental: a peaceful and healthy world, a life free from pain, loving relationships, useful work, a home—not for herself alone but for everyone. Her goals are perhaps best expressed in one of her most moving and beautiful songs, "Thoughts of Time," a song that is decades old but sounds fresh as this morning, a timeless song about time:

> Our dream is old, our dream is always new,
> A dream ever with us, it was with us from the start,
> The dream that all could live as lovers do,
> A dream coming nearer though it always seems afar—
> But to die before we see our dream come true,
>     Only that could break my heart.

# CHAPTER 21

# What Is a Folk Revival?

I can sing alone,
You can sing with me,
We can sing in harmony
In the key of C or D or E.
Songs are made for you,
Songs are made for us,
Songs are made for everyone
To join in on the chorus.

—Peggy Seeger, "One Plus One"

What is a folk revival? The scholarly literature on the subject is vast, but there is little consensus. Most definitions of "folk revival" attempt to be descriptive rather than all-inclusive; as Robert Cantwell says, we use the term "for convenience, but with an implicit sense of compromise or concession."[1] Alan Jabbour, in the foreword to one of the first scholarly essay collections on the subject, writes both as a folklorist and as a former participant in the mid-twentieth-century revival (what Neil Rosenberg calls the "great boom"): "When we speak of revival, we imply that something happening in the present somehow simultaneously resurrects the past. . . . Our revival was not so much a revival of specific artistic artifacts . . . as a revival of symbolic values. . . . We in our revival sought out—and created—a music to express simultaneously our quest for cultural roots, our admiration of democratic ideas and values, our solidarity with the culturally neglected, and our compulsion to forge our own culture for ourselves."[2] Ethnomusicologist Tamara Livingston concurs with Jabbour that music revivals involve the search for cultural meaning, but she places more emphasis on the music itself and on the sense of the music's obsolescence: "I define music revivals as any social movement with the goal of restoring and preserving a musical tradition which is believed to be disappearing or completely relegated to the past."[3] To some, the creation of new music was as essential to the folk revival as the preservation of the past. In a 1963 symposium on the folk-song revival, one of the few examinations of the subject during the great boom itself, Ben Botkin remarked, "The problem of the folksong revival is not simply to preserve traditional songs and styles but to adapt them to the needs of a new age—an industrial age in an urban, industrialized society."[4]

A distinction is frequently made, by both scholars and musicians, between traditional music and music specifically created for the revival. As discussed in chapter 10, traditional music is generally defined as music that is passed on by oral tradition, exists in variants and not as one authoritative text, and is considered the property of a community rather than an individual. Scholars and musicians also frequently cite a distinction between revival singers and traditional or source singers. Michael F. Scully describes these distinctions well: "Traditional performers are members of [the] folk and their singing is neither a commercial enterprise nor the dedicated pursuit of a hobby revolving around organizations and scheduled events. It is, instead, a more-or-less unself-conscious part of daily life. . . . Revivalists, by contrast, tend to be self-conscious folk song interpreters, not genuine, tradition-based folksingers."[5] While these distinctions have a certain amount of pragmatic validity, they are becoming increasingly harder to maintain in a literate, globalized world. In her 1985 study of the folk revival in Scotland, Ailie Munro asked forty-five singers if they considered themselves source or revival singers and found that the categories were frequently insufficient to describe the musicians' experience and background:

> Singers were "revival" if they had learned most of their songs from recorded or printed sources, from other revival singers or from source singers (several stressed the latter), and "source" if the songs had been handed down in the oral tradition, or learned in childhood. But the categories are not clear-cut. Not a few revival singers have source elements in their backgrounds, while many source singers make use of the written word—both in giving copies to other singers, and in obtaining copies of words to add to their own repertoires.[6]

At present, with worldwide access to the internet, such distinctions are breaking down even more. In his 2002 study of the U.S. folk revival, Ronald D. Cohen stresses the interplay, rather than the difference, among different types of music—rural and urban, traditional and composed, oral and literate: "With the circulation of broadsides and songsters in the nineteenth century, followed by the proliferation of songbooks in the twentieth, then the advent of phonograph records and radio, a variety of musics—hillbilly and cowboy songs, sea shanties, minstrel tunes, blues, Calypso, and much more—has been not only commercially distributed but also in continual flux. The idea of pristine songs and ballads, orally transmitted and untouched by the modern world, is hardly valid for the twentieth century, and perhaps even earlier."[7]

Now, in the twenty-first century, I do not suggest that we dispense with such concepts altogether, but we should recognize that the world does not always adapt itself to scholarly constructs. We can recognize that the songs of the folk revival are somehow distinct from traditional songs, but this distinction is always a subjective and impressionistic one, subject to constant reinterpretation. Where, indeed, should we place "The Shoals of Herring," a song of known authorship yet one that has become part of oral tradition, a song written by a singer who sang the songs he learned in childhood but also the songs that he specifically wrote for the folk revival?

While finding a definition of "folk revival" that would satisfy everyone is impossible, it is generally agreed that there were two great periods of interest in folk song, in both the United States and Great Britain, during the twentieth century: the first, in the early decades of the century, and the second, in the 1950s and 1960s. This is not to suggest that folk music was never performed, recorded, or collected during other times. In the 1930s and 1940s, great interest and attention were paid to folk music among Americans of left-wing conviction; this phenomenon has been ably chronicled by Ronald D. Cohen, Robbie Lieberman, and Richard Reuss, among others. Nor did interest in folk music end with the close of the 1960s. Michael F. Scully's *The Never-Ending Revival* pays close attention to folk music activities after the great boom, arguing convincingly that a lessening of public interest and commercial success does not mean the end of the folk revival. Some scholars, such as David King Dunaway and Molly Beer, even posit that there is a "third folk music boomlet" beginning in the late 1980s and continuing until the present day.[8] However, this "boomlet" did not make the inroads into mainstream or popular culture that occurred during the first and second folk revivals.

My criteria for the defining features of a folk revival are (1) the professionalization and commodification of previously amateur (traditional) music; (2) the attempt to place this music in new contexts; and (3) the active creation of new forms of music in the style of the old. However, none of these activities is new or even an invention of the twentieth century. The very act of naming a song as a "folk song" was itself an act of revivalism. As Dunaway aptly observes,

"Only when we feel ourselves losing the old ways do we begin to think about preserving and reviving them."[9] In the eighteenth century, Herder's fear that German peasant culture would be obliterated by increased industrialization and by the growing influence of foreign (particularly French) influence led to his invention of the term *folk song* and to his valorization of this music as a precious part of national patrimony. In Scotland, the collection and performance of traditional Scottish music followed the political union of Scotland with England and a concomitant fear that Scottish culture would be diluted and perhaps eradicated by the culture of its more powerful neighbor. So the beginning of the concept of folk song and the beginning of folk revivalism were, in many respects, one and the same. The discipline of folklore, which traces its intellectual origins to Herder, began with an attempt to revive material that seemed in danger of dying.

For many years, the discipline of folklore looked askance at folk revivals, particularly during the mid-twentieth-century "great boom." During this era, most professional folklorists ignored the folk revival in public and excoriated it in private. As Bruce Jackson memorably puts it, an academic folklorist's participation in the folk revival "was like a mildly embarrassing hobby one tolerates in a friend who is otherwise virtuous."[10] This is a rather curious position for an academic to take. The flute professor feels no shame in playing with the local orchestra; the chemistry professor is not embarrassed to enter the laboratory; the law professor does not shun the courtroom. Indeed, such activities are considered an important, even essential, part of one's profession. Why should the folklorist claim, almost as a badge of honor, to be incompetent to perform the music that he or she teaches?

Much of the hostility of academic folklorists toward folk revivals was centered on the concept of "authenticity." Academics condemned revivalists for pretending to be genuine folksingers or for singing songs that were not authentic folk songs. In this view, a revivalist is less like a law professor arguing a case in court than like a law professor acting in an episode of *Law and Order*. This anxiety was not unique to academics; it was shared by concert promoters, folk festival organizers, collectors, and musicians. As early as 1930, folk music festivals were criticized for undue modernization, changing the music in order to satisfy market demands, or selecting music according to ideological criteria. Indeed, Benjamin Filene credits the "cult of authenticity" as beginning in 1932 with John and Alan Lomax: "In a pioneering move, the Lomaxes began to promote not just the songs they gathered but the singers who sang them. In doing so they produced a web of criteria for determining what a 'true' folk singer looked and sounded like and a set of assumptions about the importance of *being* a 'true' folk singer."[11]

While folklorists of the first half of the twentieth century spent much time and energy arguing about what constituted a genuine folk song, the folklorists of the following generation problematized and analyzed the concept of authenticity as such. It is not surprising that many of these folklorists became interested in the study of folklore while participating in the folk revival—a fact they carefully hid from most of their professors.

I. Sheldon Posen, one of the many folklorists who came to the field from the folk revival, found that concepts of authenticity were important to both academics and revivalists but that the criteria were often different: revivalists focused on repertoire and performance practice, while academics focused on the context of the singing. The question of ethnic or class identity often reared its head for both groups. Posen reflects, "I wondered how I, a middle-class kid from Toronto, was warranted singing songs so removed from my own life—about nineteenth-century English sailors or seventeenth-century 'lords and ladies fair,' or of American cowboys and hill people, or even closer to home, of North Ontario shantyboys and Newfoundland fishermen."[12] Posen concludes that folk revivalists had created their own culture, with its own distinct norms and expectations, and that his participation in the folk revival was authentic because he was acting in accord with these cultural expectations: "I was doing what an urban folkie was supposed to be doing as a properly functioning member of the folksong revival."[13] Richard Blaustein, another folklorist who came to the field from the folk revival, was bemused that some revival musicians did not consider him authentic, while traditional musicians usually did: "I was distressed by pronouncements by kingpins of the urban folk music revival declaring that a performer had to be born and nurtured in a traditional community to be considered an authentic folk musician. The country fiddlers I had begun to visit and record up in western New England seemed perfectly happy to teach me what they knew regardless of my New York Jewish background. Unencumbered by purist preconceptions, they considered anyone who enjoyed and played old-time music to be one of their own kind."[14]

The concept of tradition itself, so central to the discipline of folklore, was also held up to scholarly scrutiny. Georgina Boyes, in her study of the English folk revival, shows that practices uncritically accepted as "traditional" had in fact been subject to revision and change. Morris dancing, for example, had

historically been an activity of both men and women, and both sexes participated in Morris dancing in the early days of the first folk revival. By the 1930s,
however, ideas of masculine control and fears of an "emasculated" national
culture led many proponents of Morris dancing to exclude women and to
defend this exclusion in the name of tradition. In order to revive a traditional
practice, English revivalists changed this practice for their own ideological
purposes, even while claiming that these innovations were traditional—which,
of course, they eventually became.[15] In an oft-quoted article, Richard Handler
and Jocelyn Linnekin argue that "there is no essential, bounded tradition;
tradition is a model of the past and is inseparable from the interpretation of
tradition in the present. . . . It is by now a truism that cultural revivals change
the traditions they attempt to revive."[16] Revival then is not just the attempt
to keep old cultural practices from dying out; it is the active creation of a
meaningful present through the selective valorization of past cultural items.

Both the first and second folk revivals were urban movements, but the first
in particular drew its strength from rural images, a vision of life before the
stress and anomie caused by industrialization and modernity. Before World
War I, it was possible—in Europe, at least—to cling to the notion of the Folk
as people rooted in the land since time immemorial. This image was less
feasible in the United States—a land of immigrants, adventurers, convicts,
slaves, colonizers, and colonized—so revivalists typically chose one form of
folk culture to represent the entire nation: the Anglo-American culture of the
Appalachians, the African American culture of the Deep South, or the settler/
cowboy culture of the West. The first folk revival was primarily, though not entirely, a conservative movement, frequently nationalistic, at times anti-Semitic
or racist. This right-wing conception of the Folk reached its apotheosis in Nazi
Germany, where the German peasant was seen as the true representative of
the nation and the Jew was cast as a foreign, corrupting, and urban force. Yet
left-wing interpretations of the Folk were not unknown during the first folk
revival. These interpretations celebrated images of premodern life like those
of the utopian socialists, before capitalism had alienated workers from their
products, when a master craftsman held an honored place in village life. It is
perhaps significant that the word *country* means both the rural part of a nation
and the nation itself.

After World War II, images of a rural ideal might have been comforting,
but it was clear that its moment had passed. While folklorists and folk aficionados continued to mine the riches of rural culture, there was also a focus on
celebrating the culture of the city, whether homegrown or as a place where

immigrants and country folk had relocated. In the 1963 symposium chaired by Ben Botkin, Israel (Izzy) Young went so far as to say, "Folk music of the future is going to come from the city and not from the country. The people in the country are running away from folk music. We are reviving it; not only reviving it, we are infusing it with a new life."[17] In the United States, interest in "ethnic" or "world music" also arose during and after the great boom, with groups dedicated to Irish music, Balkan music, klezmer music, Latin American music, and many others. Musicians involved in this aspect of the revival did not pretend to represent the entire country; by contrast, they sought to honor—and revive—specific strands of America's vast musical heritage. It was difficult at this point to speak of one folk revival; multiple folk revivals occurred simultaneously, and many continue to this day.

Where in a discussion of the folk revival should we place Peggy Seeger? As the daughter of Charles and Ruth Crawford Seeger, the sister of Pete and Mike Seeger, the friend of Alan Lomax, and the wife of Ewan MacColl, she was ideally positioned to be a potent force in both the American and the English folk revivals. Her influence has been extensive, yet she is difficult to categorize because her work is the sum of so many different parts. Some folk musicians achieve prominence because they excel in a popular idiom with many participants: Seamus Ennis was the ideal uilleann pipe player; Joan Baez the quintessential female vocalist; Pete Seeger the ultimate political musician and community song leader. Peggy's pathway is more singular and less traveled; indeed, it would be hard to find another musician who has incorporated so many different components into one career. She plays six instruments (her banjo playing is particularly admired); she sings with subtlety and precision; and she has written songs in a wide variety of styles and on a wide range of topics. As a formally trained musician, she combines her mastery of folk style with extensive knowledge of Western art music. Composers such as Beethoven, Bartók, and Ruth Crawford Seeger incorporated folk music into art music compositions; Peggy does the opposite, infusing her compositions and her performances of folk songs with unusual textures and sophisticated arrangements. Sometimes she uses her dual knowledge to create an unusual accompaniment to a folk song, as when she plays dissonant chords in the early portion of "The First Time Ever I Saw Your Face" and consonant chords later in the song, providing a musical resolution that mimics the course of a happy love affair, beginning with uncertainty and ending with contentment. Sometimes she writes pieces like "Different Tunes," which is more like a scene from an avant-garde opera than a traditional song. A six-minute conversation between mother and daughter, "Different Tunes" has some similarities to folk songs: it focuses on the lives of "ordinary people," and the words are relatively simple, with the kind of language used in everyday speech. However, the words are extensive, and there is little of the repetition that, in traditional songs, invites the audience to join in. Musically, "Different Tunes" does not sound like a folk song; it frequently changes melody, key, and time signature; it has a range of an octave and a half and is a performance piece that is not easy to sing.

In other compositions, Peggy pays tribute to folk tradition by deliberately using time-honored techniques. The tune of "Sing about These Hard Times" is based on an old hymn, and its lyrics feature repetitive words that make it easy for the audience to learn. When she initially sang this piece, the audience immediately joined in; though the song was new, it seemed familiar because it was based on the folk tradition. No one joins in on "Different Tunes," with its abundant lyrics, melodic and temporal variation, and wide vocal range; the audience is content to sit back and admire Peggy's virtuosity. The art music composer aims to be unique; the folk music composer aims to be familiar, easily accepted by other members of the community. Peggy Seeger can do both.

Peggy approaches singing as an actor approaches a role, a tribute to her intensive training with the Critics Group. She finds a coherent backstory for every song; like a Stanislavskian actor, she holds our attention because she believes in every word that she sings. She varies her vocal style to make it appropriate for each song, as an actor varies his or her voice to make it appropriate for the character. She uses a hard, somewhat nasal timbre on "Peacock Street," provides bluesy vocal and instrumental inflections on "You Don't Know How Lucky You Are," and adds the merest trace of a Spanish accent on "Missing." Her vocal variations are frequently more Brechtian than Stanislavskian; they are not overt imitations but rather slight suggestions of different vocal styles, a result of her complete immersion in the subject matter of the songs.

Some musicians specialize in a particular genre, but Peggy's talents encompass a wide range: ballads, children's songs, political songs, love songs, blues, instrumental pieces, and the uncategorizable songs that she wrote for *Everything Changes*. She does, however, specialize in a culture: when she sings traditional songs, they are nearly always Anglo-American ones. Her concern for authenticity is no less than that of the most rigorous folklore scholar, and this concern led her and Ewan to institute the controversial policy at the Singers Club: "You were a representative of a culture when you got on the stage."[18] In her view, a musician has a responsibility both to the music and the audience; the audience has a right to hear the music played to its best advantage and in the style appropriate to it. One can certainly argue with aspects of the policy: cultures are not tightly bounded entities, so one can represent more than one culture; and it is possible to master a musical idiom not one's own, as her brother Mike did. But the policy did not attempt to dissuade musicians like Mike Seeger, who immersed themselves in a musical culture and learned the music from its traditional masters. Rather, the policy was aimed at those who played traditional music slickly or sloppily, with an eye to the quick buck, and with little knowledge of the culture in question. As a result of the policy, many musicians learned and revived the music of their own heritage.

Peggy never calls herself a folksinger, feeling that only traditional singers deserve the title. "I sing folk songs," she says instead. Ellen Stekert calls her musical style "the new aesthetic" and considers Peggy "one of the first outstanding practitioners" of this style: "The sound of the new aesthetic group is one which developed from a merger of vocal and instrumental folk, classical, jazz, and pop styles. Almost all of the singers sing with accompaniment; they have learned to chord modal tunes, creating a bizarre and pleasing new texture to their songs, not unlike pre-Bach music. . . . I would venture to say that if the folksong movement in the cities can be said to have given anything new to urban culture, it [is] the new aesthetic."[19] Stekert is scathing toward some members of the folk revival, but she is generally respectful toward Peggy. Peggy's ability to wring praise from even the most severe critic stems from a variety of factors: a consistently high level of musical ability, her genuine love and respect for the folk tradition, and her continued focus on the songs and not the singer.

Peggy's concern for authenticity does not mean that she is opposed to change. Indeed, change is the very lifeblood of any living tradition; a tradition that does not change is one that has only been preserved, not revived. In the program of the 2000 Smithsonian Folklife Festival, Peggy writes of the challenges of being a musician on the edge of the twenty-first century: "These are heady days for music makers and songwriters. The new technologies are creating new types of musicians, people who can sculpt a song, mix sounds as a painter mixes colors. At home we can burn our own CDs, create and print the sleeves and covers, advertise and sell on the Web—in short, set up an entire recording operation ourselves (as, for instance, Ani DiFranco has done)."[20] When asked why she writes new songs, since the old songs are so good, she replies, "I am trying to speak for my time as the old songs spoke for theirs."[21]

This is the challenge for all artists: to take the tools of the past and use them to reflect the concerns of the present, to incorporate the tools of the present without destroying what has come before. The revivalists who tried to re-create the past by reviving old songs and dances were attempting the impossible; items from the past—whether old buildings or old songs—may exist in the present, but we can only know them as they are, not as they used to be. The old building may no longer reflect past glory; it may have worn steps or crumbling walls—or it may have recently gotten a fresh coat of paint. The old songs may be sung with electric instruments or in traditional a cappella style—but if we sing them now, we sing them in the present and for the present. The challenge for folk revivalists is deciding what to take from the past that has meaning and value for the present. As Georgina Boyes says, "A revival is inherently both revolutionary and conservative. It simultaneously comprehends a demand for a change in an existing situation and a requirement of reversion to an older form."[22] How can we learn from the past without lamenting that the "good old days" are over? How can we change what is wrong in the present without making mistakes that have been made before? And how can we use music to do any of this?

To Peggy, music is an essential human need. Not every culture has a word that corresponds exactly to the English word *music*, but every culture has some kind of organized artistic sound. Peggy says:

> We still hanker to sit down with a guitar, a drum, a banjo, a friend and make hands-on, spontaneous music. It's not that we have come back to the fireside—we never really left it. That's where music started, that's where it lives, and that's where it will end up if/when the lights go out. We are born with a desire to sing and make music, and we may not realize it, but part of us starves when we don't. Music makes us vibrate with the rest of the world. . . . Our new songs are a declaration of existence. They say, "We were here during our time, and this is how we felt about it."[23]

The anxiety about cultures disappearing—the anxiety that created the concept of folk culture in the first place—is perhaps a false anxiety. The very factors that threatened to obliterate folk culture—growing capitalism and growing literacy—also fostered its preservation and its revival. Preservation typically means the attempt to keep something—as much as is possible—the way it was in the past; we preserve fruit and the paintings of Leonardo da Vinci. For musicians, revival may be a nobler goal, for a song only exists when it is sung. And to sing a song is, ipso facto, to change it.

In a recent conversation, Peggy described how much her life had changed in the preceding year. Her eightieth year was filled with serious illness. "I know now," she said, "that I am old."[24] Her arthritic fingers can no longer fly across the banjo strings as they once did. Her voice lacks the depth that it once had. She wonders how much longer she can continue to tour—or fly to New Zealand to spend the summer with Irene. She spoke without self-pity or complaint, simply recognizing that her body can no longer do everything that her mind and spirit may want. "The days go by so fast," she said, and she sometimes has trouble "living in the present," because the past holds such splendid memories, and the end of the road is nearer than the beginning.[25]

And yet . . . our conversation occurred shortly after she had returned from a multicity tour throughout Britain, a tour greeted with universal acclaim from journalists, bloggers, and audience members. Clive Davies reviewed her eightieth-birthday concert at Queen Elizabeth Hall in London:

> Peggy Seeger is not the sort to indulge in geriatric sentimentality. Much like a folk-singing equivalent of Elaine Stritch, she bossed and cajoled, cracked sardonic jokes and made a point of letting the audience know when it was not keeping its end up in the singalongs.
>
> Long may she continue. This was a gloriously relaxed gathering, the singer and multi-instrumentalist joined by her sons, singer-guitarists Neill and Calum MacColl, neither of whom was in the mood to be cloyingly reverential. Seeger responded to their teasing by recalling the circumstances in which they were conceived. Game, set and match.[26]

On the tour, she performed old favorites like "The First Time Ever I Saw Your Face," but she also offered up songs from her latest album, including "Swim to the Star," the lyrical remembrance of the *Titanic* that she cowrote with Calum. Several days after our conversation, she performed at the Cambridge Folk Festival, where journalist Colin Irwin wrote that she "stole the show." Irwin ended his review of the Festival by saying, "Few matched the energy, wit and majesty of 80-year-old Peggy Seeger—who appeared at the very first Cambridge Folk Festival 51 years ago."[27]

The Cambridge Folk Festival was Peggy's last gig of the summer. She had already begun lining up gigs for the autumn and planning a new album in the style of *Everything Changes*. But it was time for a break: a three-week vacation in Africa with Irene, snorkeling and going on safari to view wildlife in Tanzania. These are not activities that one typically associates with growing old and slowing down. For Peggy Seeger, the end of the road is still a good way off. We know it's there, but it's not in view. Not yet.

# Notes

Chapter 1. Very Good Stock

1. Ann M. Pescatello, *Charles Seeger: A Life in American Music* (Pittsburgh: University of Pittsburgh Press, 1992), 15.

2. Pescatello, *Charles Seeger*, 20.

3. Letter from Charles Seeger Jr. to Charles Seeger III and Inez Wolf, January 6, 1938, Seeger, CLS, Correspondence, Family, box 1, folder 7, Music Division, Library of Congress, Washington, D.C.

4. David King Dunaway, *How Can I Keep from Singing? The Ballad of Pete Seeger* (New York: Villard Books, 2008), 31.

5. Pescatello, *Charles Seeger*, 19.

6. Richard A. Reuss, "Folk Music and Social Conscience: The Musical Odyssey of Charles Seeger," *Western Folklore* 38 (1979): 226.

7. Judith Tick, *Ruth Crawford Seeger: A Composer's Search for American Music* (New York: Oxford University Press, 1997), 54.

8. Lyn Ellen Burkett, "Linear Aggregates and Proportional Design in Ruth Crawford's *Piano Study in Mixed Accents*," in *Ruth Crawford Seeger's Worlds: Innovation and Tradition in Twentieth-Century American Music*, ed. Ray Allen and Ellie M. Hisama (Rochester, N.Y.: University of Rochester Press, 2007), 58.

9. John Seeger, telephone interview with the author, October 5, 2009.

10. Tick, *Ruth Crawford Seeger*, 172.

11. The Pierre Degeyter Club was named after the composer of "The Internationale." Since no membership lists of the Composers' Collective exist and since several members preferred anonymity or pseudonyms when dealing with a left-wing organization, it is difficult to tell exactly who was a member and who was merely an occasional visitor. I refer to all those who worked with the Composers' Collective as members.

12. Charles Louis Seeger Jr., "On Proletarian Music." *Modern Music* 11, no. 3 (1934): 122.

13. C. L. Seeger, "On Proletarian Music," 122.

14. C. L. Seeger, "On Proletarian Music," 126.

15. Pete Seeger, telephone interview with the author, October 11, 2009.

16. Reuss, "Folk Music and Social Conscience," 229.

17. Hanns Eisler, "The Birth of a Worker's Song," (1935) 1978, http://unionsong.com/reviews/peatbog.html, accessed November 6, 2009.

18. Hanns Eisler, "Birth of a Worker's Song."

19. Incorporating folk music into art music was a technique popular with the Romantics, which may explain the initial reluctance of Composers' Collective members to use it, but it had also been used effectively by modernists such as Béla Bartók, who, in addition to being an important composer, was a prominent folk song collector and ethnomusicologist.

20. Joy Calico, "'We Are Changing the World!': New German Folk Songs for the Free German Youth (1950)," in *Musical Childhoods and the Culture of Youth*, ed. Susan Boynton and Roe-Min Kok (Middletown, Conn.: Wesleyan University Press, 2006), 145.

21. In 1931 and 1932, Charles Seeger helped found the New York Musicological Society, which became the American Musicological Society in 1934 and is still the preeminent scholarly organization in the field of musicology. In 1933, he helped found the American Society for Comparative Musicology, which was allied with the German *Gesellschaft für Vergleichende Musikwissenschaft* (Society for Comparative Musicology). Neither society survived the war. The Nazis sent some of the most important German scholars, such as Erich von Hornbostel and Curt Sachs, into exile. An elderly Guido Adler was allowed to die of natural causes but not before seeing his family disappear. In 1955, the American organization was reborn as the Society for Ethno-Musicology. Once again, Charles Seeger was a founding member.

22. Pescatello, *Charles Seeger*, 135.

23. Peggy Seeger, personal interview with the author, August 23, 2008.

24. "Oral history interview" folder, Charles Louis Seeger biographical material, box 65, Music Division, Library of Congress, Washington, D.C.

25. Reuss, "Folk Music and Social Conscience," 232.

26. Carl Sands, "Songs by Auvilles Mark Step Ahead in Workers Music," *Daily Worker*, January 15, 1935.

## Chapter 2. The Early Years

1. Letter from Ruth Crawford Seeger to Dr. McCandlish, January 2, 1936, box "Seeger, Charles to Ruth, August, 1930–37," folder "Charles to Ruth, January–April, 1936," Music Division, Library of Congress, Washington, D.C.

2. Janelle Warren-Findley, introduction to "Journal of a Field Representative," *Ethnomusicology* 24, no. 2 (1980): 171.

3. Charles Seeger and Margaret Valiant, foreword to "Journal of a Field Representative," *Ethnomusicology* 24, no. 2 (1980): 179.

4. Ruth Crawford Seeger to Charles Seeger, January 2, 1936.

5. Ruth Crawford Seeger to Charles Seeger, January 2, 1936.

6. Letter from Charles Seeger Jr. to Charles Seeger III and Inez Wolf, January 6, 1938, Seeger, CLS, Correspondence, Family, box 1, folder 7, Music Division, Library of Congress, Washington, D.C.

7. Pete Seeger, telephone interview with the author, October 11, 2009.

8. Telegram from Ruth Crawford Seeger to Charles Seeger, September 1938, box "Seeger Collection, Ruth to Charles, 1931–38," folder "Ruth to Charles, August–September 1938," Music Division, Library of Congress, Washington, D.C.

9. Letter from Ruth Crawford Seeger to Charles Seeger, October 1938, box "Seeger Collection, Ruth to Charles, 1931–38," folder "Ruth to Charles," Music Division, Library of Congress, Washington, D.C.

10. Letter from Ruth Crawford Seeger to Charles Seeger, August 15, 1938, box "Seeger Collection, Ruth to Charles, 1931–38," folder "Ruth to Charles, August–September 1938," Music Division, Library of Congress, Washington, D.C.

11. Letter from Ruth Crawford Seeger to Charles Seeger, November 10, 1930, box "Seeger, Ruth to Charles, 1930–1931," folder November 1930, Music Division, Library of Congress, Washington, D.C.

12. Letter from Peggy Seeger to Charles Seeger, March 23, 1939, box "Seeger Collection, Charles to Ruth, 1938–40," folder "Charles to Ruth March–May 1939," Music Division, Library of Congress, Washington, D.C.

13. Letter from Elsie Adams Seeger to Charles and Ruth Crawford Seeger, August 16, 1938, box "Seeger Collection, Ruth to Charles, 1931–38," unmarked folder, Music Division, Library of Congress, Washington, D.C.

14. Peggy Seeger, personal interview with the author, August 23, 2008.

15. Letter from Ruth Crawford Seeger to Charles Seeger, February 11, 1939, box "Seeger Collection, Ruth to Charles, 1935–40," folder "Ruth to Charles, February–April 1939," Music Division, Library of Congress, Washington, D.C.

16. Letter from Ruth Crawford Seeger to Charles Seeger, February 12, 1939, box "Seeger Collection, Ruth to Charles, 1935–40," folder "Ruth to Charles, February–April 1939," Music Division, Library of Congress, Washington, D.C.

17. Letter from Ruth Crawford Seeger to Charles Seeger, May 21, 1939, box "Seeger Collection, Ruth to Charles, 1935–40," folder "Ruth to Charles May 1939," Music Division, Library of Congress, Washington, D.C.

18. Peggy Seeger, interview, August 23, 2008.

19. Letter from Ruth Crawford Seeger to Charles Seeger, November 6, 10:03 [*sic*], box "Seeger Collection, Ruth to Charles, 1930–31," folder "Ruth to Charles, undated," Music Division, Library of Congress, Washington, D.C.

20. Letter from Mike Seeger, "Letter dictated by Michael to Dio some time during October 1941 in the little house on Dallas Avenue, Silver Spring, Maryland," privately held.

21. Peggy Seeger, interview, August 23, 2008.

22. Peggy Seeger, interview, August 23, 2008.

23. Letter from Ruth Crawford Seeger to Charles Seeger, August 10, 1938, box "Seeger Collection, Ruth to Charles, 1931–38," folder "Ruth to Charles, August–September 1938," Music Division, Library of Congress, Washington, D.C.

24. Letter from Ruth Crawford Seeger to Charles Seeger, January 29, 1939, box "Seeger Collection, Ruth to Charles, 1935–40," folder "Ruth to Charles, January–February 1939," Music Division, Library of Congress, Washington, D.C.

25. Peggy Seeger, interview, August 23, 2008.

26. Peggy Seeger, *The Peggy Seeger Songbook: Forty Years of Songmaking* (New York: Oak, 1998), 9.

27. Peggy Seeger, *Peggy Seeger Songbook*, 8.

28. Barbara Seeger Miserantino, telephone interview with the author, September 21, 2010.

29. Peggy Seeger, interview, August 23, 2008.

30. Letter from Mike Seeger, October 1941, privately held.

31. Some Communist Party members asserted that the Molotov-Ribbentrop Pact was a canny Soviet ploy, giving the Soviet Union time to amass armaments so that it could effectively fight the Nazis.

32. David King Dunaway, *How Can I Keep from Singing? The Ballad of Pete Seeger* (New York: Villard Books, 2008), 92.

33. Letter from Ruth Crawford Seeger to Charles Seeger, May 24, 1939, box "Seeger Collection, Ruth to Charles, 1935–40," folder "Ruth to Charles May 1939," Music Division, Library of Congress, Washington, D.C.

34. Bess Lomax Hawes, "Reminiscences on *Our Singing Country*: The Crawford Seeger/Lomax Alliance," in *Ruth Crawford Seeger's Worlds: Innovation and Tradition in Twentieth-Century American Music*, ed. Ray Allen and Ellie M. Hisama (Rochester, N.Y.: University of Rochester Press, 2007), 150.

35. Judith Tick, *Ruth Crawford Seeger: A Composer's Search for American Music* (New York: Oxford University Press, 1997), 261–64.

36. Ruth Crawford Seeger to Charles Seeger, May 24, 1939.

37. Ruth Crawford Seeger, "Letter to Miss Prink," September 30, 1940, privately held.

38. Charles Seeger, "Inter-American Relations in the Field of Music," *Music Educators Journal* 27 (1941): 65.

39. Ruth Crawford Seeger, "Diary of a 'Corporating' Mother," privately held.

40. Ruth Crawford Seeger, "Diary of a 'Corporating' Mother."

41. Pete called such songs "zipper songs," in which one can zip out words such as "Mary" and "red dress" and zip in "Joe" and "blue jeans."

42. Roberta Lamb, "Composing and Teaching as Dissonant Counterpoint," in *Ruth Crawford Seeger's Worlds: Innovation and Tradition in Twentieth-Century American Music*, ed. Ray Allen and Ellie M. Hisama (Rochester, N.Y.: University of Rochester Press, 2007), 181.

43. Tick, *Ruth Crawford Seeger*, 293.

44. For more information about the musical Seeger family, see Ann Pescatello, *Charles Seeger: A Life in American Music* (Pittsburgh: University of Pittsburgh Press, 1992); Tick, *Ruth Crawford Seeger*, Dunaway's *How Can I Keep from Singing?*, Allan Winkler, *"To Everything There Is a Season": Pete Seeger and the Power of Song* (Oxford: Oxford University Press, 2011); Pete Seeger, *The Incompleat Folksinger* (New York; Simon and Schuster, 1972); Pete Seeger, *Where Have All the Flowers Gone: A Singalong Memoir* (New York: *Sing Out!* in association with W. W. Norton, 2009); and Bill Malone's *Music from the True Vine: Mike Seeger's Life and Musical Journey* (Chapel Hill: University of North Carolina Press, 2011).

### Chapter 3. Coming of Age in Chevy Chase

1. Peggy Seeger, personal interview with the author, August 23, 2008.

2. Property deed recorded August 18, 1925, Montgomery County Circuit Court land records, PBR 382, page 169, http://www.mdlandrec.com, accessed July 25, 2015.

3. Peggy Seeger, interview, August 23, 2008.

4. Peggy Seeger, interview, August 23, 2008.

5. Barbara Seeger Miserantino, telephone interview with the author, September 21, 2010.

6. R. J. B. Bosworth, *Explaining Auschwitz and Hiroshima: History Writing and the Second World War 1945–1990* (London: Routledge, 1993), 6.

7. Annette Dapp Poston, personal interview with the author, December 17, 2010.

8. Peggy Seeger, *The Peggy Seeger Songbook: Forty Years of Songmaking* (New York: Oak, 1998), 14.

9. Peggy Seeger, *Peggy Seeger Songbook*, 8.

10. David King Dunaway, *How Can I Keep from Singing? The Ballad of Pete Seeger* (New York: Villard Books, 2008), 165.

11. Peggy Seeger, interview, August 23, 2008.

12. Peggy Seeger, interview, August 23, 2008.

13. Peggy Seeger, personal interview with the author, November 7, 2008.

14. Peggy Seeger, interview, November 7, 2008.

15. Poston, interview.

16. Peggy Seeger, interview, November 7, 2008.

17. Peggy Seeger, interview, November 7, 2008.

18. Lin Frothingham Folsom, telephone interview with the author, December 16, 2010.

19. Peggy Seeger, interview, November 7, 2008.

20. Peggy Seeger, interview, November 7, 2008.

21. Folsom, interview.

22. Letter from Mike Seeger, "Letter dictated by Michael to Dio some time during October 1941 in the little house on Dallas Avenue, Silver Spring, Maryland," October 1941, privately held.

23. Folsom, interview.

24. Folsom, interview.

25. Letter from Charles Seeger Jr. to Selective Service System, November 23, 1952, box 8, Seeger, CLS, correspondence family, box 2, Music Division, Library of Congress, Washington, D.C.

26. Ray Allen, "Performing Dio's Legacy: Mike Seeger and the Urban Folk Music Revival," in *Ruth Crawford Seeger's Worlds: Innovation and Tradition in Twentieth-Century American Music*, ed. Ray Allen and Ellie M. Hisama (Rochester, N.Y.: University of Rochester Press, 2007), 227–28.

27. Peggy Seeger, interview, November 7, 2008.

28. Allen, "Performing Dio's Legacy," 226–27.

29. "Drug Store Hillbillies Shine at Warrenton Music Contest," *Washington Post*, September 15, 1952.

30. "Drug Store Hillbillies."

31. Peggy Seeger, "Teenage," privately held.

32. Peggy Seeger, interview, November 7, 2008.

33. Poston, interview.

34. Peggy Seeger, personal diary, September 16, 1953, privately held.

35. Peggy Seeger, personal diary, September 17, 1953, privately held.

### Chapter 4. A Rendezvous with Death

1. Peggy Seeger, personal diary, September 18, 1953, privately held.

2. Peggy Seeger, personal diary, September 20, 1953, privately held.

3. Peggy Seeger, personal diary, September 28, 1953, privately held.

4. Peggy Seeger, personal diary, September 30, 1953, privately held.

5. Peggy Seeger, personal diary, October 9, 1953, privately held.

6. Letter from Peggy Seeger to Seeger family, autumn 1953, privately held.

7. Letter from Peggy Seeger to Charles and Ruth Crawford Seeger, autumn 1953, privately held.

8. Letter from Charles Seeger to Peggy Seeger, October 31, 1953, privately held.

9. Matt McDade, "Mother, Son—Both Authors—Prove to Visitors at *Post* Book Fair Life with Boa Can Be Fun," *Washington Post*, November 19, 1953.

10. Peggy Seeger, personal diary, November 19, 1953, privately held.

11. Judith Tick, *Ruth Crawford Seeger: A Composer's Search for American Music* (New York: Oxford University Press, 1997), 315.

12. Peggy Seeger, personal interview with the author, November 7, 2008.

13. Peggy Seeger, personal diary, April 7, 1954, privately held.

14. Peggy Seeger, personal diary, November 19, 1953.

15. Letter to Charles Seeger, undated 1953, privately held.

16. Peggy Seeger, personal diary, December 12, 1953, privately held.

17. Peggy Seeger, personal diary, December 14–15, 1953, privately held.

18. Letter from Peggy Seeger to Charles Seeger, December 11, 1953, privately held.

19. Peggy Seeger, personal diary, December 19, 1953, privately held.

20. Peggy Seeger, personal diary, December 25, 1953, privately held.

21. Peggy Seeger, personal diary, December 31, 1953, privately held .

22. Peggy Seeger, personal diary, January 2, 1954, privately held.

23. Peggy Seeger, personal diary, January 6, 1954, privately held.

24. Peggy Seeger, personal diary, April 5, 1954, privately held.

25. Peggy Seeger, personal diary, March 15, 1954, privately held.

26. Peggy Seeger, personal diary, January 21, 1954, privately held.

27. Peggy Seeger, personal diary, April 26, 1954, privately held.

28. Peggy Seeger, personal diary, April 25, 1954, privately held.

29. Peggy Seeger, personal diary, April 13, 1954, privately held.

30. Peggy Seeger, personal diary, April 13, 1954.

31. Jay Ball, telephone interview with the author, February 8, 2011.

32. Ball, interview.

33. Letter from Ralph Rinzler to Peggy Seeger, April 27, 1954, privately held.

34. Ralph Rinzler died on July 2, 1994, at the age of fifty-nine. In 1995, Peggy wrote the song "Old Friend" in tribute to their forty-year friendship.

35. Peggy Seeger, personal diary, May 6, 1954, privately held.

36. Peggy Seeger, personal diary, June 6, 1954, privately held.

37. Peggy Seeger, personal diary, June 6, 1954.

38. Ball, interview.

39. One wonders if they had to cross state lines to acquire their silica gel holder. Birth control was illegal in Massachusetts in 1954, though experiments that would lead to the development of the pill were going on at Harvard.

40. Peggy Seeger, personal diary, July 6, 1954, privately held.

41. Peggy Seeger, personal diary, August 1, 1954, privately held.

42. Peggy Seeger, interview, November 7, 2008.

43. Peggy Seeger, interview, November 7, 2008.

44. In 1955, Folkways Records acquired and reissued *Folk Songs of Courting and Complaint*. Years later, Clark Weissman joked that the only payment he received for the record was a bumper sticker that read, "If you want to hear more of me, buy my record on Folkways" (telephone interview with the author, February 14, 2011).

45. Liner notes, *Folk Songs of Courting and Complaint*, Folkways Records FA 2049, 1955.

46. Peggy Seeger, "A Singer for My Time," in program for Smithsonian Folklife Festival 2000, 92.

47. Peggy Seeger, personal diary, February 1, 1955, privately held.

48. Peggy Seeger, personal diary, December 24, 1954, privately held.

49. Peggy Seeger, personal diary, January 10, 1955, privately held.

50. Peggy Seeger, personal diary, January 11, 1955, privately held.

51. Peggy Seeger, personal diary, January 31, 1955. In *The Incompleat Folksinger* (New York: Simon and Schuster, 1972), Pete attributes the same statement to Popeye.

52. Peggy Seeger, personal diary, January 30, 1955, privately held.

53. Peggy Seeger, personal diary, February 8, 1955, privately held.

54. Peggy Seeger, personal diary, February 11, 1955, privately held.

55. Peggy Seeger, personal diary, February 11, 1955.

56. Peggy Seeger, personal diary, March 28, 1955, privately held.

57. Peggy Seeger, personal diary, April 11, 1955, privately held.

58. Peggy Seeger, personal diary, April 11, 1955.

59. Tony, like Peggy, often sang songs that he learned from books. While a student at Harvard, he found a book of old African American songs in the Widener Library. He liked one song so much that he taught it to Peggy and her brother Pete, who taught it to several generations of Americans. The song is "Michael, Row Your Boat Ashore."

60. Memo on Swarthmore, 1955, privately held.

61. Peggy Seeger, personal diary, May 27, 1955, privately held.

62. Peggy Seeger, personal diary, June 15, 1955, privately held.

### Chapter 5. The Rover, Part One

1. Peggy Seeger, personal diary, June 17, 1955, privately held.

2. Peggy Seeger, personal diary, June 19, 1955, privately held.

3. Peggy Seeger, personal diary, June 19, 1955.

4. Peggy Seeger, personal diary, June 20, 1955, privately held.

5. Peggy Seeger, personal diary, June 21, 1955, privately held.

6. Peggy Seeger, personal diary, June 23, 1955, privately held.

7. Peggy Seeger, personal interview with the author, November 7, 2008.

8. Barbara Seeger Miserantino, telephone interview with the author, September 21, 2010.

9. Miserantino, interview, September 21, 2010.

10. Peggy Seeger, personal diary, July 29, 1955, privately held.

11. Peggy Seeger, personal diary, July 13, 1955, privately held.

12. Letter from Charles Seeger to Peggy Seeger, August 18, 1955, privately held.

13. Allan Winkler, *"To Everything There Is a Season": Pete Seeger and the Power of Song* (Oxford: Oxford University Press, 2011), 78.

14. David King Dunaway, *How Can I Keep from Singing? The Ballad of Pete Seeger* (New York: Villard Press, 2008), 213.

15. Arnold H. Lubasch, *Robeson: An American Ballad* (Lanham, MD: Scarecrow Press, 2012), 173.

16. Letter from Charles Seeger to Peggy Seeger, August 30, 1955, privately held.

17. Letter from Peggy Seeger to family, undated, summer 1955, privately held.

18. Letter from Peggy Seeger to family, undated, autumn 1955, privately held.

19. Letter from Peggy Seeger to family, undated, autumn 1955.

20. Letter from Peggy Seeger to family, undated, autumn 1955.

21. Naomi S. Seeger, email message to the author, October 20, 2011.

22. Letter from Peggy Seeger to family, undated, autumn 1955.

23. Jeremy Seeger, telephone interview with the author, April 11, 2011.

24. Peggy Seeger, personal interview, November 7, 2008.

25. Letter from Peggy Seeger to Charles Seeger, Octobvember 11, 1955, privately held.

26. The marriage ended in 1961, when Charles returned to the United States. Inez, however, had made many friends in the Netherlands and had built up a successful Dutch/English translating business. She remained in Leiden until her death in 1997, when her many friends formed an "Inez Club" to celebrate her memory.

27. Peggy Seeger, personal interview, November 7, 2008.

28. Peggy Seeger, personal interview, November 7, 2008.

29. Maurice Van de Putte, "Memories of the Winter of 1955/1956," privately held.

30. Letter from Peggy Seeger to Charles Seeger, January 10, 1956, privately held.

31. Letter from Peggy Seeger to Charles Seeger, January 10, 1956.

32. Letter from Peggy Seeger to Charles Seeger, January 10, 1956.

33. Letter from Peggy Seeger to Charles Seeger, January 10, 1956.

34. Letter from Peggy Seeger to Charles Seeger, January 10, 1956.

35. Letter from Peggy Seeger to Charles Seeger, January 10, 1956.

36. Letter from Peggy Seeger to Charles Seeger, February 7, 1956, privately held.

37. Letter from Peggy Seeger to Charles Seeger, February 7, 1956.

38. Letter from Peggy Seeger to Charles Seeger, February 7, 1956.

39. Letter from Peggy Seeger to Charles Seeger, January 28, 1956, privately held.

## Chapter 6. The First Time Ever

1. Letter from Peggy Seeger to Charles Seeger, March 29, 1956, privately held.

2. Peggy Seeger, "A Singer for My Time," in program for Smithsonian Folklife Festival 2000, 92.

3. Ewan MacColl, *Journeyman* (London: Sidgwick and Jackson, 1990), 278.

4. MacColl, *Journeyman* (1990), 278.

5. Ben Harker, *Class Act: The Cultural and Political Life of Ewan MacColl* (London: Pluto Press, 2007), 5.

6. For more on Theatre Workshop, see Howard Goorney's *The Theatre Workshop Story* (London: Eyre Methuen, 1981) and Robert Leach's *Theatre Workshop: Joan Littlewood and the Making of Modern British Drama* (Exeter: University of Exeter Press, 2006).

7. Harker, *Class Act*, 86, 90; Peter Cox, *Set into Song: Ewan MacColl, Charles Parker, Peggy Seeger and the Radio Ballads*. (London: Labatie Books, 2008), 40.

8. MacColl, *Journeyman* (1990), 254.

9. MacColl, *Journeyman* (1990), 254.

10. Looking back on her marriage with wry detachment, Jean Newlove remarks that she was married on Friday the thirteenth (email message to the author, October 28, 2011).

11. According to Ben Harker, Ewan's first child was named after his friend Hamish

Henderson, but Jean Newlove remembers choosing the name herself. It is also worth noting that "Hamish" is the Scottish form of Ewan's given name, James.

12. MacColl, *Journeyman* (1990), 357.

13. MacColl, *Journeyman* (1990), 358.

14. By 1950, Alan had collected music throughout the United States and had done extensive fieldwork in Haiti with the help of the African American folklorist and writer Zora Neale Hurston. John Szwed subtitled his biography of Alan *The Man Who Recorded the World* (New York: Viking, 2010).

15. Cecil Sharp founded the English Folk Dance Society in 1911 and was a major figure in the Folk-Song Society, which was founded in 1898. The two societies merged to form the English Folk Dance and Song Society in 1932, several years after Sharp's death.

16. Peter Kennedy was the son of Douglas Kennedy (who had succeeded Cecil Sharp as director of the English Folk Dance Society) and Helen Karpeles (the sister of Maud Karpeles, who had been Cecil Sharp's collecting partner in Appalachia). Douglas Kennedy oversaw the merger of the English Folk Dance Society with the Folk-Song Society and became the first director of the English Folk Dance and Song Society.

17. Szwed, *Alan Lomax*, 259.

18. MacColl, *Journeyman* (1990), 271.

19. The title was cleverly chosen to highlight a major contribution of British folk culture (ballads) and a major contribution of American (blues). It is also the name of a Josh White album that Alan produced in the late 1940s for the Decca record company.

20. Letter from Peggy Seeger to Charles Seeger, April 16, 1956, privately held.

21. Peggy Seeger, personal interview with the author, November 7, 2008.

22. Peggy Seeger, personal interview with the author, June 11, 2009.

23. Peggy Seeger, interview, June 11, 2009.

24. Peggy Seeger, personal diary, April 11, 1956, privately held.

25. Peggy Seeger, personal diary, April 1, 1956, privately held.

26. Peggy Seeger, interview, June 11, 2009.

27. Peggy Seeger, personal diary, April 23, 1956, privately held.

28. Letter from Peggy Seeger to Charles Seeger, April 16, 1956, privately held.

29. Letter from Charles Seeger to Peggy Seeger, April 26, 1956, privately held.

30. Letter from Charles Seeger to Peggy Seeger, April 26, 1956.

31. Letter from Peggy Seeger to Charles Seeger, April 16, 1956.

32. Letter from Peggy Seeger to Charles Seeger, June 6, 1956, privately held.

33. Shirley Collins, e-mail message to the author, November 16, 2011. Shirley would go on to have a distinguished career of her own, collecting music with Alan Lomax in the United States, performing and recording English folk music as a solo artist and with many other musicians, and writing and lecturing about folk music and her experiences. Queen Elizabeth II honored Shirley with an MBE in 2006, and Shirley was elected president of the English Folk Dance and Song Society in 2008.

34. Peggy Seeger, personal diary, April 1, 1956, privately held.

35. Television script for the Ramblers, June 18, 1956, broadcast, Ewan MacColl/Peggy Seeger Archive, Ruskin College, Oxford, England.

36. Peggy Seeger, *The Essential Ewan MacColl Songbook: Sixty Years of Songmaking* (New York: Oak, 2001), 364.

37. Letter from Charles Seeger to Peggy Seeger, July 31, 1956, privately held.

38. Letter from Charles Seeger to Peggy Seeger, July 31, 1956.

39. Peggy Seeger, personal diary, July 12, 1956, privately held.

40. The book was published in 1960, under Alan's byline, as *The Folk Songs of North America* (Garden City, N.Y.: Doubleday). Peggy transcribed the melodies and supplied the guitar chords for more than three hundred songs, while Shirley served as editorial assistant.

41. Letter from Peggy Seeger to Charles Seeger, undated 1956, privately held.

42. Peggy Seeger, interview, June 11, 2009.

### Chapter 7. The Rover, Part Two

1. Letter from Peggy Seeger to Charles Seeger, September 15, 1956, privately held.

2. Letter from Peggy Seeger to Charles Seeger, September 15, 1956.

3. Peggy Seeger, *The Essential Ewan MacColl Songbook: Sixty Years of Songmaking* (New York: Oak, 2001), 28.

4. Peggy Seeger, *Essential Ewan MacColl Songbook*, 29.

5. Ballad commonplaces are similar to the kennings of Anglo-Saxon poetry and the epithets of Homeric epic. These catchphrases are a familiar hallmark of oral literature.

6. The name "Gate of Horn" is almost certainly taken from the *Odyssey*, where the gate of horn indicates the pathway to true dreams, as opposed to the gate of ivory, which leads to false dreams. It is also a nice pun for a music club—a "gate of horn" could mean a doorway to music.

7. Letter from Peggy Seeger to Charles Seeger, May 18, 1957, privately held.

8. Peter's father, Irving Schlein, had been a student at Juilliard and a private pupil of Aaron Copland. In 1947, Irving Schlein won a music competition in which Paul Hindemith was one of the judges; Schlein went on to have a successful Broadway career working with musicians as diverse as Al Jolson and Kurt Weill. Peter would eventually arrange for all of his father's compositions to be recorded.

9. The Folklore Center lasted for more than thirty years as a haven for folk musicians in the heart of Greenwich Village, the epicenter of the New York City folk music revival.

10. Peggy Seeger, personal interview with the author, June 12, 2009.

11. Guy Carawan would later become the music director of the Highlander Folk School (now the Highlander Center) in Tennessee. He was deeply involved in the civil rights movement and was instrumental in introducing the song "We Shall Overcome" to students during that time. Both as a solo artist and with his second wife, Candie, he made many albums and documentaries of folk music.

12. Peggy Seeger, China diary, 1, privately held.

13. Peggy Seeger, China diary, 2.

14. "Youth from 102 Lands Swarms over Moscow," *Life*, August 12, 1957, 26.

15. Peggy Seeger, interview, June 12, 2009.

16. Peggy Seeger, China diary, 3.

17. Peggy Seeger, interview, June 12, 2009.

18. Guy and Candie Carawan, email message to the author, November 18, 2011.

19. They had been planning to fly from Moscow to London, but Jean suggested that they take the train instead. They gave their plane tickets to a young couple on their honeymoon and settled down for the long journey. It was a fortunate change for Jean and Ewan: the plane crashed over Denmark.

20. According to Guy Carawan and Noel Osheroff (formerly Noel Carawan), only a few members of the American delegation were initially invited to go to China, Peggy Seeger and the Carawans among them. But so many other people wanted to go along that the Chinese eventually opened the invitation to the entire American delegation. (Guy and Candie Carawan, email messages to the author, November 18, 2011 and January 31, 2012; Noel Osheroff, telephone interview with the author, April 29, 2012).

21. "Youth from 102 Lands," 26.

22. "Americans Abroad: The Mis-Guided Tour," *Time*, April 26, 1957. In the same article, *Time* reported that many members of the delegation "were no strangers to Communists or to the Communist Party line," among them Peggy Seeger. Liberal Senators Hubert Humphrey and Mike Mansfield also condemned the trip.

23. Letter from Charles Seeger to Peggy Seeger, August 21, 1957, privately held.

24. Peggy Seeger, interview, June 12, 2009.

25. Osheroff, interview, April 29, 2012.

26. Peggy Seeger, China diary, 7.

27. Peggy Seeger, China diary, 47.

28. Peggy Seeger, China diary, 12.

29. Peggy Seeger, China diary, 48.

30. Peggy Seeger, China diary, 49.

31. Letter from Peggy Seeger to Charles Seeger, October 28, 1957, privately held.

32. Peggy Seeger, personal diary, November 19, 1957, privately held.

33. Peggy Seeger, personal diary, November 15, 1957, privately held.

34. Peggy Seeger, personal diary, November 22, 1957, privately held.

35. Peggy Seeger, personal diary, November 22, 1957.

36. Ruth Crawford Seeger, *American Folk Songs for Children* (Garden City, N.Y.: Doubleday, 1948), 20.

37. Liner notes, *American Folk Songs Sung by the Seegers*, Folkways Records, 1957.

38. Alan Lomax and Peggy Seeger, *American Folk Guitar* (London: Robbins Music, 1957).

39. Letter from Peggy Seeger to Charles Seeger, January 1958, privately held.

40. Letter from Peggy Seeger to Charles Seeger, January 1958.

41. For a detailed examination of the Radio Ballads series, see Peter Cox, *Set into Song: Ewan MacColl, Charles Parker, Peggy Seeger and the Radio Ballads* (London: Labatie Books, 2008).

## Chapter 8. New Day Dawning

1. Ben Harker, *Class Act: The Cultural and Political Life of Ewan MacColl* (London: Pluto Press, 2007), 130.

2. Ewan MacColl, *Journeyman* (London: Sidgwick and Jackson, 1990), 313.

3. MacColl, *Journeyman*, 313.

4. Peggy Seeger, personal interview with the author, June 12, 2009.

5. Lawrence Aston, "The Radio-Ballads 1957–1964," liner notes, *The Ballad of John Axon*, Topic Records Ltd., 2008.

6. Peter Cox, *Set into Song: Ewan MacColl, Charles Parker, Peggy Seeger and the Radio Ballads* (London: Labatie Books, 2008), 55.

7. Coleman was primarily a jazz musician, but he also excelled at the calypso music of his West Indian homeland.

8. *The Ballad of John Axon*, Topic Records Ltd., 2008.

9. *Ballad of John Axon*.

10. Peggy Seeger, *The Essential Ewan MacColl Songbook: Sixty Years of Songmaking* (New York: Oak , 2001), 114.

11. Peggy Seeger, *Essential Ewan MacColl Songbook*, 114.

12. *Ballad of John Axon*.

13. Harker, *Class Act*, 134.

14. Cox, *Set into Song*, 59.

15. The Prix Italia is an international competition hosted by the Italian government and awarded in three categories of media: drama, music, and documentary. It began in 1948 solely devoted to radio, added television in 1957, and websites in 1998.

16. Cox, *Set into Song*, 59.

17. Cox, *Set into Song*, 60.

18. Peggy Seeger, personal diary, October 29, 1957, privately held.

19. Letter from Peggy Seeger to Charles Seeger, February 22, 1958, privately held.

20. Letter from Peggy Seeger to Charles Seeger, June 21, 1958, privately held.

21. Letter from Ewan MacColl to Peggy Seeger, n.d., Sunday 1958, privately held.

22. Peggy Seeger, *The Peggy Seeger Songbook: Forty Years of Songmaking* (New York: Oak, 1998), 41.

23. Peggy Seeger, *Peggy Seeger Songbook*, 40.

24. Peggy Seeger, *Peggy Seeger Songbook*, 43.

25. Letter from Ewan MacColl to Peggy Seeger, n.d., Wednesday 1958, privately held.

26. Letter from Peggy Seeger to Charles Seeger, December 7, 1958, privately held.

27. Letter from Ewan MacColl to Peggy Seeger, n.d., Wednesday 1958.

28. Letter from Ewan MacColl to Peggy Seeger, n.d., Thursday 1958, privately held.

29. Jean Newlove (MacColl), email message to the author, June 18, 2011.

30. Letter from Peggy Seeger to Charles Seeger, January 25, 1959, privately held.

31. Ewan had the same birthday as the Scottish national poet, Robert Burns.

### Chapter 9. At Home Abroad

1. Letter from Peggy Seeger to Charles Seeger, February 15, 1959, privately held.

2. Letter from Peggy Seeger to Charles Seeger, February 24, 1959, privately held.

3. Letter from Peggy Seeger to Penny Seeger, Spring 1959, privately held.

4. Peggy Seeger, personal interview with the author, June 12, 2009.

5. Peggy Seeger, interview, June 12, 2009.

6. Letter from Ewan MacColl to Peggy Seeger, December 24, 1958, privately held.

7. Letter from Peggy Seeger to Charles Seeger, June 22, 1959, privately held.

8. Letter from Peggy Seeger to Charles Seeger, August 1959, privately held.

9. At the time, it was the worst racial incident in Britain's history, sadly reminiscent of the 1936 Battle of Cable Street, when the British Union of Fascists marched through a predominantly Jewish neighborhood of London's East End.

10. Ewan MacColl, liner notes, *Song of a Road*, Topic Records Ltd., 2008.

11. Peggy Seeger, interview, June 12, 2009.

12. Letter from Peggy Seeger to Charles Seeger, July 9, 1959, privately held.

13. Ewan MacColl, liner notes, *Song of a Road*, Topic Records Ltd., 2008.

14. *Song of a Road*.

15. *Song of a Road*.

16. *Song of a Road*.

17. Peggy Seeger, *The Essential Ewan MacColl Songbook: Sixty Years of Songmaking* (New York: Oak, 2001), 132.

18. Peggy Seeger, interview, June 12, 2009.

19. Peter Cox, *Set into Song: Ewan MacColl, Charles Parker, Peggy Seeger and the Radio Ballads* (London: Labatie Books, 2008), 83.

20. Cox, *Set into Song*, 83.

21. Peggy Seeger, interview, June 12, 2009.

22. MacColl, *Journeyman* (London: Sidgwick and Jackson, 1990), 316.

23. Peggy Seeger, *Essential Ewan MacColl Songbook*, 140.

24. MacColl, *Journeyman*, 318.

25. Ben Harker, *Class Act: The Cultural and Political Life of Ewan MacColl* (London: Pluto Press, 2007), 147.

26. Cox, *Set into Song*, 102.

27. Letter from Charles Seeger to Peggy Seeger, May 31, 1960, privately held.

28. The BBC did not even wait to hear the finished product before deciding to enter *Singing the Fishing* in the documentary competition. The decision was made after reading the script.

29. MacColl, *Journeyman*, 326–27.

30. Letter from Peggy Seeger to Charles Seeger, October 7, 1960, privately held.

31. Robert Shelton, "Ewan MacColl, in Debut Here, Offers Concert of Folk Music," *New York Times*, December 5, 1960.

32. Though the Radio Ballads were primarily composed of new songs, they also contained a great deal of actuality and were designed as documentaries about different communities, not showcases for new songs.

33. Peggy Seeger, *The Peggy Seeger Songbook: Forty Years of Songmaking* (New York: Oak, 1998), 57.

34. *The New Briton Gazette*, Folkways Records FW 8732, 1960.

35. *New Briton Gazette*, 1960.

36. MacColl, *Journeyman*, 327.

37. There are exceptions, such as Bernice Johnson Reagon, who was an original member of the Freedom Singers (a group of civil rights activists who began singing together in 1962) and has been involved with music and political activism ever since. She went on to found the Harambee Singers in 1966 and Sweet Honey in the Rock in 1973, both of which were composed of African American women and devoted to politically focused, folk-based songs. In 1975, she received a PhD from Howard University and added a distinguished scholarly career to her musical and political activities. Her PhD dissertation is a study of the songs of the civil rights movement.

### Chapter 10. What Is a Folk Song?

1. "Folk Song Forum, No. 1: What Is a Folk Song?," May 5, 1955, BBC, Northern Ireland Home Service, transcript in folder "Broadcasts: Radio," MacColl/Seeger Archive, Ruskin College, Oxford, England.

2. "Folk Song Forum, No. 1"

3. Not all the songs in *Volkslieder* were collected from German peasants or, indeed, were collected at all; many of them came from published songbooks. Nor are they all German: there are English, Scottish, Spanish, and Lithuanian songs as well. But this very diversity only bolstered Herder's essential argument: that each people has its own recognizable folk culture.

4. The term *traditional songs* is still used to mean anonymous songs passed down from generation to generation.

5. Thomas Percy, *Reliques of Ancient English Poetry* (1765; London: J. M. Dent and Sons, 1910), 3.

6. John Finlay, *Scottish Historical and Romantic Ballads*, vol. 1 (Edinburgh: James Ballantyne, 1808), xxxiv.

7. Cecil J. Sharp, *English Folk-Song: Some Conclusions* (London: Simpkin, 1907), viii.

8. Though Cecil Sharp died in 1924 and thus never presided over the joint English Folk Dance and Song Society, his influence has been considerable. Since its inception, the headquarters of the EFDSS has been called Cecil Sharp House.

9. James Hardin, "The Archive of Folk Culture at 75: A National Project with Many Workers," *Folklife Center News* 25, no. 2 (Spring 2003): 3–4.

10. John A. Lomax and Alan Lomax, *American Ballads and Folk Songs* (1934; New York: Macmillan, 1994), xxvii.

11. Lomax and Lomax, *American Ballads and Folk Songs*, xxx.

12. Maud Karpeles, preface to *English Folk Songs from the Southern Appalachians*, collected by Cecil J. Sharp and Olive Dame Campbell, ed. Maud Karpeles, 2nd ed. (London: Oxford University Press, 1932), xvi.

13. Maud Karpeles, note to preface to *English Folk Songs from the Southern Appalachians*, collected by Cecil J. Sharp and Olive Dame Campbell, ed. Maud Karpeles, 2nd ed. (London: Oxford University Press, 1952), xx.

14. Charles Seeger to Donald Goodchild, April 6, 1937, Resettlement Administration subject file (2) folder, American Folklife Center, Library of Congress, Washington, D.C.

15. David King Dunaway, *How Can I Keep from Singing? The Ballad of Pete Seeger* (New York: Villard Books, 2008), 219.

16. John Greenway, *American Folksongs of Protest* (Philadelphia: University of Pennsylvania Press, 1953), 5.

17. Ailie Munro, *The Folk Music Revival in Scotland* (Darby, Pa.: Norwood Editions, 1985), 13.

18. Pete Seeger, *The Incompleat Folksinger* (New York: Simon and Schuster, 1972), 62.

19. For more on the American folk revival, see Robert Cantwell, *When We Were Good: The Folk Revival* (Cambridge, Mass.: Harvard University Press, 1996); Ronald D. Cohen, *Rainbow Quest: The Folk Music Revival and American Society, 1940–1970* (Amherst: University of Massachusetts Press, 2002); David Dunaway and Molly Beer, *Singing Out: An Oral History of America's Folk Revivals* (Oxford: Oxford University Press, 2010); Benjamin Filene, *Romancing the Folk: Public Memory and American Roots Music* (Chapel Hill: University of North Carolina Press, 2000); and Neil Rosenberg, ed., *Transforming Tradition: Folk Music Revivals Examined* (Urbana: University of Illinois Press, 1993).

20. Richard A. Reuss, with JoAnne C. Reuss, *American Folk Music and Left-Wing Politics, 1927–1957* (Lanham, Md.: Scarecrow Press, 2000), 9.

21. Wayland D. Hand, "The Editor's Page," *Journal of American Folklore* 61, no. 239 (1948): 82.

22. For a detailed analysis of the Nazi use of folklore, see Christa Kamenetsky, "Folklore as a Political Tool in Nazi Germany," *Journal of American Folklore* 85:221–35.

23. John Powell, "How America Can Develop a National Music," *Etude* (May 1927): 340.

24. Powell, "How America Can Develop," 340.

25. Powell, "How America Can Develop," 350.

26. Annabel Morris Buchanan, "The Function of a Folk Festival," *Southern Folklore Quarterly* 1 (1937): 34, emphasis in original.

27. David E. Whisnant, *All That Is Native and Fine: The Politics of Culture in an American Region* (Chapel Hill: University of North Carolina Press, 1983), 207.

28. Ruth Crawford Seeger, *American Folk Songs for Children* (Garden City, N.Y.: Doubleday, 1948), 21.

29. B. A. Botkin, "WPA and Folklore Research: 'Bread and Song,'" in *The Conservation of Culture: Folklorists in the Public Sector*, ed. Burt Feintuch (Lexington: University Press of Kentucky, 1988), 263.

30. B. A. Botkin, *A Treasury of American Folklore: Stories, Ballads, and Traditions of the People* (1944; New York: Crown, 1983), xxvi.

31. For more on the connection between American folk music and the Communist Party, see Robbie Lieberman, *"My Song Is My Weapon": People's Songs, American Communism, and the Politics of Culture, 1930–50* (Urbana: University of Illinois Press, 1989); and Reuss with Reuss, *American Folk Music and Left-Wing Politics*.

32. Reuss with Reuss, *American Folk Music and Left-Wing Politics*, 1.

33. Charles Louis Seeger Jr., "On Proletarian Music," *Modern Music* 11, no. 3 (1934): 122.

### Chapter 11. High Noon

1. Letter from Ewan MacColl to Peggy Seeger, undated Thursday, privately held.

2. Liner notes, *Two-Way Trip: American, Scots and English Folksongs Sung by Peggy Seeger and Ewan MacColl*, Folkways Records FW 8755, 1961.

3. Letter from Ewan MacColl to Peggy Seeger, undated Sunday, privately held.

4. Peggy Seeger, personal interview with the author, June 13, 2009.

5. Ewan MacColl, *Journeyman* (London: Sidgwick and Jackson, 1990), 288.

6. Sydney Carter, "Pop Goes the Folk Song," *English Dance and Song* (New Year 1961): 3.

7. Steve Benbow, "Going Commercial?," *English Dance and Song* (New Year 1961): 10.

8. Eric Winter, "Going Political?," *English Dance and Song* (New Year 1961): 14.

9. Ewan MacColl and Peggy Seeger, "Going American?," *English Dance and Song* (New Year 1961): 20.

10. Liner notes, *Two-Way Trip*.

11. Liner notes, *Two-Way Trip*.

12. Brian Pearson, email message to the author, June 12, 2011.

13. *Folk Britannia*, part 1: "Ballads and Blues," broadcast February 3, 2006, BBC 4.

14. Letter from Peggy Seeger to Charles Seeger, June 16, 1961, privately held.

15. Peggy Seeger, interview, June 13, 2009.

16. Peter Cox, *Set into Song: Ewan MacColl, Charles Parker, Peggy Seeger and the Radio Ballads* (London: Labatie Books, 2008), 116; MacColl, *Journeyman*, 330; Peggy Seeger, interview, June 13, 2009.

17. *The Big Hewer*, Topic Records Ltd., 2008.

18. *Big Hewer*.

19. *Big Hewer*.

20. *Big Hewer*.

21. *Big Hewer*.

22. *Big Hewer*.

23. Ben Harker, *Class Act: The Cultural and Political Life of Ewan MacColl* (London: Pluto Press), 2007, 164.

24. MacColl, *Journeyman*, 331.

25. Peggy Seeger, interview, June 13, 2009.

26. Peggy Seeger, interview, June 13, 2009.

27. Peggy Seeger, *The Peggy Seeger Songbook: Forty Years of Songmaking* (New York: Oak, 1998), 59.

28. MacColl, *Journeyman*, 333–34.

29. *On the Edge*, Topic Records Ltd., 2008.

30. *On the Edge*.

31. *On the Edge*.

32. Peggy Seeger, personal interview with the author, June 12–13, 2009.

33. Letter from Peggy Seeger to Charles Seeger, May 19, 1963, privately held.

34. Letter from Peggy Seeger to Charles Seeger, May 19, 1963.

35. Letter from Peggy Seeger to Charles Seeger, May 19, 1963.

### Chapter 12. Beginnings and Endings

1. Peggy Seeger, "Singers Club Final Night," December 6, 1991, recorded by Doc Rowe, audio cassette, Ewan MacColl/Peggy Seeger Archive, Ruskin College, Oxford, England.

2. Ewan MacColl, "Why I Am Opening a New Club," *Sing*, August 1961, 65.

3. Eric Winter, "Unaccompanied Singers," *Sing*, December 1961, 34.

4. A. L. Lloyd, "Neglecting His Duty?," *Sing*, February 1962, 56.

5. Winter, "Unaccompanied Singers," 14.

6. John Makepeace, "Discussion: A Page of Record Reviews," *Sing*, July 1962, 110.

7. Letter from Earl Robinson to Peggy Seeger, March 15, 1963, "Ewan MacColl/General Correspondence 1959–65 and undated" folder, Ewan MacColl/Peggy Seeger Archive, Ruskin College, Oxford, England.

8. Earl Robinson, ed., *Young Folk Song Book* (New York: Simon and Schuster, 1963), 108.

9. Robinson, ed., *Young Folk Song Book*, 109.

10. *A Kind of Exile*, 1971, Granada Television.

11. Liner notes, *The Fight Game*, Topic Records Ltd., 2008.

12. Letter from Peggy Seeger to Charles Seeger, May 19, 1963, privately held.

13. Liner notes, *Fight Game*.

14. *Fight Game*.

15. *Fight Game*.

16. *Fight Game.*

17. Jim Carroll, "The Critics Group" (paper presented at symposium in honor of Ewan MacColl's seventieth birthday, County Hall, London, March 1986).

18. Ewan MacColl and Peggy Seeger, "The Critics Group," audiotaped interview recorded by Jim Carroll and Pat Mackenzie, February 12, 1986, Ewan MacColl/Peggy Seeger Archive, Ruskin College, Oxford, England.

19. Brian Pearson, email message to the author, June 12, 2011.

20. Ewan MacColl, *Journeyman* (London: Sidgwick and Jackson, 1990), 306.

21. Pearson, email message, June 12, 2011.

22. Frankie Armstrong, email message to the author, November 25, 2012.

23. Frankie Armstrong with Jenny Pearson, *As Far as the Eye Can Sing* (London: Women's Press, 1992), 33.

24. As a playwright and a Marxist, Ewan was a great admirer of Bertolt Brecht. As a director, however, Ewan relied on the realism advocated by the more conservative Stanislavski.

25. Peggy Seeger, personal interview with the author, June 13, 2009.

26. Peggy Seeger, interview, June 13, 2009.

27. Peggy Seeger, interview, June 13, 2009.

28. Pearson, email message, June 12, 2011.

29. Ewan MacColl, "Folksong course," 1964, in folder "Ewan MacColl/Critics Group Transcripts," Ewan MacColl/Peggy Seeger Archive, Ruskin College, Oxford, England.

30. Armstrong, email message, November 25, 2012.

31. Jim Carroll and Pat Mackenzie, email message to the author, November 25, 2014.

32. Pearson, email message, June 12, 2011.

33. Pearson, email message, June 12, 2011.

34. Letter from Peggy Seeger to Charles Seeger, March 4, 1964, privately held.

35. *Folk Britannia*, part 1: "Ballads and Blues," February 3, 2006, BBC 4.

36. Jane Stewart had also participated in *Singing the Fishing*, along with her sister Elisabeth.

37. Ewan MacColl and Peggy Seeger, *Travellers' Songs from England and Scotland* (Knoxville: University of Tennessee Press, 1977), 2, emphasis in original.

38. In prewar eastern Europe, these outsiders were frequently prized as musicians. It was common for Jewish and Gypsy musicians to work together, with each knowing the repertoire of the other.

39. Peggy Seeger, *The Essential Ewan MacColl Songbook: Sixty Years of Songmaking* (New York: Oak, 2001), 203.

40. *The Travelling People*, Topic Records Ltd., 2008.

41. *Travelling People.*

42. Seeger, *Essential Ewan MacColl Songbook*, 204–5.

43. Seeger, *Essential Ewan MacColl Songbook*, 211. "Freeborn Man" is frequently considered one of the best songs that Ewan ever wrote. Peter Cox's book about the

Radio Ballads, *Set into Song: Ewan MacColl, Charles Parker, Peggy Seeger and the Radio Ballads* (London: Labatie Books, 2008), has this much-loved song on its cover.

44. Seeger, *Essential Ewan MacColl Songbook*, 211.

45. *Travelling People.*

46. *Travelling People.*

47. Cox, *Set into Song*, 164.

48. *Travelling People.*

49. *Travelling People.*

### Chapter 13. Different Stages

1. Letter from Peggy Seeger to Charles Seeger, March 4, 1964, privately held.

2. Letter from Peggy Seeger to Charles Seeger, January 1, 1965, privately held.

3. Brian Pearson, email message to the author, June 12, 2011.

4. The theme of death and resurrection, important in Western drama since ancient Greece, is particularly appropriate for midwinter. Christian tradition celebrates the birth of Christ and looks forward to the springtime holiday of resurrection, while in the natural world, leaves and flowers die, awaiting the rebirth of spring.

5. Frankie Armstrong, email message to the author, November 25, 2012.

6. Peggy Seeger, *The Peggy Seeger Songbook: Forty Years of Songmaking* (New York: Oak, 1998), 72.

7. Letter from Peggy Seeger to Charles Seeger, May 31, 1965, privately held.

8. Peggy Seeger, personal interview with the author, June 14, 2009.

9. Pearson, email message, June 12, 2011.

10. Letter from Peggy Seeger to Charles Seeger, May 31, 1965, privately held.

11. Letter from Peggy Seeger to Charles Seeger, May 31, 1965.

12. Letter from Peggy Seeger to Charles Seeger, May 31, 1965.

13. Letter from Peggy Seeger to Charles Seeger, May 31, 1965.

14. Peggy Seeger, *Folk Songs of Peggy Seeger* (New York: Oak, 1964), 5.

15. Peggy Seeger, *Folk Songs of Peggy Seeger*, 5.

16. Eric Winter, "True Voice of Peggy Gets Through," *Sing* 8 (April 1965): 19, capitals in original.

17. Letter from Peggy Seeger to Charles Seeger, January 8, 1966, privately held.

18. H. Thurston, "Feast of Fools," in *The Catholic Encyclopedia* (New York: Robert Appleton, 1909), http://www.newadvent.org/cathen/06132a.htm, accessed August 26, 2014.

19. A brief Google search for "Festival of Fools" shows that the tradition is currently alive and well in Europe and the United States.

20. Festival of Fools script, 1967, Ewan MacColl/Peggy Seeger Archive, Ruskin College, Oxford, England.

21. Letter from Peggy Seeger to Charles Seeger, January 8, 1966, capitals in original.

22. "Press Release, Festival of Fools," in folder "Ewan MacColl, Festival of Fools, 1965, scripts," Ewan MacColl/Peggy Seeger Archive, Ruskin College, Oxford, England.

23. *Parsley, Sage, and Politics: The Lives and Music of Peggy Seeger and Ewan MacColl*, CD 2004.

24. Brian Pearson, email message to the author, August 9, 2011.

25. Letter from Peggy Seeger to Charles Seeger, January 8, 1966.

26. Pearson, email message, August 9, 2011.

27. Newsletter number five, December 7, 1971, from bound volume "Peggy FOF 1971," Ewan MacColl/Peggy Seeger Archive, Ruskin College, Oxford, England, capitals in original.

28. Newsletter no. 1, October 25, 1971, from bound volume "Peggy FOF 1971," Ewan MacColl/Peggy Seeger Archive, Ruskin College, Oxford, England.

29. Newsletter no. 5, December 7, 1971, from bound volume "Peggy FOF 1971," Ewan MacColl/Peggy Seeger Archive, Ruskin College, Oxford, England.

30. Peggy Seeger, *Peggy Seeger Songbook* , 89.

31. Festival of Fools script, 1967, Ewan MacColl/Peggy Seeger Archive, Ruskin College, Oxford, England. In 2002, it was revealed that during the years when Thadden was leader of the National Democratic Party, he was also an agent for the British intelligence agency MI6. What a sketch Ewan could have made with that information!

32. Festival of Fools script, 1971, Ewan MacColl/Peggy Seeger Archive, Ruskin College, Oxford, England.

33. Festival of Fools script, 1967, Ewan MacColl/Peggy Seeger Archive, Ruskin College, Oxford, England.

34. Peggy Seeger, *Peggy Seeger Songbook* , 99.

35. Twelve volumes were recorded, but only ten were released.

36. Letter from Peggy Seeger to Charles Seeger, undated 1966, privately held. Peggy modeled her style of ballad singing after the American ballad singer Texas Gladden.

37. *New City Songster* 1 (1968): 2.

38. Letter from Peggy Seeger to Charles Seeger, undated 1966.

39. Peggy Seeger, email message to the author, December 6, 2012.

40. Letter from Peggy Seeger to Charles Seeger, January 8, 1966.

41. Letter from Peggy Seeger to Charles Seeger, January 8, 1966.

42. Letter from Peggy Seeger to Charles Seeger, January 8, 1966.

43. Letter from Peggy Seeger to Charles Seeger, spring 1969, privately held.

44. Pearson, email message, June 12, 2011.

45. Pearson, email message, June 12, 2011.

46. Peggy Seeger, interview, June 14, 2009.

## Chapter 14. Things Fall Apart

1. Letter from Peggy Seeger to Charles Seeger, spring 1969, privately held.

2. Letter from Peggy Seeger to Charles Seeger, spring 1969.

3. Letter from Peggy Seeger to Charles Seeger, spring 1969.

4. Calum MacColl, personal interview with the author, August 24, 2009.

5. Neill MacColl, personal interview with the author, August 25, 2009.

6. Calum MacColl, interview, August 24, 2009.

7. Calum MacColl, interview, August 24, 2009.

8. Letter from Peggy Seeger to Charles Seeger, spring 1969.

9. Letter from Peggy Seeger to Charles Seeger, March 6, 1970.

10. Letter from Peggy Seeger to Charles Seeger, September 6, 1970, privately held.

11. Letter from Peggy Seeger to Charles Seeger, September 6, 1970.

12. Letter from Peggy Seeger to Charles Seeger, September 6, 1970.

13. Peggy Seeger, *The Peggy Seeger Songbook: Forty Years of Songmaking* (New York: Oak, 1998), 83.

14. Peggy Seeger, *Peggy Seeger Songbook*, 83.

15. Peggy Seeger, *Peggy Seeger Songbook*, 85.

16. Peggy Seeger, *Peggy Seeger Songbook*, 93, emphasis in original.

17. Peggy Seeger, *Peggy Seeger Songbook*, 97.

18. Letter from Manuel Greenhill to Ewan MacColl, October 21, 1970, folder "Ewan MacColl/general correspondence, 1970," Ewan MacColl/Peggy Seeger Archive, Ruskin College, Oxford, England.

19. Letter from Barry Olivier to Ewan MacColl, October 15, 1970, folder "Ewan MacColl/general correspondence, 1970," Ewan MacColl/Peggy Seeger Archive, Ruskin College, Oxford, England.

20. "The Critics Group," folder "Ewan MacColl/Critics Group Miscellaneous Papers," Ewan MacColl/Peggy Seeger Archive, Ruskin College, Oxford, England.

21. Brian Pearson, email message to the author, August 9, 2011.

22. Peggy Seeger, *Peggy Seeger Songbook*, 110.

23. Amber Good, "'Lady, What Do You Do All Day?': Peggy Seeger's Anthems of Anglo-American Feminism" (master's thesis, University of Cincinnati, 2002), 48.

24. Frankie Armstrong, email message to the author, November 25, 2012.

25. Letter from Peggy Seeger to Charles Seeger, March 29, 1971, privately held.

26. Letter from Peggy Seeger to Charles Seeger, March 29, 1971.

27. Pearson, email message, August 9, 2011.

28. Sandra Kerr, email message to the author, January 31, 2013.

29. Letter from Peggy Seeger to Charles Seeger, June 18, 1972, privately held.

30. Pearson, email message, August 9, 2011.

31. Letter from Peggy Seeger to Charles Seeger, March 29, 1971.

32. Letter from Peggy Seeger to Charles Seeger, March 29, 1971.

33. Letter from Peggy Seeger to Charles Seeger, June 18, 1972.

34. Armstrong, email message, November 25, 2012.

35. *A Kind of Exile*, 1971, Granada.

36. *Kind of Exile*.

37. *Kind of Exile*.

38. *Kind of Exile*.

39. Peggy Seeger, personal interview with the author, May 17, 2011.

40. Peggy Seeger, interview, May 17, 2011.

41. Peggy Seeger, interview, May 17, 2011.

42. Peggy Seeger, interview, May 17, 2011.

43. Letter from Peggy Seeger to Charles Seeger, June 18, 1972.

44. Kerr, email message, January 31, 2013.

45. Armstrong, email message, November 25, 2012.

46. Pearson, email message, August 9, 2011.

47. Kerr, email message, January 31, 2013.

48. Pearson, email message, August 9, 2011.

49. Kerr, email message, January 31, 2013.

50. Letter from Peggy Seeger to Charles Seeger, June 18, 1972.

51. Kerr, email message, January 31, 2013.

52. Letter from Peggy Seeger to Charles Seeger, June 18, 1972.

53. Peggy Seeger, personal interview with the author, December 6, 2009.

54. Festival of Fools program, 1971, folder "Peggy Festival of Fools 1971," Ewan MacColl/Peggy Seeger Archive, Ruskin College, Oxford, England.

55. Letter from Peggy Seeger to Charles Seeger, June 18, 1972.

56. Letter from Peggy Seeger to Charles Seeger, June 18, 1972.

## Chapter 15. Late in the Day

1. Frankie Armstrong, email message to the author, November 25, 2012.

2. Sandra Kerr, email message to the author, January 31, 2013.

3. Peggy Seeger, personal interview with the author, June 13, 2009.

4. Peggy Seeger, personal interview with the author, December 6, 2009.

5. Neill MacColl, personal interview with the author, August 25, 2009.

6. "Report of a Meeting with Former Members of the Critics Group Held at the Co-Op Centre on Wednesday, 22 November 1972 at 7 PM," from "Ewan MacColl/Critics Group, Dissolution: papers," Ewan MacColl/Peggy Seeger Archive, Ruskin College, Oxford.

7. Letter from Peggy Seeger to Charles Seeger, June 18, 1972, privately held.

8. Peggy Seeger, interview, December 6, 2009.

9. Letter from Peggy Seeger to Charles Seeger, September 16, 1972, privately held.

10. Peggy Seeger, interview, December 6, 2009.

11. Calum MacColl, personal interview with the author, August 24, 2009.

12. Peggy Seeger, interview, December 6, 2009.

13. Letter from Peggy Seeger to Charles Seeger, April 14, 1973, privately held.

14. Calum MacColl, interview, August 24, 2009.

15. Letter from Peggy Seeger to Charles Seeger, May 1, 1974, privately held.

16. Peggy Seeger, *The Peggy Seeger Songbook: Forty Years of Songmaking* (New York: Oak, 1998), 116.

17. Letter from Peggy Seeger to Charles Seeger, May 1, 1974.

18. Letter from Peggy Seeger to Charles Seeger, May 1, 1974, capitals in original.

19. Peggy Seeger, *The Essential Ewan MacColl Songbook: Sixty Years of Songmaking* (New York: Oak, 2001), 151.

20. Peggy Seeger, interview, December 6, 2009.

21. Peggy Seeger, interview, December 6, 2009.

22. Peggy Seeger, *Peggy Seeger Songbook*,141.

23. Frederick Engels, *The Origin of the Family, Private Property, and the State* (1884; New York: Pathfinder Press, 1972), 75.

24. Peggy Seeger, interview, December 6, 2009. Socialist feminists have long used the metaphor of "an unhappy marriage" to describe the relationship between socialism and feminism. Socialists complained that feminists focused on the concerns of privileged, middle-class women, while feminists complained that socialists were blind to the gender components of oppression.

25. Peggy Seeger, interview, December 6, 2009.

26. Peggy Seeger, *Essential Ewan MacColl Songbook*, 82.

27. Peggy Seeger, *Essential Ewan MacColl Songbook*, 83.

28. Peggy Seeger, *Peggy Seeger Songbook*, 113.

29. Neill MacColl, interview, August 25, 2009.

30. Neill MacColl, interview, August 25, 2009.

31. Neill MacColl, interview, August 25, 2009. Neill is alluding to the sign that Woody Guthrie attached to his guitar, which read, "This machine kills fascists."

32. Peggy Seeger, *Peggy Seeger Songbook*, 127.

33. Calum MacColl, interview, August 24, 2009.

34. Neill MacColl, interview, August 25, 2009.

35. Peggy Seeger, personal interview with the author, May 17, 2011.

36. Letter from Peggy Seeger to Charles Seeger, May 1, 1974.

37. Letter from Peggy Seeger to Charles Seeger, undated 1974, privately held.

38. Letter from Peggy Seeger to Charles Seeger, September 1975, privately held.

39. Letter from Peggy Seeger to Charles Seeger, September 1975, capitals in original.

40. Liner notes, *Penelope Isn't Waiting Any More*, Blackthorne Records BR 1050, 1976.

41. Liner notes, *Penelope Isn't Waiting Any More*.

42. Letter from Amalgamated Metal Worker's Union to Peggy Seeger and Ewan MacColl, November 11, 1976, folder "General correspondence 1976," Ewan MacColl/Peggy Seeger Archive, Ruskin College, Oxford.

43. Peggy Seeger, interview, December 6, 2009.

44. Ewan MacColl and Peggy Seeger, *Travellers' Songs from England and Scotland* (Knoxville: University of Tennessee Press, 1977), 15.

45. Peggy Seeger, interview, December 6, 2009.

46. Peggy Seeger, *Peggy Seeger Songbook*,133.

47. Marcus Wohlsen, "Charles Seeger Inaugurates New Era of Music," *Illumina-*

*tions: Berkeley's Online Magazine of Research in the Arts and Humanities* (2005), http:// illuminations.berkeley.edu/archives/2005/history.php? volume =4, accessed June 25, 2013.

48. Liner notes, *American Folksongs for Children*, Rounder Records 8001, 1978.

49. Peggy Seeger, *Peggy Seeger Songbook*,142.

50. Letter from Peggy Seeger to Charles Seeger, August 8, 1978, privately held.

51. Peggy Seeger, personal interview with the author, December 7, 2009.

52. Ann M. Pescatello, *Charles Seeger: A Life in American Music* (Pittsburgh: University of Pittsburgh Press, 1992), 281.

53. Gilbert Chase, "An Exagmination Round His Factification for Incamination of Work in Progress (Review Essay and Reminiscence)," *Yearbook of the International Folk Music Council* 11 (1979): 143.

54. Mantle Hood, "Reminiscent of Charles Seeger," *Yearbook of the International Folk Music Council* 11 (1979): 79, emphasis in original.

55. Peggy Seeger, interview, December 7, 2009.

56. Peggy Seeger, *Peggy Seeger Songbook*, 161.

57. Ewan MacColl, *Journeyman* (London: Sidgwick and Jackson, 1990), 380.

58. Peggy Seeger, interview, December 7, 2009.

## Chapter 16. The Day Is Ending

1. Peggy Seeger, personal interview with the author, April 9, 2010.

2. Ewan MacColl, *Journeyman* (London: Sidgwick and Jackson, 1990), 378, 380.

3. Peggy Seeger, personal interview with the author, December 7, 2009.

4. Peggy Seeger, interview, December 7, 2009.

5. Jim Carroll, "Editorial," *Lark*, January 1980, 4–5.

6. Liner notes, *Kilroy Was Here*, Blackthorne Records BR 1063, 1980.

7. Peggy Seeger, *The Essential Ewan MacColl Songbook: Sixty Years of Songmaking* (New York: Oak, 2001), 110.

8. Peggy Seeger, *The Peggy Seeger Songbook: Forty Years of Songmaking* (New York: Oak, 1998), 166.

9. Peggy Seeger, *Peggy Seeger Songbook*, 165.

10. Peggy Seeger, *Peggy Seeger Songbook*, 169.

11. Calum MacColl, personal interview with the author, August 24, 2009.

12. Peggy Seeger, interview, December 7, 2009.

13. *Kirsty: The Life and Songs of Kirsty MacColl*, BBC 2, www.bbc.co.uk.

14. Peggy Seeger, interview, April 9, 2010.

15. *Rhythms of the World*, unedited material from program on Ewan MacColl, videotape, roll number SL 4-28, 79-46-78, Ewan MacColl/Peggy Seeger Archive, Ruskin College, Oxford, England.

16. Kitty MacColl, personal interview with the author, August 24, 2009.

17. Liner notes, *From Where I Stand*, Folkways Records FW 8563, 1982.

18. Peggy Seeger, *Peggy Seeger Songbook*, 170.

19. Peggy Seeger, *Peggy Seeger Songbook*, 173.

20. Peggy Seeger, *Peggy Seeger Songbook*, 166.

21. Kitty MacColl, interview, August 24, 2009.

22. Kitty MacColl, interview, August 24, 2009.

23. Jean Stead, "The Greenham Common Peace Camp and Its Legacy," *Guardian*, September 5, 2006, www.theguardian.com/uk/2006/sep/05/Greenham5, accessed August 30, 2014.

24. Peggy Seeger, email message to the author, October 3, 2013.

25. Peggy Seeger, *Peggy Seeger Songbook*, 176.

26. Peggy Seeger, email message, October 3, 2013.

27. Peggy Seeger, *Peggy Seeger Songbook*, 177.

28. Peggy Seeger, *Peggy Seeger Songbook*, 178.

29. Kitty MacColl, interview, August 24, 2009.

30. Kitty MacColl, interview, August 24, 2009.

31. Calum MacColl, interview, August 24, 2009.

32. Album cover, *Freeborn Man*, Blackthorne Records BR 1065, 1983.

33. *The Good Old Way*, BBC 2, Betamax, 1983, Ewan MacColl/Peggy Seeger Archive, Ruskin College, Oxford, England.

34. *Ewan MacColl and Peggy Seeger*, film directed by Jane Muir, videotape, mid-1980s, Ewan MacColl/Peggy Seeger Archive, Ruskin College, Oxford, England.

35. *Ewan MacColl and Peggy Seeger*.

36. Huw Beynon, introduction to *Digging Deeper: Issues in the Miners' Strike* (London: Verso, 1985), 5.

37. *Daddy, What Did You Do in the Strike?* Blackthorne BSC 1, 1984.

38. *Daddy, What Did You Do?*

39. *Daddy, What Did You Do?*

40. *Daddy, What Did You Do?*

41. *Daddy, What Did You Do?*

42. *Daddy, What Did You Do?*

43. *Daddy, What Did You Do?*

44. Peggy Seeger, *Peggy Seeger Songbook*, 190.

45. Peggy Seeger, *Peggy Seeger Songbook*, 191.

46. Calum MacColl, interview, August 24, 2009.

47. Ewan updated *Uranium 235* as new events occurred. When the play was published in *Agit-prop to Theatre Workshop* in 1986, he wrote a new ending, which describes the dangers of even the most peaceful uses of nuclear power.

48. Peggy Seeger, *Essential Ewan MacColl Songbook*, 373. "The Joy of Living" shows Ewan's continued ability to use commonplaces. The first stanza contains the wonderfully evocative line, "days in the sun and the tempered wind and the air like wine." The phrase "air like wine" was popular in travel posters during Ewan's youth; it also appears in John Masefield's poem "The West Wind."

49. Neill MacColl, personal interview with the author, August 25, 2009.

50. Peggy Seeger, interview, April 9, 2010.

51. Peggy Seeger, interview, April 9, 2010.

52. Peggy Seeger, *Peggy Seeger Songbook*, 232–34.

53. Peggy Seeger, *Peggy Seeger Songbook*, 196.

54. Peggy Seeger, *Peggy Seeger Songbook*, 241.

55. Peggy Seeger, interview, April 9, 2010.

56. Peggy Seeger, interview, April 9, 2010.

57. Peggy Seeger, *Peggy Seeger Songbook*, 281.

58. Lydia Hamessley, "Peggy Seeger: From Traditional Folksinger to Contemporary Songwriter," in *Ruth Crawford Seeger's Worlds: Innovation and Tradition in Twentieth-Century American Music*, ed. Ray Allen and Ellie M. Hisama (Rochester, N.Y.: University of Rochester Press, 2007), 259.

59. Hamessley, "Peggy Seeger," 259.

60. Irene Pyper-Scott, personal interview with the author, June 6, 2010.

61. Irene Pyper-Scott, interview, June 6, 2010.

62. Peggy Seeger, interview, April 9, 2010.

63. Peggy Seeger, interview, April 9, 2010.

64. Peggy Seeger, liner notes, *American Folk Songs for Christmas*, Rounder Records 0268/0269, 1989.

65. Peggy Seeger, *Essential Ewan MacColl Songbook*, 356. Thatcher's poll tax proved no more popular than the one enacted in the fourteenth century. Riots ensued, and between one-fifth and one-quarter of the population simply refused to pay. Less than a year after Ewan's death, Margaret Thatcher resigned, and her successor abolished the poll tax.

66. Peggy Seeger, *Peggy Seeger Songbook*, 248.

67. There is one mistake in "Naming of Names": Mother Jones is included in a list of people who were murdered. Irish-American labor activist Mary Harris "Mother" Jones retired from activism while in her nineties and died when she was close to one hundred years old.

68. Interestingly, Kirsty's first child is also called Jamie. Ewan's first son and two of his grandsons all received a form of his given name.

69. Peggy Seeger, interview, April 9, 2010.

70. Peggy Seeger, interview, April 9, 2010.

### Chapter 17. The Long Road Home

1. Calum MacColl, personal interview with the author, August 24, 2009.

2. Peggy Seeger, personal interview with the author, April 9, 2010.

3. Irene Pyper-Scott, personal interview with the author, June 6, 2010.

4. Peggy Seeger, interview, April 9, 2010.

5. Peggy Seeger, interview, April 9, 2010.

6. Peggy Seeger, personal interview with the author, April 11, 2010.

7. Peggy Seeger, interview, April 9, 2010.

8. Peggy Seeger, *The Peggy Seeger Songbook: Forty Years of Songmaking* (New York: Oak, 1998), 243.

9. Peggy Seeger, interview, April 9, 2010.

10. Peggy Seeger, interview, April 11, 2010.

11. Calum MacColl, interview, August 24, 2009.

12. Calum MacColl, interview, August 24, 2009.

13. Neill MacColl, personal interview with the author, August 25, 2009.

14. Kitty MacColl, personal interview with the author, August 24, 2009.

15. A new edition of *Journeyman*, with a new introduction by Peggy, was published by Manchester University Press in 2009.

16. Peggy Seeger, introduction to *Journeyman* by Ewan MacColl (London: Sidgwick and Jackson, 1990), 6.

17. Peggy Seeger, personal diary, June 28, 1991, privately held.

18. Peggy Seeger, personal diary, June 20, 1991, privately held.

19. Peggy Seeger, personal diary, June 15, 1991, privately held.

20. Peggy Seeger, personal diary, June 30, 1991, privately held.

21. Peggy Seeger, interview, April 11, 2010.

22. Peggy Seeger, interview, April 11, 2010.

23. Peggy Seeger, interview, April 11, 2010.

24. Liner notes, *Peggy Seeger, the Folkways Years 1955–1992: Songs of Love and Politics*, Smithsonian Folkways CD SF 40048, 1992.

25. Peggy Seeger, email message to the author, June 22, 2015.

26. Peggy Seeger, personal diary, January 25, 1992, privately held.

27. Peggy Seeger, interview, April 11, 2010.

28. Peggy Seeger, interview, April 9, 2010.

29. Peggy Seeger, interview, April 11, 2010.

30. Sonya Cramer, personal interview with the author, April 1, 2014.

### Chapter 18. Heading for Home

1. Peggy Seeger, personal interview with the author, April 11, 2010.

2. Peggy Seeger, interview, April 11, 2010.

3. Peggy Seeger, *The Peggy Seeger Songbook: Forty Years of Songmaking* (New York: Oak, 1998), 251.

4. Peggy Seeger, *Peggy Seeger Songbook*, 251.

5. Kitty MacColl, personal interview with the author, August 24, 2009.

6. Peggy Seeger, email message to the author, July 27, 2014.

7. Peggy Seeger, *Peggy Seeger Songbook*, 335.

8. Peggy Seeger, *Peggy Seeger Songbook*, 329.

9. Letter from Peggy Seeger to Ann McKay, August 18, 1997, privately held.

10. Peggy Seeger, *Peggy Seeger Songbook*, 40.

11. Helen Brown, *Daily Telegraph*, March 16, 2002, www.peggyseeger.com/raves/songbook-reviews, accessed September 2, 2014.

12. Peggy Seeger, personal diary, July 19, 2000, privately held.

13. Peggy Seeger, *Peggy Seeger Songbook*, 293.

14. *Love Will Linger On*, Appleseed Recordings 1039, 2000.

15. *Love Will Linger On*.

16. Liner notes, *Love Will Linger On*.

17. For a moving account of Kirsty's life and death, see Jean MacColl's book *Sun on the Water: The Brilliant Life and Tragic Death of Kirsty MacColl* (London: John Blake, 2008).

18. Peggy Seeger, *The Essential Ewan MacColl Songbook: Sixty Years of Songmaking* (New York: Oak, 2001), 419.

19. Peggy Seeger, *Essential Ewan MacColl Songbook*, 22.

20. The song was initially written to raise money for Christine's medical expenses.

21. Peggy Seeger, personal diary, February 9, 2001, privately held.

22. *Love Call Me Home*, Appleseed Recordings APR CD 1087, 2005.

23. *Peaceful Woman, Fighting Hard*, Timely Productions, 2002.

24. For a fascinating account of Robert Burns's song collecting activities, see Mary Ellen B. Lewis, "'The Joy of My Heart': Robert Burns as Folklorist," *Scottish Studies* 20 (1976): 45–67.

25. Peggy Seeger, email message to the author, July 19, 2014.

26. Peggy Seeger, *Essential Ewan MacColl Songbook*, 295.

27. *Peaceful Woman, Fighting Hard*.

28. Neill MacColl, personal interview with the author, August 25, 2009.

29. Calum MacColl, personal interview with the author, August 24, 2009.

30. Liner notes, *Heading for Home*, Appleseed Recordings APR CD 1076, 2003.

31. Calum MacColl, interview, August 24, 2009. This story has clearly become a family legend. When I interviewed Kitty, she asked, "He's [Calum] told you the balls story?" (August 24, 2009)

32. Peggy Seeger, email message, July 27, 2014, emphasis in original.

33. Kerry Harvey-Piper, Skype interview with the author, August 4, 2014.

34. Peggy Seeger, personal interview, May 20, 2011.

35. *Heading for Home*.

36. "About Peggy," http://www.peggyseeger.com/about/whats-new/2003, accessed August 11, 2016.

37. *Crazy Quilt*, Timely Productions, 2008. Massey has written about his experience in *Kill! Kill! Kill!*, published with the French journalist Natasha Saulnier. Some people in the antiwar movement have distanced themselves from Massey, saying that he was harming their cause with inaccurate information. Massey's initial claims did contain inconsistencies, as he himself later admitted and attributed to post-traumatic

stress disorder, for which he was treated following his discharge from the Marine Corps. But he never backed down from his fundamental assertion: that U.S. troops were responsible for the death of Iraqi civilians.

38. "February 2005," http://www.peggyseeger.com/about/whats-new/2005, accessed August 11, 2016.

39. "February 2005."

40. Liner notes, *Three Score and Ten*, Appleseed Recordings APR CD 1100, 2007.

41. *Three Score and Ten*.

42. *Three Score and Ten*.

43. Remaking religious songs for political purposes has a long history in the United States. Joe Hill used popular hymns as the basis of many of his songs; "In the Sweet By-and-By" became "Pie in the Sky When You Die." During the civil rights movement, many songs of the African American church were altered to reflect a focus on civil rights; "We Shall Overcome" is the most famous example. While Joe Hill's use of hymns was primarily satiric, civil rights workers felt that the use of sacred music showed the holiness of their cause. Peggy's usage is somewhere in between: she does not parody religious songs, but she does imbue them with secular meanings.

44. *Crazy Quilt*.

### Chapter 19. Old New England

1. Irene Pyper-Scott, personal interview with the author, June 6, 2010.

2. The 2013 Marriage (Same Sex Couples) Act legalized marriage for same-sex couples in England and Wales. Scotland passed a similar law in 2014. On June 26, 2015, the U.S. Supreme Court legalized same-sex marriage throughout the country.

3. Peggy Seeger, personal interview with the author, April 11, 2010.

4. Neil Rosenberg, "Family Values Seeger Style" (paper presented at "How Can I Keep from Singing? The Seeger Family Tribute," Library of Congress, Washington, D.C., March 16, 2007).

5. Millie Rahn, "The 'It Changed My Life' Syndrome: The Folk Revival" (paper presented at "How Can I Keep from Singing? The Seeger Family Tribute," Library of Congress, Washington, D.C., March 16, 2007).

6. "March," http://www.peggyseeger.com/about/whats-new/2006-2007, accessed August 12, 2016.

7. Peggy Seeger, interview, April 11, 2010.

8. Elias Bouquillon, telephone interview with the author, September 7, 2014.

9. Bouquillon, interview, September 7, 2014.

10. Peggy Seeger, interview, April 11, 2010.

11. Pyper-Scott, interview, June 6, 2010.

12. Peggy Seeger, interview, April 11, 2010.

13. "April–May," http://www.peggyseeger.com/about/whats-new/2006-2007, accessed August 11, 2016.

14. This song raises the question: Are songs about abandoned women sad because the woman has lost her lover or because the man forgot to pay child support?

15. This is the kind of ambiguity found in the "signal songs" of the Underground Railroad, in which seemingly innocuous religious words signaled the route to earthly freedom.

16. *Bring Me Home*, Appleseed Recordings APR CD 1106, 2008.

17. *Crazy Quilt*, Timely Productions, 2008.

18. *Crazy Quilt*. Peggy took the theme of "Dick and the Devil" from the old Irish song "The Devil and Bailiff McGlynn," in which the devil comes to earth looking for damned souls and ends up carrying off the bailiff. Ewan rewrote this song as "The Devil and Ganger McGlynn," about Irish workers in London. Ewan's version is extremely derivative of its model, using the same tune and many of the same words. Peggy's song is very different; she wrote a new tune and different words. All these songs are modern descendants of Chaucer's "The Friar's Tale."

19. *Crazy Quilt*.

20. *Obama Is the One for Me*, Timely Productions, 2008.

21. http://www.peggyseeger.com/about/whats-new/2008-2009/22b%20breast cancerribbon.gif/view, accessed August 11, 2016.

22. http://www.peggyseeger.com/about/whats-new/2008-2009/24-NEU-students concert.JPG/view, accessed August 11, 2016.

23. "Peggy's Madison Avenue Square Letter to Pete," http://www.peggyseeger .com/about/about-my-family/peggys-madison-avenue-square-letter-to-pete, accessed August 11, 2016.

24. Bill C. Malone, *Music from the True Vine: Mike Seeger's Life and Musical Journey* (Chapel Hill: University of North Carolina Press, 2011), 168.

25. Malone, *Music from the True Vine*, 169.

26. Peggy Seeger, interview, April 11, 2010.

## Chapter 20. Everything Changes

1. Liner notes, *Fly Down Little Bird*, Appleseed Recordings APR CD 1125, 2011.

2. Liner notes, *Fly Down Little Bird*, emphasis in original.

3. "Declaration of the Occupation of New York City," September 29, 2011, http:// www.nycga.net/resources/documents/declaration/, accessed June 30, 2016.

4. This line refers to economic divisions between the top 1 percent of the population and the remaining 99 percent. One of the rallying cries of the Occupy movements was, "We are the 99 percent."

5. "The Anticapitalist Roadshow," http://www.redmagic.co.uk/anticap/index .htm, accessed June 30, 2016.

6. Frankie Armstrong, email message to the author, December 8, 2012.

7. Peggy Seeger, email message to the author, September 3, 2014.

8. Peggy Seeger, email message to the author, August 15, 2012.

9. Nick Dent-Robinson, "Peggy Seeger: Interview," August 27, 2012, www.penny blackmusic.co.uk, accessed September 18, 2012.

10. "Folksploitation," http://broadcasteruk.com/folksploitation, accessed June 30, 2016.

11. Peggy Seeger, email message to the author, November 18, 2012.

12. Greg Haymes, "Peggy and Pete Seeger at Proctors, 5/12/13," http://www.peggy seeger.com/raves/concert-reviews, accessed June 30, 2016.

13. Douglas Martin, "Toshi Seeger, Wife of Folk-Singing Legend, Dies at 91," *New York Times*, July 11, 2013, http:// tinyurl.com/hs7pda7, accessed July 14, 2014.

14. Peggy Seeger, "Peggy Seeger News," email message to the author, December 16, 2013.

15. Peggy Seeger, "Peggy Seeger News," email message to the author, August 22, 2013.

16. Peggy Seeger Facebook page, January 29, 2014, https://www.facebook.com /PeggySeegerMusic.

17. Dorian Lynskey, "Pete Seeger: The Man Who Brought Politics to Music," *Guardian*, January 28, 2014, http://www.theguardian.com/music/2014/jan/28/pete -seeger-man-brought-politics-to-music, accessed June 30, 2016.

18. Mark Guarino, "Peggy Seeger Keeps the Folk Music Flame Burning Brightly," March 16, 2014, http:// tinyurl.com/jaeduto, accessed June 30, 2016.

19. Pete Seeger, telephone interview with the author, April 7, 2009.

20. Peggy Seeger Facebook page, January 29, 2014, https://www.facebook.com /PeggySeegerMusic.

21. Kerry Harvey-Piper, email message to the author, July 11, 2014.

22. Peggy Seeger, email message, September 3, 2014.

23. *Everything Changes*, Signet Music, 2013.

24. Track notes, *Everything Changes*.

25. *Everything Changes*.

26. *Everything Changes*.

27. *Everything Changes*.

28. Peggy Seeger, email message, September 3, 2014.

29. *Everything Changes*.

30. Liner notes, *Everything Changes*.

31. David Lowenthal, *The Past Is a Foreign Country* (Cambridge: Cambridge University Press, 1985), 8.

32. Judith Tick, *Ruth Crawford Seeger: A Composer's Search for American Music* (New York: Oxford University Press, 1997), 11.

33. Ray Allen and Ellie M. Hisama, eds., *Ruth Crawford Seeger's Worlds: Innovation and Tradition in Twentieth-Century American Music* (Rochester, N.Y.: University of Rochester Press, 2007).

34. Judith Tick, telephone interview with the author, July 14, 2014.

35. Peggy Seeger, Skype interview with the author, July 20, 2014.

36. *Rhythms of the World*, unedited material from program on Ewan MacColl, videotape, roll number: SL 115-222, Ewan MacColl/Peggy Seeger Archive, Ruskin College, Oxford, England.

37. Ken Hunt, *Q* magazine, http://www.peggyseeger.com/listen-buy/an-odd -collection/an-odd-collection-reviews, accessed August 11, 2016.

38. Neil Johnston, "Neil Johnston's Festival Notebook," *Belfast Telegraph*, November 8, 2002, http://www.peggyseeger.com/raves/concert-reviews/, accessed June 30, 2016.

39. "Letters," http://www.peggyseeger.com/raves/letters, accessed June 30, 2016.

40. Julian Owen, "Peggy Seeger, Chapel Arts, Bath—Review," October 22, 2013, http://www.bigissue.com/reviews/live-reviews/3144/peggy-seeger-chapel-arts-bath -review, accessed June 30, 2016.

## Chapter 21. What Is a Folk Revival?

1. Robert Cantwell, *When We Were Good: The Folk Revival* (Cambridge, Mass.: Harvard University Press, 1996), 15.

2. Neil Rosenberg, introduction to *Transforming Tradition: Folk Music Revivals Examined* (Urbana: University of Illinois Press, 1993), 2; Alan Jabbour, foreword to *Transforming Tradition*, xii–xiii.

3. Tamara E. Livingston, "Music Revivals: Towards a General Theory," *Ethnomusicology* 43 (1999): 68.

4. Ben A. Botkin, moderator, "The Folksong Revival: A Symposium," *New York Folklore Quarterly* 19 (1963): 83.

5. Michael F. Scully, *The Never-Ending Revival: Rounder Records and the Folk Alliance* (Urbana: University of Illinois Press, 2008), 8–9.

6. Ailie Munro, *The Folk Music Revival in Scotland* (Darby, Penn.: Norwood Editions, 1985), 88.

7. Ronald D. Cohen, *Rainbow Quest: The Folk Music Revival and American Society, 1940–1970* (Amherst: University of Massachusetts Press, 2002), x.

8. David King Dunaway and Molly Beer, *Singing Out: An Oral History of America's Folk Music Revivals* (Oxford: Oxford University Press, 2010), 3.

9. Dunaway, introduction to Dunaway and Beer, *Singing Out*, 1.

10. Bruce Jackson, "The Folksong Revival," in *Transforming Tradition: Folk Music Revivals Examined*, ed. Neil V. Rosenberg (Urbana: University of Illinois Press, 1993), 75.

11. Benjamin Filene, *Romancing the Folk: Public Memory and American Roots Music* (Chapel Hill: University of North Carolina Press, 2000), 49, emphasis in original.

12. I. Sheldon Posen, "On Folk Festivals and Kitchens: Questions of Authenticity in the Folksong Revival," in *Transforming Tradition: Folk Music Revivals Examined*, ed. Neil V. Rosenberg (Urbana: University of Illinois Press, 1993), 134.

13. Posen, "On Folk Festivals and Kitchens," 136.

14. Richard Blaustein, "Rethinking Folk Revivalism: Grass-roots Preservationism

and Folk Romanticism," in *Transforming Tradition: Folk Music Revivals Examined*, ed. Neil V. Rosenberg (Urbana: University of Illinois Press, 1993), 258–59.

15. Georgina Boyes, *The Imagined Village: Culture, Ideology and the English Folk Revival* (Manchester: Manchester University Press, 1993).

16. Richard Handler and Jocelyn Linnekin, "Tradition, Genuine or Spurious," *Journal of American Folklore* 97 (1984): 276.

17. Botkin, "Folksong Revival," 107.

18. Peggy Seeger, Skype interview with the author, July 29, 2015.

19. Ellen J. Stekert, "Cents and Nonsense in the Urban Folksong Movement: 1930–66," in *Transforming Tradition: Folk Music Revivals Examined*, ed. Neil V. Rosenberg (Urbana: University of Illinois Press, 1993), 99–100.

20. Peggy Seeger, "A Singer for My Time," program of Smithsonian Folklife Festival 2000, 95.

21. Peggy Seeger, "Singer for My Time," 95.

22. Boyes, *Imagined Village*, 3.

23. Peggy Seeger, "Singer for My Time," 95.

24. Peggy Seeger, Skype interview, July 29, 2015.

25. Peggy Seeger, Skype interview, July 29, 2015.

26. Clive Davies, "Peggy Seeger at Queen Elizabeth Hall," *Times* (London), June 10, 2015, http://www.thetimes.co.uk/tto/arts/music/livereviews/article4465056.ece, accessed June 30, 2016.

27. Colin Irwin, "Joan Baez and Joan Armatrading, Cambridge Folk Festival, review: 'A Generous Slice of Folk History,'" *Telegraph* (London), August 3, 2015, http://tinyurl.com/zju5an2, accessed June 30, 2016.

# References Cited

## Published Sources

Allen, Ray. "Performing Dio's Legacy: Mike Seeger and the Urban Folk Music Revival." In Allen and Hisama, *Ruth Crawford Seeger's Worlds*, 224–51.

Allen, Ray, and Ellie M. Hisama, eds. *Ruth Crawford Seeger's Worlds: Innovation and Tradition in Twentieth-Century American Music*. Rochester, N.Y.: University of Rochester Press, 2007.

"Americans Abroad: The Mis-Guided Tour." *Time*, August 26, 1957, 15.

Armstrong, Frankie, with Jenny Pearson. *As Far as the Eye Can Sing*. London: Women's Press, 1992.

Benbow, Steve. "Going Commercial?" *English Dance and Song* (New Year 1961): 8–11.

Beynon, Huw. Introduction to *Digging Deeper: Issues in the Miners' Strike*, edited by Huw Beynon, 1–26. London: Verso, 1985.

Blaustein, Richard. "Rethinking Folk Revivalism: Grass-roots Preservationism and Folk Romanticism." In Rosenberg, *Transforming Tradition*, 258–74.

Bosworth, R. J. B. *Explaining Auschwitz and Hiroshima: History Writing and the Second World War 1945–1990*. London: Routledge, 1993.

Botkin, B. A. "The Folksong Revival: A Symposium." *New York Folklore Quarterly* 19 (1963): 83–142.

———. *A Treasury of American Folklore: Stories, Ballads, and Traditions of the People*. 1944; New York: Crown, 1983.

———. *A Treasury of Western Folklore*. New York: Crown, 1951.

———. "WPA and Folklore Research: 'Bread and Song.'" In *The Conservation of Culture: Folklorists and the Public Sector*, edited by Burt Feintuch, 258–63. Lexington: University Press of Kentucky, 1988.

Boyes, Georgina. *The Imagined Village: Culture, Ideology and the English Folk Revival*. Manchester: Manchester University Press, 1993.

Brown, Helen. Review in *Daily Telegraph*, March 16, 2002. www.peggyseeger.com /raves/songbook-reviews, accessed September 2, 2014.

Buchanan, Annabel Morris. "The Function of a Folk Festival." *Southern Folklore Quarterly* 1 (1937): 29–34.

Burkett, Lyn Ellen. "Linear Aggregates and Proportional Design in Ruth Crawford's *Piano Study in Mixed Accents*." In Allen and Hisama, *Ruth Crawford Seeger's Worlds*, 57–72.

Calico, Joy. "'We Are Changing the World!': New German Folk Songs for the Free German Youth (1950)." In *Musical Childhoods and the Culture of Youth*, edited by Susan Boynton and Roe-Min Kok, 145–67. Middletown, Conn.: Wesleyan University Press, 2006.

Cantwell, Robert. *When We Were Good: The Folk Revival*. Cambridge, Mass.: Harvard University Press, 1996.

Carroll, Jim. "Editorial." *Lark*, January 1980, 1–4.

Carter, Sydney. "Pop Goes the Folk Song." *English Dance and Song* (New Year 1961): 3–6.

Chase, Gilbert. "An Exagmination Round His Factification for Incamination of Work in Progress (Review Essay and Reminiscence)." *Yearbook of the International Folk Music Council* 11 (1979): 138–44.

Child, Francis James. *The English and Scottish Popular Ballads*. Boston: Houghton Mifflin, 1898.

Cohen, Ronald D. *Rainbow Quest: The Folk Music Revival and American Society, 1940–1970*. Amherst: University of Massachusetts Press, 2002.

Cohen, Ronald D., and Rachel Clare Donaldson. *Roots of the Revival: American and British Folk Music in the 1950s*. Urbana: University of Illinois Press, 2014.

Cox, Peter. *Set into Song: Ewan MacColl, Charles Parker, Peggy Seeger and the Radio Ballads*. London: Labatie Books, 2008.

Davies, Clive. "Peggy Seeger at Queen Elizabeth Hall," *Times* (London), June 10, 2015. http://www.thetimes.co.uk/tto/arts/music/livereviews/article4465056.ece, accessed June 30, 2016.

"Drug Store Hillbillies Shine at Warrenton Music Contest." *Washington Post*, September 15, 1952.

Dunaway, David King. *How Can I Keep from Singing? The Ballad of Pete Seeger*. New York: Villard Books, 2008.

Dunaway, David King, and Molly Beer. *Singing Out: An Oral History of America's Folk Music Revivals*. Oxford: Oxford University Press, 2010.

Engels, Frederick. *The Origin of the Family, Private Property, and the State*. 1884; New York: Pathfinder Press, 1972.

Filene, Benjamin. *Romancing the Folk: Public Memory and American Roots Music*. Chapel Hill: University of North Carolina Press, 2000.

Finlay, John. *Scottish Historical and Romantic Ballads.* Vol. 1. Edinburgh: James Ballantyne, 1808.

Friedan, Betty. *The Feminine Mystique.* New York: W. W. Norton, 1963.

Good, Amber. "'Lady, What Do You Do All Day?': Peggy Seeger's Anthems of Anglo-American Feminism." MM thesis, University of Cincinnati, 2002.

Goorney, Howard. *The Theatre Workshop Story.* London: Eyre Methuen, 1981.

Goorney, Howard, and Ewan MacColl, eds. *Agit-Prop to Theatre Workshop.* Manchester: Manchester University Press, 1986.

Greenway, John. *American Folksongs of Protest.* Philadelphia: University of Pennsylvania Press, 1953.

Guarino, Mark. "Peggy Seeger Keeps the Folk Music Flame Burning Brightly." *Chicago Sun-Times,* March 16, 2014. http://tinyurl.com/jaeduto, accessed June 30, 2016.

Gyorgy, Anna, and friends. *No Nukes: Everyone's Guide to Nuclear Power.* Montreal: Black Rose Books, 1979.

Hamessley, Lydia. "Peggy Seeger: From Traditional Folksinger to Contemporary Songwriter." In Allen and Hisama, *Ruth Crawford Seeger's Worlds,* 252–87.

Hand, Wayland D. "The Editors' Page." *Journal of American Folklore* 61, no. 239 (1948): 82.

Handler, Richard, and Jocelyn Linnekin. "Tradition, Genuine or Spurious." *Journal of American Folklore* 97 (1984): 273–90.

Hardin, James. "The Archive of Folk Culture at 75: A National Project with Many Workers." *Folklife Center News* 25, no. 2 (Spring 2003): 3–4.

Harker, Ben. *Class Act: The Cultural and Political Life of Ewan MacColl.* London: Pluto Press, 2007.

Hawes, Bess Lomax. "Reminiscences on *Our Singing Country*: The Crawford Seeger/ Lomax Alliance." In Allen and Hisama, *Ruth Crawford Seeger's Worlds,* 148–52.

Hood, Mantle. "Reminiscent of Charles Seeger." *Yearbook of the International Folk Music Council* 11 (1979): 76–81.

Irwin, Colin. "Joan Baez and Joan Armatrading, Cambridge Folk Festival, review: 'A Generous Slice of Folk History.'" *Telegraph* (London), August 3, 2015. http://tinyurl.com/zju5an2, accessed June 30, 2016.

Jabbour, Alan. Foreword to *Transforming Tradition: Folk Music Revivals Examined,* edited by Neil V. Rosenberg. Urbana: University of Illinois Press, 1993.

Jackson, Bruce. "The Folksong Revival." In Rosenberg, *Transforming Tradition,* 73–83.

Johnston, Neil. "Neil Johnston's Festival Notebook." *Belfast Telegraph,* November 8, 2002. http://www.peggyseeger.com/raves/concert-reviews/, accessed June 30, 2016.

Kamenetsky, Christa. "Folklore as a Political Tool in Nazi Germany." *Journal of American Folklore* 85 (1972): 221–35.

Karpeles, Maud. Note to preface. In *English Folk Songs from the Southern Appala-*

*chians*, collected by Cecil J. Sharp and Olive Dame Campbell, edited by Maud Karpeles, 2nd ed., xx. London: Oxford University Press, 1952.

———. Preface to *English Folk Songs from the Southern Appalachians*, collected by Cecil J. Sharp and Olive Dame Campbell, edited by Maud Karpeles, 2nd ed., xii–xx. London: Oxford University Press, 1932.

Lamb, Roberta. "Composing and Teaching as Dissonant Counterpoint." In Allen and Hisama, *Ruth Crawford Seeger's Worlds*, 169–95.

Leach, Robert. *Theatre Workshop: Joan Littlewood and the Making of Modern British Drama*. Exeter: University of Exeter Press, 2006.

Lewis, Mary Ellen B. "'The Joy of My Heart': Robert Burns as Folklorist." *Scottish Studies* 20 (1976): 45–67.

Lieberman, Robbie. *"My Song Is My Weapon": People's Songs, American Communism, and the Politics of Culture, 1930–50*. Urbana: University of Illinois Press, 1989.

Livingston, Tamara E. "Music Revivals: Towards a General Theory." *Ethnomusicology* 43 (1999): 66–85.

Lloyd, A. L. "Neglecting His Duty?" *Sing* 6 (February 1962): 56.

Lomax, Alan. *The Folk Songs of North America*. Garden City, N.Y.: Doubleday, 1960.

Lomax, Alan, and Peggy Seeger. *American Folk Guitar*. London: Robbins Music, 1957.

Lomax, John A., and Alan Lomax. *American Ballads and Folk Songs*. 1934; New York: Macmillan, 1994.

———. *Folk Song USA*. New York: Grosset and Dunlap, 1947.

———. *Our Singing Country*. New York: Macmillan, 1941.

Lowenthal, David. *The Past Is a Foreign Country*. Cambridge: Cambridge University Press, 1985.

Lubasch, Arnold H. *Robeson: An American Ballad*. Lanham, MD: Scarecrow Press, 2012.

Lunsford, Bascom Lamar, and Lamar Stringfield, compilers and arrangers. *30 and 1 Folksongs from the Southern Mountains*. New York: C. Fischer, 1929.

Lynskey, Dorian. "Pete Seeger: The Man Who Brought Politics to Music." *Guardian*, January 28, 2014. http://www.theguardian.com/music/2014/jan/28/pete-seeger-man-brought-politics-to-music, accessed June 30, 2016.

MacColl, Ewan. *Folk Songs and Ballads of Scotland*. New York: Oak, 1965.

———. *Journeyman*. London: Sidgwick and Jackson, 1990.

———. *Journeyman*. 2nd ed. Manchester: Manchester University Press, 2009.

———. "Why I Am Opening a New Club." *Sing* 5 (August 1961): 65.

MacColl, Ewan, and Peggy Seeger. *Ewan MacColl–Peggy Seeger Songbook*. New York: Oak, 1963.

———. "Going American?" *English Dance and Song* (New Year 1961): 19–20.

———. *The Singing Island: A Collection of English and Scots Folksongs*. London: Mills Music, 1960.

———. *Songs for the Sixties*. London: Workers' Music Association, 1961.

———. *Till Doomsday in the Afternoon*. Manchester: Manchester University Press, 1986.

———. *Travellers' Songs from England and Scotland*. Knoxville: University of Tennessee Press, 1977.

MacColl, Ewan, and Peggy Seeger with Ben Bright. *Shellback: Reminiscences of Ben Bright, Mariner. History Workshop* pamphlets, item 13 [1970s].

MacColl, Jean. *Sun on the Water: The Brilliant Life and Tragic Death of Kirsty MacColl*. London: John Blake, 2008.

Malone, Bill C. *Music from the True Vine: Mike Seeger's Life and Musical Journey*. Chapel Hill: University of North Carolina Press, 2011.

Makepeace, John. "Discussion: A Page of Record Reviews." *Sing* 6 (July 1962): 110.

Martin, Douglas. "Toshi Seeger, Wife of Folk-Singing Legend, Dies at 91." *New York Times*, July 11, 2013. http://tinyurl.com/hs7pda7, accessed July 14, 2014.

Massey, Jimmy, with Natasha Saulnier. *Kill! Kill! Kill!* Paris: Éditions du Panama, 2005.

McDade, Matt. 1953. "Mother, Son—Both Authors—Prove to Visitors at *Post* Book Fair Life with Boa Can Be Fun." *Washington Post*, November 19, 1953.

Munro, Ailie. *The Folk Music Revival in Scotland*. Darby, Penn.: Norwood Editions, 1985.

*New City Songster*. Vol. 1. 1968.

Percy, Thomas. *Reliques of Ancient English Poetry*. 1765; London: J. M. Dent and Sons, 1910.

Pescatello, Ann M. *Charles Seeger: A Life in American Music*. Pittsburgh: University of Pittsburgh Press, 1992.

Posen, I. Sheldon. "On Folk Festivals and Kitchens: Questions of Authenticity in the Folksong Revival." In Rosenberg, *Transforming Tradition*, 127–36.

Powell, John. "How America Can Develop a National Music." *Etude* (May 1927): 342–50.

Reuss, Richard A. "Folk Music and Social Conscience: The Musical Odyssey of Charles Seeger." *Western Folklore* 38 (1979): 221–38.

Reuss, Richard A., with JoAnne C. Reuss. *American Folk Music and Left-Wing Politics, 1927–1957*. Lanham, MD: Scarecrow Press, 2000.

Robinson, Earl, ed. *Young Folk Song Book*. New York: Simon and Schuster, 1963.

Rosenberg, Neil V., ed. *Transforming Tradition: Folk Music Revivals Examined*. Urbana: University of Illinois Press, 1993.

Sandburg, Carl. *The American Songbag*. New York: Harcourt, Brace, 1927.

Sands, Carl. "Songs by Auvilles Mark Step Ahead in Workers Music." *Daily Worker*, January 15, 1935.

Scully, Michael F. *The Never-Ending Revival: Rounder Records and the Folk Alliance*. Urbana: University of Illinois Press, 2008.

Seeger, Anthony. Foreword to *Understanding Charles Seeger: Pioneer in American Musicology*. Urbana: University of Illinois Press, 1999.

Seeger, Charles Louis, Jr. "Inter-American Relations in the Field of Music." *Music Educators Journal* 27 (1941): 17–18, 64–65.

———. "On Proletarian Music." *Modern Music* 11, no. 3 (1934): 121–27.

———. "On the Principles of Musicology." *Musical Quarterly* 10 (1924):244–50.

Seeger, Charles, and Margaret Valiant. Foreword to "Journal of a Field Representative" (1937). *Ethnomusicology* 24, no. 2 (1980): 178–80.

———. "Journal of a Field Representative" (1937). *Ethnomusicology* 24, no. 2 (1980): 180–210.

Seeger, Peggy. *The Essential Ewan MacColl Songbook: Sixty Years of Songmaking*. New York: Oak, 2001.

———. *The Five-String Banjo American Folk Styles*. New York: Hargail Music Press, 1960.

———. *Folk Songs of Peggy Seeger*. New York: Oak, 1964.

———. *The Peggy Seeger Songbook: Forty Years of Songmaking*. New York: Oak, 1998.

———. "A Singer for My Time." In program for Smithsonian Folklife Festival 2000, 91–96

Seeger, Pete. *How to Play the 5-String Banjo*. New York: People's Songs, 1948.

———. *The Incompleat Folksinger*. New York: Simon and Schuster, 1972.

———. *Where Have All the Flowers Gone: A Singalong Memoir*. New York: *Sing Out!* in association with W. W. Norton, 2009.

Seeger, Ruth Crawford. *American Folk Songs for Children*. Garden City, N.Y.: Doubleday, 1948.

———. *Animal Folk Songs for Children*. Garden City, N.Y.: Doubleday, 1950.

———. *American Folk Songs for Christmas*. Garden City, N.Y.: Doubleday, 1953.

Sharp, Cecil J. *English Folk Songs from the Southern Appalachians*. London: Oxford University Press, 1932.

———. *English Folk-Song: Some Conclusions*. London: Simpkin, 1907.

Shelton, Robert. "Ewan MacColl, in Debut Here, Offers Concert of Folk Music." *New York Times*, December 5, 1960.

Stead, Jean. 2006. "The Greenham Common Peace Camp and Its Legacy." *Guardian*, September 5, 2006. https:// www.theguardian.com/uk/2006/sep/05/Greenham5, accessed August 30, 2014.

Stekert, Ellen J. "Cents and Nonsense in the Urban Folk Song Movement: 1930–66." In Rosenberg, *Transforming Tradition*, 84–106.

Szwed, John. 2010. *Alan Lomax: The Man Who Recorded the World*. New York: Viking, 2010.

Thurston, H. 1909. "Feast of Fools." In *The Catholic Encyclopedia*. New York: Robert Appleton. Accessed August 26, 2014, at New Advent, http://www.newadvent.org /cathen/06132a.htm.

Tick, Judith. *Ruth Crawford Seeger: A Composer's Search for American Music*. New York: Oxford University Press, 1997.

Warren-Findley, Janelle. Introduction to "Journal of a Field Representative." *Ethnomusicology* 24, no. 2 (1980): 169–78.

Whisnant, David E. *All That Is Native and Fine: The Politics of Culture in an American Region*. Chapel Hill: University of North Carolina Press, 1983.

Winkler, Allan M. *"To Everything There Is a Season": Pete Seeger and the Power of Song*. Oxford: Oxford University Press, 2011.

Winter, Eric. "Going Political?" *English Dance and Song* (New Year 1961): 12–14.

———. "Unaccompanied Singers." *Sing* 6 (December 1961): 14.

———. "True Voice of Peggy Gets Through." *Sing* 8 (April 1965): 19.

Wohlsen, Marcus. 2005. "Charles Seeger Inaugurates New Era of Music." In *Illuminations: Berkeley's Online Magazine of Research in the Arts and Humanities*. http://illuminations.berkeley.edu/archives/2005/history.php?volume =4, accessed June 25, 2013, URL no longer active.

"Youth from 102 Lands Swarms over Moscow." *Life*, August 12, 1957, 22–27.

### Archival Sources

American Folklife Center. Library of Congress, Washington, D.C.

Peggy Seeger/Ewan MacColl Archive. Ruskin College, Oxford, England.

Seeger Collection. Music Division. Library of Congress, Washington, D.C.

### Recordings

*Alan Lomax and the Ramblers with Ewan MacColl and Peggy Seeger*. Decca Records. 1956.

*Almost Commercially Viable*. Golden Egg Productions SB 71204. 1992.

*America at Play*. EMI CLP 1174. 1958.

*American Folksongs for Children*. Rounder Records 8001. 1978.

*American Folk Songs for Christmas*. Folkways Records FC 7553. 1957.

*American Folk Songs for Christmas*. Rounder Records 0268/0269. 1989.

*American Folk Songs Sung by the Seegers*. Folkways Records. 1957.

*American History in Ballad and Song*. Folkways Records 5801. 1960.

*American Song Train*. PYE NIXA NPL 18013. 1958.

*The Amorous Muse*. Argo ZDA 84. 1968.

*The Angry Muse*. Argo ZFB 65. 1968.

*Animal Folk Songs for Children*. Folkways Records. 1957.

*Animal Folk Songs for Children*. Rounder Records ROUN 11543/44. 1992.

*As We Were a-Sailing*. Argo ZDA 137. 1970.

*At the Present Moment*. Rounder ROUN 4003. 1973.

*Bad Lads and Hard Cases: British Ballads of Crime and Criminals*. Riverside RLP 12-632. 1956.

*The Ballad of Jimmy Massey*. Timely Productions. 2005.
*The Ballad of John Axon*. Topic Records Ltd. TSCD 801. 2008.
*The Best of Peggy Seeger*. Prestige International 13005. Early 1960s.
*The Big Hewer*. Topic Records Ltd. TSCD 804. 2008.
*Black and White: The Definitive Ewan MacColl Collection*. Cooking Vinyl COOK 038. 1990.
*Bless 'Em All and Other British Army Songs*. Riverside RLP 12-641. 1957.
*Blood and Roses*, vols. 1–5. Blackthorne Records BR 79-83. 1979–86.
*The Body Blow*. Topic Records Ltd. TSCD 805. 2008.
*Bold Sportsmen All*. Topic Records 10T 36. 1958.
*Bothy Ballads of Scotland*. Folkways Records FW 08759. 1961.
*Bring Me Home*. Appleseed Recordings APR CD 1106. 2008.
*Broadside Ballads, Volume 1 (London: 1600–1700)*. Folkways Records FW 3043. 1962.
*Broadside Ballads, Volume 2 (London: 1600–1700)—Female Frolicks and Politicks*. Folkways Records FW 3044. 1962.
*Celebrating Subversion*. Fuse Records. 2012.
*Classic Scots Ballads*. Tradition Records. 1959.
*Chorus from the Gallows*. Topic Records 12T16. 1960.
*Classic Peggy Seeger*. Fellside FECD 105. 1996.
*Cold Snap*. Blackthorne BR 1057. 1977.
*Come Along, John*. Topic Records TOP 18. 1957.
*Crazy Quilt*. Timely Productions. 2008.
*Daddy, What Did You Do in the Strike?* Blackthorne BSC 1.
*Different Therefore Equal*. Blackthorne Records BR 1061/Folkways Records FS 8561. 1979.
*Early in the Spring*. Topic Records TOP 73. 1962.
*Eleven American Ballads and Songs*. Topic Records TOP 10T9. 1957.
*The Elliotts of Birtley: A Musical Portrait of a Durham Mining Family*. Folkways Records FG 3565. 1962.
*English and Scottish Love Songs*. Riverside RLP 12-656. 1958.
*Enough Is Enough*. Timely Productions. 2006.
*Everything Changes*. Signet Music. 2013.
*Ewan MacColl Sings British Industrial Ballads*. Vanguard VRS-9090. 1961.
*Familiar Faces*. Blackthorne Records BR 1069. 1988.
*The Female Frolic*. Argo ZDA 82. 1968.
*The Fight Game*. Topic Records Ltd. TSCD 807. 2008.
*Fly Down Little Bird*. Appleseed Recordings APR CD 1125. 2011.
*Folksongs and Ballads*. Riverside RLP 12-655. 1958.
*Folk-Song Saturday Night*. Kapp KL-1110. 1958.
*Folk Songs of Courting and Complaint*. Folkways Records FA 2049. 1955.
*Folksploitation*. Red Grape Records. 2012.

*Folkways Record of Contemporary Songs.* Folkways FW 08736. 1973.
*Freeborn Man.* Blackthorne Records BR 1065. 1983.
*Freight Train.* Topic Records TRC 107. 1958.
*From Where I Stand.* Folkways Records FW 8563. 1982.
*Heading for Home.* Appleseed Recordings APR CD 1076. 2003.
*Hot Blast.* Blackthorne Records BR 1059/Folkways Records FW 8710. 1978.
*Items of News.* Blackthorne Records BR 1067. 1986.
*Kilroy Was Here.* Blackthorne Records BR 1063. 1980.
*Living Folk.* Albatross VPA 8093.
*The Long Harvest,* vols. 1–10. Argo DA 66–75. 1966–68.
*Love Call Me Home.* Appleseed Recordings APR CD 1087. 2005.
*Love Will Linger On.* Appleseed Recordings 1039. 2000.
*A Lover's Garland.* Prestige International 13061. 1962.
*Manchester Angel.* Topic Records 12T 147. 1966.
*Matching Songs of Britain and America.* Riverside RLP 12-637. 1957.
*A Merry Progress to London.* Argo ZDA 46. 1966.
*Naming of Names.* Cooking Vinyl COOK 036. 1990.
*The New Briton Gazette.* Folkways Records FW 8732. 1960.
*The New Briton Gazette, Volume 2.* Folkways Records FW 8734. 1962.
*No Tyme Lyke the Present.* Larrikin EMC 2556. 1976.
*Now Is the Time for Fishing.* Folkways FG 3507. 1961.
*Obama Is the One for Me.* Timely Productions. 2008.
*An Odd Collection.* Rounder CD 4031. 1996.
*On the Edge.* Topic Records Ltd. TSCD 806. 2008.
*Our Singing Heritage.* Elektra RLPL 151. 1958.
*Outback Ballads.* Topic Records 12T51. 1960.
*The Paper Stage,* vols. 1–2. Argo ZDA 98–99. 1968.
*Parsley, Sage, and Politics: The Lives and Music of Peggy Seeger and Ewan MacColl.* CD 2004. 1985.
*Peaceful Woman, Fighting Hard.* Timely Productions. 2002.
*Peggy Alone.* Argo ZDA 81. 1967.
*Peggy 'n' Mike.* Argo ZDA 80. 1967.
*Peggy Seeger Live.* Appleseed Recordings APR CD 1129. 2012.
*Peggy Seeger Sings and Plays American Folksongs for Banjo.* Folk Lyric FL 114. Early 1960s.
*Peggy Seeger Teaches Guitar Accompaniment for Folk Songs, Ballads, and Originals.* DVD-PEG-GT21. 2012.
*Peggy Seeger, the Folkways Years 1955–1992: Songs of Love and Politics.* Smithsonian Folkways CD SF 40048. 1992.
*Penelope Isn't Waiting Any More.* Blackthorne Records BR 1050. 1976.
*Period Pieces.* Tradition Records TCD 1078. 1998.

*Poetry and Song*, vols. 1–14. Argo DA 50–63, ZDA 50–63, ZPL 1094–1107. 1967–68.

*Popular Ballads.* Folk Lyric FL 120. Early 1960s.

*Popular Scottish Songs.* Folkways Records FW 8757. 1960/1961.

*Primary Transmission.* Red Grape Records. 2007.

*Saturday Night at the Bull & Mouth.* Blackthorne BR 1055. 1977.

*Scots Drinking Songs.* Riverside RLP 12-605. 1956.

*Second Shift.* Topic Records 10T 25. 1958.

*Shine like a Star.* Topic Records TOP 38. 1957.

*Shuttle and Cage: Industrial Folk Ballads.* Topic Records 10T 13. 1957.

*Singing the Fishing.* Topic Records Ltd. TSCD 803. 2008.

*Solo Flight.* Argo ZFB 12. 1972.

*A Song for You and Me.* Prestige International 13058. 1962.

*Song of a Road.* Topic Records Ltd. TSCD 802. 2008.

*Songs against the Bomb.* Topic Records 12001. 1959.

*Songs for October 2004.* Timely Productions. 2004.

*Songs of Robert Burns.* Folkways FW 8758. 1959.

*Songs of Struggle.* AMWU 91. 1976.

*Songs of Two Rebellions: The Jacobite Wars of 1715 and 1745.* Folkways 8756. 1960.

*Steam Whistle Ballads.* Topic Records 12T 104. 1958.

*Still I Love Him.* Topic Records 10T 50. 1958.

*Sweet Thames Flow Softly.* Argo ZDA 47. 1966.

*Thar She Blows.* Riverside RLP 12-635. 1957.

*The Three Sisters.* Prestige International PR-INT 13029. 1957.

*The Travelling People.* Topic Records Ltd. TSCD 808. 2008.

*Three Score and Ten.* Appleseed Recordings APR CD 1100. 2007.

*Troubled Love.* Topic Records TOP 72. 1962.

*Two-Way Trip: American, Scots and English Folksongs sung by Peggy Seeger and Ewan MacColl.* Folkways Records FW 8755. 1961.

*Voices*, vols. 1–6. Argo DA 91–96. 1968.

*The Wanton Muse.* Argo DA 85. 1968.

*Waterloo-Peterloo.* Argo ZFB 68. 1968.

*We Are the Engineers/I'm Gonna Be an Engineer.* AUEW 1. 1975.

*We Sing America.* PYE NIXA NPT 19029. 1958.

*Whaler out of New Bedford.* Folkways Records FS 3850. 1962.

*White Wind, Black Tide.* Blackthorne BSC 2. 1986.

*Who's Going to Shoe Your Pretty Little Foot?* Topic Records 12T 113. 1964.

*The World of Ewan MacColl and Peggy Seeger.* Argo SPA-A 102. 1970.

*The World of Ewan MacColl and Peggy Seeger, Volume 2.* Argo SPA-A 216. 1972.

*Ye Mariners All.* Argo ZDA 138. 1971.

## Radio Broadcasts

*Landmarks.* BBC Midland Home Service. 1964.
*Lonesome Train.* CBS. March 21–22, 1944.
*Love Call Me Home: Peggy Seeger's Song of the Soul.* Northern Spirit Radio. May 2, 2010.
*My People and Your People.* BBC Home Service. July 22, 1959.
*Not Known in Denmark Street.* BBC Third Programme. 1962.
*Romeo and Juliet.* BBC Home Service for Schools. May 18 and 25, 1966.
*The Song Carriers.* BBC. Mid-1960s.

## Television Programs

*The Ballad of Ewan MacColl.* BBC 2. 1990.
*Before the Mast.* BBC 2. December 1971.
*The Big Hewer.* BBC 2. 1974.
*Daddy, What Did You Do in the Strike?* Granada Television. 1985.
*The Fight Game.* BBC 2. 1973.
*Folk Britannia,* part 1: "Ballads and Blues." BBC 4. February 3, 2006.
*Four People: A Ballad Film.* Dir. Guy Brenton. Morse Films/Ballad Films. 1962.
*The Good Old Way.* BBC 2. 1983.
*A Kind of Exile.* Granada Television. 1971.
*Kirsty: The Life and Songs of Kirsty MacColl.* BBC 2. 2001. http://www.bbc.co.uk.
*Sing in the New.* Granada Television. December 31, 1962.

## Internet Sources

"About Peggy." http://www.peggyseeger.com/about/whats-new/2003, accessed August 11, 2016.
"The Anticapitalist Roadshow." http://www.redmagic.co.uk/anticap/index.htm, accessed June 30, 2016.
"April–May." http://www.peggyseeger.com/about/whats-new/2006-2007, accessed August 11, 2016.
"Composer Elie Siegmeister: A Conversation with Bruce Duffie." 1987. http://www.kcstudio.com/sieg 2.html, accessed November 19, 2009.
"Declaration of the Occupation of New York City." 2011. http://www.nycga.net/resources/documents/declaration/, accessed June 30, 2016.
Dent-Robinson, Nick. "Peggy Seeger: Interview." August 27, 2012. http://www.peggyseeger.com/raves/interviews/nick-dent-robinson-27-08-2012, accessed September 18, 2012.
Eisler, Hanns. "The Birth of a Worker's Song." (1935) 1978. http://unionsong.com/reviews/peatbog.html, accessed November 6, 2009.

"February 2005." http://www.peggyseeger.com/about/whats-new/2005, accessed August 11, 2016.

"Folksploitation." http://broadcasteruk.com/folksploitation, accessed June 30, 2016.

Haymes, Greg. "Peggy and Pete Seeger at Proctors, 5/12/13." http://blog.timesunion .com/localarts/peggy-and-pete-seeger-at-proctors-51213/28003/, accessed June 30, 2016.

Hunt, Ken. *Q* magazine. http://www.peggyseeger.com/listen-buy/an-odd-collection /an-odd-collection-reviews/, accessed August 11, 2016.

"June–July." http://www.peggyseeger.com/about/whats-new/2006-2007, accessed August 11, 2016.

"Letters." http://www.peggyseeger.com/raves/letters, accessed June 30, 2016.

"March." http://www.peggyseeger.com/about/whats-new/2006-2007, accessed August 12, 2016.

Owen, Julian. "Peggy Seeger, Chapel Arts, Bath—Review." October 22, 2013. http:// www.bigissue.com/reviews/live-reviews/3144/peggy-seeger-chapel-arts-bath -review, accessed June 30, 2016.

Peggy Seeger Facebook page. https://www.facebook.com/PeggySeegerMusic, January 29, 2014.

"Peggy's Madison Avenue Square Letter to Pete." http://tinyurl.com/j6aucjb, accessed August 11, 2016.

Property deed recorded August 18, 1925. Montgomery County Circuit Court land records, PBR 382, page 169. http://www.mdlandrec.com, accessed July 25, 2015, website no longer available.

"Timely #01—Songs for October 2004." http://tinyurl.com/z2b9u5x, accessed August 11, 2016.

http://www.peggyseeger.com/about/whats-new/2008–2009/22b%20breastcancer ribbon.gif/view, accessed August 11, 2016.

http://www.peggyseeger.com/about/whats-new/2008–2009/24-NEU-students concert.JPG, accessed August 11, 2016.

## Conference Presentations

Cantwell, Robert. "The Politics of Pete." Presented at "How Can I Keep from Singing? The Seeger Family Tribute." March 16, 2007, Library of Congress, Washington, D.C.

Carroll, Jim. "The Critics Group." Paper presented at symposium in honor of Ewan MacColl's Seventieth birthday. March 1986, County Hall, London.

Greer, Taylor Aitkin. "The Legacy of Charles Seeger: Defying and Defining Tradition." Presented at "How Can I Keep from Singing? The Seeger Family Tribute." March 16, 2007, Library of Congress, Washington, D.C.

Rahn, Millie. "The 'It Changed My Life' Syndrome: The Folk Revival." Presented at "How Can I Keep from Singing? The Seeger Family Tribute." March 16, 2007, Library of Congress, Washington, D.C.

Rosenberg, Neil. "Family Values Seeger Style." Presented at "How Can I Keep from Singing? The Seeger Family Tribute." March 16, 2007, Library of Congress, Washington, D.C.

Seeger, Mike, with Ray Allen. "Integrating Documentation, Presentation and Performance." Presented at "How Can I Keep from Singing? The Seeger Family Tribute." March 16, 2007, Library of Congress, Washington, D.C.

Tick, Judith. "Ruth Crawford Seeger's Legacy." Presented at "How Can I Keep from Singing? The Seeger Family Tribute." March 16, 2007, Library of Congress, Washington, D.C.

# General Index

Photos appear on unnumbered pages following page 186 and are indexed by their order in the plate page sequence.

Adler, Guido, 20, 306n21
Almanac Singers, 33, 37, 107
Amalgamated Metal Workers' Union, 209
American Conservatory of Music, 13
American Folklore Society, 139
*American Songbag* (Sandburg), 14, 25
Anti-Capitalist Roadshow, 281, 283
anticommunism: academic folklore and, 139; folk music as target, 143; Moscow/China trip and, 99–100, 316n22; Pete Seeger HUAC testimony, 69, 75–76, 88, 137, 143, 153, 155; post–World War II ethos and, 42–43; Seegers as target, 51–52, 60. *See also* Communist Party
antinuclear movement: Beckenham Anti-Nuclear Group (BANG), 222–26, 233; Campaign for Nuclear Disarmament (CND), 131, 220, 223; Cold War Europe and, 120; Ewan and Peggy approaches to, 231; "Four-Minute Warning" approach, 219–20; Frances Crowe as activist for, 258–60; "The Invader" treatment of, 212–13; "The Plutonium Factor" treatment of, 219; Trafalgar Square action of 1959, 120, plate 6; *Uranium 235* (Ewan play), 85, 231, 330n47. *See also* peace movement
Archive of American Folk Song, 43, 135
Armstrong, Frankie: in the Anti-Capitalist Roadshow, 281; Critics Group and, 191, 199,

243; on Ewan, 168; in *The Female Frolic*, 182; on the Festival of Fools, 192–93, 196; in *The Other Music*, 220; on Peggy's lectures, 165–66; on the workers' theater troupe, 193
Axon, Gladys, 108–9, 112
Axon, John, 107–13

Baez, Joan, 96, 161–62, 164, 275, 300
Ball, Jay, 59, 60–62, 64, 69
"Ballad of Jimmy Massey" (song), 263–64, 333–34n37
"Ballad of Springhill, The" (song), 115–16, 130, 155
ballad opera, 121, 127
ballads: *Blood and Roses* series, 214, 220, 221, 231; as dramatic genre, 177; early exposure to, 2, 29; "Fair Ellender," 104; fondness for, 175, 222, 270; "The House Carpenter," 65; influence on compositions, 114–16, 156, 190, 212, 240, 250, 260, 263; *The Long Harvest* series, 183; "The Rich Irish Lady," 104
Ballads and Blues Club (London), 86–87, 106, 144–45, plate 4, 314n19
Balls, Ronnie, 125, 128
Bartók, Béla, 300, 306n19
Becher, Johannes R., 20
Beckenham Anti-Nuclear Group (BANG), 223, 226, 233
Beer, Molly, 296
Behan, Dominic, 153
Belfrage, Cedric, 100
Belfrage, Sally, 100
Benbow, Steve, 147

Bennett, Martyn, 283
Benton, Thomas Hart, 20, 22
Bertha (housekeeper), 28
Bettelheim, Bruno, 42
Blackthorne Records, 208–9, 210, 214, 226
Blaustein, Richard, 298
Blitzstein, Marc, 16, 17
Boggs, Dock, 276
Botkin, Benjamin, 27, 44, 142–43, 295, 300
Bouquillon, Elias, 270–71
boxing profession (Radio Ballad subject), 162–63
Boyes, Georgina, 298, 303
Bragg, Billy, 239, 264–65, 275
Brecht, Bertolt, 18–19, 323n24
Bridson, Geoffrey, 121
Bright, Ben, 203, 213
Britten, Benjamin, 153
Broadcaster (musician), 282–83
Broonzy, Big Bill, 87, 96
Brown, Helen, 253
Buchan, Norman and Janey, 93
Buchanan, Annabel Morris, 141–42
Burkett, Lyn Ellen, 15
Burns, Robert, 259, 333n24

Calico, Joy H., 20
Cameron, Isla, 87, 106, 144
Campbell, Alex, 117, 153
Cantwell, Robert, 269, 294
Caravan, Guy, 97–100, 102, 106, **plate 5**, 315n11
Caravan, Noel (Noel Osheroff), 97, 100, 102, 316n20
Carroll, Jim, 164, 168, 217
Carter, Sydney, 146–47
Carthy, Eliza, 264
Carthy, Martin, 87, 150, 220, 264, 271
Cash, Johnny, 95
Chase, Gilbert, 213
Child, Francis James, 139, 169
Chile, Pinochet regime in, 233
civil rights movement, 42, 132, 196, 265, 315n11, 319n37
Clancy Brothers, 94
Clayton, Paul, 106
coal mining (Radio Ballad subject), 150–52, 154
Cohen, Ronald D., 295–96
Cohen, Rufus (son of Penny), 245
Coleman, Fitzroy, 82, 106, 111, 144

Collett, Valborg, 13
Collins, Judy, 162
Collins, Shirley, 89–91, 169, 314n33
Communist Party: Almanac Singers and, 37; Charles Seeger affiliation, 18, 22, 33, 60; Composers' Collective, 17–21, 25, 305n11, 306n19; *Daily Worker* music writings, 18; Ewan MacColl affiliation, 84, 88–89; folk music approaches and, 143; Pete Seeger affiliation, 33, 60; Pierre Degeyter Club, 17, 305n11; World War II isolationism and, 33. *See also* anticommunism
Composers' Collective, 17–21, 25, 305n11, 306n19
Copland, Aaron, 17, 19
Corwin, Norman, 107–8, 124
Cotten, Elizabeth "Libba," 41, 189, 244, 276
counterculture, 181
Cowell, Henry, 8, 11, 14, 16, 17, 213
Cowell, Sydney, 239
Cox, Harry, 165, 220
Cox, Peter, 171, 323n43
Cramer, Sonya (daughter of Penny), 236, 245, 247
Crawford, Carl (maternal uncle), 12, 62
Crawford, Clara (maternal grandmother), 12–13
Crawford, Clark (maternal grandfather), 11–12
Critics Group, The: breakup effect on Ewan, 199–200, 208; dissolution of, 196–98; Festival of Fools productions, 177–79, 189, 191–94; founding, 164–68; productions and recordings, 174, 177–86, 189, 203; reconciliation among members, 243; songwriting and, 270; vocal style and, 301
Cronin, Elisabeth, 165
Crowe, Frances, 258–60
Culver, Ted, 174

Daly, Brian, 154
Damrosch, Frank, 10–11, 21
Davidson, Ian, 245
Davies, Clive, 304
Dawson, Alice, 201, 207
Dent-Robinson, Nick, 282–83
Desai, Jayaben, 214
Dickens, Hazel, 222, 276
"Different Tunes" (song), 233, 240, 253, 300–301
Dion, Celine, 95
Dobie, Frank, 138–39

Donnellan, Philip, 203, 220
Dornbush, Adrian J., 22
Dorson, Richard, 138–39
Dubliners (band), 115
Dunaway, David King, 33, 137, 269, 296–97
Dunlop, Mona, 16
Dunson, Josh, 249
Dylan, Bob, 96, 155, 161, 164, 286

economy, labor and. *See* labor and economy
Edson, Constance (stepmother), 7–11, 17, 21, 91–92
Edwards, Alf, 149, 154
Eisler, Hanns, 18–20, 42, 83
Eliot, T. S., 9
Elliott, Ramblin' Jack, 120, 161, 275
El Salvador, political violence in, 231
"Emily" (song), 204, 212, 292
Emrich, Duncan, 43
Engel, Carl, 135
English Folk Dance and Song Society (EFDSS), 135, 137, 146–47, 177, 232, 314n15
Ennis, Seamus, 82, 87, 106, 123, 300
environmental movement, 212, 222–26, 230–31, 240, 251
Epstein, Freyda, 249
ethnomusicology, 44, 153, 294–95, 306n19, 306n21. *See also* folk music; musicology

family life: in Beckenham, 153, 158–59, 173, 191, 200–203, 205–8, 241–42; Betsy Miller and, 116, 118–20, 129, 153, 158–59, 188–89, 206, 221; in Cambridge apartment, 63–64, 66–67, 69–71; in Chevy Chase house, 1, 38, 39–53, 62, **plate 2**; children's duties, 41–42; Christmas celebration, 29, 58, 66, 68; father-children relationships, 45; financial austerity, 17, 21–22, 26, 29; housekeepers, 28, 30, 40–41, 43, 46, 188–89, 201, 207; Margaret Taylor and, 66–67, 70, 72–74; Peggy views on, 56, 185, 188; Puritan radicalism, 53, 143; religious belief and practice, 58, 67–68, 80; Seeger family photos, **plates 1–2**; in Silver Spring house, 28–38. *See also entries for specific family members*
Faulkner, John, 169, 197–98
Federal Music Project, 27, 35
feminism: Calum views of, 226, 260–61; Critics Group and, 191–93; domestic violence as song topic, 204, 212, 214,

240–41, 292; Ewan-Peggy relationship and, 128, 129–30, 131–32, 176, 193, 204–5, 226; Inez domestic role and, 77–78; Irene Pyper-Scott relationship and, **plate 10**, 226, 232–38; Jade women's singing group, 232–33, 237–38, 253; proposed women's Radio Ballad, 204–5; Rosie the Riveter model and, 42; Ruth Crawford Seeger and, 28, 29–30, 36, 45–46; socialist, 204, 208, 328n24; women in *John Axon*, 111; women in *Singing the Fishing*, 127–28, 131; women in *Song of a Road*, 123–24; Women's Peace Camp at Greenham Common, 223–26, 233.
—Peggy Seeger compositions: "Darling Annie," 192; "Emily," 204, 212; "Housewife's Alphabet," 204; "I'm Gonna Be an Engineer," 192–93, 198, 203–5, 214, 244, 253, 265, 292; "The Invader," 212–13; "The Judge's Chair," 250–51; "Lady, What Do You Do All Day," 204; "My Friend Pat," 240–41; *Needs Must When the Devil Drives* (film music), 232–33; "Nightshift," 192; "Nine Month Blues," 204; "Talking Matrimony Blues," 204; "Winnie and Sam," 204
Ferris, Paul, 124
Festival of Fools, 177–82, 187, 191–93, 196–98, 293, 324n19
Filene, Benjamin, 297–98
Finlay, John, 134
"First Time Ever I Saw Your Face, The" (song): awards, 202; dissemination of, 86, 95; Earl Robinson on, 161–62; inspiration for, 3, 94–96, 292; "Love Unbidden" references to, 234–35; lyrics, 95; in *My People and Your People*, 121; Peggy performances and recordings of, 96, 172, 189, 244, 254, 265, 282–83, 300, 304; Roberta Flack recording of, 95, 187–88, 200, 202; structure of, 95–96
Fischer, Ernst, 270
Flack, Roberta, 95, 187–88, 200, 202
Fleming, Jacky, 253
Folk Alliance, 293
folk music: academic folklore and, 133–40, 294–99; Appalachia significance for, 93, 103, 135–36, 142; authenticity and, 22, 134–36, 138–40, 147–50, 297–98, 301–3; Charles Seeger views on, 10, 18, 22, 24–25, 27, 140, 142–43; folk song definition, 133, 143, 160; Mike Seeger interest in, 3, 50, 103–4, 149, 211–12, 236, 258; Pete Seeger and, 44–45;

political theories of, 140, 142–43; radio broadcasts of, 86–87, 107; Resettlement Administration use of, 24–25; romantic nationalism and, 139–43, 297; Ruth Crawford Seeger arrangements/adaptations, 14, 25–26, 34–35; Ruth Crawford Seeger influence from, 37; in Seeger household, 31–32; at UC Berkeley, 8
—Collections: Alan Lomax and, 314n14; *American Folk Songs for Children* (Ruth Crawford Seeger), 37, 43–44, 103–4, 142, 211; *Animal Folk Songs for Children* (Ruth Crawford Seeger), 44, 105, 243, 245; Charles Seeger influences from, 20–21; *The Essential Ewan MacColl Songbook*, 256–57; *Ewan MacColl–Peggy Seeger Songbook*, 176; folk revival and, 138–39, 295; *Folk Songs and Ballads of Scotland* (Peggy and Ewan), 176; *The Folk Songs of North America* (Peggy transcriptions), 130, 315n40; Hanns Eisler and Johannes R. Becher collection, 20; history of, 134–36, 259; *The Peggy Seeger Songbook*, 249, 252–53; Ruth Crawford Seeger arrangements/adaptations, 26, 34–35; Ruth Crawford Seeger transcriptions, 14, 26; Shirley Collins and, 314n33; *The Singing Island* (Peggy and Ewan), 118, 130; *Songs for the Sixties* (Peggy and Ewan), 159
folk revival: antiquarian approach in, 68–69, 135–37, 298–99; Asheville as site for, 257; British, 83, 85–87, 89, 90, 132, 135–37, 169; defining features of, 295–99; *Folk Britannia* retrospective film, 150, 169; folk clubs and, ix, 87, 106, 144–50, 173, 186; Folklore Center role in, 97, 315n9; *Folksploitation* approach to, 282–83; hootenannies, 55, 63; Peggy songwriting course, 270–71; retrospective programs on, 150, 169, 220, 226–27; scholarship on, 294–95, 299, 302, 309n44, 319n37, 320n19, 321n31; schools and, 136; Singers Club policy, 144–50, 160–61, 301–2; theatrical performance and, 166–67, 173–75, 177–82, 187, 191–94, 196–98, 301; urban folklore and, 27, 59, 64, 86, 137, 295–96, 298–300; Warrenton, Va., country music contest, 50
Folsom, Lin Frothingham, 47–49
Foster, Bertha, 12–13
Foster, Jeremy, 51–52, 55, 58, 62, 63, 66
Frankenstein, Alfred, 14
Freedman, Jean, **plate 12**
Freedom Singers, 319n37

Gilbert, Ronnie, 44
Gilles (college boyfriend of Peggy), 63–64, 66, 67–68, 70–71, 74–75
Gladden, Texas, 2
Goldstein, Kenneth, 138, 193
Good, Amber, 192
Gordon, Robert Winslow, 138
Great Depression: European fascism/Nazism and, 33; "homesteads" of farmers and workers, 23–25; Seeger family austerity, 5, 11, 17, 21–22. *See also* New Deal
Greenbriar Boys, 61, 161
Greene, Felix, 193
Greenhill, Manny, 191
Greenway, John, 138–39
Greer, Taylor Aitken, 269
Grimm Brothers (Jacob and Wilhelm), 19, 134
Grossman, Albert, 96
Gunning, Sarah Ogan, 132, 176, 262
Guthrie, Arlo, 275
Guthrie, Woody, 32, 37, 44, 83, 87, 90, 132, 143

Hamessley, Lydia, 234–35
Hamilton, Diane, 94, 103
Hand, Wayland, 139
Handler, Richard, 299
Hansen, Susan Forbes, 289
Harker, Ben, 83, 126, 313n11
Harris, Emmylou, 275
Harrison, Mamie, 40, 189
Harvey-Piper, Kerry (wife of Calum), 261, 286
Haufrecht, Herbert, 25
Havens, Richie, 275
Hawes, Bess Lomax, 34
Hayeem, Benji, 59
Hays, Lee, 44, 75
Heaney, Joe, 165, 169
Hellerman, Fred, 44
Henderson, Hamish, 85, 132, 137–38, 239, 313–14n11
Herder, Johann Gottfried, 133–34, 139–40, 297, 319n3
Herrmann, John, 272
Herz, Djane Lavoie, 13–14
Herzog, George, 26
Higgins, Lizzie, 283
Hill, Joe, 19–20, 132, 334n43
Hindemith, Paul, 8
Hinton, Carmelita, 47, 49
Ho Chi Minh, 185
Hogan, Muriel, 222
Hood, Mantle, 213

Hornbostel, Erich von, 306n21
HUAC. *See* anticommunism
Hunt, Ken, 292
Hurston, Zora Neale, 314n14

Idoine, Lucienne, 116
"I Have a Rendezvous with Death" (song, Alan Seeger), 9
"I'm Gonna Be an Engineer" (song), 192–93, 198, 203–5, 214, 244, 253, 265, 292
Industrial Workers of the World (IWW), 8
Institute of Musical Art (Julliard School), 10, 17, 21
International Folk Music Council (IFMC), 138
Iraq War, 263–64, 333–34n37
Irish Folklore Commission, 137
Irwin, Colin, 304
Ives, Burl, 107
Ives, Charles, 16

Jabbour, Alan, 294
Jackson, Aunt Molly, 21, 22, 24, 132, 182, 250, 272
Jackson, Bruce, 297
Jade (singing group), 232–33, 237–38, 253
Jagger, Mick, 87
James, Mary Ann, 40–41, 43, 46
jazz: in *Ballads and Blues* programs, 87; Charles Seeger views on, 9; John and Alan Lomax disdain for, 136; in *John Axon*, 112; in Peggy's recordings, 245–46, 288, 302; Polish audience requests for, 102; Resettlement Administration and, 24
Jenkins, Hezekiah, 280
Johnson, James, 259
Jones, Jennifer, 233
Jones, Mary Harris "Mother," 331n67
"Judge's Chair, The" (song), 250–51

Kahn, Alfie, 154
Kahn, Si, 222
Karpeles, Helen, 314n16
Karpeles, Maud, 93–94, 116, 135–36, 314n16
Kennedy, Douglas, 314n16
Kennedy, Peter, 86, 133, 314n16
Kerr, Sandra, 158–59, 166–67, 182, 186, 193–94, 196–98, 199, 243, 281
Killen, Louis (Louisa Jo Killen), 149, 156, 165, 220, 239
King, Charlie, 222
Kitson, Dave, 226
Kittredge, George Lyman, 21

Korean War, 49, 103
Korson, George, 139
Kristofferson, Kris, 275

Laban, Rudolf, 84, 167
labor and economy: balancing work and family, 26, 28, 30, 34–35, 36–37, 40–41, 43, 191–92, 204–5; Britain miners' strike of 1984, 227–31, 233; Charles Seeger labor observations, 8, 23–24; China and the Soviet Union, 101–2; coal mining in *The Big Hewer*, 150–52, 154, 203, 228–29; engine driving in *The Ballad of John Axon*, 110–13; feminist approach to, 204–5, 214; Festival of Fools and, 192–93; fishermen in *Singing the Fishing*, 125–28, 131, 152, 154, 203; folk music as progressive tool, 20–21, 105, 143; Granada series, 90; industrialization as Radio Ballad theme, 124; Occupy Wall Street and, 279–81, 335n4; peace movement and, 259; as Peggy composition theme, 131–32; protest songs and, 190; road building in *Song of a Road*, 121–24, 157; women in British trade union movement, 214, 232
labor songs, 149, 153, 264–65, 273; American, 19–21, 90, 131–32, 265, 273, 280
Lampell, Millard, 107–8
Lange, Don, 222
Larner, Sam, 125–28, 152, 165, 220
Lassiter, Christine, 257–58, 265, 333n20
Lavoie-Herz, Djane, 13–14
Leach, MacEdward, 139
Leadbelly (Huddie Ledbetter), 26, 44, 45, 87, 145
Lennon, John, 87
Lessing, Doris, 153
Levy, Heniot, 13
Leydi, Roberto, 184
Lieberman, Robbie, 296
Lindsay, Hugh and Sally, 80–81
Linnekin, Jocelyn, 299
Lippman, Dave, 280
Littlewood, Joan, 84, 193
Livingston, Tamara, 294
Lloyd, A. L. "Bert": as *Ballads and Blues* artist, 86–87; death of, 221; in *The Other Muse* folk revival documentary, 220; Peggy collaboration with, 106, 116, 130; Peggy-Ewan relationship and, 116, 119; Pete Seeger benefit concert and, 153; Singers Club policy and, 144, 149, 161; *Whaler out of New*

*Bedford* score and, 149; as working-class artist, 86, 108

Lomax, Alan: *American Ballads and Folk Songs*, 20, 26, 135–36; *American Folk Guitar* (with Peggy), 105; British folk revival and, 86–87, 90, 220; collaboration with Charles and Ruth Crawford Seeger, 3, 29, 30, 34, 43; collaboration with Peggy, 105–6; death of, 264; Ewan MacColl and, 85–86, 108, 232, 239; on folk music, 135–37, 297–98; as folk music collector, 3, 20–21, 26, 130, 135–36, 314n14, 314n19, 314n33; as Seeger family friend, 2, 22, 43–44, 80–83, 300; views on transcription, 34–35

Lomax, Anna, 89

Lomax, Elizabeth, 89

Lomax, John, 20–21, 22, 26, 43, 86, 135–36

London Co-operative Society, 173–74, 200

"Love Call Me Home" (song), 257–58

"Love Unbidden" (song), 234–35

Lowenthal, David, 289

Lunsford, Bascom Lamar, 25, 26

Lynskey, Dorian, 284–85

Lyttelton, Humphrey, 87

MacColl, Calum (son): birth of Kitty and, 200–202; *Black and White* Ewan tribute selections, 242; childhood, 158–59, 175, 188–89, 200–202, 206; collaborations with Broadcaster, 282–83; death of Ewan and, 239, 241; family performances and recordings, **plate 9**, 216, 228, 236; *Home* trilogy, 260–62; Irene Pyper-Scott relationship and, 242; mastery of folk instruments, 210, 236; political views, 205, 231, 260–61; productions with Peggy and Irene, 245, 249, 253–54, 255–56, 266, 286–87; Queen Elizabeth Hall concert, 304; rock music interests, 220–21; song written for, 260

MacColl, Ewan, **plates 7–9**; antiwar writing by, 174–76, 181–82, 185–86; *Black and White* retrospective recording, 242; British Conservative Party and, 218–19; as Critics Group leader, 164–68, 177–84, 191–94, 196–98, 199–200; death and remembrance of, 238, 239; dramatic approach to folk music, 105, 151–52, 164–69, 227; environmental movement and, 230–31; Ewan MacColl/Peggy Seeger Archive, 278; feminism and, 128, 131–32, 193, 204–5, 226; folk influences

in songwriting, 95–96, 108–13, 127, 137, 157–58; as folk music "purist," 90, 130, 133–34, 160–61; health issues, 193–94, 207–8, 213, 215, 216, 221, 231–33; labor advocacy, 111–12, 122, 130–32, 155, 227–31, 237; leftist folk music approach, 83–87, 131–32, 143, 170–72, 184–85, 208, 212; Marxist background, 84, 88–89, 99, 143; Peggy early relationship with, 13, 83, 88–97, 99, 113–17, 118–20; Singers Club policy and, 144–50, 160–61, 301–2; theater background, 84–88, 166–67, 178, 194, 323n24; upbringing, 82–84, 90
—Selected works: *The Ballad of John Axon* (Radio Ballad), 108–13, 121–27; *The Big Hewer* (Radio Ballad), 150–52, 154, 203, 228–29; *The Body Blow* (Radio Ballad), 155; *Burning Light* (television documentary), 129; "Dirty Old Town," 86, 90, 187, 270–71; *On the Edge* (Radio Ballad), 156–58; Festival of Fools productions, 177–82, 187, 191–93, 196–98, 324n19, 325n31; *The Fight Game* (Radio Ballad), 162–64, 203; *Journeyman* (autobiography), 242; "The Joy of Living," 95, 231–32, 242, 330n48; "Manchester Rambler," 84–85, 90, 109; *Ours the Fruit* (play), 174–75; "The Shoals of Herring," 86, 127, 189, 296; *Singing the Fishing* (Radio Ballad), 125–28, 131, 152, 154; *Song of a Road* (Radio Ballad), 121–27, 157; "Sweet Thames, Flow Softly," 95, 182, 189; *The Travelling People* (Radio Ballad), 169–72. *See also* "First Time Ever I Saw Your Face, The" (song)

MacColl, Hamish (son of Ewan and Jean Newlove)): birth and childhood, 85, 88, 89, 92, 313–14n11; family tensions and, 94, 116–17, 118–20, 129, 153, 191

MacColl, Jamie (son of Neill), 238, 331n68

MacColl, Kirsty (daughter of Ewan and Jean Newlove)), 120, 153, 209, 221, 238, 241, 256, 331n68

MacColl, Kitty (daughter), **plates 8, 11**; childhood, 200–202, 207, 210, 215, 216, 221, 223, 225; Ewan's illness, death, and aftermath, 231, 233, 241–43; musical life, 236, 245, 249–51, 253, 254, 256, 260–62; political views, 223, 225, 261; songs composed for, 218, 233, 290

MacColl, Neill (son): *Black and White* Ewan tribute selections, 242; childhood, 118–20, 129, 153, 158–59, 175, 188, 200–201, 205–6; Ewan's illness, death, and aftermath, 215,

232, 241–42; family performances and recordings, **plate 9**, 209, 216; *Home* trilogy, 260, 262; marriage to Kate St. John, **plate 12**, 286; mastery of folk instruments, 210; on Peggy's vocal style, 64; productions with Peggy and Irene, 244–45, 249, 253–54, 256, 287; Queen Elizabeth Hall concert, 304; rock music interests, 205–6, 220–21; song written for, 191
MacDiarmid, Hugh (Christopher Grieve), 93
MacDowell, Marian, 15, 16
MacDowell Colony (New Hampshire), 14–15, 16
MacGregor, Ian, 229
MacGregor, Jimmie, 93
Mackenzie, Pat, 168
Makem, Tommy, 94
Malone, Bill, 276, 309n44
Massey, Jimmy, 263–64, 333–34n37
McCarthyism. *See* anticommunism
McCurdy, Ed, 99, 129
McDonagh, Maggie, 165
McKay, Ann, 252
McNaughtan, Adam, 93
Mellencamp, John, 275
Miller, Betsy (mother of Ewan), 116, 118–20, 129, 153, 158–59, 188–89, 207, 221
Mills, Susan, 2, 82–83, 89
Morris, Denis, 121–22
Morrison, Van, 87
Mountain Dance and Folk Festival (Asheville, N.C.), 25
Muir, Jane, 227
mumming plays, 174–75, 177, 324n4
Munro, Ailie, 295
musicology: Charles Seeger and, 8, 10, 20, 60, 213, 306n21; comparative, 20; dissonant counterpoint, 8, 14, 15–16. *See also* ethnomusicology

National Coal Board, 129, 175
Nazism: Great Depression and, 33; postwar neo-, 180; rise of, 17, 18–20, 33, 139–40, 299; Travellers and, 171–72; use of folk culture, 18–20, 139–40, 299. *See also* World War II
New Deal: Charles and Ruth Crawford Seeger views on, 5, 22, 23–24, 33–34, 142–43; Special Skills Division philosophy, 5, 23–24; Works Progress Administration, 27–28, 142–43. *See also* Resettlement Administration

New Lost City Ramblers, 161, 177
Newlove (MacColl), Jean (wife of Ewan): Ewan death and, 238; Ewan marriage to, 84–85; Ewan-Peggy early relationship and, 88–89, 92, 94, 114, 116–17; Godstone Road household and, 118–20, 129; Kirsty death and, 256; reflections on her marriage, 313n10; Soviet Union trip, 99; Stanley Avenue household and, 153
New School for Social Research, 11, 17, 21
Nice, Mahala, 209

Obama, Barack, 274–75
O'Boyle, Sean, 133
O'Casey, Sean, 153
Occupy Wall Street/Occupy St. Paul, 279–81, 335n4
O'Connor, Jim, 194, 243
Odetta (singer), 96
O'Rourke, Michael, 227
Orr, Mary, 227
Osheroff, Noel (Noel Carawan), 97, 100, 102, 316n20
Owen, Julian, 293

Paley, Tom, 177
Pan American Union, 35–36, 52
Parker, Charles: *The Ballad of John Axon* production, 107–10, 113; *The Big Hewer* production, 150; *The Body Blow* production, 154–55; Critics Group founding and, 164, 167; death, 220; *On the Edge* production, 156–57; *The Fight Game* production, 162–63; "Folk and Song" weekend, 153; *Not Known in Denmark Street* production, 155–56; *Singing the Fishing* production, 125–26, 128; *Song of a Road* production, 116, 121–22, 124–25; *The Travelling People* production, 169, 172; as *Whaler out of New Bedford* singer, 149
Paul, Alice, 15
Paxton, Tom, 275
peace movement: Charles Seeger pacifist views, 8–9, 49–50; Greenham Common Women's Peace Camp, 223–26, 233; Iraq War and, 263–64, 333–34n37; *Peaceful Woman, Fighting Hard*, 258–60; Vietnam War and, 174–76, 178, 181–82, 185–86, 190, 196, 203, 258. *See also* antinuclear movement
Pearson, Brian: on Critics Group antiwar

activism, 185–86; Critics Group dissolution, 196, 199; as Critics Group member, 165, 167–68; Critics Group reconciliation, 243; Critics Group theater productions, 174–75, 193–94; on the Festival of Fools, 178–79, 192; as Singers Club patron, 150

People's Songs (organization), 44, 69, 132

Percy, Thomas, 134

Pescatello, Ann, 211, 309n44

Petrie, Grace, 281

Pinochet regime in Chile, 233

plays. *See* theater

polio (Radio Ballad subject), 154–55

Popular Front, 22

popular music: Charles Seeger views on, 9, 17, 24, 45; covers of Ewan's songs, 95, 187–88, 200, 202; Festival of Fools parody of, 187; "The First Time Ever" appeal and, 96; *Folksploitation* and, 282–83; Kirsty's interest in, 221, 256; Neill and Calum's interest in, 210, 220–21; working-class tastes and, 24, 217

Posen, I. Sheldon, 298

Poston, Annette Dapp, 43, 46, 51

Powell, Enoch, 190–91

Powell, John, 140–42

Powell (Scheider), Nina, 78–79

Presley, Elvis, 95

Pyper-Scott, Irene, **plate 10**; death of Ewan and, 239, 243; move to Asheville, 249, 252, 267; New Zealand house, 268–69, 271, 275, 277, 284, 304; Peggy civil union ceremony, 268–69; Peggy performances/recordings with, 237–38, 240, 243–46, 253–56, 260, 264–65, 271; Peggy relationship with, 226, 232–38, 240, 242, 249–50, 252, 268, 269, 271; personal background, 226

Pyper's Place coffeehouse, 252, 263, 267

Quarrymen, The (music group), 87

race and racialsm: in Chevy Chase, 39; civil rights movement, 42, 132, 265, 315n11, 319n37; folklore views, 140–43; politics of, 185; postwar British violence, 120–21; in Seeger household, 30, 40–41; South African apartheid, 185, 198, 203, 212, 226, 231, 233, 242

Radio Ballads: albums influenced by, 222, 227–30, 242, 260; *The Ballad of John Axon* (1958), 107–13, 121–25, 127; BBC television

adaptations (1972–74), 203; *The Big Hewer* (1961), 150–52, 154, 203, 228, 229; *The Body Blow* (1961), 154–55; *On the Edge* (1963), 156–58; *The Fight Game* (1963), 162–64, 203; folk music radio broadcasts, 110, 121–24, 126–28; *Singing the Fishing* (1960), 125–28, 131, 152, 154, 203; *Song of a Road* (1959), 121–27, 157; *The Travelling People* (1964), 169–72; women's, proposed (1970s), 204–5; *The World of Ewan MacColl and Peggy Seeger, Vol. 2* (1972), 203

Radley, Jean-Pierre, 59, 61–62, 64

Rahn, Millie, 269

Ramblers, The (music group), 3, 82–83, 89–91, 94

Randolph, Vance, 139

Reagon, Bernice Johnson, 275, 319n37

Reece, Florence, 132

Resettlement Administration, 5, 22–26. *See also* New Deal

Reuss, Richard, 296, 321n31

Rinzler, Ralph: as accompanist on Peggy's recordings, 104–6; Ballads and Blues Club performance, **plate 4**; death, 247; "Old Friend" tribute to, 251–52, 311n34; Peggy European travels and, 103, 116; Peggy meeting with, 61; as Seeger family friend, 61, 66, 76, 97; as Smithsonian Folklife Festival founder, 61, 254

Ritchie, Jean, 87

road building (Radio Ballad subject), 121–27, 157

Robertson, Jeannie, 93

Robertson, Sidney, 25

Robeson, Paul, 44, 75, 120, 153, **plate 6**

Robinson, Earl, 17, 19–20, 107, 161–62

Robinson, Robert, 124

romantic nationalism, 140–43, 297

Rosen, Mike, 194

Rosenberg, Neil, 269, 294

Rosselson, Leon, 281

Rudhyar, Dane, 14

Rueb, Anneke, 78

Ruskin College, 213, 243; Ewan MacColl/ Peggy Seeger Archive, 278

Russell, Bertrand, 8

Sachs, Curt, 306n21

Saletan, Tony, 59, 69, 312n59

Samuel, Raphael, 213

Sandburg, Carl, 14, 25, 26, 44

Sanders, Barry, 270
Saville, Ian, 281
Schlein, Irving, 315n8
Schlein, Peter, 97, 315n8
Schoenberg, Arnold, 8, 18
Schwarz, Tracy, 177
Scott, Irene. *See* Pyper-Scott, Irene
Scully, Michael F., 295–96
Seeger, Alan (paternal uncle), 6, 9, 49, 271–72
Seeger (Miserantino), Barbara (sister): childhood, 1, 26, 28–29, 31–32, 36, 40–41, 45, 56–58, 62–63, **plates 1–2**; Mar relationship with, 73–74; move to Cambridge, 67, 70; Peggy recordings with, 68, 103, 245
Seeger, Charles (father), **plate 2**; anticommunism and, 52, 76–77, 88–89; birth and upbringing, 5–7; California move, 71, 72–74; as composer, 7–9, 17–18, 20–21, 34–35; Composers' Collective, 17–21, 306n19; death, 213–14; early exposure to folk music, 10, 18–19, 20–22; Federal Music Project position, 27–28, 35; as folk music arranger/adapter, 34–35; folk music as family vocation, 43–44; on folk music as living tradition, 142, 291; as folk music collector, 24–27, 136–37; folk music cultural tolerance approach, 140, 142–43; Latin American music, 7, 35–36, 52; marriage to Constance Edson, 7–10, 16–17, 91–92; marriage to Margaret (Mar) Taylor, 1, 63, 66–67, 70–71, 129, 153; marriage to Ruth Crawford, 17; Marxist folk music approach and, 17–19, 24; as musicologist, 8–10, 15, 17, 20–21, 44, 153, 213–14, 306n21; pacifism, 8–9, 49–50; Peggy relationship with, 45, 58–60, 88–89, 213–14, 290; personality, 30–31; principled character of, 8–9, 27, 290; Resettlement Administration folk music approach, 5, 22–26; Seeger family tribute, 269; support for Pete, 75–76; as teacher, 8–9, 10, 11, 12, 13, 20, 56, 60; working-class sympathies, 8–9; World War II political views, 33–34
—Letters from Peggy (1953–79, in chronological order): on her upbringing, 55–56; on Ruth's illness and death, 56–58; on Ewan, 89, 91; on China and the Soviet Union, 102; on the birth of Neill, 119; on the British peace movement, 120; on the miners' strike, 150; on the birth of Calum,

159; on folk music as class ideology, 168–69; on visiting the United States, 173, 189–90; on the Vietnam War, 175–76, 185, 190; on Ewan's talents, 176; on touring, 129, 184; on her stature in the British revival, 184–85; on family struggles, 187, 189, 207–8, 213; on the Festival of Fools, 193–94; on the Critics Group breakup, 197–98, 200; on the birth of Kitty, 200–201
—Letters to Peggy (1953–79, in chronological order): on Pete's HUAC testimony, 75–76; on Ewan's political ties, 88–89; on Ewan, 91; on travel in China, 100; on the birth of Neill, 119
—Selected works: *Folk Songs of Courting and Complaint* liner notes, 64; *Folk Song U.S.A.* (music editor), 43; "Inter-American Relations in the Field of Music," 36; "John Hardy" adaptation, 34–35; "Journal of a Field Representative," 23–24; "On Proletarian Music," 17–18; *Treasury of American Folklore* (music consultant), 143
Seeger, Charles, Sr. (paternal grandfather), 5–7, 11, 27
Seeger, Charles, III (half-brother), 8, 27, 32, 45, 49, 67, 76–78, 264, 313n26
Seeger, Chris (son of Mike), 276
Seeger, Elizabeth "Elsie" (paternal aunt), 6, 53, 54, 58
Seeger, Ellie (wife of John), 62
Seeger, Elsie Adams (paternal grandmother), 6, 11, 17, 21–22, 27
Seeger, Jeremy (son of Charles III), 77
Seeger, Jeremy (son of Mike), 276
Seeger, John (half-brother), 8, 16, 45, 49, 62, 277
Seeger, Kim (son of Mike), 236, 276
Seeger, Mike (brother): *American Folk Songs Sung by the Seegers*, 103–5; birth, 17; childhood, 22, 23–24, 28–32, 35, 38, 40–41, **plates 1–2**; Conscientious Objector status, 49–50, 103; death, 275–76; early musical experiences, 43, 45, 50; education, 47, 49–50; folk music performance, 50, 61, 177; marriage to Alexia Smith, 249; mastery of Appalachian music, 50, 103–4, 149, 269, 276, 302; New Lost City Ramblers, 161, 177; Peggy performances with, 177; Peggy recordings with, 183, 211–12, 236, 245, 258–59, 264–65, 278–79; Peggy relationship with, 28–29, 48, 50, 60

Seeger, Naomi S. (daughter of Charles III),
76–77
Seeger, Peggy: awards, 128, 232, 275, 287, 293;
as banjo player, 2, 50, 82–83, 130; Charles
relationship with, 45, 55–60, 66–67, 70,
72–74, 88–89, 91, 213–14, 290; dual national
identity, 119, 129, 147–49, 189–90, 194–96,
222, 246, 247, 277; Dutch language study,
1, 74; education, 43, 45–49, 51–52, 55–63,
67, 70, 77, 81; Ewan Marxist background
and, 88–89, 143, 155; feminism importance
for, 191–92, 203–6, 226, 232, 250–51; Irene
Pyper-Scott relationship, **plate 10**, 226,
232–38, 240, 242, 249–50, 252, 268–69, 271;
miners' strike and, 228–31; musical training,
32, 43, 44, 58; musical transcriptions,
43–44; Occupy Wall Street and, 279–81;
personality, 30–31, 48, 51, 59–60, 66–70,
206–7; political convictions, 184–86, 189–
91, 195–96, 222–26, 231; Russian language
study, 63, 70, 77–78, 98; Ruth relationship
with, 56, 233, 289–91; Seeger family
politics, 68–69, 290; songwriting approach,
270–71; stature as folk artist, 161–62, 184–85,
221–22, 254, 292, 300; theory of authentic
performance, 145–49, 300–302; traditional
form as creative source and, 114–15, 130–32,
136–37, 143, 155–156, 168–69, 227, 302–3;
vocal style development, 48, 64–65, 104–6,
157, 161–62. *See also* family life
—Chronology: birth and childhood (1935–53),
21–22, 28–32, 35, 38–53, **plates 1–2**; P Street
apartment (1937), 26; Silver Spring house
(1938–44), 28–31; Chevy Chase house
(1944–54), 1, 38, 39–41, 43, 45–47, 60, 62,
**plate 2**; Putney School (1950–51), 47–49;
Bethesda-Chevy Chase High School (1951–
53), 49–52; Radcliffe College (1953–55), 52,
55–62, 63, 70, 81; death of Ruth Crawford
Seeger (1953), 56–58; Cambridge apartment
(1954–55), 63, 67, 70–71, **plate 3**; California
trip (1955), 72–74; Leiden, the Netherlands
(1955), 1, 67, 76–78; the Netherlands/
Belgium/Germany/Denmark (1955–56),
78–81, **plate 4**; London move (1956), 1–3,
82–92; Ewan MacColl early relationship
(1956–59), 82–83, 88–97, 99, 113–17, 118–20;
European scooter trip (1956), 93; U.S. trip
(1957), 96–97; Moscow/China/Poland/Paris
trip (1957), 97–103, **plates 5–6**, 316nn19–20,
316n22; exile in France (1958), 113–17; Radio

Ballads (1958–64), 109–13, 121–29, 131, 150–
52, 154–58, 162–63, 169–72, 293; marriage
to Alex Campbell (1959), 117, 153; birth
of Neill MacColl (1959), 118–19; Singers
Club founding (1961), 144–50; Beckenham
house purchase (1961), 153; birth of Calum
MacColl (1963), 158–59; *Young Folk Song
Book* profile (1963), 161–62; Critics Group
founding (1963), 164–68, 174–75, 203, 270;
Critics Group theater productions (1965),
177–86, 189, 191–94; U.S. trip (1970), 189–
91; Critics Group breakup (1972), 196–98,
199–200, 208; birth of Kitty MacColl
(1972), 200–201; Blackthorne Records
(1976), 208–9; Peggy and Ewan marriage
(1977), 210; Charles Seeger celebration
(1977), 211; death of Charles Seeger (1979),
213–14; Greenham Common Women's
Peace Camp (1981–2000), 224–26; miners'
strike (1984), 227–31; Irene Pyper-Scott,
early relationship (1988), 232–38; death of
Ewan (1989), 199, 238, 239, 241–46; move
to Asheville (1994–2006), 248–49, 252, 257,
266–67; move to Boston and Northeastern
University (2006–10), 266, 268–71, 277;
Irene New Zealand move (2007), 268–69,
271, 275, 277; return to England (2010),
277, 278; University of Salford honorary
doctorate (2011), 293; Folk Alliance Lifetime
Achievement Award (2015), 293
Seeger (Cohen), Penny (sister): Cambridge
apartment life, 63, 67, 70; childhood, 38,
40–41, 51, 56, 58, 62, 72, 76, **plates 1–2**;
death, 247; death of Ruth and, 57–58; Peggy
recordings with, 68, 103, 236, 245
Seeger, Pete (half-brother): Army service,
30, 37–38, 49, **plate 1**; *At 89* Grammy
award, 275; as banjo player, 25–26, 32,
50; Beacon, N.Y., residence, 60, 62–63,
70, 76, 94, 97; childhood, 6, 9–11, 16–18;
children's recordings by, 137; Communist
Party affiliation, 33, 60, 88; death, 284–85;
education, 32; as folksinger, 3, 44–45,
48–49, 55, 69, 96–97, 132; on folk song
revival, 138; HUAC and, 69, 75–76, 88,
137, 143, 153, 155; legacy of, 284–85, 300;
marriage to Toshi Ohta, 27, 30, 38; North
Carolina folk music trip, 10, 25–26, 248;
Peggy performances/recordings with, 53,
55, 61, 129, 153, 264–265, 283–284; political
folk songs and, 33, 37, 44, 69, 132, 265,

279; political views, 18, 33, 37, 44, 75, 269; relationship with father, 45 —Selected works: *How to Play the 5-String Banjo*, 50; "If I Had a Hammer," 44; "Take It from Doctor King," 265

Seeger, Ruth Crawford (mother): Charles meeting and marriage, 11, 14–15, 16–17; childrearing by, 25, 28–32, 35–37, 41, 45, 48, **plate 2**, 289–92; Clarendon, Va., house, 23, 25; as composer, 3, 11, 13–17, 26, 34–36, 57, 269, 290–91, 300; death, 56–59, 290; *Everything Changes* as tribute to, 288–91; exposure to folk music, 14, 20; folk music as cultural resource, 26, 27, 34–35, 291; folk music as family routine, 31–32, 43–44; folk music in school curricula, 36–37, 43–44, 136; folk music progressive approach, 14, 140, 142–43; Guggenheim fellowship, 16–17, 28; legacy of, 269, 290–91; Peggy relationship with, 56, 233, 289–91; personality, 30–31, 290; as piano teacher, 12–14, 30, 34, 40, 51, 56, 60; political views, 17, 33–34, 140, 142–43; as school music teacher, 37–38, 43, 52; transcriptions, 26, 30, 34–35, 38, 43–44; upbringing, 11–12, 46 —Selected works: *American Folk Songs for Children*, 37, 43–44, 103–4, 142, 211; *American Folk Songs for Christmas*, 44, 56, 68–69, 103, 236, 245; *Animal Folk Songs for Children*, 44, 105, 243, 245; *Folk Song U.S.A.* (music editor, with Charles Seeger), 43; *Our Singing Country* (music editor), 26, 34–36; "Rissolty, Rossolty," 34–35, 51; String Quartet 1931, 17

Seeger, Tinya (daughter of Pete and Toshi), 70, 284

Seeger, Toshi (wife of Pete), 27, 30, 38, 62–63, 70, 76, 97, 284

Sharp, Cecil, 26, 86, 93, 133–36, 142, 146–47, 314nn15–16, 319n8

Siegmeister, Elie, 17, 20

Silverstein, Deborah, 222

Singers Club: Bob Dylan appearance, 155; closing of, 160; Ewan illness/death and, 221, 243; Festival of Fools and, 178, 198; founding of, 144–50, 160–61; Irene's presence, 226; Jade founding and, 232; Jean Freedman visits to, ix–x; MacColl-Seeger family performances at, **plate 9**, 188, 200, 210; as *New City Songster* sales point, 184; organizational work for, 173; policy of,

144–50, 160–61, 217, 301–2; Sandra Kerr meeting, 158; *St. George and the Dragon* performance, 175

*Sing* magazine, 147, 177

*Sing Out!* magazine, 132

Sitnick, Leni, 252

skiffle, 87, 90, 144–46

Small, Fred, 244

Smith, Alexia (wife of Mike), 249, 276

Smith, Hobart, 2

Smithsonian Folklife Festival, 61, 254, 302

Sokoloff, Nikolai, 35

"Song of Myself" (song), 190, 244

South African apartheid, ix, 185, 198, 203, 212, 226, 231, 233, 242

Spanish Civil War, 19, 22, 132, 229

Springsteen, Bruce, 275

Stanislavski, Constantine, 166, 301, 323n24

Stekert, Ellen, 106, 302

Stewart, Belle and Jane, 169, 323n36

Stewart, Jackie, 187

Stewart, Rod, 187

Stewart family (Travellers), 209–10, 217–18

St. John, Kate (wife of Neill MacColl), **plate 12**, 286

Stringfield, Lamar, 26

Sugar, Maurice, 280

Swarbrick, Dave, 149

Swarthmore Folk Festival, 61, 69–70

"Swim to the Star" (song), 286–87, 304

Szwed, John, 314n14

Taylor, Margaret "Mar" (stepmother), 1, 21, 63, 66–67, 70–71, 72–74, 100, 153, 263

Thatcher, Margaret, ix, 218–19, 227–28, 230, 237, 240, 331n65

theater: Ewan background in, 84–88, 166–67, 178, 231, 313n6, 323n24, 330n47; Festival of Fools productions, 177–82, 187, 191–93, 196–98, 293, 324n19; *Ours the Fruit* (Drury Lane, London), 173–74; Stantonbury Campus Drama Group, 209; *St. George and the Dragon*, 174–75, 177, 324n4

Thompson, Stith, 138–39

"Thoughts of Time" (song), 210–11, 244–45, 255–56, 293

Thurston, Herbert, 177

Tick, Judith, 34–35, 266, 269, 291

Torvik, Nathan, 282

Travellers (ethnic group), 159, 169–72, 209–10, 217–18

Truesdale, Adelaide and Alfred, 28, 30
Tugwell, Rexford, 26

U2, 115
ultramodernism, 14, 21, 26

Valiant, Margaret, 24, 28
Van de Putte, Maurice, 79
Van Ronk, Dave, 106
Vidor, Mike, 48–49, 55, 59
Vietnam War: as "Agent Orange Song" theme, 222; as "The Battle of Ho Chi Minh" theme, 185–86; decline and end of, 203; Ewan and Peggy opposition to, 175–76, 190, 196; as Festival of Fools theme, 178, 181–82; "Peaceful Woman, Fighting Hard" and, 258; as *St. George and the Dragon* theme, 174–75
Vloeberghs, Josef Ernst, 78–80

Wade, Bonnie, 211
Wallace, Henry, 44
Walton, Blanche, 15
Warshaw, Jack, 185
Waterson, Norma, 264

Watersons (music group), 271
Watton, Harry, 171–72
Weavers (music group), 44–45, 52, 78, 82
Weidig, Adolf, 13–14
Weissman, Clark, 59, 60–61, 64, 69
White Top Folk Festival (Virginia), 25, 140–42
Wilde, Oscar, 235
Winter, Eric, 147, 160–61
Wolf, Inez (wife of Charles Seeger III), 27, 76–78, 80, 313n26
Workers Music Co-Operative (Dublin), 232
Works Progress Administration, 27–28, 142–43. *See also* New Deal
World War I, 8–9
World War II: aftermath of, 42–43, 258; "Crooked Cross" commentary on, 131; neo-Nazism after, 180; Pan American Union role, 35–36; Peggy experience with, 138; political folk music on, 37, 132; rise of Nazism, 17, 18–20, 33–34, 139–40, 299; Travellers compared to Nazi victims, 171–72; U.S. isolationism in, 33; views of Europe after, 79, 102. *See also* Nazism

Young, Israel "Izzy," 97, 300

# Index of Selected Recordings and Publications by Peggy Seeger

**1954**
*Folk Songs of Courting and Complaint*, 60–62, 64–66, 103–6, 157, 161

**1956**
*Alan Lomax and the Ramblers*, 94

**1957**
*America at Play* (with Guy Carawan), 106
*American Folk Guitar* (with Alan Lomax), 105–6
*American Folk Songs for Christmas* (with Barbara and Penny Seeger), 68–69, 103, 236
*American Folk Songs Sung by the Seegers* (with Barbara, Penny, and Mike Seeger), 103–5
*American Song Train* (Alan Lomax production), 106
*Animal Folk Songs for Children*, 105
*Come Along, John* (with Barbara and Penny Seeger), 103
*Eleven American Ballads and Songs*, 105
*Folk-Song Saturday Night* (Alan Lomax production), 106
*Matching Songs of Britain and America* (with Ewan), 105
*Our Singing Heritage* (with other folksingers), 106
*Shine Like a Star* (with Barbara and Penny Seeger), 103
*The Three Sisters* (with Barbara and Penny Seeger), 103
*We Sing America* (with Guy Carawan), 106

**1958**
*The Ballad of John Axon*, 107–13, 121–25, 127
*Bold Sportsmen All* (with Ewan and A. L. Lloyd), 106
*English and Scottish Love Songs* (with Ewan, Isla Cameron, and Ralph Rinzler), 106
*Folksongs and Ballads*, 106
*Freight Train*, 106
*Second Shift* (with Ewan), 106
*Steam Whistle Ballads* (with Ewan), 106
*Still I Love Him* (with Ewan and Isla Cameron), 106

**1959**
*Classic Scots Ballads* (with Ewan), 94, 120
*Song of a Road*, 121–27, 157
*Songs against the Bomb* (with others), 120
*Songs of Robert Burns* (with Ewan), 120

**1960**
*American History in Ballad and Song* (with others), 130
BBC series on Mark Twain, 128–29
*The Best of Peggy Seeger* (early 1960s), 159
*Burning Light* (television documentary), 129
*Chorus from the Gallows* (with Ewan), 130, 159
*The Five-String Banjo American Folk Styles*, 130
*The Folk Songs of North America* (transcriptions), 130
*The New Briton Gazette* (with Ewan), 130–32
*Outback Ballads* (with A. L. Lloyd), 130

*Peggy Seeger Sings and Plays American Folksongs for Banjo* (early 1960s), 159
*Popular Ballads* (early 1960s), 159, 161
*Popular Scottish Songs* (with Ewan), 130, 159
*The Singing Island* (with Ewan), 118, 130
*Singing the Fishing*, 125–28, 131, 152, 154, 203
*Songs of Two Rebellions* (with Ewan), 130

1961
*The Big Hewer*, 150–52, 154, 203, 228, 229
*Bothy Ballads of Scotland* (with Ewan), 152
*The Elliots of Birtley* (co-producer), 152
*Ewan MacColl Sings British Industrial Ballads*, 152
*Four People* (film score), 154
*Now Is the Time for Fishing* (co-producer), 152
*Songs for the Sixties* (with Ewan), 159
*Two-Way Trip* (with Ewan), 147–49, 152

1962
*The Body Blow*, 154–55
*Broadside Ballads, London: 1600–1700*, vols. 1 and 2 (with Ewan), 155
*Early in the Spring*, 155
*A Lover's Garland*, 159
*The New Briton Gazette*, vol. 2 (with Ewan), 155–56
*Sing In the New* (television program, with Ewan and other artists), 156
*A Song for You and Me*, 159
*Troubled Love*, 155
*Whaler out of New Bedford* (with Ewan, A. L. Lloyd, and others), 149

1963
*Ewan MacColl–Peggy Seeger Songbook*, 176
*The Fight Game*, 162–64, 203
*On the Edge*, 156–58

1964
*Folk Songs of Peggy Seeger*, 176
*An Impression of Love* (television program, with Ewan), 172
*Landmarks* (radio series, with Ewan and Charles Parker), 172, 182
*The Song Carriers* (radio series, with Ewan and Charles Parker), 172, 182
*The Travelling People*, 169–72
*Who's Going to Shoe Your Pretty Little Foot?* (with Tom Paley), 177

1965
*Folk Songs and Ballads of Scotland* (with Ewan, transcription and editing), 176

1966
*The Long Harvest*, 10 vols. (with Ewan), 183
*Manchester Angel* (with Ewan), 183
*A Merry Progress to London* (with Ewan and the Critics Group), 182
*Romeo and Juliet* (radio drama, with Ewan and the Critics Group), 182
*Sweet Thames Flow Softly* (with Ewan and the Critics Group), 182

1967
*Peggy Alone*, 183–84
*Peggy 'n' Mike* (with Mike Seeger), 183
*Poetry and Song* (with Ewan and the Critics Group), 182

1968
*The Amorous Muse* (with Ewan), 183
*The Angry Muse* (with Ewan and the Critics Group), 182, 186
*The Female Frolic* (with Frankie Armstrong and Sandra Kerr), 182
*New City Songster* magazine (1968–85), 184, 187, 198, 226
*The Paper Stage* (with Ewan and the Critics Group), 183
*Voices* (with Ewan and the Critics Group), 183
*The Wanton Muse* (with Ewan and the Critics Group), 183
*Waterloo-Peterloo* (with Ewan and the Critics Group), 182

1970
*As We Were a-Sailing* (with Ewan and the Critics Group), 189
*Living Folk* (with Ewan and the Critics Group), 189
*Shellback* (1970s, with Ewan and Ben Bright), 213
*The World of Ewan MacColl and Peggy Seeger*, 189

1971
*Before the Mast* (soundtrack, with Ewan and the Critics Group), 203
*A Kind of Exile* (documentary on Peggy), 162, 194–96

*Ye Mariners All* (with Ewan and the Critics Group), 194

**1972**
*Solo Flight* (with Ewan and the Critics Group), 203
*The World of Ewan MacColl and Peggy Seeger,* vol. 2 (with the Critics Group), 203

**1973**
*At the Present Moment* (with Ewan), 203
*Folkways Record of Contemporary Songs* (with Ewan), 203

**1976**
*No Tyme Like the Present* (with Ewan), 209
*Penelope Isn't Waiting Any More,* 208–9, 214, 249
*Songs of Struggle* (with Ewan), 209

**1977**
*American Folk Songs for Children* (with Mike Seeger), 211–12, 258
*Cold Snap* (with Ewan, Calum, and Neill), 210
*Saturday Night at the Bull & Mouth* (with Ewan, Calum, and Neill), 210
*Travellers' Songs from England and Scotland* (with Ewan), 209–10

**1978**
*Hot Blast* (with Ewan), 212

**1979**
*Blood and Roses,* vol. 1 (with Ewan), 214
*Different Therefore Equal,* 214

**1980**
*Kilroy Was Here* (with Ewan), 218–20
*Stories and Songs of a Scots Family Group* (BBC television program, with Ewan and others), 217–18

**1981**
*Blood and Roses,* vol. 2 (with Ewan), 220
*The Other Music* (television program, with Ewan and other folk artists), 220

**1982**
*Blood and Roses,* vol. 3 (with Ewan), 221
*From Where I Stand,* 221–23

**1983**
*Freeborn Man* (with Ewan), 226
*The Good Old Way* (television documentary), 226–27

**1984**
*Daddy, What Did You Do in the Strike?* (with Ewan and Calum), 228–30
*Parsley, Sage and Politics* (radio documentary and CD), 227

**1986**
*Blood and Roses,* vols. 4 and 5 (with Ewan), 231
*Items of News* (with Ewan), 231
*Till Doomsday in the Afternoon* (with Ewan), 210
*White Wind, Black Tide* (with Ewan), 231

**1988**
*Familiar Faces,* 233

**1989**
*American Folk Songs for Christmas* (with Ewan, Calum, Kitty, Kim, and Sonya), 236
*Needs Must When the Devil Drives* (film music), 232

**1990**
*Journeyman* (introduction to Ewan's autobiography), 242
*Naming of Names* (with Ewan and Jade), 237–38, 242

**1992**
*Almost Commercially Viable* (with Irene), 243, 245–46
*Animal Folk Songs for Children* (with Irene, Neill, Calum, Kitty, Mike, Barbara, Penny, Kim, Sonya, and Rufus), 243, 245
*Peggy Seeger, The Folkways Years 1955–1992,* 243–45

**1996**
*An Odd Collection,* 249–52, 292

**1998**
*The Peggy Seeger Songbook,* 249, 252–53
*Period Pieces* (with Neill, Calum, Kitty, Irene, and Jade), 253–54

2000
*Love Will Linger On* (with Irene, Neill,
 Calum, and Kitty), 254–56

2001
*The Essential Ewan MacColl Songbook*, 249,
 256–57
*Peaceful Woman, Fighting Hard*, 258–60

2003
*Heading for Home*, 260–63

2004
*Songs for October 2004*, 263

2005
*Love Call Me Home*, 265–66

2006
*Enough Is Enough*, 266

2007
*Primary Transmission* (with Calum and
 Broadcaster), 282

*Three Score and Ten*, 264–65

2008
*Bring Me Home*, 272–73, 275
*Crazy Quilt*, 273–74

2011
*Fly Down Little Bird* (with Mike Seeger),
 278–79

2012
*Celebrating Subversion* (with the Anti-
 Capitalist Roadshow), 281
*Folksploitation* (with Broadcaster), 282–83
*Peggy Seeger Live*, 282
*Peggy Seeger Teaches Guitar Accompaniment
 for Folk Songs, Ballads, and Originals*, 283

2014
*Everything Changes*, 286–92, 301

JEAN R. FREEDMAN earned a Ph.D. in folklore from
Indiana University. She is the author of *Whistling in
the Dark: Memory and Culture in Wartime London*.

# Music in American Life

Only a Miner: Studies in Recorded Coal-Mining Songs  *Archie Green*
Great Day Coming: Folk Music and the American Left  *R. Serge Denisoff*
John Philip Sousa: A Descriptive Catalog of His Works  *Paul E. Bierley*
The Hell-Bound Train: A Cowboy Songbook  *Glenn Ohrlin*
Oh, Didn't He Ramble: The Life Story of Lee Collins, as Told to Mary Collins
    *Edited by Frank J. Gillis and John W. Miner*
American Labor Songs of the Nineteenth Century  *Philip S. Foner*
Stars of Country Music: Uncle Dave Macon to Johnny Rodriguez
    *Edited by Bill C. Malone and Judith McCulloh*
Git Along, Little Dogies: Songs and Songmakers of the American West  *John I. White*
A Texas-Mexican *Cancionero*: Folksongs of the Lower Border  *Américo Paredes*
San Antonio Rose: The Life and Music of Bob Wills  *Charles R. Townsend*
Early Downhome Blues: A Musical and Cultural Analysis  *Jeff Todd Titon*
An Ives Celebration: Papers and Panels of the Charles Ives Centennial Festival-
    Conference  *Edited by H. Wiley Hitchcock and Vivian Perlis*
Sinful Tunes and Spirituals: Black Folk Music to the Civil War  *Dena J. Epstein*
Joe Scott, the Woodsman-Songmaker  *Edward D. Ives*
Jimmie Rodgers: The Life and Times of America's Blue Yodeler  *Nolan Porterfield*
Early American Music Engraving and Printing: A History of Music Publishing in America
    from 1787 to 1825, with Commentary on Earlier and Later Practices  *Richard J. Wolfe*
Sing a Sad Song: The Life of Hank Williams  *Roger M. Williams*
Long Steel Rail: The Railroad in American Folksong  *Norm Cohen*
Resources of American Music History: A Directory of Source Materials from Colonial
    Times to World War II  *D. W. Krummel, Jean Geil, Doris J. Dyen, and Deane L. Root*
Tenement Songs: The Popular Music of the Jewish Immigrants  *Mark Slobin*
Ozark Folksongs  *Vance Randolph; edited and abridged by Norm Cohen*
Oscar Sonneck and American Music  *Edited by William Lichtenwanger*
Bluegrass Breakdown: The Making of the Old Southern Sound  *Robert Cantwell*
Bluegrass: A History  *Neil V. Rosenberg*
Music at the White House: A History of the American Spirit  *Elise K. Kirk*
Red River Blues: The Blues Tradition in the Southeast  *Bruce Bastin*
Good Friends and Bad Enemies: Robert Winslow Gordon and the Study of
    American Folksong  *Debora Kodish*
Fiddlin' Georgia Crazy: Fiddlin' John Carson, His Real World, and the
    World of His Songs  *Gene Wiggins*
America's Music: From the Pilgrims to the Present (rev. 3d ed.)  *Gilbert Chase*
Secular Music in Colonial Annapolis: The Tuesday Club, 1745–56  *John Barry Talley*
Bibliographical Handbook of American Music  *D. W. Krummel*
Goin' to Kansas City  *Nathan W. Pearson Jr.*
"Susanna," "Jeanie," and "The Old Folks at Home": The Songs of Stephen C. Foster
    from His Time to Ours (2d ed.)  *William W. Austin*
Songprints: The Musical Experience of Five Shoshone Women  *Judith Vander*

"Happy in the Service of the Lord": Afro-American Gospel Quartets in Memphis
  *Kip Lornell*
Paul Hindemith in the United States   *Luther Noss*
"My Song Is My Weapon": People's Songs, American Communism, and the Politics
  of Culture, 1930–50   *Robbie Lieberman*
Chosen Voices: The Story of the American Cantorate   *Mark Slobin*
Theodore Thomas: America's Conductor and Builder of Orchestras, 1835–1905
  *Ezra Schabas*
"The Whorehouse Bells Were Ringing" and Other Songs Cowboys Sing
  *Collected and Edited by Guy Logsdon*
Crazeology: The Autobiography of a Chicago Jazzman   *Bud Freeman,
  as Told to Robert Wolf*
Discoursing Sweet Music: Brass Bands and Community Life in Turn-of-the-
  Century Pennsylvania   *Kenneth Kreitner*
Mormonism and Music: A History   *Michael Hicks*
Voices of the Jazz Age: Profiles of Eight Vintage Jazzmen   *Chip Deffaa*
Pickin' on Peachtree: A History of Country Music in Atlanta, Georgia   *Wayne W. Daniel*
Bitter Music: Collected Journals, Essays, Introductions, and Librettos   *Harry Partch;
  edited by Thomas McGeary*
Ethnic Music on Records: A Discography of Ethnic Recordings Produced in the
  United States, 1893 to 1942   *Richard K. Spottswood*
Downhome Blues Lyrics: An Anthology from the Post–World War II Era   *Jeff Todd Titon*
Ellington: The Early Years   *Mark Tucker*
Chicago Soul   *Robert Pruter*
That Half-Barbaric Twang: The Banjo in American Popular Culture   *Karen Linn*
Hot Man: The Life of Art Hodes   *Art Hodes and Chadwick Hansen*
The Erotic Muse: American Bawdy Songs (2d ed.)   *Ed Cray*
Barrio Rhythm: Mexican American Music in Los Angeles   *Steven Loza*
The Creation of Jazz: Music, Race, and Culture in Urban America   *Burton W. Peretti*
Charles Martin Loeffler: A Life Apart in Music   *Ellen Knight*
Club Date Musicians: Playing the New York Party Circuit   *Bruce A. MacLeod*
Opera on the Road: Traveling Opera Troupes in the United States, 1825–60
  *Katherine K. Preston*
The Stonemans: An Appalachian Family and the Music That Shaped Their Lives
  *Ivan M. Tribe*
Transforming Tradition: Folk Music Revivals Examined   *Edited by Neil V. Rosenberg*
The Crooked Stovepipe: Athapaskan Fiddle Music and Square Dancing in Northeast
  Alaska and Northwest Canada   *Craig Mishler*
Traveling the High Way Home: Ralph Stanley and the World of Traditional
  Bluegrass Music   *John Wright*
Carl Ruggles: Composer, Painter, and Storyteller   *Marilyn Ziffrin*
Never without a Song: The Years and Songs of Jennie Devlin, 1865–1952
  *Katharine D. Newman*
The Hank Snow Story   *Hank Snow, with Jack Ownbey and Bob Burris*

Milton Brown and the Founding of Western Swing   *Cary Ginell, with special assistance from Roy Lee Brown*

Santiago de Murcia's "Códice Saldívar No. 4": A Treasury of Secular Guitar Music from Baroque Mexico   *Craig H. Russell*

The Sound of the Dove: Singing in Appalachian Primitive Baptist Churches *Beverly Bush Patterson*

Heartland Excursions: Ethnomusicological Reflections on Schools of Music   *Bruno Nettl*

Doowop: The Chicago Scene   *Robert Pruter*

Blue Rhythms: Six Lives in Rhythm and Blues   *Chip Deffaa*

Shoshone Ghost Dance Religion: Poetry Songs and Great Basin Context   *Judith Vander*

Go Cat Go! Rockabilly Music and Its Makers   *Craig Morrison*

'Twas Only an Irishman's Dream: The Image of Ireland and the Irish in American Popular Song Lyrics, 1800–1920   *William H. A. Williams*

Democracy at the Opera: Music, Theater, and Culture in New York City, 1815–60 *Karen Ahlquist*

Fred Waring and the Pennsylvanians   *Virginia Waring*

Woody, Cisco, and Me: Seamen Three in the Merchant Marine   *Jim Longhi*

Behind the Burnt Cork Mask: Early Blackface Minstrelsy and Antebellum American Popular Culture   *William J. Mahar*

Going to Cincinnati: A History of the Blues in the Queen City   *Steven C. Tracy*

Pistol Packin' Mama: Aunt Molly Jackson and the Politics of Folksong   *Shelly Romalis*

Sixties Rock: Garage, Psychedelic, and Other Satisfactions   *Michael Hicks*

The Late Great Johnny Ace and the Transition from R&B to Rock 'n' Roll *James M. Salem*

Tito Puente and the Making of Latin Music   *Steven Loza*

Juilliard: A History   *Andrea Olmstead*

Understanding Charles Seeger, Pioneer in American Musicology   *Edited by Bell Yung and Helen Rees*

Mountains of Music: West Virginia Traditional Music from *Goldenseal* *Edited by John Lilly*

Alice Tully: An Intimate Portrait   *Albert Fuller*

A Blues Life   *Henry Townsend, as told to Bill Greensmith*

Long Steel Rail: The Railroad in American Folksong (2d ed.)   *Norm Cohen*

The Golden Age of Gospel   *Text by Horace Clarence Boyer; photography by Lloyd Yearwood*

Aaron Copland: The Life and Work of an Uncommon Man   *Howard Pollack*

Louis Moreau Gottschalk   *S. Frederick Starr*

Race, Rock, and Elvis   *Michael T. Bertrand*

Theremin: Ether Music and Espionage   *Albert Glinsky*

Poetry and Violence: The Ballad Tradition of Mexico's Costa Chica   *John H. McDowell*

The Bill Monroe Reader   *Edited by Tom Ewing*

Music in Lubavitcher Life   *Ellen Koskoff*

Zarzuela: Spanish Operetta, American Stage   *Janet L. Sturman*

Bluegrass Odyssey: A Documentary in Pictures and Words, 1966–86   *Carl Fleischhauer and Neil V. Rosenberg*

That Old-Time Rock & Roll: A Chronicle of an Era, 1954–63   *Richard Aquila*
Labor's Troubadour   *Joe Glazer*
American Opera   *Elise K. Kirk*
Don't Get above Your Raisin': Country Music and the Southern Working Class
   *Bill C. Malone*
John Alden Carpenter: A Chicago Composer   *Howard Pollack*
Heartbeat of the People: Music and Dance of the Northern Pow-wow   *Tara Browner*
My Lord, What a Morning: An Autobiography   *Marian Anderson*
Marian Anderson: A Singer's Journey   *Allan Keiler*
Charles Ives Remembered: An Oral History   *Vivian Perlis*
Henry Cowell, Bohemian   *Michael Hicks*
Rap Music and Street Consciousness   *Cheryl L. Keyes*
Louis Prima   *Garry Boulard*
Marian McPartland's Jazz World: All in Good Time   *Marian McPartland*
Robert Johnson: Lost and Found   *Barry Lee Pearson and Bill McCulloch*
Bound for America: Three British Composers   *Nicholas Temperley*
Lost Sounds: Blacks and the Birth of the Recording Industry, 1890–1919   *Tim Brooks*
Burn, Baby! BURN! The Autobiography of Magnificent Montague
   *Magnificent Montague with Bob Baker*
Way Up North in Dixie: A Black Family's Claim to the Confederate Anthem
   *Howard L. Sacks and Judith Rose Sacks*
The Bluegrass Reader   *Edited by Thomas Goldsmith*
Colin McPhee: Composer in Two Worlds   *Carol J. Oja*
Robert Johnson, Mythmaking, and Contemporary American Culture
   *Patricia R. Schroeder*
Composing a World: Lou Harrison, Musical Wayfarer   *Leta E. Miller and
   Fredric Lieberman*
Fritz Reiner, Maestro and Martinet   *Kenneth Morgan*
That Toddlin' Town: Chicago's White Dance Bands and Orchestras, 1900–1950
   *Charles A. Sengstock Jr.*
Dewey and Elvis: The Life and Times of a Rock 'n' Roll Deejay   *Louis Cantor*
Come Hither to Go Yonder: Playing Bluegrass with Bill Monroe   *Bob Black*
Chicago Blues: Portraits and Stories   *David Whiteis*
The Incredible Band of John Philip Sousa   *Paul E. Bierley*
"Maximum Clarity" and Other Writings on Music   *Ben Johnston, edited by Bob Gilmore*
Staging Tradition: John Lair and Sarah Gertrude Knott   *Michael Ann Williams*
Homegrown Music: Discovering Bluegrass   *Stephanie P. Ledgin*
Tales of a Theatrical Guru   *Danny Newman*
The Music of Bill Monroe   *Neil V. Rosenberg and Charles K. Wolfe*
Pressing On: The Roni Stoneman Story   *Roni Stoneman, as told to Ellen Wright*
Together Let Us Sweetly Live   *Jonathan C. David, with photographs by Richard Holloway*
Live Fast, Love Hard: The Faron Young Story   *Diane Diekman*
Air Castle of the South: WSM Radio and the Making of Music City   *Craig P. Havighurst*
Traveling Home: Sacred Harp Singing and American Pluralism   *Kiri Miller*
Where Did Our Love Go? The Rise and Fall of the Motown Sound   *Nelson George*

Lonesome Cowgirls and Honky-Tonk Angels: The Women of Barn Dance Radio
  *Kristine M. McCusker*
California Polyphony: Ethnic Voices, Musical Crossroads  *Mina Yang*
The Never-Ending Revival: Rounder Records and the Folk Alliance  *Michael F. Scully*
Sing It Pretty: A Memoir  *Bess Lomax Hawes*
Working Girl Blues: The Life and Music of Hazel Dickens  *Hazel Dickens and
  Bill C. Malone*
Charles Ives Reconsidered  *Gayle Sherwood Magee*
The Hayloft Gang: The Story of the National Barn Dance  *Edited by Chad Berry*
Country Music Humorists and Comedians  *Loyal Jones*
Record Makers and Breakers: Voices of the Independent Rock 'n' Roll Pioneers
  *John Broven*
Music of the First Nations: Tradition and Innovation in Native North America
  *Edited by Tara Browner*
Cafe Society: The Wrong Place for the Right People  *Barney Josephson,
  with Terry Trilling-Josephson*
George Gershwin: An Intimate Portrait  *Walter Rimler*
Life Flows On in Endless Song: Folk Songs and American History  *Robert V. Wells*
I Feel a Song Coming On: The Life of Jimmy McHugh  *Alyn Shipton*
King of the Queen City: The Story of King Records  *Jon Hartley Fox*
Long Lost Blues: Popular Blues in America, 1850–1920  *Peter C. Muir*
Hard Luck Blues: Roots Music Photographs from the Great Depression  *Rich Remsberg*
Restless Giant: The Life and Times of Jean Aberbach and Hill and Range Songs
  *Bar Biszick-Lockwood*
Champagne Charlie and Pretty Jemima: Variety Theater in the Nineteenth Century
  *Gillian M. Rodger*
Sacred Steel: Inside an African American Steel Guitar Tradition  *Robert L. Stone*
Gone to the Country: The New Lost City Ramblers and the Folk Music Revival
  *Ray Allen*
The Makers of the Sacred Harp  *David Warren Steel with Richard H. Hulan*
Woody Guthrie, American Radical  *Will Kaufman*
George Szell: A Life of Music  *Michael Charry*
Bean Blossom: The Brown County Jamboree and Bill Monroe's Bluegrass Festivals
  *Thomas A. Adler*
Crowe on the Banjo: The Music Life of J. D. Crowe  *Marty Godbey*
Twentieth Century Drifter: The Life of Marty Robbins  *Diane Diekman*
Henry Mancini: Reinventing Film Music  *John Caps*
The Beautiful Music All Around Us: Field Recordings and the American Experience
  *Stephen Wade*
Then Sings My Soul: The Culture of Southern Gospel Music  *Douglas Harrison*
The Accordion in the Americas: Klezmer, Polka, Tango, Zydeco, and More!
  *Edited by Helena Simonett*
Bluegrass Bluesman: A Memoir  *Josh Graves, edited by Fred Bartenstein*
One Woman in a Hundred: Edna Phillips and the Philadelphia Orchestra
  *Mary Sue Welsh*

The Great Orchestrator: Arthur Judson and American Arts Management   *James M. Doering*
Charles Ives in the Mirror: American Histories of an Iconic Composer   *David C. Paul*
Southern Soul-Blues   *David Whiteis*
Sweet Air: Modernism, Regionalism, and American Popular Song   *Edward P. Comentale*
Pretty Good for a Girl: Women in Bluegrass   *Murphy Hicks Henry*
Sweet Dreams: The World of Patsy Cline   *Warren R. Hofstra*
William Sidney Mount and the Creolization of American Culture   *Christopher J. Smith*
Bird: The Life and Music of Charlie Parker   *Chuck Haddix*
Making the March King: John Philip Sousa's Washington Years, 1854–1893   *Patrick Warfield*
In It for the Long Run   *Jim Rooney*
Pioneers of the Blues Revival   *Steve Cushing*
Roots of the Revival: American and British Folk Music in the 1950s   *Ronald D. Cohen and Rachel Clare Donaldson*
Blues All Day Long: The Jimmy Rogers Story   *Wayne Everett Goins*
Yankee Twang: Country and Western Music in New England   *Clifford R. Murphy*
The Music of the Stanley Brothers   *Gary B. Reid*
Hawaiian Music in Motion: Mariners, Missionaries, and Minstrels   *James Revell Carr*
Sounds of the New Deal: The Federal Music Project in the West   *Peter Gough*
The Mormon Tabernacle Choir: A Biography   *Michael Hicks*
The Man That Got Away: The Life and Songs of Harold Arlen   *Walter Rimler*
A City Called Heaven: Chicago and the Birth of Gospel Music   *Robert M. Marovich*
Blues Unlimited: Essential Interviews from the Original Blues Magazine   *Edited by Bill Greensmith, Mike Rowe, and Mark Camarigg*
Hoedowns, Reels, and Frolics: Roots and Branches of Southern Appalachian Dance   *Phil Jamison*
Fannie Bloomfield-Zeisler: The Life and Times of a Piano Virtuoso   *Beth Abelson Macleod*
Cybersonic Arts: Adventures in American New Music   *Gordon Mumma, edited with commentary by Michelle Fillion*
The Magic of Beverly Sills   *Nancy Guy*
Waiting for Buddy Guy   *Alan Harper*
Harry T. Burleigh: From the Spiritual to the Harlem Renaissance   *Jean E. Snyder*
Music in the Age of Anxiety: American Music in the Fifties   *James Wierzbicki*
Jazzing: New York City's Unseen Scene   *Thomas H. Greenland*
A Cole Porter Companion   *Edited by Don M. Randel, Matthew Shaftel, and Susan Forscher Weiss*
Foggy Mountain Troubadour: The Life and Music of Curly Seckler   *Penny Parsons*
Blue Rhythm Fantasy: Big Band Jazz Arranging in the Swing Era   *John Wriggle*
Bill Clifton: America's Bluegrass Ambassador to the World   *Bill C. Malone*
Chinatown Opera Theater in North America   *Nancy Yunhwa Rao*
The Elocutionists: Women, Music, and the Spoken Word   *Marian Wilson Kimber*
May Irwin: Singing, Shouting, and the Shadow of Minstrelsy   *Sharon Ammen*
Peggy Seeger: A Life of Music, Love, and Politics   *Jean R. Freedman*